Great Holiness Classics
Volume 2

GREAT HOLINESS CLASSICS
in Six Volumes

Volume 1
Holiness Teaching—New Testament Times to Wesley

Volume 2
The Wesley Century

Volume 3
Leading Wesleyan Thinkers

Volume 4
The 19th-Century Holiness Movement

Volume 5
Holiness Preachers and Preaching

Volume 6
Holiness Teaching Today

✳ GREAT HOLINESS CLASSICS ✳

VOLUME 2

The Wesley Century

(1725-1825)

Edited by
T. Crichton Mitchell

Volume Advisors:
Arlo Newell
David Cubie

BEACON HILL PRESS OF KANSAS CITY
KANSAS CITY, MISSOURI

Copyright 1984
Beacon Hill Press of Kansas City

ISBN: 0-8341-0910-7
    0-8341-0909-3 series

Printed in the United States of America

10 9 8 7 6 5 4 3 2 1

Editorial Board

Dr. Mark B. Moore, *Chairman*
Dr. William M. Greathouse
Mr. Bud Lunn
Dr. Leslie Parrott
Dr. W. T. Purkiser
Dr. Richard Taylor
Rev. John M. Nielson

Executive Editor: Dr. A. F. Harper
Associate Editor: Dr. J. Fred Parker

Advisory Board

Dr. J. D. Abbott
Colonel Milton Agnew
Dr. William Arnett
Dr. Myron Augsburger
Dr. Frank Baker
Dr. Don Bastian
Dr. Charles Carter
Dr. Frank Carver
Dr. Allen Coppedge
Dr. Leo Cox
Dr. David Cubie
Dr. Alex Deasley
Dr. Don Demaray
Dr. Melvin Dieter
Dr. Morton Dorsey
Dr. H. Ray Dunning
Dr. George Failing
Dr. Eldon Fuhrman
Dr. Myron Goldsmith

Dr. J. Kenneth Grider
Dr. Norval Hadley
Dr. Merne Harris
Dr. Leon Hynson
Dr. Dennis Kinlaw
Dr. John A. Knight
Dr. Richard Lovelace
Mrs. Evelyn Mottweiler
Dr. Wayne G. McCown
Dr. Herb McGonigle
Dr. Arlo Newell
Dr. Jose C. Rodriquez
Dr. Delbert Rose
Dr. Bill Strickland
Dr. Willard Taylor
Dr. R. Duane Thompson
Dr. George A. Turner
Dr. Mildred B. Wynkoop

Permission to quote from the following copyrighted version of the Bible is acknowledged with appreciation:

The Holy Bible, New International Version, copyright © 1978 by the New York International Bible Society.

Contents

Foreword	7
Understanding *Great Holiness Classics*	8
Concepts and Identifying Terms	12
Abbreviations Used in This Volume	15
Editor's Introduction to Volume 2	17

CHAPTER 1: JOHN WESLEY AND HIS ROOTS ... 21
    Thomas à Kempis
    William Law
    John Wesley, the Man

CHAPTER 2: SELECTED SERMONS ... 43
    Wesley's Preaching
    Key Sermons by Wesley
        The Circumcision of the Heart (1733)
        The Pure in Heart (1739)
        The Marks of the New Birth (1741)
        Catholic Spirit (1749)
        Original Sin (1759)
        On Sin in Believers (1763)
        The Scripture Way of Salvation (1765)
        The Repentance of Believers (1767)
        On Perfection (1788)
        On Patience (1788)
        The More Excellent Way (1788)
        On the Wedding Garment (1790)

CHAPTER 3: A PLAIN ACCOUNT OF CHRISTIAN
      PERFECTION ... 155

CHAPTER 4: EXPOSITIONS, HYMNS, LETTERS, AND
      TREATISES ... 223
    Notes on the Old and New Testaments
    Holiness in the Hymns

The Letters of John Wesley
Appeals to Men of Reason and Religion
Social Implications of Entire Sanctification

CHAPTER 5: WESLEY'S CLOSE ASSOCIATES 303
Charles Wesley (1707-88)
Adam Clarke, LL.D. (1760-1832)
Richard Watson (1781-1833)

CHAPTER 6: JOHN FLETCHER 381
Fletcher's Thought
The Heart of Fletcher's Teaching

CHAPTER 7: FRANCIS ASBURY AND HIS ASSOCIATES IN AMERICA 457
Francis Asbury
Asbury's Associates
Phillip Gatch • William Watters • William Thatcher • Freeborn Garrettson • Ezekiel Cooper • Daniel Hitt • William McKendree

Foreword

John Wesley is acknowledged and acclaimed as the chief architect of the doctrine of entire sanctification or Christian perfection as understood within the Holiness Movement. However, the truth this tenet expresses derives from the very heart of Scripture, and the experience and life it enshrines have been known and exemplified by the saints of every age.

Nor did Wesley give final and complete formulation of this truth. Theology is an ongoing process; it endeavors to interpret truth in language and thought-forms relevant to each succeeding generation. The creativity of the Spirit is evident in the unfolding of the doctrine from Wesley to the present. The truth of Christian holiness is so grand it defies any finality of expression.

Furthermore, since saints within every Christian tradition have found this Kingdom treasure, their witness to holiness reflects the variety of these traditions. The truth of perfect love is like a sparkling diamond—to appreciate its full beauty and brilliance we must view it from many angles.

This series of classics is designed to provide the modern reader a compact library of holiness literature. Herein you will find, along with appropriate editorial introductions and comments, many of the significant primary documents of the Holiness Movement. I commend these volumes as a devotional treasure for those who seek spiritual enrichment as well as a resource library for teachers and preachers who would deepen and enlarge their understanding of this central truth of Scripture.

—WILLIAM M. GREATHOUSE
General Superintendent
Church of the Nazarene

Understanding the Great Holiness Classics

Holiness

Christian holiness is a scriptural teaching to be understood and a relationship with God to be experienced. God is a holy God, and He asks His people to be like Him in this respect.

In the Old Testament we read, "Ye shall be holy: for I the Lord your God am holy" (Lev. 19:2). In teaching us about our responsibilities to God, Jesus summarized the first chapter of the Sermon on the Mount with the admonition: "Be ye therefore perfect, even as your Father which is in heaven is perfect" (Matt. 5:48).

Every sincere Christian wants to know what it means to be as holy as God asks us to be. Every follower of Christ feels at times yearnings to be more Christlike, to somehow realize the Christian perfection Jesus sets before us.

It is this ideal and goal taught in the Scriptures that has, across the centuries, stirred every devout Christian who has sought and experienced God's sanctifying grace. In John Wesley's *A Plain Account of Christian Perfection* he records his own experience of discovering this truth: "I tell you, as plain as I can speak, where and when I found this. I found it in the oracles of God, in the Old and New Testament, when I read them with no other view or desire, but to save my own soul" (*WW,* 11:444).

The Holiness Classics

Following in the tradition of Wesley and other devout persons who have sought and preached Christian holiness, the publishers conceived and launched this series of six volumes of *Great Holiness Classics.* The desire and purpose was, in Wesley's words, to "spread scriptural holiness over these lands" in the 20th century.

The commission given to the editors states that desire.

> To provide a representative compilation of the best holiness literature in a format readily accessible to the average minister, thus providing: (1) the preservation of the essential elements of our holiness heritage; (2) an overview of the broad scope of the holi-

ness message; (3) a norm for holiness theology, proclamation, and practice; (4) a succinct reference work on holiness; and (5) a revival of the best of the out-of-print holiness classics.

What Is a Classic?

A classic work comes from the past, but simply being old does not make it classic. To be classic, a work must have enduring excellence. Its content must be so true and persuasive that succeeding generations read it and are moved to accept the truth and to shape their lives by it. Seeking after holiness as taught in a classic, one finds the truths verified both in Scripture and in his own experience with God. A work is classic because its truths are central to revealed and to experiential Christianity.

It is this verifying of previous experience that keeps a classic alive in the consciousness of the Christian community. There is here a principle somewhat parallel to the scientific method. In science we accept as true an experiment that can be repeated under similar conditions with the same results.

Because a holiness classic represents such a verifiable and biblical promise of spiritual fulfillment, it becomes a typical example of true teaching and a dependable model of Christian experience. Other persons who ponder the Scripture and perform the experiment report comparable experiences of God. The accumulating testimony verifies the classic nature of the document.

A classic thus becomes an authoritative commentary on scriptural truth. It contains guidance that can be depended on to result in sound action and blessed results. The work therefore becomes a norm for future generations. It affirms to the reader, "If you approach God as I did and respond to Him, as by His Word and Spirit He led me to respond, you will discover that He works in your life as I testify He has worked in mine."

In a letter to Dr. Middleton, Wesley cites this appeal to holy living as characteristic of the Christian Fathers: "What the Scripture promises, I enjoy. Come and see what Christianity has done here; and acknowledge it is of God" (*WW*, 10:79).

Selection of Materials

The editors have been guided by these concepts of classic holiness writings. Works that have spoken to succeeding generations have endured; therefore, we have included them. Writings that present views widely held by other holiness writers are to be considered classic. A work that stimulates the reader to try the grand experiment is classical. In Christian literature, writings that most faithfully reflect biblical teachings are classical in the best sense of being truly Christian norms.

The materials here selected as classic, then, (1) reflect accurately the teachings of the Bible, (2) have a broad and common base of Christian testimony, (3) and are in line with the best thinking of Christian leaders who have enjoyed the experience of God's sanctifying grace.

What we have chosen, we believe gives a true account of God's plan for holy living. These writings offer a norm for Christian life that reflects God's will for His children. They lead to the greatest personal fulfillment and inspire believers to make their most effective contribution to the extension of God's kingdom.

Truth with Tolerance

Not all sincere Christians understand Bible holiness in the same way. What is here reflected is generally called the Wesleyan interpretation of entire sanctification. Even within the circle of those who follow Wesley there are some differences of interpretation. The statement of "Concepts and Identifying Terms" was drawn up as a way to reflect the widely accepted positions of the Wesleyan, Methodist tradition.

We recognize and appreciate guides to holy living from other traditions as in the Moravian, Quaker, Mennonite, and modern Keswick movements. Much of what is here included crosses all denominational boundaries. It will therefore speak to the spirits of evangelical Christians from most of the historic orthodox communions.

In order to avoid being too restrictive in our selections, we have sought the advice of a broad group of nearly 50 Bible scholars and churchmen whose names appear in the lists of editors, and of members of the editorial advisory boards. These persons have all been involved in a continuing consultation on the choice of materials to be included. We trust that the broad consensus further assures our choice of truly classic materials.

Editorial Policy

The editors were instructed to select writings "judged by the quality of the material and its ability to speak to this generation."

Because many of the holiness classics, especially in the first two volumes, come from an earlier period of writing, we were further given "the right to excerpt and edit the materials, updating archaic usage as needed."

Our goal has been, insofar as is possible, to let the writers speak for themselves. In excerpting we have tried to be completely faithful to the writer's views, deleting only dated, irrelevant, or duplicated materials. Our concern has always been to present as clearly as possible what the writer believed, experienced, and taught about Christian holiness.

In order to make our selections as clear as possible for today's reader we have: (1) modernized some spelling and punctuation, (2) divided some long paragraphs for greater ease in reading, (3) prepared brief introductions and analyses of the writings included, and we have also (4) inserted center heads, side heads, and cut-in headings as brief indications of content in order to guide the reader who is looking for specific aspects of holiness teaching.

For the historical scholar who wishes to follow in our footsteps and form his own judgment of our accuracy, we have: (1) indicated our sources by title, date, edition, and page numbers from which the selection is taken (where relevant for accuracy, we have used the earliest editions of the text); (2) retained original paragraph numbers to aid the reader in locating the source of our quotations; (3) used ellipses to indicate where material has been omitted; and (4) retained italics that appear in the originals, to show what the writers sought to emphasize.

Our Prayer

The prayer of the editors and publishers is that all who read these classics of holy living may come to understand "the way of God more perfectly" (Acts 18:26).

We pray "that Christ may dwell in your hearts by faith; that ye, being rooted and grounded in love, may be able to comprehend with all saints what is the breadth, and length, and depth, and height; and to know the love of Christ, which passeth knowledge, that ye might be filled with all the fulness of God.

"Now unto him that is able to do exceeding abundantly above all that we ask or think, according to the power that worketh in us, unto him be glory in the church by Christ Jesus throughout all ages, world without end. Amen" (Eph. 3:17-21).

—A. F. HARPER
Executive Editor

Concepts and Identifying Terms

At the beginning of the project the editors were mandated to "strive for balance, reflecting the various facets of holiness—crisis and process, practice and proclamation, etc."

In order to guide us and to test the inclusiveness and balance of materials chosen, it seemed necessary to devise an instrument for reminder and measurement. We therefore developed the following list of concepts and identifying terms.

The statements are designed to indicate the teachings of the church. The identifying terms are planned as a kind of shorthand device for highlighting these truths throughout the set and in the indexes.

We believe the statements faithfully reflect what the Bible teaches and what the Church has believed and taught across the centuries. The terms are biblical and/or classical in the sense that they represent the language the Church has used to describe the various facets of the experience of God's sanctifying grace.

For convenient reference, we have used these code words as cut-in heads on pages where the related concepts are explored.

A. Doctrinal

1. The requirement of entire sanctification is rooted in God's holiness. — **God's Holiness**
2. The need for entire sanctification is seen in the remaining presence of inbred sin, or carnality, in believers. The experience of entire sanctification includes cleansing from this original sin. — **Carnality/ Cleansing**
3. Entire sanctification is a gift of God's grace. — **Grace**
4. God provides the gift in the atonement of Christ. — **Atonement**

5. To be sanctified wholly means to receive grace to love God with your whole heart and to love your neighbor as yourself. — **Perfect Love**
6. At conversion, Christians receive God's Holy Spirit in regeneration, sometimes described as initial sanctification. To be sanctified wholly means to be baptized, or filled with the Holy Spirit, as happened to the disciples in the Upper Room. — **Holy Spirit**
7. God offers the ministry of the indwelling Holy Spirit to make us more Christlike. — **Christlikeness**
8. We believe the doctrine of entire sanctification is taught in the Bible and is consistent with other salvation truths of Scripture. — **Scriptural**
9. Entire sanctification is God's call to all Christians. — **For All Christians**
10. Entire sanctification is experienced as a second blessing of grace subsequent to regeneration. — **Second Blessing**
11. Because entire sanctification is God's gift in response to faith, it occurs in a moment of time, just as God's forgiveness comes in an instant. — **In a Moment**
12. Entire sanctification is also known as Christian perfection, perfect love, heart purity, the baptism with the Holy Spirit, being filled with the Spirit, the fullness of the blessing, full salvation, the deeper life, Christian holiness, scriptural holiness, the rest of faith, and the promise of the Father. — **Names**

B. Steps to Seeking and Finding

13. The new birth is a prerequisite to entire sanctification. — **New Birth**
14. Conviction of need is a condition for the personal quest after holiness. — **Hunger**
15. Full consecration is both a precondition and a gracious fruit of entire sanctification. — **Consecration**
16. Faith grounded on the full-orbed purpose of Christ's death, and the fullest consecration of — **Faith**

which we are capable, is the human condition for entire sanctification.

17. God gives the witness of His Spirit when we are sanctified wholly. — **Assurance**

C. **Living the Life of Holiness**

18. Christians grow in likeness to Christ, both before and after entire sanctification. Successful growth requires obedience, trust, deep devotion, and personal discipline. — **Growth**
19. Being filled with the Spirit makes a difference in a Christian's attitudes. — **Attitudes**
20. Holiness tends toward fulfillment of life and wholeness of human personality. — **Wholeness**
21. Though sanctified wholly, men and women are still limited by their imperfections in judgment, personality, and conduct; they are still subject to all sorts of temptation. — **Humanity**
22. Dangers to which the sanctified are especially vulnerable include spiritual pride and setting standards too high. — **Dangers**

D. **Proclamation—Witnessing**

23. Testifying to God's work of entire sanctification honors God and spreads the truth. — **Witnessing**
24. The truth of entire sanctification and a holy life is to be proclaimed through preaching. — **Preaching**
25. Understanding of the truth of Christian holiness and hunger for the experience are communicated through teaching. — **Teaching**
26. The truth of Christian holiness is spread through written testimony, exposition, and exhortation. — **Writing**
27. We document and prove holiness by living holy lives and by Christian ethical behavior. — **Ethics**

Abbreviations Used in This Volume

CHUPCM	*Collection of Hymns for the Use of the People Called Methodists.* London: John Mason, 1849.
EPPWM	*Ecclesiastical Principles and Policies of the Wesleyan Methodists.* London: Pierce, 1854.
FW	*Fletcher's Works.* 9 vols. London: Wesleyan Conference Office, 1877.
HAM	*History of American Methodism.* Nashville: Abingdon Press, 1964.
HMCB	*History of the Methodist Church in Britain.* London: Epworth Press, 1965.
JFA	*Journal of Francis Asbury.* Nashville: Abingdon Press, 1958.
JJW	*Journal of John Wesley.* Edited by Curnock. London: Epworth Press, 1938.
JWNT	*John Wesley's New Testament.* Anniversary ed. Philadelphia: John C. Winston Co., 1953.
LJW	*Letters of John Wesley.* Edited by Telford. London: Epworth Press, 1931.
NHM	*New History of Methodism.* London: Hodder and Stoughton, 1909.
PWJCW	*Poetical Works of John and Charles Wesley.* Edited by Osborn. London: Wesleyan-Methodist Conference Office, 1868-72.
RWW	*Richard Watson's Works.* London: John Mason, 1858.
SS	*Standard Sermons of John Wesley.* Edited by Sugden. London: Epworth Press, 1921.
SSB	*Standard Sermons of John Wesley.* Edited by Burwash.
WN	*Wesley's Explanatory Notes upon the New Testament.* London: William Bower, 1755.
WSJB	*Wesley's Sermons.* 3 vols. Edited by Rev. John Beecham. London: Wesleyan Conference Office, 1866.
WW	*Wesley's Works,* 3rd edition. London: John Mason, 1829.
WW, Amer.	*Wesley's Works,* American edition. Edited by Emory.

John Wesley (1703-91)

Editor's Introduction to Volume 2

The 18th century was the watershed of the modern Holiness Movement and of its literature. Into that century God poured rivers of living water, and out of that century flowed streams of power and inspiration.

No era exists in historical isolation, but some are granted providential dispensations that give them unique significance among the centuries. The 18th century was such a time.

In that period it pleased God to send a widespread, penetrating, and elevating revival of spiritual religion such as had never previously been known by His European and American church. With that wind of the Spirit came a renewal of the divine call to the preaching and teaching of scriptural holiness.

From one angle this was the revival of the Reformation, but it went both deeper and further. It brought the recovered doctrine of justification by faith alone to its biblical and reasonable completeness in the complementary truth of entire sanctification by faith alone. It restored a whole gospel to the whole church for the whole world and the whole person.

The holiness preachers of the 18th century knew their indebtedness to those who had gone before, especially to the Reformers and the Apostolic Fathers.

The Wesley brothers acknowledged their debt particularly to the early Fathers of the first five Christian centuries. John translated some of their writings and gave 13 reasons why they should be studied.[1] Charles borrows their ideas, even words, and transplants them into his hymns.[2]

The Methodist preachers believed, experienced, and preached the gospel of biblical holiness. They hungered and thirsted and were

---

1. Cf. *The Epistles of the Apostolical Fathers*, comp. J. Wesley (London: Houlston and Stoneman, 1845). Cf. also *WW*, 10:238-43.

2. Cf. Henry Bett, *The Hymns of Methodism* (London: Epworth Press, 1913), 98.

satisfied. In the blood and sweat of their welfare work they exemplified and mediated the doctrine of love made perfect. Their lives and their literature show that although there is a doctrine of heart holiness, holiness is more than a doctrine. It is living the life that pleases God in conformity with His will declared in His Word and made possible by His indwelling Spirit. Holiness is a life-style molded by the Holy Spirit in the heart made clean by the power of the blood of Jesus.

From the writings of a few of these men I have selected some that must be looked upon as classic. They belong to the first generation of writers in the modern period of Christian history, and to the first generation of writers in the Holiness Movement. These selections are classic in the sense of clarity, pungency, and purity of biblical doctrine. They are classic also in the sense of age; they are vintage works; indeed, they are definitive and formative for the later generations of holiness authors and teachers.

As long as New Testament holiness is being preached, the names of Law, the Wesleys, Fletcher, Clarke, Benson, Watson, and Hunt will head the list.

I have titled this period of holiness literature *The Wesley Century*. The dates do not synchronize with Wesley's birth and death (1703-91). But 1725 may be circled as the inaugural of holiness literature. That was the year in which William Law published the little book *A Serious Call to a Devout and Holy Life*. The book compelled Wesley to drive a probe deep into his soul, examine the motives of his life, and scrutinize his intentions. That book has been a conscience goad and a life guide for serious-minded Christians for over 250 years. In its many editions it has been a serious call to a devout and holy life to thousands of people. Its birth year seems a natural starting point in a presentation of the holiness literature of the 18th century.

The concluding year of 1825 is chosen more arbitrarily, but it virtually closes the first decade of the Methodist holiness movement without its founders. Charles Wesley died in 1788; George Whitefield "joined the ship's company" in heaven in 1770. Mr. Wesley finished his course with joy in 1791. It took very little time for a strong leadership to emerge, but the years 1791-1825 were extremely crucial not only to Methodist policy and organization, but also to the publication of holiness literature.

Wesley never flagged in what he understood to be a crucial part of his work, namely the production and sale of religious literature. He wrote books and pamphlets by the score; he borrowed, edited, and circulated the writings of others; his saddlebags symbolize the Methodist publishers and all later holiness publishing houses. He appointed, supervised, and guided editor after editor. When he died he left, as probably the liveliest and most enduring resource of a holiness preacher, the Methodist Publishing House. Since his death, the offspring of Methodism—Primitive Methodists, Free Methodists, Wesleyans, United Methodists, Nazarenes, and others—have given priority to the terribly decisive matter of Christian literature. Wesley died at the end of the 18th century; the 19th became undoubtedly the most fruitful and crowded period of the production of substantial writings on "second blessing holiness."

The editor of Methodism when Wesley died was James Creighton. He was a most able and painstaking writer who passed his duties on to George Story in 1791. Story lived until 1818, dying at the age of 80. His story is in volume 5 of *The Lives of Early Methodist Preachers,* where Benson adds: "He was an old disciple and faithful laborer in the Lord's vineyard. His piety was genuine, and uniformly evidenced by a life and conversation unblamable and holy. . . . He believed and loved our doctrines."[3]

Joseph Benson brings to its end the period of Methodist holiness literature directly associated with Wesley. His work covered the years 1804-21 as editor of the Methodist Book Room. He it was who edited and piloted through the press the first octavo edition of *Wesley's Works.* A man of outstanding ability as scholar and author, he had taught alongside John Fletcher at Trevecca College. He also authored a justly appreciated commentary, plus biographies of both John and Mary Fletcher. His obituary declares that "few ministers in modern times have been so successful in the conversion of sinners to God. His applications at the end of his sermons were energetic and impressive almost beyond belief."

—T. CRICHTON MITCHELL

---

3. *The Lives of Early Methodist Preachers,* Thomas Jackson, ed. (London: Wesleyan Conference Office, 1865-66), 5:240.

1

JOHN WESLEY AND HIS ROOTS

Thomas à Kempis (1380-1471)
The Imitation of Christ

William Law (1686-1761)
A Serious Call to a Devout and Holy Life

John Wesley, the Man (1703-91)

1 John Wesley and His Roots

Thomas à Kempis
(1380-1471)

The influence of the 15th-century monk Thomas à Kempis on the 18th-century apostle of England is striking indeed.

Thomas Hemerken became known as Thomas à Kempis, from the name of his hometown, Kempen, Prussia. He was a child of medieval Catholicism in revolt against decadent Catholic religion. Born in 1380 at Kempen of a humble Catholic family, he received his education under the disciples of Gerhard Groote at the Deventer school of the Brethren of the Common Life—precursors of the Protestant Reformation. He was influenced especially by Florentius Radewyn who later directed him to a brother-school at Mount Saint Agnes. For 72 years à Kempis lived there, becoming a priest in 1413 and subprior in 1425 and 1448. He copied the complete Bible for the house of Mount Saint Agnes and had the habit of distributing Bible portions written on small slips of paper to those who could read them in their homes.

Thomas à Kempis began the writing of *De Imitatione Christi* in 1413 and completed it in 1441. He died in 1471 but his little "golden treatise," as Wesley describes it, lives on.

> Its keynote is peace, and it embodies that great spiritual culture which began with Augustine. . . .
> Thomas à Kempis concentrated it all in his wonderful book, and while reacting against formalism, and aridness on the one hand, saved spiritual religion from becoming extreme mysticism on the other.[1]

John Wesley's first reaction to à Kempis was annoyance rather than pleasure. Nevertheless à Kempis moved Wesley to examine deeply his motives and his intentions:

> I saw that giving even all my life to God (supposing it possible

---

1. Rev. D. Butler, *Thomas à Kempis: A Religious Study* (Edinburgh and London: Oliphant, Anderson, and Ferrier, 1908).

to do this and go no farther) would profit me nothing unless I gave my heart, yea, all my heart to Him.

I saw that "simplicity of intention and purity of affections," one desire in all we speak or do, and one desire ruling all our tempers, are indeed "the wings of the soul: without which she can never ascend to the mount of God."[2]

The book's effect on Wesley, as on many other famous Englishmen, was thus powerful. He wanted very much to put *De Imitatione Christi* into the hands and hearts of "the people called Methodists." In 1735 he published his own edition—the 16th in English. From that edition we present four excerpts.

The Imitation of Christ

Wesley's Preface

It is impossible for anyone to know the usefulness of this treatise till he has read it in such a manner as it deserves: instead of heaping up commendations on it, which those who have so read it do not want, and those who have not, will not believe, I have transcribed a few plain directions on how to read this (or indeed any other religious book) with improvement.

I. Assign some stated time every day for this pious employment. If any indispensable business unexpectedly robs you of your hour of retirement, take the next hour for it. When such large portions of each day are so willingly bestowed on bodily refreshments, can you scruple allotting some little time daily for the improvement of your immortal soul?

II. Prepare yourself for reading by purity of intention, whereby you singly aim at your soul's benefit; and then in a short ejaculation beg God's grace to enlighten your understanding, and dispose your heart for receiving what you read: and that you may both know what He requires of you, and seriously resolve to execute His will when known.

III. Be sure to read not cursorily and hastily but leisurely and seriously and with great attention, with proper intervals and pauses

---

2. *WW*, 11:366.

that you may allow time for the enlightenings of divine grace. Stop frequently to recollect what you have read and consider how to reduce it to practice. Further, let your reading be continued and regular, not rambling and desultory. It shows a vitiated palate to taste of many dishes without fixing upon or being satisfied with any; not but that it will be of great service to read over and over those passages which more nearly concern yourself and more closely affect your own practice or inclinations, especially if you add a particular examination upon each.

IV. Labour for a temper, correspondent to what you read; otherwise it will prove empty and unprofitable while it only enlightens your understanding without influencing your will or inflaming your affections. Therefore intersperse here and there pious aspirations to God and petitions for His grace. Select also any remarkable sayings or advices; treasure them up in your memory to ruminate and consider on, which you may either in time of need draw forth as arrows from a quiver against temptations, against this or that vice which you are more particularly addicted to; or make use of as incitements to humility, patience, the love of God, or any other virtue.

V. Conclude all with a short ejaculation to God that He would preserve and prosper this good seed sown in your heart, that it may bring forth its fruit in due season. And think not this will take up too much of your time for you can never bestow it to so good advantage.

—Preface, 7-8

Purity of Mind and Simplicity of Intention

1. Simplicity and purity are the two wings by which a person is lifted up above all earthly things. Simplicity is in the intention, purity is in the affection. Simplicity tends to God, purity apprehends and tastes Him.

No action will hinder you if you are inwardly free from inordinate affection. If you intend and seek nothing but the will of God and the good of your neighbour, you will enjoy eternal liberty; for if your heart be right, every creature will be a looking glass of life and a text of holy doctrine. There is no creature so lowly but represents the goodness of God.

2. Heart purity sees and senses things clearly and directly, discerning the seen and the unseen things of heaven and hell; for we judge outward things according to our inward condition. If there is real joy

in the world, it is the pure heart that possesses it; but the evil conscience feels tribulation and affliction.

As when iron is put into the fire its rust is burned away and it becomes bright like fire, so is the heart that commits itself entirely to God. It is purified from all and transmuted into the likeness of God. When the heart cools toward God, seeking Him becomes a burden; but when we begin to forget ourselves that burden becomes a light thing indeed.

—Book II, Chap. IV, 28 ff.

Temptation

So long as we live in this world we cannot be without temptation. Hence it is written in Job that the life of a man is a warfare upon earth. Everyone therefore ought to take care of his own temptations and watch in prayer lest he be deceived by the devil, who never sleeps but goes about seeking whom he may devour.

Temptations are often very profitable to men, though they may be troublesome and grievous, for in them a man is humbled, purified, and instructed. All the saints have passed through and profited by many tribulations and temptations, and they that could not bear them became reprobates and fell away. There is no place where there are no temptations, and there is no man immune from temptation in this life. When one temptation goes away another comes, and we shall ever have something to suffer. Many people try to get away from temptations only to fall more grievously into them. By flight alone we cannot overcome, but by patience and humility we conquer all our enemies.

He that only avoids them outwardly and does not pluck them up by the roots shall profit little; indeed, temptations will soon return to him worse than before. By patience, with God's help, you will more easily overcome than by harsh and disquieting self-effort. Often take counsel in temptations, and don't deal roughly with him that is tempted.

Temptation begins in inconstancy of mind and little confidence in God. As a ship without a rudder is tossed to and fro with the waves, so the negligent man is tempted in many ways. Fire tries iron, and temptation a just man. We know not often what we are able to do, but temptation shows us what we are.

We must be watchful, especially in the beginning of the temptation, for the enemy is then more easily overcome if he is not allowed to enter our hearts but is resisted at his first knock. Wherefore one said, "Withstand the beginning for an after remedy comes too late."

First there cometh to the mind a simple evil thought; then a strong imagination; afterwards delight; and lastly consent, and so by little and little our malicious enemy getteth entrance whilst he is not resisted at the beginning. The longer one is slack in resisting, the weaker he becomes daily and the enemy stronger against him.

Some suffer the greatest temptation in the beginning of their conversion, others in the latter end. Others, again, are much troubled almost throughout their life. Some are but slightly tempted according to the wisdom which weighs the states of men and orders all things for the good of His elect.

We ought therefore, when we are tempted, to pray the more fervently to God who will surely make with the temptation a way to escape that we may be able to bear it. Let us therefore humble ourselves under the hand of God in all temptations and tribulations, for He will exalt the humble in spirit.

In temptations and afflictions man is proved how much he has profited. Neither is it any such great thing if a man be devout and fervent when he feels no affliction, but if he bears himself patiently in time of adversity there is hope then of great proficiency. Some are exempt from great temptations and are overcome in small ones that, being humbled, they may never trust themselves in great matters who are baffled in such small things.

—Book I, Chap. X, 14 ff.

Bearing the Cross After Jesus

Lord Jesus, as Thou hast said and promised so let it come to pass. I have received the cross, I have received it from Thy hand. I will bear it, and bear it till death, as Thou has laid it upon me. Truly the life of a Christian is in the cross, but yet it is a guide to paradise. I have begun. I may not go back, neither is it fit to leave that which I have undertaken.

Let us then take courage, my brethren, and go forward together. Jesus will be with us. For Jesus' sake we have undertaken His cross, for Jesus' sake let us persevere therein. He will be our helper, who is our guide and forerunner. Behold, our King goeth before us and will also fight for us. Let us follow Him manfully. Let us not be dismayed, but be ready to die manfully in the battle.

Let us not blemish our glory by flying from the cross.

—Book III, Chap. XXXIX, 75 ff.

William Law
(1686-1761)

Despite John Wesley's disagreement with William Law and his severe criticism of him, Law's writings made Wesley look more closely at the nature of his intentions as a seeker after that "holiness without which it is impossible to see God." Law was an exceedingly important link in the spiritual pilgrimage of both John Wesley and his brother Charles.

Thomas Coke wrote: "The great Mr. Law . . . enforced by his excellent pen that essential doctrine of the Gospel the necessity of the inspiration of the Holy Ghost. . . . This considerable writer was the great fore-runner of the Revival which followed, and did more to promote it than any other individual."[3]

William Law's father was a grocer at King's Cliffe in Northampton, England, and there William was born on February 3, 1686. His parents were Church of England people who saw to it that their son was reared among the Orthodox and traditional Anglican influences. William went to Emmanuel College, Cambridge, at 19 years of age, graduated in 1708 and was ordained in 1711.

When a new dynasty was thrust on England, numbers of clergymen of the Church of England refused to transfer their allegiance from one monarch to the other. William Law joined their ranks by refusing the oath of allegiance to King George I. This was as genuine a proof of his religion as of his politics in that it demanded that he relinquish his University Fellowship to which he had been elected in 1711. Thus, without a pulpit, Law took up his pen and produced writings that impacted the religious world of his day.

In 1726 he published *Christian Perfection,* and in 1728, *A Serious Call to a Devout and Holy Life,* the book that virtually stunned the Oxford Holy Club led by the Wesleys. Law became counselor-in-chief to the Wesley brothers in the years of their "legal night" as

---

3. John Henry Overton, *The Evangelical Revival in the Eighteenth Century* (New York: Randolph and Company, 1886), 7 ff.

Charles Wesley put it. They visited him, walking from Oxford to London to do so.

The Wesleys broke with him later on the grounds that he had failed to point them to the Lamb of God and the power of the Evangel, but John Wesley never lost his high opinion of Law's *Serious Call*. Lumping together Law's two most famous books, which he had read while at Lincoln College, Wesley wrote: "I was much offended at several parts of both, yet they convinced me more and more of the exceeding height and breadth and depth of the law of God. The light flowed in so mightily upon my soul that everything appeared in a new view. I cried to God for help."[4]

The *Serious Call* is just that! The author was sick of the laxity of his contemporary church and society. He frowned upon many of the ways of religion, so Wesley carefully examined his friendships. Law advocated the importance of isolation and strict control of pleasure, so Wesley trimmed his recreational life down to the core. Following Thomas à Kempis, Law urged strict use of time; so Wesley first rose at seven, then six, five, and finally four every morning. He maintained the habit to the end of his long life as beneficial to health and spiritual discipline.

But chiefly it was Law's emphases on singleness of will and purity of intention that gripped and held Wesley. On this aspect of holiness, Law seems at least as memorable as Søren Kierkegaard with his "purity of heart is to will one thing."

Echoes of William Law are heard in many places in Wesley's preaching, especially in his messages on the Sermon on the Mount. Indeed Standard Sermon XXIII is actually based on chapters IV and VI of Law's *Serious Call* and contains extended quotations from it.[5]

William Law offers much counsel and seems to lay down a great many rules, but he is not a mere moralist. He is endeavoring to have us raise our sights and focus on a life of entire devotement to God. His last book concludes with these words:

> Therefore all that Christ was, did, suffered, dying in the flesh, and ascending into heaven, was for the sole end, to purchase for all his followers a new birth, new life, and new light, in and by the Spirit of God restored to them and living in them as their support,

---

4. *LJW*, 8:238.
5. *SS*, 1:473, 489.

Comforter, and Guide into all truth. And this was His, "Lo, I am with you alway, even unto the end of the world."[6]

John Wesley, the father of the modern Holiness Movement, certainly did not forsake, nor did he forget the pungent ethical teaching of William Law. He placed Law's works on the book list for Society classes. In 1743 he published an edited version of Law's book on *Perfection* and did the same with the *Serious Call* in 1744.

A Serious Call to a Devout and Holy Life

SINCERITY OF INTENTION

Let a man but have so much piety as to intend to please God in all the actions of his life, as the happiest and best thing in the world and then he will never swear more. It will be as impossible for him to swear, whilst he feels this intention within himself, as it is impossible for a man that intends to please his prince to go up and abuse him to his face.

It seems but a small and necessary part of piety to have such a sincere intention as this; and that he has no reason to look upon himself as a disciple of Christ who is not thus far advanced in piety. And yet it is purely for want of this degree of piety that you see such a mixture of sin and folly in the lives even of the better sort of people. It is for want of this intention that you see men that profess religion, yet live in swearing and sensuality; that you see clergymen given to pride, and covetousness, and worldly enjoyments. It is for want of this intention that you see women that profess devotion yet living in all the folly and vanity of dress, wasting their time in idleness and pleasures, and in all such instances of state and equipage as their estates will reach. For let but a woman feel her heart full of this intention and she will find it as impossible to patch or paint as to curse or swear; she will no more desire to shine at balls or assemblies, or make a figure amongst those that are most finely dressed than she will desire to dance upon a rope to please spectators. She will know that the one is as far from the the wisdom and excellency of the Christian spirit as the other.

It was this general intention that made the primitive Christians such eminent instances of piety, and made the goodly fellowship of the

---

6. *LJW,* 8:258.

saints, and all the glorious army of martyrs and confessors. And if you will here stop and ask yourselves why you are not as pious as the primitive Christians were, your own heart will tell you that it is neither through ignorance nor inability but purely because you never thoroughly intended it. You observe the same Sunday worship that they did, and you are strict in it because it is your full intention to be so. And when you as fully intend to be like them in their ordinary common life, when you intend to please God in all your actions, you will find it as possible to be strictly exact in the service of the Church. And when you have this intention to please God in all your actions as the happiest and best thing in the world, you will find in you as great an aversion to everything that is vain and impertinent in common life, whether of business or pleasure, as you now have to any thing that is profane. You will be as fearful of living in any foolish way, either of spending your time or your fortune, as you are now fearful of neglecting the public worship.

Practical Effects of Sincerity

Now, who that lacks this general sincere intention can be reckoned a Christian? And yet if it was among Christians, it would change the whole face of the world. True piety and exemplary holiness would be as common and visible as buying and selling or any trade in life.

1. Let a clergyman be but thus pious and he will converse as if he had been brought up by an apostle. He will no more think and talk of noble preferment than of noble eating or a glorious chariot. He will no more complain of the frowns of the world, or a small cure [pastoral charge], or the want of a patron than he will complain of the want of a laced coat or a running horse. Let him but intend to please God in all his actions as the happiest and best thing in the world, and then he will know that there is nothing noble in a clergyman but a burning zeal for the salvation of souls; nor anything poor in his profession but idleness and a worldly spirit.

2. Again, let a tradesman but have this intention, and it will make him a saint in his shop; his everyday business will be a course of wise and reasonable actions, made holy to God by being done in obedience to His will and pleasure. He will buy and sell, and labour and travel, because by so doing he can do some good to himself and others. But then, as nothing can please God but what is wise, and reasonable, and holy, so he will neither buy nor sell, nor labour in any other manner,

nor to any other end, but such as may be shown to be wise, and reasonable, and holy.

He will therefore consider not what arts, or methods, or application, will soonest make him richer and greater than his brethren, or remove him from a shop to a life of state and pleasure; but he will consider what arts, what methods, what application can make worldly business most acceptable to God, and make a life of trade a life of holiness, devotion, and piety. This will be the temper and spirit of every tradesman; he cannot stop short of these degrees of piety whenever it is his intention to please God in all his actions as the best and happiest thing in the world. And on the other hand, whoever is not of this spirit and temper in his trade and profession, and does not carry it on only so far as is best subservient to a wise, and holy, and heavenly life, it is certain that he has not this intention; and yet without it, who can be shown to be a follower of Jesus Christ?

3. Again, let the gentleman of birth and fortune but have this intention and you will see how it will carry him from every appearance of evil to every instance of piety and goodness. He cannot live by chance or as humour and fancy carry him because he knows that nothing can please God but a wise and regular course of life. He cannot live in idleness and indulgence, in sports and gaming, in pleasures and intemperance, in vain expenses and high living; because these things cannot be turned into means of piety and holiness, or made so many parts of a wise and religious life. As he thus removes from all appearance of evil, so he hastens and aspires after every instance of goodness.

He does not ask what is allowable and pardonable but what is commendable and praiseworthy. He does not ask whether God will forgive the folly of our lives, the madness of our pleasures, the vanity of our expenses, the richness of our equipage, and the careless consumption of our time; but he asks whether God is pleased with these things, or whether these are the appointed ways of gaining His favor. He does not inquire whether it be pardonable to hoard up money, to adorn ourselves with diamonds, and gild our chariots whilst the widow and the orphan, the sick and the prisoner, want to be relieved; but he asks whether God has required these things at our hands, whether we shall be called to account at the last day for the neglect of them because it is not his intent to live in such ways as, for aught we know, God may perhaps pardon; but to be diligent in such ways as we know that God will infallibly reward.

He will not therefore look at the lives of Christians to learn how he ought to spend his estate, but he will look into the Scriptures and make every doctrine, parable, precept, or instruction that relates to rich men a law to himself in the use of his estate.

He will have nothing to do with costly apparel because the rich man in the Gospel was clothed with purple and fine linen. He denies himself the pleasures and indulgences which his estate could procure because our blessed Saviour saith, "Woe unto you that are rich! for ye have received your consolation" (Luke vi. 24). He will have but one rule for charity and that will be to spend all that he can that way because the Judge of quick and dead hath said that all that is so given is given to Him.

He will have no hospitable table for the rich and wealthy to come and feast with him, in good eating and drinking; because our blessed Lord saith, "When thou makest a dinner . . . call not thy friends, nor thy brethren, neither thy kinsmen, nor thy rich neighbours; lest they also bid thee again, and a recompence be made thee. But when thou makest a feast, call the poor, the maimed, the lame, the blind: and thou shalt be blessed; for they cannot recompense thee: for thou shalt be recompensed at the resurrection of the just" (Luke xiv. 12-14).

He will waste no money in gilded roofs, or costly furniture. He will not be carried from pleasure to pleasure in expensive state and equipage, because an inspired apostle hath said that "all that is in the world, the lust of the flesh, the lust of the eyes, and the pride of life, is not of the Father, but is of the world" (1 John ii. 16).

The Life That Pleases God

1. The Proper Use of Estate

Let not anyone look upon this as an imaginary description of charity that looks fine in the notion but cannot be put in practice. For it is so far from being an imaginary, impracticable form of life that it has been practiced by great numbers of Christians in former ages who were glad to turn their whole estates into a constant course of charity. And it is so far from being impossible now that if we can find any Christians that sincerely intend to please God in all their actions as the best and happiest thing in the world, whether they be young or old, single or married, men or women, if they have but this intention, it will be impossible for them to do otherwise. This one principle will infallibly carry them to this height of charity and they will find themselves unable to stop short of it.

For how is it possible for a man that intends to please God in the use of his money and intends it because he judges it to be his greatest happiness; how is it possible for such a one, in such a state of mind, to bury his money in needless, impertinent finery, in covering himself or his horses with gold, whilst there are any works of piety and charity to be done with it or any ways of spending it well?

This is as strictly impossible as for a man that intends to please God in his words to go into company on purpose to swear and lie. For as all waste and unreasonable expense is done designedly, and with deliberation, so no one can be guilty of it whose constant intention is to please God in the use of his money.

I have chosen to explain this matter by appealing to this intention because it makes the case so plain and because everyone that has a mind may see it in the clearest light, and feel it in the strongest manner only by looking into his own heart. For it is as easy for every person to know whether he intends to please God in all his actions as for any servant to know whether this be his intention toward his master. Everyone also can as easily tell how he lays out his money and whether he considers how to please God in it as he can tell where his estate is and whether it be in money or land. So that here is no plea left for ignorance or frailty as to this matter. Everybody is in the light and everybody has power. And no one can fail except he that is not so much a Christian as to intend to please God in the use of his estate.

2. Sincerity in Devotion

You see two persons: one is regular in public and private prayer and the other is not. Now the reason of this difference is not this, that one has strength and power to observe prayer, and the other has not. But the reason is that one intends to please God in the duties of devotion and the other has no intention about it. Now the case is the same in the right or wrong use of our time and money. You see one person throwing away his time in sleep and idleness, in visiting and diversions, and his money in the most vain and unreasonable expenses. You see another careful of every day, dividing his hours by rules of reason and religion, and spending all his money in works of charity. Now the difference is not owing to this, that one has strength and power to do thus and the other has not; but it is owing to this, that one intends to please God in the right use of all his time and all his money and the other has no intention about it.

3. Sincerity with Ourselves

Here, therefore, let us judge ourselves sincerely. Let us not vainly content ourselves with the common disorders of our lives, the vanity of our expenses, the folly of our diversions, the pride of our habits, the idleness of our lives, and the wasting of our time, fancying that these are such imperfections as we fall into through the unavoidable weakness and frailty of our natures. But let us be assured that these disorders of our common life are owing to this, that we have not so much Christianity as to intend to please God in all the actions of our life as the best and happiest thing in the world. So that we must not look upon ourselves in a state of common and pardonable imperfection, but in such a state as wants the first and most fundamental principle of Christianity, that is, an intention to please God in all our actions.

And if anyone was to ask himself, how it comes to pass that there are any degrees of sobriety which he neglects, any practices of humility which he wants, any method of charity which he does not follow, any rules of redeeming time which he does not observe, his own heart will tell him that it is because he never intended to be so exact in those duties. For whenever we fully intend it, it is as possible to conform to all this regularity of life as it is possible for a man to observe times of prayer.

So that the fault does not lie here, that we desire to be good and perfect, but through the weakness of our nature fall short of it; but it is because we have not piety enough to intend to be as good as we can, or to please God in all the actions of our life. This we see is plainly the case of him that spends his time in sports when he should be in church. It is not his want of power but his want of intention or desire to be there.

And the case is plainly the same in every other folly of human life. She that spends her time and money in the unreasonable ways and fashions of the world does not do so because she wants power to be wise and religious in the management of her time and money, but because she has no intention or desire of being so. When she feels this intention she will find it as possible to act up to it as to be strictly sober and chaste because it is her care and desire to be so.

This doctrine does not suppose that we have no need of divine grace or that it is in our own power to make ourselves perfect. It only supposes that through the want of a sincere intention of pleasing God in all our actions we fall into such irregularities of life as by the ordinary means of grace we should have power to avoid; and that we have not that perfection which our present state of grace makes us capable of because we do not so much as intend to have it. It only teaches us that the reason why you see no real mortification or self-denial, no eminent charity, no profound humility, no heavenly affection, no true contempt of the world, no Christian meekness, no sincere zeal, no eminent piety in the common lives of Christians is because they do not so much as intend to be exact and exemplary in these virtues.

See: *Classics of Western Spirituality* (New York: Paulist Press, 1978), 56-63.
A Serious Call to a Devout and Holy Life (Grand Rapids: Baker Book House, 1977), 37-49.

* * *

John Wesley, the Man
(1703-91)

R. Newton Flew writes:
> A certain river on the continent rises from a mysterious spring which wells up from beneath an ancient cathedral. Within a quarter of a mile from its source the river has become so strong and forceful that a great mill is worked by it. It was with such a mysterious suddenness that the stream of Methodism appeared in the world. In an incredibly short space of time that stream had become a practical force.[7]

Flew sees the river's origin to be at Aldersgate in 1738, but the spring lies farther back and deeper down. There is no doubt that Wesley's ancestry and parentage had providentially much to do with the person he became and the work he did. Likewise there is no doubt that the river sprang from hidden springs in God.

---

7. R. Newton Flew, *The Idea of Perfection in Christian Theology* (London: Oxford University Press, 1934), 313.

The stream became a mighty river. We may without exaggeration assert that more than two score religious movements in the modern world trace their origins to Wesley and 18th-century Methodism. Within the space of 50 years there were at least 160,000 members in the Methodist Society. Seventy thousand of these were alive when Wesley died; a further 70,000 had died before him. There were also 65,000 Methodists in America. It was therefore with good reason that Wesley took as his text at the foundation laying of his new City Road Chapel in 1777, "What Hath God Wrought!"[8]

Wesley, at the age of 35, was led to where he could get the Bread of Life. He spent the next 53 years leading others to the same Source; also selecting, training, and sending men across land and sea with the same glad good news.

John Wesley was in no doubt as to why he was alive. It was to save as many souls as he could and to multiply that number by extending his ministry through the efforts of his noble helpers. To this he gave himself with zeal and singlemindedness. The churchmen of his own day were left standing breathless and shocked. Even 250 years later mobile men of the 20th century raise incredulous eyebrows. He was "out of breath pursuing souls" because he looked upon it as his one reason for existence. He could never do it halfheartedly or cautiously.

One learned critic traced Wesley's zeal and passion to his heredity. Writing to Wesley, he said:

> The son of a Wesley and an Annesley is in no danger of lukewarmness, but ought to take great care on the side of impetuosity and zeal. The tempter will never make you a saunterer or a sluggard, but if you are not upon your guard, may possibly before you are aware, make you a Quaker.[9]

John Wesley's ancestors were nonconformists on both the father's and the mother's side. They refused to knuckle under to the prejudicial laws favoring the Church of England. Great-grandfather Bartholemew Wesley was expelled from his charge under the 1662 Act of Uniformity. Grandfather John Wesley, M.A., son of Bartholemew, was imprisoned at Worcester on false charges, released, but later charged before the Bishop of Bristol for irregular preaching. He was sent to jail in Blandford for "not using the liturgy," and finally

---

8. *WW*, 7:419.
9. Letter from "John Smith" quoted from Moore's *Life of Wesley*, by Albert C. Outler, *John Wesley* (New York: Oxford University Press, 1964), 4.

thrown out of his living in 1662, for conscience' sake. Rejected by the Church of England, he was cast on the goodwill of the Presbyterians and Baptists who, he says, "treated him with much kindness." "Among them," he writes, "I preached almost every day." Two very small boys shared their parents' ostracism. One was Matthew Wesley; the other was Samuel, who became rector of Epworth and father of John Wesley, the Methodist.

It is not difficult to see the power of heredity in the founder of Methodism. Although Samuel returned to the church that had cast out his father, even he had strong traces of the dour independent spirit.

On Wesley's maternal side Dr. Annesley was "the St. Paul of Nonconformity." And here once again, although Annesley's daughter Su-

John Wesley visiting his mother's grave

sanna returned to the Church of England, nonconformity was in her blood. She held services in her kitchen when her husband was away from home on church business and also lent her support to the first of Methodism's lay preachers.

Early Life

Samuel and Susanna Wesley eventually made their home in Epworth in Lincolnshire where Samuel was rector, and here in June 1703 was born their 13th child, John Benjamin Wesley, the only Wesley child with a middle name.

At five years John started his formal education in the kitchen school of Susanna and also began to participate in her evening family counseling program. John's special evening was Thursday. He left home in 1714 to become a foundation scholar at Charterhouse School in London, noted for its severe discipline. In 1720 he went up to Oxford University's Christ Church College. By 1724 his spiritual and religious life was deepening and he had turned decisively toward the ministry of the Church of England.

Through the reading of the Catholic à Kempis, the Anglican Taylor, and the Presbyterian Scougal, Wesley came to a personal spiritual crisis in 1725. The crisis was so emphatic that various writers look upon that year as the year of Wesley's conversion. Certainly it was a watershed year for him. His life, ever methodical, became even more rigorously disciplined in the areas of self-examination, the keeping of a record as to how he used his time, and the whole matter of purity of intention in all his thoughts and actions. In 1727 Law's *Serious Call* intensified his devotional life.

Wesley meanwhile excelled in his studies and in 1726 was appointed Greek Lecturer. But in 1727 his father took ill at Epworth and for two years Wesley spent his life as the elder man's assistant.

Oxford and the Holy Club

In 1729 he was required to resume his duties at Oxford as a Fellow of Lincoln College. On his return there he found a few undergraduates who had formed themselves into a prayer, study, and goodwill group, headed by Charles Wesley. Before long Charles had willingly relinquished the leadership to John and soon the group was nicknamed "The Holy Club." They read and studied the Greek New Testament, the early Church Fathers, the classics of Christian devotion and history. They visited the prisoners in Oxford jail, fed and clothed the needy, and educated some of the children of Oxford's poor people.

The Holy Club, however, dwindled in numbers from over 20 to only 5 in 1733. One of the five was George Whitefield. Wesley ventured at this time to publish his little book of prayers and his *Christian Pattern*, a kind of rehash of à Kempis' *Imitation of Christ*.

To the New World

In 1735, following the death of his father, Wesley was offered and accepted the post of chaplain to the settlers in the new colony of Georgia under its founder and first governor, General Oglethorpe. But his work there, although conscientiously and diligently executed, brought satisfaction neither to him nor to the objects of his ministrations. He did much good and probably underestimated his contribution to Georgia's colonial religion. But he also made enemies and finally left Georgia under a cloud because of silly delays in legal proceedings. Wesley left Georgia late in 1737 in distress of soul, still trying to work his own passage to heaven. In Georgia he had, however, published the first *Methodist Hymnbook* in Charleston, 1737. He included mostly the hymns of his older contemporary Isaac Watts and some of his own fine translations of German hymns. In Georgia also he had learned how to preach in the open air and in the languages of the settlers, especially German, which he had learned aboard ship en route to the new world.

Returning from Georgia disillusioned and somewhat dejected, Wesley struggled on in his quest for real religion. The Moravians, especially Peter Böhler, a missionary under appointment to Georgia, brought him much light. Largely through their influence he was enabled to "trust in Christ, Christ alone for salvation" on May 24, 1738.

The Evangelist

After an unsatisfying visit to Moravian headquarters in Germany, Wesley responded affirmatively to the call of George Whitefield to continue Whitefield's open-air ministry in Bristol. Thus, in the spring of 1739 he was thrust into the greatest evangelistic ministry in the history of the Christian church in England.

Wesley's message to the masses is tersely but eloquently summarized in the words of his brother Charles:

> *To me, with thy dear name is given*
> *Pardon, and holiness, and heaven!*

Wesley stands as the apostle of 18th-century Britain; a combination of St. Francis, St. Ignatius Loyola, and William Tyndale. He was unwearied in labor and travel—250,000 miles on horseback over the worst roads in Europe. God gave him an organizing genius, intrepid courage in the face of wild mobs, and a keen logical mind. All were set on fire by the Spirit of God. His publications fill shelf after shelf in our libraries. His theology, after two centuries of analysis, criticism, and popularizing, remains as the basic standard of doctrine for "the people called Methodists"—and a half score other "peoples" beside.

John Wesley preaching from the steps of a market cross

2

SELECTED SERMONS

Wesley's Preaching
Preface to *Sermons on Several Occasions*

Key Sermons by Wesley
The Circumcision of the Heart
The Pure in Heart
The Marks of the New Birth
Catholic Spirit
Original Sin
On Sin in Believers
The Scripture Way of Salvation
The Repentance of Believers
On Perfection
On Patience
The More Excellent Way
On the Wedding Garment

2 Selected Sermons

Wesley's Preaching

In 1746 Wesley published his first volume of sermons, titled *Sermons on Several Occasions*. In the Preface he notes that these sermons reflect what he had been preaching for eight or nine years. By this dating he means us to understand that 1738, the year of the great change (his Aldersgate experience), was a hinge year in his preaching ministry and in his spiritual life.

The Preface is greatly beloved by all who know it. It reflects the master motive and the candid mood of all of Wesley's preaching: a clear presentation of biblical truths he had been preaching since his conversion.

Preface to *Sermons on Several Occasions*[1]

1. The following sermons contain the substance of what I have been preaching for between eight and nine years last past. During that time I have frequently spoken in public on every subject in the ensuing collection. I am not conscious that there is any one point of doctrine on which I am accustomed to speak in public which is not here incidentally, if not professedly, laid before every Christian reader. Every serious man who peruses these will therefore see in the clearest manner what these doctrines are which I embrace and teach as the essentials of true religion.

2. But I am throughly sensible that these are not proposed in such a manner as some may expect. Nothing here appears in an elaborate, elegant, or oratorical dress. If it had been my desire or design to write thus, my leisure would not permit. But in truth I, at present, designed nothing less; for I now write as I generally speak, *ad populum*: to the bulk of mankind, to those who neither relish nor understand the art of speaking, but who, notwithstanding, are competent

---

1. *The Works of John Wesley*, reprint, third edition (Kansas City: Beacon Hill Press of Kansas City, 1948), 5:1-6. The Preface follows a 47-page biography of Wesley.

judges of those truths which are necessary to our present and future happiness. I mention this that curious readers may spare themselves the labour of seeking for what they will not find.

3. I design plain truth for plain people. Therefore, of set purpose, I abstain from all nice and philosophical speculations; from all perplexed and intricate reasonings; and, as far as possible, from even the show of learning unless in sometimes citing the original Scripture. I labour to avoid all words which are not easy to be understood, all which are not used in common life; and, in particular, those kinds of technical terms that so frequently occur in bodies of divinity—those modes of speaking which men of reading are intimately acquainted with, but which to common people are an unknown tongue. Yet I am not assured that I do not sometimes slide into them unawares. It is so extremely natural to imagine that a word which is familiar to ourselves is so to all the world.

4. Nay, my design is, in some sense, to forget all that ever I have read in my life. I mean to speak, in the general, as if I had never read one author, ancient or modern (always excepting the inspired). I am persuaded that on the one hand this may be a means of enabling me more clearly to express the sentiments of my heart, while I simply follow the chain of my own thoughts without entangling myself with those of other men; and that, on the other I shall come with fewer weights upon my mind, with less of prejudice and prepossession either to search for myself or to deliver to others the naked truths of the gospel.

5. To candid, reasonable men I am not afraid to lay open what have been the inmost thoughts of my heart. I have thought, I am a creature of a day, passing through life as an arrow through the air. I am a spirit come from God and returning to God: just hovering over the great gulf till a few moments hence I am no more seen! I drop into an unchangeable eternity! I want to know one thing—the way to heaven: how to land safe on that happy shore. God himself has condescended to teach the way; for this very end He came from heaven. He hath written it down in a book! At any price, give me the book of God! I have it: here is knowledge enough for me. Let me be *homo unius libri* [a man of one Book]. Here then I am, far from the busy ways of men. I sit down alone; only God is here. In His presence I open, I read His book for this end—to find the way to heaven. Is there a doubt concerning the meaning of what I read? Does anything appear dark or intricate? I lift up my heart to the Father of Lights—"Lord, is it not

Thy word, 'If any man lack wisdom, let him ask of God?' Thou 'givest liberally, and upbraidest not.' Thou hast said, 'If any be willing to do thy will, he shall know.' I am willing to do: let me know Thy will." I then search after and consider parallel passages of Scripture, "comparing spiritual things with spiritual." I meditate thereon, with all the attention and earnestness of which my mind is capable.[2] If any doubt still remains, I consult those who are experienced in the things of God; and then, the writings whereby, being dead, they yet speak. And what I thus learn, that I teach.

6. I have accordingly set down in the following sermons what I find in the Bible concerning the way to heaven; with a view to distinguish this way of God from all those which are the inventions of men. I have endeavoured to describe the true, the scriptural, experimental religion, so as to omit nothing which is a real part thereof, and to add nothing thereto which is not. And herein it is more especially my desire, first to guard those who are just setting their faces toward heaven (and who, having little acquaintance with the things of God, are the more liable to be turned out of the way), from formality, from mere outside religion, which has almost driven heart religion out of the world; and, secondly, to warn those who know the religion of the heart, the faith which worketh by love, lest at any time they make void the law through faith, and so fall back into the snare of the devil.

7. By the advice and at the request of some of my friends, I have prefixed to the other sermons contained in this volume, three sermons of my own, and one of my brother's, preached before the university of Oxford. My design required some discourses on those heads. And I preferred these before any others as being a stronger answer than any which can be drawn up now, to those who have frequently asserted that we have changed our doctrine of late and do not preach now what we did some years ago. Any man of understanding may now judge for himself, when he has compared the latter with the former sermons.

8. But some may say I have mistaken the way myself although I take upon me to teach it to others. It is probable many will think this, and it is very possible that I have. But I trust wheresoever I have

---

2. In his *A Plain Account of Christian Perfection,* Wesley points out that it was this kind of Bible study that led him to believe in entire sanctification: "I tell you, as plain as I can speak, where and when I found this. I found it in the oracles of God, in the Old and New Testament; when I read them with no other view or desire, but to save my own soul" (*WW,* 11:444).

mistaken, my mind is open to conviction. I sincerely desire to be better informed. I say to God and man, "What I know not, teach thou me!"

9. Are you persuaded you see more clearly than I? It is not unlikely that you may. Then treat me as you would desire to be treated yourself upon a change of circumstances. Point me out a better way than I have yet known. Show me it is so by plain proof of Scripture. And if I linger in the path I have been accustomed to tread, and am therefore unwilling to leave it, labour with me a little; take me by the hand, and lead me as I am able to bear. But be not displeased if I entreat you not to beat me down in order to quicken my pace. I can go but feebly and slowly at best; then, I should not be able to go at all. May I not request of you, further, not to give me hard names in order to bring me into the right way. Suppose I were ever so much in the wrong. I doubt this would not set me right. Rather, it would make me run so much the farther from you and so get more and more out of the way.

10. Nay, perhaps if you are angry so shall I be too; and then there will be small hopes of finding the truth. If once anger arise (as Homer somewhere expresses it), this smoke will so dim the eyes of my soul that I shall be able to see nothing clearly. For God's sake, if it be possible to avoid it, let us not provoke one another to wrath. Let us not kindle in each other this fire of hell; much less blow it up into a flame. If we could discern truth by that dreadful light, would it not be loss rather than gain? For, how far is love—even with many wrong opinions—to be preferred before truth itself without love! We may die without the knowledge of many truths and yet be carried into Abraham's bosom. But if we die without love what will knowledge avail? Just as much as it avails the devil and his angels!

The God of love forbid we should ever make the trial! May He prepare us for the knowledge of all truth by filling our hearts with all His love and with all joy and peace in believing!

Key Sermons by Wesley

The sermons that follow belong to the main current of the preaching of John Wesley. They have been selected, not for their homiletical excellence, nor because they are what some would hail as "the best sermons of John Wesley." They have been chosen because they contain the essence of what Wesley himself described as "the grand depositum which God has lodged with the people called Methodists."

This distinctive element in Wesley's theology is his teaching on Christian perfection, which he much preferred to define as perfect love. In his judgment, this consisted in complete freedom from all sin and the presence and fruit of the Holy Spirit in the soul and life.

The selected sermons are here presented in the order in which they were prepared and preached. They represent the mature thought of John Wesley. Although *The Circumcision of the Heart* was preached on New Year's Day 1733 five and a half years previous to his evangelical conversion, it was solidly reaffirmed by Wesley himself as to its doctrinal content 32 years later on May 14, 1765:

> January 1, 1733, I preached the sermon on *The Circumcision of the Heart,* which contains all that I now teach concerning salvation from all sin, and loving God with an undivided heart. . . . This was then, as it is now, my idea of Perfection, though I should have started at the word.[3]

It is notable that this reaffirmation was made in the year in which Wesley published *A Plain Account of Christian Perfection,* and in which he preached his classic sermon *The Scripture Way of Salvation.*

We can be confident that these sermons here presented reflect Wesley's matured thinking on the doctrine and experience of Christian perfection. What he had written and preached in 1733 he firmly and consistently maintained to the end of his long life. In 1790, a few months before his death, "on the brink of the great gulf" as he would say, he wrote to Robert Carr Brackenbury:

> I am glad Brother D—— has more light with regard to full sanctification. This doctrine is the grand depositum which God has lodged with the people called Methodists; and for the sake of propagating this chiefly, He appears to have raised us up.[4]

And even closer to death he wrote to John Booth: "Whenever you have opportunity of speaking to believers, urge them to go on to Perfection. Spare no pains; and God, our own God, still give you His blessing!"[5]

---

3. *WW,* 3:213.
4. *WW,* 13:9.
5. *WW,* 13:154.

List of Sermons in This Volume

(Presented in chronological order)

Title	Date	Source[6]
The Circumcision of the Heart	1733	5:202-12
The Pure in Heart	1739	5:278-94
The Marks of the New Birth	1741	5:212-23
Catholic Spirit	1749	5:492-504
Original Sin	1759	6:54-65
On Sin in Believers	1763	5:144-56
The Scripture Way of Salvation	1765	6:43-54
The Repentance of Believers	1767	5:156-70
On Perfection	1788	6:411-24
On Patience	1788	6:484-92
The More Excellent Way	1788	7:26-37
On the Wedding Garment	1790	7:311-17

The Circumcision of the Heart
1733

Although Wesley wrote and preached this, the first of his University sermons, more than five years before his conversion, he continued to maintain that it was definitive of his doctrine of purity of heart. It was chosen as the opening sermon in the second published volume of sermons although it had been chronologically much earlier than the others. It was placed by Wesley among his Standard Sermons, appearing in 1748 in the second volume.

In a letter to John Newton dated May 14, 1765, Wesley refers dogmatically to this sermon as his continuing conviction, integral to his teaching. He said, "[It] contains all that I now teach concerning salvation from *all* sin, and loving God with an *undivided* heart. . . . This was then, as it is now, my idea of Perfection, though I should have started at the word."[7]

Again, in his Journal for September 1, 1778, Wesley writes of this

---

6. For convenience only Beacon Hill Press of Kansas City reprint of the *Works of John Wesley*, 1978, is here listed.

7. *LJW*, 4:299; and *JJW*, 5:117.

sermon: "I know not that I can write a better sermon on the Circumcision of the heart than I did five-and-forty years ago.... Forty years ago I knew and preached every Christian doctrine which I preach now."[8] Thus we have in 1733, 1748, 1765, and 1778, four affirmations that leave no room for doubting that *The Circumcision of the Heart* conveys Wesley's conviction on the subject of purity of heart.

If we compare Wesley's declarations on these occasions as to what he means by "the circumcision of the heart" with his other reference such as his note on Rom. 2:28-29 and the sermon on *Grieving the Holy Spirit*,[9] we gain a strong impression of the radical nature of his concept of purity of heart. It is:

> ... the putting away of all inward impurity. This is seated in the spirit, the inmost soul, renewed by the Spirit of God.[10]
> ... salvation from all sin and loving God with an undivided heart
> ... giving the whole heart, the whole life, to God.[11]
>
> One design, one desire, one love ... pursuing the one end of our life in all our words and actions.[12]

THE CIRCUMCISION OF THE HEART

Circumcision is that of the heart, in the spirit, and not in the letter (Rom. ii. 29).

1. It is the melancholy remark of an excellent man, that he who now preaches the most essential duties of Christianity runs the hazard of being esteemed, by a great part of his hearers, a "setter forth of new doctrines." Most men have so *lived away* the substance of that religion, the profession whereof they still retain, that no sooner are any of those truths proposed which difference [differentiate] the Spirit of Christ from the spirit of the world, than they cry out, "Thou bringest strange things to our ears; we would know what these things mean": though he is only preaching to them "Jesus and the resurrection," with the necessary consequence of it—If Christ be risen, ye ought then to die unto the world, and to live wholly unto God.

2. A hard saying this to the natural man, who is alive unto the

---

8. *JJW*, 6:209.
9. *WW*, 7:485.
10. *WN*, Rom. 2:28-29.
11. *LJW*, 4:299.
12. *JJW*, 5:17.

world and dead unto God; and one that he will not readily be persuaded to receive as the truth of God, unless it be so qualified in the interpretation as to have neither use nor significancy left. He "receiveth not the" words "of the Spirit of God," taken in their plain and obvious meaning; "they are foolishness unto him: neither" indeed "can he know them, because they are spiritually discerned." They are perceivable only by that spiritual sense, which in him was never yet awakened; for want of which he must reject, as idle fancies of men, what are both the wisdom and the power of God.

3. The "circumcision is that of the heart, in the spirit, and not in the letter"—that the distinguishing mark of a true follower of Christ, of one who is in a state of acceptance with God, is not either outward circumcision, or baptism, or any other outward form, but a right state of soul, a mind and spirit renewed after the image of Him that created it—is one of those important truths that can only be spiritually discerned. And this the Apostle himself intimates in the next words, "Whose praise is not of men, but of God." As if he had said, "Expect not, whoever thou art, who thus followest thy great Master, that the world, the men who follow him not, will say, 'Well done, good and faithful servant!'" Know that the circumcision of the heart, the seal of thy calling, is foolishness with the world. Be content to wait for thy applause till the day of thy Lord's appearing. In that day shalt thou have praise of God in the great assembly of men and angels."

I design, first, particularly to inquire wherein this circumcision of the heart consists; and, secondly, to mention some reflections that naturally arise from such an inquiry.

I.

1. I am, first, to inquire wherein that circumcision of the heart consists, which will receive the praise of God. In general we may observe, it is that habitual disposition of soul which in the sacred writings is termed holiness; and which directly implies the being cleansed from sin, "from all filthiness both of flesh and spirit"; and, by consequence, the being endued with those virtues which were also in Christ Jesus; the being so "renewed in the spirit of our mind" as to be "perfect as our Father in heaven is perfect."

2. To be more particular: circumcision of heart implies humility, faith, hope, and charity. Humility, a right judgment of ourselves, cleanses our minds from those high conceits of our own perfections, from that undue opinion of our own abilities and attainments, which

are the genuine fruit of a corrupted nature. This entirely cuts off that vain thought, "I am rich and wise and have need of nothing," and convinces us that we are by nature "wretched and poor, and miserable, and blind, and naked." It convinces us that in our best estate we are of ourselves all sin and vanity; that confusion, and ignorance, and error reign over our understanding; that unreasonable, earthly, sensual, devilish passions usurp authority over our will; in a word, that there is no whole part in our soul, that all the foundations of our nature are out of course.

3. At the same time we are convinced that we are not sufficient of ourselves to help ourselves; that without the Spirit of God we can do nothing but add sin to sin; that it is He alone who worketh in us by His almighty power, either to will or do that which is good; it being as impossible for us even to think a good thought without the supernatural assistance of His Spirit as to create ourselves, or to renew our whole souls in righteousness and true holiness.

4. A sure effect of our having formed this right judgment of the sinfulness and helplessness of our nature is a disregard of that "honour which cometh of man," which is usually paid to some supposed excellency in us. He who knows himself neither desires nor values the applause which he knows he deserves not. It is therefore "a very small thing with him, to be judged by man's judgment." He has all reason to think, by comparing what it has said either for or against him, with what he feels in his own breast, that the world as well as the god of this world was "a liar from the beginning." And even as to those who are not of the world, though he would choose, if it were the will of God, that they should account of him as of one desirous to be found a faithful steward of his Lord's goods, if haply this might be a means of enabling him to be of more use to his fellow servants. Yet, as this is the one end of his wishing for their approbation, so he does not at all rest upon it: for he is assured that whatever God wills He can never want instruments to perform, since He is able, even of these stones, to raise up servants to do His pleasure.

5. This is that lowliness of mind which they have learned of Christ, who follow His example and tread in His steps. And this knowledge of their disease whereby they are more and more cleansed from one part of it, pride and vanity, disposes them to embrace with a willing mind the second thing implied in circumcision of the heart: that faith which alone is able to make them whole, which is the one medicine given under heaven to heal their sickness.

6. The best guide of the blind, the surest light of them that are in darkness, the most perfect instructor of the foolish, is faith. But it must be such a faith as is "mighty through God, to the pulling down of strongholds," to the overturning all the prejudices of corrupt reason, all the false maxims revered among men, all evil customs and habits, all that "wisdom of the world which is foolishness with God"; as "casteth down imaginations," reasonings, "and every high thing that exalteth itself against the knowledge of God, and bringeth into captivity every thought to the obedience of Christ."

7. "All things are possible to him that" thus "believeth." "The eyes of his understanding being enlightened," he sees what is his calling; even to glorify God, who hath bought him with so high a price, in his body and his spirit, which now are God's by redemption as well as by creation. He feels what is "the exceeding greatness of his power," who, as He raised up Christ from the dead, so is able to quicken us, dead in sin, "by his Spirit which dwelleth in us." "This is the victory which overcometh the world, even our faith"; that faith which is not only an unshaken assent to all that God hath revealed in Scripture—and in particular to those important truths, "Jesus Christ came into the world to save sinners"; "He bare our sins in his own body on the tree"; "He is the propitiation for our sins, and not for ours only, but also for the sins of the whole world" [*Note*: The following part of this paragraph is now added to the Sermon formerly preached.]—but likewise the revelation of Christ in our hearts; a divine evidence or conviction of His love, His free, unmerited love to me a sinner; a sure confidence in His pardoning mercy, wrought in us by the Holy Ghost; a confidence, whereby every true believer is enabled to bear witness, "I know that my Redeemer liveth," that I have an "Advocate with the Father," and that "Jesus Christ the righteous" is my Lord, and "the propitiation for my sins." I know He hath "loved me, and given himself for me"; He hath reconciled me, even me, to God; and I "have redemption through his blood, even the forgiveness of sins."

8. Such a faith as this cannot fail to show evidently the power of Him that inspires it, by delivering His children from the yoke of sin, and "purging their consciences from dead works"; by strengthening them so, that they are no longer constrained to obey sin in the desires thereof; but instead of "yielding their members unto it, as instruments of unrighteousness," they now "yield themselves" entirely "unto God, as those that are alive from the dead."

9. Those who are thus by faith born of God have also strong

consolation through hope. This is the next thing which the circumcision of the heart implies; even the testimony of their own spirit with the Spirit which witnesses in their hearts that they are children of God. Indeed it is the same Spirit who works in them that clear and cheerful confidence that their heart is upright toward God; that good assurance that they now do, through His grace, the things which are acceptable in His sight; that they are now in the path which leadeth to life and shall, by the mercy of God, endure therein to the end. It is He who giveth them a lively expectation of receiving all good things at God's hand; a joyous prospect of that crown of glory which is reserved in heaven for them.

ASSURANCE

By this anchor a Christian is kept steady in the midst of the waves of this troublesome world and preserved from striking upon either of those fatal rocks—presumption or despair. He is neither discouraged by the misconceived severity of his Lord, nor does he "despise the riches of his goodness." He neither apprehends the difficulties of the race set before him to be greater than he has strength to conquer, nor expects them to be so little as to yield in the conquest till he has put forth all his strength. The experience he already has in the Christian warfare, as it assures him his "labour is not in vain" if "whatever his hand findeth to do, he doeth it with his might"; so it forbids his entertaining so vain a thought as that he can otherwise gain any advantage; as that any virtue can be shown, any praise attained by faint hearts and feeble hands; or, indeed, by any but those who pursue the same course with the great Apostle of the Gentiles. "I," says he, "so run, not as uncertainly; so fight I, not as one that beateth the air; but I keep under my body, and bring it into subjection; lest, by any means, when I have preached to others, I myself should be a castaway."

10. By the same discipline is every good soldier of Christ to inure himself to endure hardship. Confirmed and strengthened by this, he will be able not only to renounce the works of darkness, but every appetite too, and every affection which is not subject to the law of God. For "every one," saith St. John, "who hath this hope, purifieth himself even as he is pure." It is his daily care, by the grace of God in Christ and through the blood of the covenant, to purge the inmost recesses of his soul from the lusts that before possessed and defiled it; from uncleanness, and envy, and malice, and wrath; from every passion and temper that is after the flesh, that either springs from or cherishes his native corruption. As well knowing, that he whose very body is the temple of God ought to admit into it

GROWTH

nothing common or unclean; and that holiness becometh that house forever where the Spirit of holiness vouchsafes to dwell.

PERFECT LOVE

11. Yet lackest thou one thing, whosoever thou art, that to a deep humility and a steadfast faith hast joined a lively hope, and thereby in a good measure cleansed thy heart from its inbred pollution. If thou wilt be perfect, add to all these, charity; add love, and thou hast the circumcision of the heart. "Love is the fulfilling of the law, the end of the commandment." Very excellent things are spoken of love; it is the essence, the spirit, the life of all virtue. It is not only the first and great command, but it is all the commandments in one. "Whatsoever things are just, whatsoever things are pure, whatsoever things are amiable," or honourable; "if there be any virtue, if there be any praise," they are all comprised in this one word—love. In this is perfection, and glory, and happiness. The royal law of heaven and earth is this: "Thou shalt love the Lord thy God with all thy heart, and with all thy soul, and with all thy mind, and with all thy strength."

12. Not that this forbids us to love anything besides God: it implies that we love our brother also. Nor yet does it forbid us (as some have strangely imagined) to take pleasure in anything but God. To suppose this is to suppose the Fountain of holiness is directly the author of sins; since He has inseparably annexed pleasure to the use of those creatures which are necessary to sustain the life He has given us. This, therefore, can never be the meaning of His command.

What the real sense of it is, both our blessed Lord and His Apostles tell us too frequently, and too plainly, to be misunderstood. They all with one mouth bear witness that the true meaning of those several declarations, "The Lord thy God is one Lord"; "Thou shalt have no other gods but me"; "Thou shalt love the Lord thy God with all thy strength"; "Thou shalt cleave unto him"; "The desire of thy soul shall be to his name," is no other than this: The one perfect Good shall be your one ultimate end. One thing shall ye desire for its own sake—the fruition of Him that is All in all. One happiness shall ye propose to your souls, even an union with Him that made them; the having "fellowship with the Father and the Son"; the being joined to the Lord in one Spirit.

ONE GOAL

One design you are to pursue to the end of time—the enjoyment of God in time and in eternity. Desire other things so far as they tend to this. Love the creature as it leads to the Creator. But in every step you take, be this the glorious point that terminates your view. Let every affection, and thought, and word, and work, be subordinate to this. Whatever ye desire or fear, whatever ye seek or shun, whatever ye think, speak, or do, be it in order to your happiness in God, the sole End as well as Source of your being.

13. Have no end, no ultimate end, but God. Thus our Lord: "One thing is needful"; and if thine eye be singly fixed on this one thing, "thy whole body shall be full of light." Thus St. Paul: "This one thing I do; I press toward the mark, for the prize of the high calling in Christ Jesus." Thus St. James: "Cleanse your hands, ye sinners; and purify your hearts, ye double-minded." Thus St. John: "Love not the world, neither the things that are in the world. For all that is in the world, the lust of the flesh, the lust of the eye, and the pride of life, is not of the Father, but is of the world." The seeking happiness in what gratifies either the desire of the flesh, by agreeably striking upon the outward senses; the desire of the eye, of the imagination, by its novelty, greatness, or beauty; or the pride of life, whether by pomp, grandeur, power, or, the usual consequence of them, applause and admiration—"is not of the Father," cometh not from, neither is approved by, the Father of spirits, "but of the world." It is the distinguishing mark of those who will not have Him to reign over them.

II.

1. Thus have I particularly inquired what that circumcision of heart is which will obtain the praise of God. I am, in the second place, to mention some reflections that naturally arise from such an inquiry as a plain rule whereby every man may judge of himself whether he be of the world or of God.

And, first, it is clear from what has been said, that no man has a title to the praise of God unless his heart is circumcised by humility; unless he is little, and base, and vile in his own eyes; unless he is deeply convinced of that inbred "corruption of his nature," "whereby he is very far gone from original righteousness," being prone to all evil, averse to all good, corrupt and abominable; having a "carnal mind which is enmity against God, and is not subject to the law of God, nor indeed can be"; unless he continually feels in his inmost soul that without the Spirit of God resting upon him, he can neither think, nor desire, nor speak, nor act anything good, or well-pleasing in His sight.

No man, I say, has a title to the praise of God till he feels his want of God; nor indeed, till he seeketh that "honour which cometh of God" only; and neither desires nor pursues that which cometh of man, unless so far only as it tends to this.

2. Another truth, which naturally follows from what has been said, is that none shall obtain the honour that cometh of God, unless his heart be circumcised by faith; even a "faith of the operation of God"; unless, refusing to be any longer led by his senses, appetites, or passions, or even by that blind leader of the blind so idolized by the world, natural reason, he lives and walks by faith; directs every step as "seeing him that is invisible"; "looks not at the things that are seen, which are temporal, but at the things that are not seen, which are eternal"; and governs all his desires, designs, and thoughts, all his actions and conversations, as one who is entered in within the veil where Jesus sits at the right hand of God.

3. It were to be wished that they were better acquainted with this faith, who employ much of their time and pains by laying another foundation; in grounding religion on the eternal *fitness* of things, on the intrinsic *excellence* of virtue, and the *beauty* of actions flowing from it; on the *reasons* as they term them, of good and evil, and the *relations* of beings to each other. Either these accounts of the grounds of Christian duty coincide with the scriptural, or not. If they do, why are well-meaning men perplexed and drawn from the weightier matters of the law by a cloud of terms whereby the easiest truths are explained into obscurity? If they are not, then it behooves them to consider who is the author of this new doctrine; whether he is likely to be an angel from heaven, who preacheth another gospel than that of Christ Jesus; though if he were, God, not we, hath pronounced His sentence: "Let him be accursed."

4. Our gospel, as it knows no other foundation of good works than faith or of faith than Christ, clearly informs us we are not His disciples while we either deny Him to be the Author, or His Spirit to be the Inspirer and Perfecter, both of our faith and works. "If any man have not the Spirit of Christ, he is none of his." He alone can quicken those who are dead unto God, can breathe into them the breath of Christian life and so prevent, accompany, and follow them with His grace as to bring their good desires to good effect. And, "as many as are thus led by the Spirit of God, they are the sons of God." This is God's short and plain account of true religion and virtue; and "other foundation can no man lay."

CHRISTLIKENESS

5. From what has been said we may, thirdly, learn that none is truly "led by the Spirit" unless that "Spirit bear witness with his spirit, that he is a child of God"; unless he see the prize and the crown before

him and "rejoice in hope of the glory of God." So greatly have they erred who have taught that in serving God we ought not to have a view to our own happiness! Nay, but we are often and expressly taught of God to have "respect unto the recompense of reward"; to balance the toil with the "joy set before us," these "light afflictions" with that "exceeding weight of glory." Yea, we are "aliens to the covenant of promise," we are "without God in the world," until God, "of his abundant mercy, hath begotten us again unto a living hope of the inheritance incorruptible, undefiled, and that fadeth not away."

ASSURANCE

6. But if these things are so, it is high time for those persons to deal faithfully with their own souls, who are so far from finding in themselves this joyful assurance that they fulfil the terms, and shall obtain the promises of that covenant, as to quarrel with the covenant itself and blaspheme the terms of it; to complain they are too severe; and that no man ever did or shall live up to them. What is this but to reproach God as if He were a hard Master, requiring of His servants more than He enables them to perform?—as if He had mocked the helpless works of His hands by binding them to impossibilities; by commanding them to overcome, where neither their own strength nor His grace was sufficient for them?

FOR ALL CHRISTIANS

7. These blasphemers might almost persuade those to imagine themselves guiltless, who, in the contrary extreme, hope to fulfil the commands of God without taking any pains at all. Vain hope! that a child of Adam should ever expect to see the kingdom of Christ and of God without striving, without agonizing, first "to enter in at the strait gate"; that one who was "conceived and born in sin" and whose "inward parts are very wickedness," should once entertain a thought of being "purified as his Lord is pure," unless he tread in His steps and "take up his cross daily," unless he "cut off his right hand" and "pluck out the right eye, and cast it from him"; that he should ever dream of shaking off his old opinions, passions, tempers, of being "sanctified throughout in spirit, soul, and body," without a constant and continued course of general self-denial!

8. What less than this can we possibly infer from the above-cited words of St. Paul, who, living "in infirmities, in reproaches, in necessities, in persecutions, in distresses" for Christ's sake; who, being full of "signs and wonders, and mighty deeds," who, having been "caught up into the third heaven"; yet reckoned, as a late author strongly expresses it, that all his virtues would be insecure, and even his salvation

in danger without this constant self-denial? "So run I," says he, "not as uncertainly; so fight I, not as one that beateth the air": by which he plainly teaches us that he who does not thus run, who does not thus deny himself daily, does run uncertainly and fighteth to as little purpose as he that "beateth the air."

9. To as little purpose does he talk of "fighting the fight of faith," as vainly hope to attain the crown of incorruption (as we may, lastly, infer from the preceding observations), whose heart is not circumcised by love. Love, cutting off both the lust of the flesh, the lust of the eye, and the pride of life—engaging the whole man, body, soul, and spirit, in the ardent pursuit of that one object—is so essential to a child of God, that without it, whosoever liveth is counted dead before Him. "Though I speak with the tongues of men and of angels, and have not love, I am as sounding brass, or a tinkling cymbal. Though I have the gift of prophecy, and understand all mysteries, and all knowledge; and though I have all faith, so as to remove mountains, and have not love, I am nothing." Nay, "though I give all my goods to feed the poor, and my body to be burned, and have not love, it profiteth me nothing."

PERFECT LOVE

10. Here, then, is the sum of the perfect law; this is the true circumcision of the heart. Let the spirit return to God that gave it, with the whole train of its affections. "Unto the place from whence all the rivers came," thither let them flow again. Other sacrifices from us He would not; but the living sacrifice of the heart He hath chosen. Let it be continually offered up to God through Christ in flames of holy love. And let no creature be suffered to share with Him: for He is a jealous God. His throne will He not divide with another: He will reign without a rival. Be no design, no desire admitted there, but what has Him for its ultimate object. This is the way wherein those children of God once walked, who being dead still speak to us: "Desire not to live but to praise His name: let all your thoughts, words, and works tend to His glory. Set your heart firm on Him, and on other things only as they are in and from Him. Let your soul be filled with so entire a love of Him that you may love nothing but for His sake." "Have a pure intention of heart, a steadfast regard to His glory in all your actions." "Fix your eye upon the blessed hope of your calling, and make all the things of the world minister unto it." For then, and not until then, is that "mind in us which was also in Christ Jesus"; when, in every motion of our heart, in every word of our tongue, in every work of our hands, we "pursue nothing but in rela-

LORDSHIP

tion to him, and in subordination to his pleasure"; when we, too, neither think, nor speak, not act, to fulfil our "own will, but the will of him that sent us"; when, whether we "eat, or drink, or whatever we do, we do all to the glory of God."

The Pure in Heart
1739 (Excerpts)

Blessed are the pure in heart: for they shall see God (Matt. v. 8).

1. How excellent things are spoken of the love of our neighbour! It is the "fulfilling of the law," "the end of the commandment." Without this, all we have, all we do, all we suffer, is of no value in the sight of God. But it is that love of our neighbour which springs from the love of God: otherwise itself is nothing worth. It behooves us, therefore, to examine well upon what foundation our love of our neighbour stands; whether it is really built upon the love of God; whether we do "love him because he first loved us"; whether we are pure in heart: for this is the foundation which shall never be moved. "Blessed are the pure in heart: for they shall see God."

2. "The pure in heart" are they whose hearts God hath "purified even as he is pure"; who are purified, through faith in the blood of Jesus, from every unholy affection; who, being "cleansed from all filthiness of flesh and spirit, perfect holiness in the" loving "fear of God." They are, through the power of His grace, purified from pride by the deepest poverty of spirit; from anger, from every unkind or turbulent passion, by meekness and gentleness; from every desire but to please and enjoy God, to know and love Him more and more, by that hunger and thirst after righteousness which now engrosses their whole soul: so that now they love the Lord their God with all their heart, and with all their soul, and mind, and strength.

CLEANSING

3. But how little has this purity of heart been regarded by the false teachers of all ages! They have taught men barely to abstain from such outward impurities as God hath forbidden by name; but they did not strike at the heart; and by not guarding against, they in effect countenanced inward corruptions.

A remarkable instance of this our Lord has given us in the following words: "Ye have heard that it was said by them of old time, Thou shalt not commit adultery" (v. 27); and, in explaining this, those blind leaders of the blind only insisted on men's abstaining from the outward act. "But I say unto you, That whosoever looketh on a woman to lust after her hath committed adultery with her already in his heart" (v. 28); for God requireth truth in the inward parts: He searcheth the heart and trieth the reins; and if thou incline unto iniquity with thy heart, the Lord will not hear thee.

4. And God admits no excuse for retaining anything which is an occasion of impurity. Therefore, "if thy right eye offend thee, pluck it out, and cast it from thee: for it is profitable for thee that one of thy members should perish, and not that thy whole body should be cast into hell" (v. 29). If persons as dear to thee as thy right eye be an occasion of thy thus offending God, a means of exciting unholy desire in thy soul, delay not; forcibly separate from them. "And if thy right hand offend thee, cut it off, and cast it from thee: for it is profitable for thee that one of thy members should perish, and not that thy whole body should be cast into hell" (v. 30). If any who seem as necessary to thee as thy right hand be an occasion of sin, of impure desire; even though it were never to go beyond the heart, never to break out in word or action; constrain thyself to an entire and final parting. Cut them off at a stroke. Give them up to God. Any loss, whether of pleasure, or substance, or friends, is preferable to the loss of thy soul.

Two steps only it may not be improper to take before such an absolute and final separation. First, try whether the unclean spirit may not be driven out by fasting and prayer, and by carefully abstaining from every action, and word, and look, which thou hast found to be an occasion of evil. Secondly, if thou art not by this means delivered, ask counsel of him that watcheth over thy soul, or, at least, of some who have experience in the ways of God, touching the time and manner of that separation; but confer not with flesh and blood, lest thou be "given up to a strong delusion to believe a lie."

5. Nor may marriage itself, holy and honourable as it is, be used as a pretence for giving a loose to our desires. Indeed, "it hath been said, Whosoever will put away his wife, let him give her a writing of divorcement" and then all was well; though he alleged no cause, but that he did not like her or liked another better. "But I say unto you, That whosoever shall put away his wife, saving for the cause of fornication" (that is, adultery; the word *wopveia* signifying unchastity in

general, either in the married or unmarried state), "causeth her to commit adultery," if she marry again: "and whosoever shall marry her that is put away committeth adultery" (vv. 31-32).

All polygamy is clearly forbidden in these words, wherein our Lord expressly declares that for any woman who has a husband alive, to marry again is adultery. By parity of reason, it is adultery for any man to marry again so long as he has a wife alive, yea, although they were divorced; unless that divorce had been for the cause of adultery. In that only case there is no scripture which forbids to marry again.

6. Such is the purity of heart which God requires and works in those who believe on the Son of His love. And "blessed are" they who are thus "pure in heart: for they shall see God." He will "manifest himself unto them," not only "as he doth not unto the world," but as He doth not always to His own children. He will bless them with the clearest communications of His Spirit, the most intimate "fellowship with the Father and with the Son." He will cause His presence to go continually before them, and the light of His countenance to shine upon them. It is the ceaseless prayer of their heart, "I beseech Thee, show me Thy glory"; and they have the petition they ask of Him. They now see Him by faith (the veil of flesh being made as it were transparent), even in these His lowest works, in all that surrounds them, in all that God has created and made. They see Him in the height above, and in the depth beneath; they see Him filling all in all. The pure in heart see all things full of God. They see Him in the firmament of heaven; in the moon, walking in brightness; in the sun, when He rejoiceth as a giant to run His course. They see Him "making the clouds his chariots, and walking upon the wings of the wind." They see Him "preparing rain for the earth, and blessing the increase of it; giving grass for the cattle, and green herb for the use of man." They see the Creator of all, wisely governing all and "upholding all things by the word of his power." "O Lord our Governor, how excellent is thy name in all the world!"

7. In all His providences relating to themselves, to their souls or bodies, the pure in heart do more particularly see God. They see His hand ever over them for good; giving them all things in weight and measure, numbering the hairs of their head, making a hedge round about them and all that they have, and disposing all the circumstances of their life according to the depth both of His wisdom and mercy.

8. But in a more especial manner they see God in His ordinances. Whether they appear in the great congregation, to "pay him the hon-

our due unto his name," "and worship him in the beauty of holiness"; or "enter into their closets," and there pour out their souls before their "Father which is in secret"; whether they search the oracles of God, or hear the ambassadors of Christ proclaiming glad tidings of salvation; or, by eating of that bread, and drinking of that cup, "show forth his death till he come" in the clouds of heaven; in all these appointed ways, they find such a near approach as cannot be expressed. They see Him, as it were, face to face, and "talk with him, as a man talketh with his friend"; a fit preparation for those mansions above, wherein they shall see Him as He is.

The Marks of the New Birth
1741 (Abridged)

This sermon was first preached on April 3, 1741, and used frequently thereafter. It was preached in Epworth at 5 a.m. on the day when Wesley was refused access to the Sacrament of Communion at the "very table where I had myself so often distributed the bread of life."[13]

Wesley included it in the second volume of the 1748 edition of his *Sermons*. It is placed there because Wesley is laying the foundation upon which the holy life is based; he is showing the new birth as the foundation for the fully sanctified life. Here he also emphasizes the presence and witness of the Holy Spirit in the regenerate life, and makes it clear that regeneration is indeed "newness of life in Christ Jesus."

THE MARKS OF THE NEW BIRTH

So is every one that is born of the Spirit (John iii. 8).

1. How is everyone that is "born of the Spirit"—that is, born again—born of God? What is meant by the being born again, the being born of God, or being born of the Spirit? What is implied in the being a son or a child of God, or having the Spirit of adoption? . . .

---

13. *JJW*, 3:61 ff.

2. Perhaps it is not needful to give a definition of this, seeing the Scripture gives none. But as the question is of the deepest concern to every child of man, since "except a man be born again," born of the Spirit, "he cannot see the kingdom of God," I propose to lay down the marks of it in the plainest manner, just as I find them laid down in Scripture.

I.

1. The first of these, and the foundation of all the rest, is faith. So St. Paul, "Ye are all the children of God by faith in Christ Jesus" (Gal. iii. 26). So St. John, "To them gave he power" (*right* or *privilege,* it may rather be translated) "to become the sons of God, even to them that believe on his name; which were born," when they believed, "not of blood, nor of the will of the flesh," not by natural generation, "nor of the will of man," like those children adopted by men, in whom no inward change is thereby wrought, "but of God" (John i. 12-13). And again, in his General Epistle, "Whosoever believeth that Jesus is the Christ is born of God" (1 John v. 1).

2. But it is not a barely notional or speculative faith that is here spoken of by the Apostles. It is not a bare assent to this proposition, "Jesus is the Christ"; nor indeed to all the propositions contained in our creed, or in the Old and New Testament. It is not merely an assent to any or all these credible things, as credible. To say this, were to say (which who could hear?) that the devils were born of God; for they have this faith. . . . Yet, notwithstanding this faith, they are still "reserved in chains of darkness unto the judgment of the great day."

3. For all this is no more than a dead faith. The true, living, Christian faith, which whosoever hath is born of God, is not only assent, an act of the understanding; but a disposition, which God hath wrought in his heart; "a sure trust and confidence in God that, through the merits of Christ, his sins are forgiven, and he reconciled to the favour of God." This implies that a man first renounce himself; that, in order to be "found in Christ," to be accepted through Him, he totally rejects all "confidence in the flesh." "Having nothing to pay," having no trust in his own works or righteousness of any kind, he comes to God as a lost, miserable, self-destroyed, self-condemned, undone, helpless sinner. He comes as one whose mouth is utterly stopped, and who is altogether "guilty before God." Such a sense of sin . . . together with a full conviction . . . that of Christ only cometh our salvation, and an earnest desire of that salvation must precede a

living faith. We trust in Him who "for us paid our ransom by his death, and for us fulfilled the law in his life." This faith then, whereby we are born of God, is "not only a belief of all the articles of our faith, but also a true confidence of the mercy of God, through our Lord Jesus Christ."

4. An immediate and constant fruit of this faith whereby we are born of God ... is power over sin; power over outward sin of every kind; over every evil word and work; for wheresoever the blood of Christ is thus applied, it "purgeth the conscience from dead works"; and over inward sin, for it purifieth the heart from every unholy desire and temper. This fruit of faith St. Paul has largely described in the sixth chapter of his Epistle to the Romans. "How shall we," saith he, "who" by faith "are dead to sin, live any longer therein?" "Our old man is crucified with Christ, that the body of sin might be destroyed, that henceforth we should not serve sin." "Likewise, reckon ye yourselves to be dead unto sin, but alive unto God, through Jesus Christ our Lord. Let not sin therefore reign" even "in your mortal body," "but yield yourselves unto God, as those that are alive from the dead." "For sin shall not have dominion over you. God be thanked, that ye were the servants of sin, but being made free," the plain meaning is, God be thanked that though ye were in time past the servants of sin, yet now "being free from sin, ye are become the servants of righteousness."

5. The same ... is as strongly asserted by St. John; particularly with regard to the former branch of it, namely, power over outward sin. After he had been crying out as one astonished at the depth of the riches of the goodness of God, "Behold, what manner of love the Father hath bestowed upon us, that we should be called the sons of God! Beloved, now are we the sons of God, and it doth not yet appear what we shall be: but we know that, when he shall appear, we shall be like him; for we shall see him as he is" (1 John iii. 1-2), he soon adds, "Whosoever is born of God doth not commit sin; for his seed remaineth in him: and he cannot sin, because he is born of God" (v. 9). But some men will say, "True: whosoever is born of God doth not commit sin *habitually.*" *Habitually!* Whence is that? I read it not. It is not written in the Book....

6. [Let] ... the Apostle interpret his own words by the whole tenor of his discourse. In the fifth verse of this chapter he had said, "Ye know that he," Christ, "was manifested to take away our sins; and in him is no sin." What is the inference he draws from this? "Whosoever abideth in him sinneth not: whosoever sinneth hath not seen him,

neither known him" (1 John iii. 6). To his enforcement of this important doctrine, he premises a highly necessary caution: "Little children, let no man deceive you" (v. 7); for many will endeavour so to do; to persuade you that you may be unrighteous, that you may commit sin, and yet be children of God; "He that doeth righteousness is righteous, even as he is righteous. He that committeth sin is of the devil; for the devil sinneth from the beginning." Then follows, "Whosoever is born of God doth not commit sin; for his seed remaineth in him: and he cannot sin, because he is born of God." "In this," adds the Apostle, "the children of God are manifest, and the children of the devil." By this plain mark (the committing or not committing sin) are they distinguished from each other. To the same effect are those words in his fifth chapter, "We know that whosoever is born of God sinneth not; but he that is begotten of God keepeth himself, and that wicked one toucheth him not" (v. 18).

7. Another fruit of this living faith is peace. For, "being justified by faith," having all our sins blotted out, "we have peace with God through our Lord Jesus Christ" (Rom. v. 1). This indeed our Lord himself, the night before His death, solemnly bequeathed to all His followers. "Peace," saith He, "I leave with you" (you who "believe in God," and "believe also in me"); "my peace I give unto you: not as the world giveth, give I unto you. Let not your heart be troubled, neither let it be afraid" (John xiv. 27). And again, "These things have I spoken unto you, that in me ye might have peace" (John xvi. 33). This is that "peace of God which passeth all understanding," that serenity of soul which it hath not entered into the heart of a natural man to conceive, and which it is not possible for even the spiritual man to utter. And it is a peace which all the powers of earth and hell are unable to take from him. Waves and storms beat upon it, but they shake it not; for it is founded upon a rock. It keepeth the hearts and minds of the children of God, at all times and in all places. Whether they are in ease or in pain, in sickness or health, in abundance or want, they are happy in God. In every state they have learned to be content, yea, to give thanks unto God through Christ Jesus; being well assured, that "whatsoever is, is best," because it is His will concerning them: so that in all the vicissitudes of life their "heart standeth fast, believing in the Lord."

II.

1. A second scriptural mark of those who are born of God, is hope. Thus St. Peter, speaking to all the children of God who were

then scattered abroad, saith, "Blessed be the God and Father of our Lord Jesus Christ, which according to his abundant mercy, hath begotten us again unto a lively hope" (1 Pet. i. 3). . . . A *lively* or *living* hope, saith the Apostle; because there is also a *dead* hope, as well as a dead faith; a hope which is not from God, but from the enemy of God and man; as evidently appears by its fruits; for, as it is the offspring of pride, so it is the parent of every evil word and work; whereas, every man that hath in him this living hope, is "holy as he that calleth him is holy"; every man that can truly say to his brethren in Christ, "Beloved, now are we the sons of God, and we shall see him as he is," "purifieth himself, even as he is pure."

2. This hope [termed in the Epistle to the Hebrews, chap. x. 22, . . . and chap. vi. 11, in our translation, "the full assurance of faith, and the full assurance of hope"] . . . implies first, the testimony of our own spirit, or conscience, that we walk "in simplicity and godly sincerity"; secondly, the testimony of the Spirit of God, "bearing witness with," or to, "our spirit, that we are the children of God," "and if children, then heirs, heirs of God, and joint-heirs with Christ."

ASSURANCE

3. . . . Who is it that is here said to bear witness? Not our spirit only, but another; even the Spirit of God: He it is who "beareth witness with our spirit." What is it He beareth witness of? "That we are the children of God; and if children, then heirs; heirs of God, and joint-heirs with Christ" (Rom. viii. 16-17); "if so be that we suffer with him . . . that we may also be glorified together." And in whom doth the Spirit of God bear this witness? In all who are the children of God. By this very argument does the Apostle prove, in the preceding verses, that they are so: "As many," saith he, "as are led by the Spirit of God, they are the sons of God." "For ye have not received the spirit of bondage again to fear; but ye have received the spirit of adoption, whereby we cry, Abba, Father!" It follows, "The Spirit itself beareth witness with our spirit, that we are the children of God" (Rom. viii. 14-16).

4. The variation of the phrase in the 15th verse is worthy our observation: "Ye have received the Spirit of adoption, whereby we cry, Abba, Father!" *Ye,* as many as are the sons of God, have, in virtue of your sonship, received that self-same Spirit of adoption, whereby *we* cry, Abba, Father. *We,* the apostles, prophets, teachers; . . . *we,* through whom you have believed, the "ministers of Christ, and stewards of the mysteries of God." As *we* and *you* have one Lord, so we

have one Spirit: as we have one faith, so we have one hope also. We and you are sealed with one "Spirit of promise," the earnest of *your* and of *our* inheritance: the same Spirit bearing witness with your and with our spirit, "that we are the children of God."

5. And thus is the Scripture fulfilled, "Blessed are they that mourn: for they shall be comforted." For it is easy to believe, that though sorrow may precede this witness of God's Spirit with our spirit . . . yet as soon as any man feeleth it in himself, his "sorrow is turned into joy." Whatsoever his pain may have been before; yet as soon as that "hour is come, he remembereth the anguish no more, for joy" that he is born of God.

It may be many of *you* have now sorrow because you are "aliens from the commonwealth of Israel"; because you are conscious to yourselves that you have not this Spirit; that you are "without hope and without God in the world." But when the Comforter is come, "then your heart shall rejoice"; yea, "your joy shall be full," and "that joy no man taketh from you" (John xvi. 22). "We joy in God," will ye say, "through our Lord Jesus Christ, by whom we have now received the atonement"; "by whom we have access into this grace," this state of grace, of favour, or reconciliation with God, "wherein we stand, and rejoice in hope of the glory of God" (Rom. v. 2). . . .

It is not for the tongue of man to describe this joy in the Holy Ghost. It is "the hidden manna, which no man knoweth, save he that receiveth it." But this we know, it not only remains but overflows in the depth of affliction. . . . When sufferings most abound, the consolations of His Spirit do much more abound; insomuch that the sons of God "laugh at destruction when it cometh." . . .

III.

1. A third scriptural mark of those who are born of God, and the greatest of all, is love; even "the love of God shed abroad in their hearts, by the Holy Ghost which is given unto them" (Rom. v. 5). "Because they are sons, God hath sent forth the Spirit of his Son into their hearts, crying, Abba, Father!" (Gal. iv. 6). By this Spirit, continually looking up to God as their reconciled and loving Father, they cry to Him for their daily bread, for all things needful, whether for their souls or bodies. They continually pour out their hearts before Him, knowing "they have the petitions which they ask of him" (1 John v. 15). Their delight is in Him. He is the joy of their heart; their "shield," and their "exceeding great reward." The desire of their soul

is toward Him; it is their "meat and drink to do his will"; and they are "satisfied as with marrow and fatness, while their mouth praiseth him with joyful lips" (Ps. lxiii. 5).

2. And, in this sense also, "Every one who loveth him that begat, loveth him that is begotten of him" (1 John v. 1). His spirit rejoiceth in God his Saviour. He "loveth the Lord Jesus Christ in sincerity." He is so "joined unto the Lord," as to be one spirit. . . .

3. The necessary fruit of this love of God, is the love of our neighbour; of every soul which God hath made; not excepting our enemies; not excepting those who are now "despitefully using and persecuting us"; a love whereby we love every man as ourselves; as we love our own souls. Nay, our Lord has expressed it still more strongly, teaching us to "love one another, even as he hath loved us." Accordingly, the commandment written in the hearts of all those that love God is no other than this, "As I have loved you, so love ye one another." Now, "herein perceive we the love of God, in that he laid down his life for us" (1 John iii. 16). "We ought," then, as the Apostle justly infers, "to lay down our lives for the brethren."

If we feel ourselves ready to do this, then do we truly love our neighbour. Then "we know that we have passed from death unto life, because we" thus "love the brethren" (v. 14). "Hereby know we" that we are born of God, that we "dwell in him, and he in us, because he hath given us his" loving "spirit" (1 John iv. 13). For "love is of God; and every one that" thus "loveth is born of God, and knoweth God" (v. 7).

4. But some may possibly ask, "Does not the Apostle say, 'This is the love of God, that we keep his commandments'?" (1 John v. 3). Yea, and this is the love of our neighbour also, in the same sense as it is the love of God. But what would you infer from hence? that the keeping the outward commandments is all that is implied in loving God with all your heart, with all your mind, and soul, and strength, and in loving your neighbour as yourself? that the love of God is not an affection of the soul, but merely an *outward service?* and that the love of our neighbour is not a disposition of heart, but barely a course of *outward works?* . . . The plain indisputable meaning of that text is, this is the sign or proof of the love of God, of our keeping the first and great commandment, to keep all the rest of His commandments. For true love, if it be once shed abroad in our heart, will constrain us so to do; since, whosoever loves God with all his heart, cannot but serve Him with all his strength.

5. A second fruit, then, of the love of God . . . is universal obedience to Him we love, and conformity to His will; obedience to all the commands of God, internal and external; obedience of the heart and of the life; in every temper, and in all manner of conversation. And one of the tempers most obviously implied herein is, the being "zealous of good works"; the hungering and thirsting to do good, in every possible kind, unto all men; the rejoicing to "spend and be spent for them," for every child of man; not looking for any recompense in this world, but only in the resurrection of the just.

IV.

1. Thus have I plainly laid down those marks of the new birth, which I find laid down in Scripture. Thus doth God himself answer that weighty question, What is it to be born of God? Such, if the appeal be made to the oracles of God, is "every one that is born of the Spirit." This it is, in the judgment of the Spirit of God, to be a son or a child of God. It is, so to *believe* in God, through Christ, as "not to commit sin," and to enjoy at all times, and in all places, that "peace of God which passeth all understanding." It is, so to *hope* in God through the Son of His love, as to have not only the "testimony of a good conscience," but also the Spirit of God "bearing witness with your spirits, that ye are the children of God"; whence cannot but spring the rejoicing in Him through whom ye "have received the atonement." It is so to *love* God, who hath thus loved you, as you never did love any creature: so that ye are constrained to love all men as yourselves; with a love not only ever burning in your hearts, but flaming out in all your actions and conversations, and making your whole life one "labour of love," one continued obedience to those commands, "Be ye merciful, as God is merciful"; "Be ye holy, as I the Lord am holy"; "Be ye perfect, as your Father which is in heaven is perfect."

2. Who then are ye that are *thus* born of God? Ye "know the things which are given to you of God." Ye well know that ye are the children of God, and "can assure your hearts before him." And every one of you who has observed these words cannot but feel and know of a truth, whether at this hour (answer to God and not to man!) you are thus a child of God or no. The question is not what you were made in baptism (do not evade); but, what are you now? Is the Spirit of adoption now in your heart? To your own heart let the appeal be made. I ask not, whether you *were* born of water and of the Spirit; but are you *now* the temple of the Holy Ghost which dwelleth in you? I allow

you were "circumcised with the circumcision of Christ"; . . . but does the Spirit of Christ and of glory *now* rest upon you? Else "your circumcision is become uncircumcision."

3. Say not then in your heart, I *was once* baptized [Wesley is speaking of infant baptism], therefore I *am now* a child of God. Alas, that consequence will by no means hold. How many are the baptized gluttons and drunkards, the baptized liars and common swearers, the baptized railers and evil speakers, the baptized whoremongers, thieves, extortioners? What think you? Are these now the children of God? Verily, I say unto you, whosoever you are, unto whom any one of the preceding characters belong, "Ye are of your father the devil, and the works of your father ye do." Unto you I call in the name of Him whom you crucify afresh, and in His words to your circumcised predecessors, "Ye serpents, ye generation of vipers, how can ye escape the damnation of hell?"

4. How, indeed, except ye be born again! For ye are now dead in trespasses and sins. To say, then, that ye cannot be born again, that there is no new birth but in baptism, is to seal you all under damnation, to consign you to hell, without help, without hope. . . . And it is mere mercy, free, undeserved mercy, that *we* are not now in unquenchable fire. You will say, "But we are washed"; we were born again "of water and of the Spirit." So *were* they: this, therefore, hinders not at all, but that ye may *now* be even as they. Know ye not, that "what is highly esteemed of men is an abomination in the sight of God"? Come forth, ye "saints of the world," ye that are honoured of men, and see who will cast the first stone at them, at these wretches not fit to live upon the earth, these common harlots, adulterers, murderers. Only learn ye first what that meaneth, "He that hateth his brother is a murderer" (1 John iii. 15). "He that looketh on a woman to lust after her hath committed adultery with her already in his heart" (Matt. v. 28). "Ye adulterers and adulteresses, know ye not that the friendship of the world is enmity with God?" (James iv. 4).

5. "Verily, verily, I say unto you, ye" also "must be born again." "Except ye" also "be born again, ye cannot see the kingdom of God." Lean no more on the staff of that broken reed, that we *were* born again in baptism. Who denies that ye were then made children of God, and heirs of the kingdom of heaven? But, notwithstanding this, ye are now children of the devil. Therefore, ye must be born again. And let not Satan put it into your heart to cavil at a word, when the thing is clear. Ye have heard what are the marks of the children of God: all ye

who have them not on your souls, baptized or unbaptized, must needs receive them, or without doubt ye will perish everlastingly. And if ye have been baptized, your only hope is this, that those who were made the children of God by baptism, but are now the children of the devil, may yet again receive "power to become the sons of God"; that they may receive again what they have lost, even the "Spirit of adoption, crying in their hearts, Abba, Father!"

Amen, Lord Jesus! May every one who prepareth his heart yet again to seek Thy face, receive again that Spirit of adoption, and cry out, "Abba, Father!" Let him now again have power so to believe in Thy name as to become a child of God; as to know and feel he hath "redemption in thy blood, even the forgiveness of sins," and that he "cannot commit sin, because he is born of God." Let him be now "begotten again unto a living hope," so as to "purify himself as thou art pure"; and "because he is a son," let the Spirit of love and of glory rest upon him, cleansing him "from all filthiness of flesh and spirit," and teaching him to "perfect holiness in the fear of God"!

Catholic Spirit
1749 (Outlined Excerpts)

This sermon has captured many hearts, and the attention of many more. It was preached first at Newcastle and then in Bristol in 1749. Published in 1750, it was republished in 1755 accompanied by Charles Wesley's impressive and meaningful hymn:

> *Weary of all this wordy strife,*
>   *These notions, forms, and modes, and names,*
> *To Thee, the Way, the Truth, the Life*
>   *Whose love my simple heart inflames,*
> *Divinely taught, at last I fly*
> *With Thee and Thine to live and die.*[14]

Wesley lifted the text (2 Kings 10:15) from its context and uses its characters as foils for his purpose. The personalities of the story were of anything but catholic spirits—perhaps not even toward each other. However, each saw a potential ally in the other. From this facet of the

---

14. *PWJCW*, 6:71-72. The hymn has seven stanzas.

story Wesley fastens on a text as a motto for one of his most persuasive sermons.

"Catholic Spirit" breathes the loving oneness that marked so much of early Methodism; oneness not of mere opinion or outward form, but the spirit of people whose hearts were first knotted on Jesus Christ. And to all such this sermon still makes its appeal.

CATHOLIC SPIRIT

And when he was departed thence, he lighted on Jehonadab the son of Rechab coming to meet him: and he saluted him, and said to him, Is thine heart right, as my heart is with thy heart? And Jehonadab answered, It is. If it be, give me thine hand (2 Kings x. 15).

Introduction

1. Even those who do not love all mankind acknowledge they ought to do so. Not in the manner of the old-time Zealots who reconstructed the command to read "Thou shalt love thy relation, acquaintance, friend, and hate thine enemy." But as the Lord interpreted it: loving enemies and those who injure you, thus showing to everyone that you are children of your Father in heaven whose love is poured on all men, good and evil, just and unjust alike.

2. However, there is a special love which we owe to all them that love God. David expressed it thus, "All my delight is upon the saints . . ." And a greater than David said, "A new commandment I give unto you, that you love one another as I have loved you." The apostle John often strongly insisted on this also: "This is the message," said he, "that we should love one another" (1 John iii. 11; cf. also v. 16, and iv. 7-11).

3. Everyone approves of this but experience contradicts their approval: even Christians fail in this. And why? First, because they cannot think alike; and therefore, secondly because they cannot all walk alike. They allow their sentiments to rule even the small points of practice. But should opinions be allowed to prevent union in affection? Though we cannot think alike, may we not love alike? May we not be of one heart even when not of one opinion? Certainly we may! In this all God's children may unite despite smaller differences. Even when keeping these opinions they may forward one another in love and good works.

4. Even such a character as Jehu is worth heeding at this point by every serious Christian. He met Jehonadab and "he saluted him, and said to him, Is thine heart right, as my heart is with thy heart? And Jehonadab answered, It is. If it be, give me thine hand."

I. The Question Stated

Let us consider the question proposed by Jehu to Jehonadab: "Is thine heart right, as my heart is with thy heart?"

A. The question does not concern opinions. Jehonadab certainly held some uncommon opinions peculiar to himself but affecting many others, especially his own posterity. This is evident from what Jeremiah later said of Jehonadab's descendants: "We will drink no wine: for Jehonadab our father, the son of Rechab, commanded us, Ye shall drink no wine, neither you nor your sons for ever. Neither shall ye build house, nor sow seed, nor plant vineyard, nor have any; but all your days ye shall dwell in tents. And we have obeyed him" (Jer. xxxv. 6-8).

Yet Jehu, although a zealot in spirit and action, did not concern himself with these things: he left Jehonadab to hold his own opinions. Indeed neither man bothered about the opinions of the other.

1. Probably many good men have peculiar opinions just as singular as Jehonadab's. For while we know *in part* it is certain that we will not all see eye to eye; that is, as it has always been, one of the shortcomings and weaknesses of human understanding in religion as in everything else.

2. And what is more, since not believing an opinion is the same thing as not holding it, every man will believe his own opinions to be true! Yet no one can ever be sure that all his opinions put together are absolutely true. To be ignorant of many things and mistaken in other things is the human lot. And who really knows the extent of his own ignorance? He knows it only in a general way, not in a specific way. Therefore wise men will allow others that same liberty of thinking which he expects to be allowed himself. He bears with those whose opinions differ from his own. Desiring only to be united in love, he asks only one question: "Is thy heart right, as my heart is with thy heart?"

B. Nor does the question concern forms of worship.

1. Here again Jehonadab was different from almost everyone else. He and his people and his posterity worshiped God at Jerusalem; Jehu did not, for he was more politically minded than religiously

minded. True, he destroyed the worshipers of Baal, but he found it convenient to worship Jeroboam's golden calf! (2 Kings x. 29).

2. Upright men realize that where there are varying opinions about God there will be various ways of worship. And men have differed in nothing as much as in their opinions about God, thus they have differed in their ways of worship. If this were true only about the heathen it would be little more than we might expect, but it is strange to find it also in the Christian world where we all agree that "God is Spirit; and they that worship Him must worship Him in spirit and in truth," and yet we vary about as much in our ways of worship as do the heathen!

3. No man can choose another man's way to worship. Everyone must follow and obey his own conscience with complete sincerity: he must follow whatever light he has, for each man must give an account of himself to God.

4. Christians too must remember this. We are by the very nature of the church obliged to be a member of a particular congregation, and this implies a particular form of worship. But which it shall be is a matter of personal decision and conscience. I used to zealously maintain that Christians born in England ought to be Anglicans, but I have good reasons for being now less zealous for this opinion. For one thing, if that had been true we would not have been delivered from Popery; there would have been no Reformation in England. So, although this is my mode of worship, and I am sure it is truly primitive and apostolic, my belief is no rule for anyone else.

5. "Is thine heart right?" Therefore I do not ask him with whom I would unite in love "which is your church? are your prayer forms like mine? Were you baptized thus, or thus?" Indeed although I am clear as to the sacraments for myself, I do not ask him whether he observes any! My only question is "Is thine heart right, as my heart is with thy heart?" "Is your faith filled with love?"

a. Toward God? Do you love God "with all thy heart, and with all thy mind, and with all thy soul, and with all thy strength"? Is God the centre of your soul, the sum total of all your desires? Are you laying up your treasure in heaven and counting all else dung and dross? Has the love of God cast the love of the world out of your heart?

Do you love God such as to do His will in everything and at all times doing everything, either in word or deed in the name of the Lord Jesus; giving thanks unto God, even the Father through Him? And being more afraid of God's displeasure than of either death or hell, do you exercise yourself to have a conscience void of offence toward God or man?

    b. Toward your neighbour? Do you love all mankind without exception, as you love yourself? Is your soul full of goodwill toward *your* enemies and toward the unthankful and unholy enemies of God? Do you really yearn deeply over them and even wish yourself temporarily *"accursed"* for their sake? Do you prove your love by blessing them that curse you and praying for them that despitefully use you and persecute you?

    And does your love go out in good works to neighbour or stranger, friend or enemy, whether good or bad? Do you do them *all* the good you can in every way that you can, to the uttermost of your power? I trust every Christian can answer "Yes," or that he is sincerely desirous of it and willing to follow on until he attains it. If so, then, "Thy heart is right as my heart is with thy heart."

II. The Plea Made. "Give me thy hand!"

    A. I do not ask that you disregard opinions. I neither want nor expect that. Keep your opinion and I will keep mine, and just as steadily as ever. I don't even want to dispute them. Let all opinions alone on one side and the other: simply "Give me your hand."

    B. Neither do I ask you to worship in the way I do. In this we must be absolutely sincere: you must hold fast to whatever form of worship you believe God wants—Episcopal, Presbyterian, Independent—or whatever; and I will do the same.

    I believe the Episcopal form to be scriptural and apostolical; and that infants ought to be baptized; that forms of prayer are of excellent use, and that I ought to observe the memorial of the Lord's Supper. But if you think otherwise on these things, act according to the light you have.

    Put all these smaller points on one side: let them disappear: "If thine heart is as my heart," that is, if you really do love God and all mankind, I ask no more: "Give me your hand."

    C. Love me. That is what I really am asking for. And love me not simply in a general sort of way as you might do someone about whom you know nothing. I am not satisfied with this kind of love, I desire tender affection. I want you to love me as a brother in Christ; as a fellow-citizen of the New Jerusalem; as a fellow-soldier in the same war under the same commander; as a companion in suffering, and as a joint-heir of the glory of Christ.

1. Love me with the love described in 1 Corinthians, chapter 13; the love that is longsuffering and kind, that lightens and bears my burden; that does not envy any success God may give me in His work; that thinks no evil and will even get rid of all jealousy and evil surmising; that can cover my faults and always put the best possible construction on what I do or say, believing in my purity of intention in whatever circumstance. Love me, believing and hoping that whatever I may lack His mercy will supply.

2. Pray for me; earnestly commend me to God and wrestle with Him on my behalf. Get as close to God as you can and plead of Him that my heart may be more as your heart by being right with His; and that I may have a fuller conviction of the unseen things, a stronger view of God's love in Christ Jesus, a steadier walk by faith, and a more earnest grip on eternal life. Pray that my heart may constantly be full of God's love, making me increasingly zealous of good works to all men, and keeping me from even the appearance of evil.

3. Provoke me in the faith that works by love. Follow up your prayer for me by taking reasonable opportunity to speak to me in love, whatever you really believe to be for my soul's health. Quicken me in God's work: tell me how I may do it better. Check and correct me when you think that I am doing my own thing rather than His will. O speak and spare not whatever you think will help me mend my faults, strengthen my weakness, build me up in love, or make me in any way more fit for the Master's use.

4. Join me in the work of God. So far as in conscience you can (retaining your own opinions and your own ways of worship) join with me in the work of God, and let us go on hand in hand. Wherever you go speak honourably of God's work and kindly of His messengers whoever they may be. And do not only sympathise with them, but help them cheerfully and effectually when they are in difficulty or distress. Then they will glorify God on your behalf.

On this head let us observe two things. First: all that I seek from him whose heart is right with mine, *that* I am ready to give to him as God enables me. And second: I am not making this claim on my own behalf only, but for all those whose heart is right toward God and man, so that we may love one another as Christ has loved us.

Conclusion

From all I have said we may learn by inference what is a catholic spirit.

1. It is not indifference to opinion. A man of a truly catholic spirit knows what he believes and is firmly established in Christian doctrine. He does not limp between two opinions nor try to blend them into one. A catholic spirit does not mean a muddy mind. A catholic spirit does not mean jumbling all opinions together. First learn the first elements of the gospel of Christ, and then you shall learn to be of a truly catholic spirit.

2. It is not indifference as to public worship. This would be a curse, an unspeakable hindrance to the worshiping of God in spirit and in truth. But the man of a truly catholic spirit assessing all things in the presence of God has no misgiving concerning his mode of worship. He is convinced that it is scriptural and rational, therefore he sticks to it and blesses God for the opportunity of so doing.

3. Therefore also a catholic spirit does not mean indifference in congregational life. A man of catholic spirit is as established in his congregation as in his principles. He partakes of all the ordinances of God in the congregation. There he receives the Lord's Supper, pours out his soul in public prayer and praise. There he rejoices to hear the gospel of God's grace. With his brethren he seeks God by fasting and with them he watches over souls. These are his family and as God helps him he cares for them and provides that they may have all the things that are needful for life and godly living.

4. A catholic spirit nevertheless goes out to all men everywhere; those he knows and those he does not know. His strong, cordial affection embraces neighbours and strangers, friends and enemies. For love alone gives the title to this character: *catholic love is a catholic spirit.*

5. In the strictest sense, therefore, a man of a catholic spirit is one who in the manner we have described gives his hand to all whose hearts are right with his heart. He is one who knows how to value and praise God for all the advantages he enjoys with regard to the knowledge of the things of God, the true scriptural manner of worshiping Him, and above all his union with a congregation fearing God and working righteousness. He is one who while keeping and guarding these things, nevertheless loves as friends, brethren, and fellow Christians and fellow heirs all others of whatever opinion, worship, or congregation, who believe in the Lord Jesus Christ; who love God and man; who is careful to abstain from evil and is zealous of good works. A man of catholic spirit is one who is ready to spend and be spent to strengthen and to help temporally and spiritually all and any of God's people. He is even ready to lay down his life for their sake.

Appeal

O man of God, think on these things! If you are already in this way, go on! If you have mistook the path, bless God for bringing you back! And now run the race set before you, in the royal way of universal love. Beware of being shaken in your mind or limited in your love. Keep an even pace, rooted in the faith once delivered to the saints, and grounded in love—*truly catholic love*—until you are swallowed up in love for ever and ever!

Original Sin
1759 (Excerpts)

This sermon was intended to be an antidote to the unorthodox teaching of Dr. John Taylor, a Presbyterian preacher and teacher of considerable ability and charm. Taylor's scholarship was oustanding and he made many converts in the midlands and southern parts of England.

Taylor was the minister of the then famous Octagon Chapel in Norwick, which Wesley described as "perhaps the most elegant one in Europe. It is eight-square built of the finest brick . . . in the highest taste and is as clean as any noblemen's saloon."[15]

Wesley had previously encountered Taylor's teaching and his disciples in the northern midlands and now immediately associated the magnificence of Taylor's chapel with the pastor's distorted view of man and sin. Wesley asks, "How can it be thought that the old, coarse gospel should find admission here?"[16] Wesley believed Dr. Taylor did not accept the deity of Christ, nor did he believe the orthodox doctrine of Original Sin, that is, that every human being is born with a corrupt human nature. This doctrine was to Wesley "the fundamental point which differences heathenism from Christianity."[17]

It was to counter such views that Wesley had published his treatise on *The Doctrine of Original Sin* in 1757 and now in 1759 condensed part of it as the sermon reproduced here.

---

15. *JJW*, 4:244.
16. Ibid.
17. *SS*, 2:223. Compare also Wesley's letter to Trelawney, *LJW*, 7:27-28, and his letter to Dr. Taylor, *LJW*, 4:66 ff.

Wesley held no personal antipathy toward Taylor, but he desired to protect the Methodists from the evil results of Taylor's teaching, hence both the treatise and the sermon on *Original Sin*.[18] He declared later, "I have reason to believe he [Dr. Taylor] was convinced of his mistake before he died, but to acknowledge this publicly was too hard a task for him."[19]

Original Sin

And God saw that the wickedness of man was great in the earth, and that every imagination of the thoughts of his heart was only evil continually (Gen. vi. 5).

1. How widely different is this from the fair pictures of human nature which men have drawn in all ages! The writings of many of the ancients abound with gay descriptions of the dignity of man. . . .

2. Nor have Heathens alone . . . but many likewise of them that bear the name of Christ, and to whom are entrusted the oracles of God, spoken as magnificently concerning the nature of man, as if it were all innocence and perfection. . . . And it must be acknowledged, that, if their accounts of him be just, man is still but "a little lower than the angels"; or, as the words may be more literally rendered, "a little less than God."

3. Is it any wonder that these accounts are very readily received by the generality of men? For who is not easily persuaded to think favourably of himself? Accordingly, writers of this kind are most universally read, admired, applauded. . . . So that it is now quite unfashionable to talk otherwise, to say anything to the disparagement of human nature; which is generally allowed, notwithstanding a few infirmities, to be very innocent, and wise, and virtuous!

4. But in the meantime what must we do with our Bibles?—for they will never agree with this. These accounts, however pleasing to flesh and blood, are utterly irreconcilable with the scriptural. The Scripture avers, that "by one man's disobedience all men were constituted sinners"; that "in Adam all died," spiritually died, lost the life and the image of God; that fallen, sinful Adam then "begat a son in his own likeness"—nor was it possible he should beget him in any other; for "who can bring a clean thing out of an unclean?"—that con-

---

18. See also *LJW*, 3:180, 208; 8:20.
19. *LJW*, 4:28.

sequently we, as well as other men, were by nature "dead in trespasses and sins," "without hope, without God in the world," and therefore "children of wrath"; that every man may say, "I was shapen in wickedness, and in sin did my mother conceive me"; that "there is no difference," in that "all have sinned and come short of the glory of God," of that glorious image of God wherein man was originally created.... Just agreeable this, to what is declared by the Holy Ghost... "God saw," when He looked down from heaven before, "that the wickedness of man was great in the earth"; so great, that "every imagination of the thoughts of his heart was only evil continually."

This is God's account of man: from which I shall take occasion, first, to show what men were before the flood; secondly, to inquire, whether they are not the same now; and, thirdly, to add some inferences.

I.

1. I am, first, by opening the words of the text, to show what men were before the flood. And we may fully depend on the account here given: for God saw it, and He cannot be deceived. He "saw that the wickedness of man was great" ... of men universally. The word includes the whole human race, every partaker of human nature. And it is not easy for us to compute their numbers, to tell how many thousands and millions they were.... Yet, among all this inconceivable number, only "Noah found favour with God." He alone (perhaps including part of his household) was an exception from the universal wickedness, which, by the just judgment of God, in a short time after brought on universal destruction. All the rest were partakers in the same guilt, as they were in the same punishment.

2. "God saw all the imaginations of the thoughts of his heart"—of his soul, his inward man, the spirit within him, the principle of all his inward and outward motions. He "saw all the imaginations"—it is not possible to find a word of a more extensive signification. It includes whatever is formed, made, fabricated within; all that is or passes in the soul; every inclination, affection, passion, appetite; every temper, design, thought. It must of consequence include every word and action, as naturally flowing from these fountains, and being either good or evil according to the fountain from which they severally flow.

3. Now God saw that all this, the whole thereof, was evil—contrary to moral rectitude; contrary to the nature of God, which

necessarily includes all good; contrary to the divine will, the eternal standard of good and evil; contrary to the pure, holy image of God, wherein man was originally created, and wherein he stood when God, surveying the works of His hands, saw them all to be very good; contrary to justice, mercy, and truth, and to the essential relations which each man bore to his Creator and his fellow creatures.

4. But was there not good mingled with the evil? Was there not light intermixed with the darkness? No, none at all: "God saw that the whole imagination of the heart of man was only evil." It cannot indeed be denied, but many of them, perhaps all, had good motions put into their hearts; for the Spirit of God did then also "strive with man" . . . But still "in his flesh dwelt no good thing"; all his nature was purely evil: it was wholly consistent with itself, and unmixed with anything of an opposite nature.

5. However, it may still be a matter of inquiry, "Was there no intermission of this evil? Were there no lucid intervals, wherein something good might be found in the heart of man?" We are not here to consider, what the grace of God might occasionally work in his soul; and, abstracted from this, we have no reason to believe there was any intermission of that evil. . . . He never deviated into good.

II.

Such is the authentic account of the whole race of mankind which He who knoweth what is in man, who searcheth the heart and trieth the reins, hath left upon record for our instruction. Such were all men before God brought the flood upon the earth. We are, secondly, to inquire whether they are the same now.

1. And this is certain, the Scripture gives us no reason to think any otherwise of them. On the contrary, all the above-cited passages of Scripture refer to those who lived after the flood. It was above a thousand years after, that God declared by David concerning the children of men, "They are all gone out of the way" of truth and holiness; "there is none righteous, no, not one." And to this bear all the prophets witness, in their several generations. So Isaiah, concerning God's peculiar people . . . "The whole head is sick, and the whole heart faint. From the sole of the foot even unto the head there is no soundness; but wounds, and bruises, and putrifying sores." The same account is given by all the Apostles, yea, by the whole tenor of the oracles of God. From all these we learn, concerning man in his natural state, unassisted by the grace of God, that "every imagination of the thoughts of his heart is" still "evil, only evil," and that "continually."

2. And this account of the present state of man is confirmed by daily experience. It is true, the natural man discerns it not: and this is not to be wondered at. So long as a man born blind continues so, he is scarce sensible of his want. Much less, could we suppose a place where all were born without sight, would they be sensible of the want of it. In like manner, so long as men remain in their natural blindness of understanding, they are not sensible of their spiritual wants, and of this in particular. But as soon as God opens the eyes of their understanding, they see the state they were in before; they are then deeply convinced, that "every man living," themselves especially, are, by nature, "altogether vanity"; that is, folly and ignorance, sin and wickedness.

3. We see, when God opens our eyes, that we were before . . . *without God,* or, rather, *atheists in the world.* We had, by nature, no knowledge of God, no acquaintance with Him. It is true, as soon as we came to the use of reason, we learned "the invisible things of God, even his eternal power and Godhead, from the things that are made." From the things that are seen we inferred the existence of an eternal, powerful Being, that is not seen. But still, although we acknowledged His being, we had no acquaintance with Him. As we know there is an Emperor of China, whom yet we do not know; so we knew there was a King of all the earth, yet we know Him not. Indeed we could not by any of our natural faculties. By none of these could we attain the knowledge of God. We could no more perceive Him by our natural understanding than we could see Him with our eyes. For "no one knoweth the Father but the Son, and he to whom the Son willeth to reveal him. And no one knoweth the Son but the Father, and he to whom the Father revealeth him."

4. We read of an ancient king, who, being desirous to know what was the *natural language* of men, in order to bring the matter to a certain issue, made the following experiment: he ordered two infants, as soon as they were born, to be conveyed to a place prepared for them, where they were brought up without any instruction at all, and without ever hearing a human voice. And what was the event? Why, that when they were at length brought out of their confinement, they spoke no language at all; they uttered only inarticulate sounds, like those of other animals. Were two infants in like manner to be brought up from the womb without being instructed in any religion, there is little room to doubt but . . . the event would be just the same. . . .

5. And having no knowledge, we can have no love of God: we

cannot love Him we know not. Most men *talk* indeed of loving God, and perhaps imagine they do; at least, few will acknowledge they do not love Him: but the fact is too plain to be denied. No man loves God by nature, any more than he does a stone, or the earth he treads upon. What we love we delight in: but no man has naturally any delight in God. In our natural state we cannot conceive how anyone should delight in Him. We take no pleasure in Him at all; He is utterly tasteless to us. To love God! It is far above, out of our sight. We cannot, naturally, attain unto it.

6. We have by nature, not only no love, but no fear of God. It is allowed, indeed, that most men have, sooner or later, a kind of senseless, irrational fear, properly called "superstition" . . . Yet even this is not natural, but acquired; chiefly by conversation or from example. By nature "God is not in all our thoughts": we leave Him to manage His own affairs, to sit quietly, as we imagine, in heaven, and leave us on earth to manage ours; so that we have no more of the fear of God before our eyes, than of the love of God in our hearts.

7. Thus are all men "atheists in the world." But Atheism itself does not screen us from idolatry. In his natural state, every man born into the world is a rank idolater. . . . We have set up our idols in our hearts; and to these we bow down and worship them: we worship ourselves, when we pay that honour to ourselves which is due to God only. Therefore all pride is idolatry; it is ascribing to ourselves what is due to God alone. And although pride was not made for man, yet where is the man that is born without it? But hereby we rob God of His unalienable right, and idolatrously usurp His glory.

8. But pride is not the only sort of idolatry which we are all by nature guilty of. Satan has stamped his own image on our heart in self-will also. "I will," said he, before he was cast out of heaven. . . . I will do my own will and pleasure, independently of that of my Creator. The same does every man born into the world say, and that in a thousand instances; nay, and avow it too, without ever blushing upon the account, without either fear or shame. Ask the man, "Why did you do this?" He answers, "Because I had a mind to it." . . . The will of God, meantime, is not in his thoughts, is not considered in the least degree; although it be the supreme rule of every intelligent creature, whether in heaven or earth, resulting from the essential, unalterable relation which all creatures bear to their Creator.

9. So far we bear the image of the devil, and tread in his steps. But at the next step we leave Satan behind; we run into an idolatry

whereof he is not guilty: I mean love of the world, which is now as natural to every man as to love his own will. What is more natural to us than to seek happiness in the creature, instead of the Creator—to seek that satisfaction in the works of His hands, which can be found in God only? What more natural than "the desire of the flesh"? that is, of the pleasure of sense in every kind?

Men indeed talk magnificently of despising these low pleasures, particularly men of learning and education. They affect to sit loose to the gratification of those appetites wherein they stand on a level with the beasts that perish. But it is mere affectation; for every man is conscious to himself, that in this respect he is, by nature, a very beast. Sensual appetites, even those of the lowest kind, have, more or less, the dominion over him. They lead him captive; they drag him to and fro, in spite of his boasted reason. The man, with all his good breeding, and other accomplishments, has no preeminence over the goat: nay, it is much to be doubted, whether the beast has not the preeminence over him. Certainly he has, if we may hearken to one of their modern oracles, who very decently tells us,

> *Once in a season beasts too taste of love;*
> *Only the beast of reason is its slave,*
> *And in that folly drudges all the year.*

A considerable difference indeed, it must be allowed, there is between man and man, arising (beside that wrought by preventing grace) from difference of constitution and of education. But, notwithstanding this, who, that is not utterly ignorant of himself, can here cast the first stone at another? Who can abide the test of our blessed Lord's comment on the Seventh Commandment: "He that looketh on a woman to lust after her hath committed adultery with her already in his heart"? So that one knows not which to wonder at most, the ignorance or the insolence of those men who speak with such disdain of them that are overcome by desires which every man has felt in his own breast; the desire of every pleasure of sense, innocent or not, being natural to every child of man.

10. And so is "the desire of the eye"; the desire of the pleasures of the imagination. These arise either from great, or beautiful, or uncommon objects—if the two former do not coincide with the latter; for perhaps it would appear, upon a diligent inquiry, that neither grand nor beautiful objects please any longer than they are new; that when the novelty of them is over, the greatest part, at least, of the

pleasure they give is over; and in the same proportion as they become familiar, they become flat and insipid. But let us experience this ever so often, the same desire will remain still. The inbred thirst continues fixed in the soul; nay, the more it is indulged, the more it increases, and incites us to follow after another, and yet another object; although we leave every one with an abortive hope, and a deluded expectation. . . .

11. A third symptom of this fatal disease—the love of the world, which is so deeply rooted in our nature—is "the pride of life"; the desire of praise, of the honour that cometh of men. This the greatest admirers of human nature allow to be strictly natural; as natural as the sight, or hearing, or any other of the external senses. And are they ashamed of it, even men of letters, men of refined and improved understanding? So far from it that they glory therein! They applaud themselves for their love of applause. . . .

But would one imagine that these men had ever heard of Jesus Christ or His Apostles; or that they knew who it was that said, "How can ye believe who receive honour one of another, and seek not the honour which cometh of God only?" But if this is really so, if it be impossible to believe, and consequently to please God, so long as we receive or seek honour one of another, and seek not the honour which cometh of God only; then in what a condition are all mankind! the Christians as well as Heathens! since they all seek honour one of another! since it is as natural for them so to do, themselves being the judges, as it is to see the light which strikes upon their eye, or to hear the sound which enters their ear; yea, since they account it a sign of a virtuous mind, to seek the praise of men, and of a vicious one to be content with the honour that cometh of God only!

III.

1. I proceed to draw a few inferences from what has been said. And, first, from hence we may learn one grand fundamental difference between Christianity, considered as a system of doctrines, and the most refined Heathenism. Many of the ancient Heathens have largely described the vices of particular men. . . . But still as none of them were apprised of the fall of man, so none of them knew of his total corruption. They knew not that all men were empty of all good, and filled with all manner of evil. They were wholly ignorant of the entire depravation of the whole human nature, of every man born into the world, in every faculty of his soul, not so much by those particular

vices which reign in particular persons, as by the general flood of Atheism and idolatry, of pride, self-will, and love of the world.

CARNALITY

This, therefore, is the first grand distinguishing point between Heathenism and Christianity. The one acknowledges that many men are infected with many vices, and even born with a proneness to them; but supposes withal, that in some the natural good much overbalances the evil: the other declares that all men are "conceived in sin," and "shapen in wickedness"—that hence there is in every man a "carnal mind, which is enmity against God; which is not, cannot be, subject to" His "law"; and which so infects the whole soul, that "there dwelleth in" him, "in his flesh," in his natural state, "no good thing"; but "every imagination of the thoughts of his heart is evil," only evil, and that "continually."

2. Hence we may, secondly, learn, that all who deny this, call it "original sin," or by any other title, are but Heathens still, in the fundamental point which differences Heathenism from Christianity. . . . But here is the *shibboleth:* Is man by nature filled with all manner of evil? Is he void of all good? Is he wholly fallen? Is his soul totally corrupted? Or, to come back to the text, is "every imagination of the thoughts of his heart only evil continually"? Allow this, and you are so far a Christian. Deny it, and you are but an Heathen still.

CLEANSING

3. We may learn from hence, in the third place, what is the proper nature of religion, of the religion of Jesus Christ. It is . . . God's method of *healing a soul* which is thus diseased. Hereby the great Physician of souls applies medicines to heal this sickness; to restore human nature, totally corrupted in all its faculties. God heals all our Atheism by the knowledge of himself, and of Jesus Christ whom He hath sent; by giving us faith, a divine evidence and conviction of God, and of the things of God—in particular, of this important truth, "Christ loved *me,* and gave himself for *me.*"

By repentance and lowliness of heart, the deadly disease of pride is healed; that of self-will by resignation, a meek and thankful submission to the will of God; and for the love of the world in all its branches, the love of God is the sovereign remedy. Now, this is properly religion, "faith" thus "working by love"; working the genuine meek humility, entire deadness to the world, with a loving, thankful acquiescence in, and conformity to, the whole will and word of God.

4. Indeed, if man were not thus fallen, there would be no need of all this. There would be no occasion for this work in the heart, this renewal in the spirit of our mind. The superfluity of godliness would

then be a more proper expression than the "superfluity of naughtiness." For an outside religion, without any godliness at all, would suffice to all rational intents and purposes. It does, accordingly, suffice, in the judgment of those who deny this corruption of our nature. . . . According to them, religion is only a well-ordered train of words and actions. And they speak consistently with themselves; for if the inside be not full of wickedness, if this be clean already, what remains, but to "cleanse the outside of the cup"? Outward reformation, if their supposition be just, is indeed the one thing needful.

5. But ye have not so learned the oracles of God. Ye know that He who seeth what is in man gives a far different account both of nature and grace, of our fall and our recovery. Ye know that the great end of religion is to renew our hearts in the image of God, to repair that total loss of righteousness and true holiness which we sustained by the sin of our first parent. Ye know that all religion which does not answer this end, all that stops short of this, the renewal of our soul in the image of God, after the likeness of Him that created it, is no other than a poor farce, and a mere mockery of God, to the destruction of our own soul.

O beware of all those teachers of lies, who would palm this upon you for Christianity! Regard them not, although they should come unto you with all the deceivableness of unrighteousness; with all smoothness of language, all decency, yea, beauty and elegance of expression, all professions of earnest goodwill to you, and reverence for the Holy Scriptures. Keep to the plain, old faith, "once delivered to the saints," and delivered by the Spirit of God to our hearts. Know your disease! Know your cure! Ye were born in sin: Therefore, "ye must be born again," born of God. By nature ye are wholly corrupted. By grace ye shall be wholly renewed. In Adam ye all died: in the second Adam, in Christ, ye all are made alive. "You that were dead in sins hath he quickened": He hath already given you a principle of life, even faith in Him who loved you and gave himself for you! Now, "go on from faith to faith," until your whole sickness be healed; and all that "mind be in you which was also in Christ Jesus"!

On Sin in Believers
1763 (Abridged)

This sermon Wesley considered to be of great significance in understanding his message of Christian holiness. Of sin in believers he wrote:

> It is ... not a question of mere curiosity; or ... of little importance.... Rather it is a point of the utmost moment to every serious Christian; the resolving of which very nearly concerns both his present and eternal happiness.[20]

Wesley prepared the sermon in March 1763 for the purpose of removing "a mistake which some were labouring to propagate—that there is no sin in any that are justified."[21]

If Wesley seemed to suggest in some earlier sermons a more radical work in the believer's heart in the crisis of justification than the Scriptures warranted, this sermon will serve as an excellent corrective of that impression.

Analysis of the Sermon

1. The core of the question: Is there or is there not sin remaining in the heart of the born-again person? Paragraphs 2 and 3 maintain that the primitive church and Wesley's own denomination firmly declare that sin remains in the regenerate believer. Paragraphs 3 and 4 make a similar claim for the Greek, Roman Catholic, and all Reformed European churches.

Paragraphs 5 through 7 maintain that the Moravians have gone clean over to the other extreme of offering freedom from both the dominion and being of inward and outward sin in conversion.

2. Two contrary principles in the regenerate believer. In paragraph 4 Wesley insists that there is a very real and radical change wrought in the believer at justification. This answers the extreme views of the Greek and Roman churches, and indeed of all who minimize the revolutionary effect of conversion. Section II presents Wes-

---

20. I. Paragraph 1. Intro. to the sermon, *SS*, 2:361.
21. Ibid., 360; and *JJW*, 5:10.

ley's teaching on the remains of sin in believers, pressed home by arguments from Scripture and experience.

3. In part IV Wesley answers objections to his proposition by means of imaginary conversations with the objectors.

4. The bottom line. In part V with firm tenacity, Wesley restates his conviction that sin remains in justified persons, demanding of them constant vigilance and discipline.

ON SIN IN BELIEVERS

If any man be in Christ, he is a new creature (2 Cor. v. 17).

I.

1. Is there then sin in him that is in Christ? Does sin *remain* in one that believes in Him? Is there any sin in them that are born of God, or are they wholly delivered from it? Let no one imagine this to be a question of mere curiosity; or, that it is of little importance whether it be determined one way or the other. . . .

2. . . . I do not know that ever it was controverted in the primitive church. Indeed there was no room for disputing concerning it, as all Christians were agreed. And so far as I have ever observed the whole body of ancient Christians who have left us anything in writing declare with one voice that even believers in Christ, till they are "strong in the Lord and in the power of his might," have need to "wrestle with flesh and blood," with an evil nature, as well as "with principalities and powers."

3. And herein our own church . . . exactly copies after the primitive; declaring in her ninth article, "Original sin is the corruption of the nature of every man, whereby man is in his own nature inclined to evil, so that the flesh lusteth contrary to the spirit. And this infection of nature doth remain, yea in them that are regenerated; whereby the lust of the flesh . . . is not subject to the law of God. And although there is no condemnation for them that believe, yet this lust hath of itself the nature of sin."

CLEANSING

4. The same testimony is given by all other churches; not only by the Greek and Romish church, but by every reformed church in Europe, of whatever denomination. . . .

5. To avoid this extreme, many well-meaning men . . . affirm that "all true believers are not only saved from the *dominion* of sin, but

from the *being* of inward as well as outward sin, so that it no longer *remains* in them." And . . . many of our countrymen imbibed the same opinion, that even the corruption *is no more,* in those who believe in Christ. . . .

II.

1. For the sake of those who really fear God and desire to know "the truth as it is in Jesus," it may not be amiss to consider the point with calmness and impartiality. In doing this I use indifferently the words *regenerate, justified,* or *believers;* since, though they have not precisely the same meaning, . . . yet they come to one and the same thing; as every one that believes is both justified and born of God.

2. By sin, I here understand inward sin; any sinful temper, passion, or affection; such as pride, self-will, love of the world, in any kind or degree; such as lust, anger, peevishness; any disposition contrary to the mind which was in Christ.

3. The question is not concerning *outward sin:* whether a child of God *commit sin* or no. We all agree and earnestly maintain, "He that committeth sin is of the devil." We agree, "Whosoever is born of God doth not commit sin." Neither do we now inquire, whether inward sin will *always* remain in the children of God; whether sin will continue in the soul as long as it continues in the body: nor yet do we inquire whether a justified person may *relapse* either into inward or outward sin; but simply this, Is a justified or regenerate man freed from *all sin* as soon as he is justified? Is there then no sin in his heart?—nor ever after, unless he fall from grace?

4. We allow that the state of a justified person is inexpressibly great and glorious. He is born again, "not of blood, nor of the flesh, nor of the will of man, but of God." He is a child of God, a member of Christ, an heir of the kingdom of heaven. "The peace of God, which passeth all understanding, keepeth his heart and mind in Christ Jesus." His very body is a "temple of the Holy Ghost," and a "habitation of God through the Spirit." He is "created anew in Christ Jesus": he is *washed,* he is *sanctified.* His heart is purified by faith; he is cleansed "from the corruption that is in the world"; "the love of God is shed abroad in his heart by the Holy Ghost which is given unto him." And so long as he "walketh in love" (which he may always do), he worships God in spirit and in truth. He keepeth the commandments of God, and doeth those things that are pleasing in his sight; so exercising himself as to "have a conscience void of offence towards

God and towards man"; and he has power both over outward and inward sin even from the moment he is justified.

III.

1. But was he not then freed from all sin so that there is no sin in his heart? . . . I cannot believe it; because St. Paul says the contrary. He is speaking to believers, and describing the state of believers in general, when he says, "The flesh lusteth against the Spirit, and the Spirit against the flesh: these are contrary the one to the other" (Gal. v. 17). Nothing can be more express. The apostle here directly affirms that the flesh, evil nature, opposes the Spirit, even in believers; that even in the regenerate there are two principles, "contrary the one to the other."

CARNALITY

2. Again: when he writes to the believers at Corinth, to those who were sanctified in Christ Jesus (1 Cor. i. 2), he says, "I, brethren, could not speak unto you, as unto spiritual, but as unto carnal, as unto babes in Christ. Ye are yet carnal: for whereas there is among you envying and strife, are ye not carnal?" (1 Cor. iii. 1-3). Now here the Apostle speaks unto those who were unquestionably believers . . . as being still, in a measure, carnal. He affirms there was envying (an evil temper), occasioning strife among them, and yet does not give the least intimation that they had lost their faith. Nay, he manifestly declares they had not; for then they would not have been babes in Christ. And (what is most remarkable of all) he speaks of being carnal, and babes in Christ, as one and the same thing; plainly showing that every believer is (in a degree) carnal while he is only a babe in Christ.

3. Indeed this grand point that there are two contrary principles in believers, nature and grace, the flesh and the Spirit, runs through all the epistles of St. Paul, yea, through all the Holy Scriptures; almost all the directions and exhortations therein are founded on this supposition; pointing at wrong tempers or practices in those who are, notwithstanding, acknowledged by the inspired writers to be believers. And they are continually exhorted to fight with and conquer these, by the power of the faith which was in them.

4. And who can doubt but there was faith in the angel of the church of Ephesus when our Lord said to him, "I know thy works, and thy labour, and thy patience: thou hast patience, and for my name's sake hast laboured and hast not fainted" (Rev. ii. 2-4). But was there, meantime, no sin in his heart? Yea, or Christ would not have

added, "Nevertheless I have somewhat against thee, because thou hast left thy first love." . . .

5. The angel of the church at Pergamos, also, is exhorted to *repent,* which implies sin, though our Lord expressly says, "Thou hast not denied my faith" (vv. 13, 16). And to the angel of the church in Sardis, he says, "Strengthen the things which remain, that are ready to die." The good which remained was *ready to die* but was not actually dead (Rev. iii. 2). So there was still a spark of faith even in him; which he is accordingly commanded to *hold fast* (v. 3).

6. Once more: when the Apostle exhorts believers to "cleanse themselves from all filthiness of flesh and spirit" (2 Cor. vii. 1), he plainly teaches that those believers were not yet cleansed therefrom.

Will you answer, "He that abstains from all appearances of evil," does [in fact] "cleanse himself from all filthiness." Not in any wise. For instance: a man reviles me: I feel resentment, which is filthiness of spirit; yet I say not a word. Here I "abstain from all appearance of evil"; but this does not cleanse me from that filthiness of spirit as I experience to my sorrow.

7. And as this position, "There is no sin in a believer, no carnal mind, no bent to backsliding," is thus contrary to the word of God, so it is to the experience of His children. These continually feel a heart bent to backsliding; a natural tendency to evil; a proneness to depart from God and cleave to the things of earth. They are daily sensible of sin remaining in their heart, pride, self-will, unbelief; and of sin cleaving to all they speak and do, even their best actions and holiest duties. Yet at the same time they "know that they are of God"; they cannot doubt of it for a moment. They feel His Spirit clearly "witnessing with their spirit, that they are the children of God." They "rejoice in God through Christ Jesus, by whom they have now received the atonement." So that they are equally assured that sin is in them and that "Christ is in them the hope of glory."

8. "But can Christ be in the same heart where sin is?" Undoubtedly He can. Otherwise it never could be saved therefrom. Where the sickness is, there is the physician,

> *Carrying on his work within,*
> *Striving till he cast out sin.*

Christ indeed cannot *reign* where sin *reigns;* neither will He *dwell* where any sin is *allowed.* But He *is* and *dwells* in the heart of every believer who is *fighting against* all sin; although it be not yet purified, according to the purification of the sanctuary.

9. It has been observed before that the opposite doctrine, that there is no sin in believers, is quite new in the church of Christ . . . I do not remember to have seen the least intimation of it either in any ancient or modern writer; unless perhaps in some of the wild, ranting Antinomians. And these likewise say and unsay, acknowledging there is sin *in their flesh* although no *sin in their heart*. But whatever doctrine is *new* must be *wrong;* for the *old* religion is the only *true* one; and no doctrine can be right unless it is the very same "which was from the beginning."

10. One argument more against this new, unscriptural doctrine, may be drawn from the dreadful consequences of it. One says, "I felt anger today." Must I reply, "Then you have no faith?" Another says, "I know what you advise is good, but my will is quite averse to it." Must I tell him, "Then you are an unbeliever, under the wrath and the curse of God?" What will be the natural consequence of this? Why, if he believe what I say, his soul will not only be grieved and wounded but perhaps utterly destroyed; inasmuch as he will "cast away" that "confidence which hath great recompense of reward": and having cast away his shield, how shall he "quench the fiery darts of the wicked one"? How shall he overcome the world?—seeing "this is the victory that overcometh the world, even our faith." He stands disarmed in the midst of his enemies, open to all their assaults. What wonder, then, if he be utterly overthrown; if they take him captive at their will; yea, if he fall from one wickedness to another, and never see good any more?

I cannot therefore by any means receive this assertion, that there is no sin in a believer from the moment he is justified; first, because it is contrary to the whole tenor of Scripture; secondly, because it is contrary to the experience of the children of God; thirdly, because it is absolutely new, never heard of in the world till yesterday; and, lastly, because it is naturally attended with the most fatal consequences; not only grieving those whom God hath not grieved, but perhaps dragging them into everlasting perdition.

IV.

1. However, let us give a fair hearing to the chief arguments of those who endeavour to support it. And it is, first, from Scripture they attempt to prove that there is no sin in a believer. They argue thus: "The Scripture says, Every believer is born of God, is clean, is holy, is sanctified, is pure in heart, has a new heart, is a temple of the Holy Ghost. Now, as 'that which is born of the flesh is flesh,' is altogether

evil, so 'that which is born of the Spirit is spirit,' is altogether good. Again, a man cannot be clean, sanctified, holy, and at the same time unclean, unsanctified, unholy. He cannot be pure and impure, or have a new and an old heart together. Neither can his soul be unholy while it is a temple of the Holy Ghost." . . .

Let us now examine it part by part. And (1) "That which is born of the Spirit is spirit, is altogether good." I allow the text but not the comment. For the text affirms this and no more, that every man who is "born of the Spirit," is a spiritual man. He is so. But so he may be, and yet not be altogether spiritual. The Christians at Corinth were spiritual men; else they had been no Christians at all; and yet they were not altogether spiritual: they were still, in part, carnal—"But they were fallen from grace." St. Paul says, no. They were even then babes in Christ. (2) "But a man cannot be clean, sanctified, holy, and at the same time unclean, unsanctified, unholy." Indeed he may. So the Corinthians were. "Ye are washed," says the Apostle, "ye are sanctified"; namely, from "fornication, idolatry, drunkenness," and all other outward sin (1 Cor. vi. 9-11): and yet, at the same time in another sense of the word, they were unsanctified; they were not washed, not inwardly cleansed from envy, evil surmising, partiality.

"But sure they had not a new heart and an old heart together." It is most sure they had; for at that very time their hearts were *truly*, yet not *entirely* renewed. Their carnal mind was nailed to the cross; yet it was not wholly destroyed. "But could they be unholy while they were 'temples of the Holy Ghost'?" Yes; that they were temples of the Holy Ghost is certain (1 Cor. vi. 19); and it is equally certain they were, in some degree, carnal, that is, unholy.

2. "However, there is one scripture more which will put the matter out of question: 'If any man be [a believer] in Christ, he is a new creature. Old things are passed away; behold all things are become new" (2 Cor. v. 17). Now, certainly, a man cannot be a new creature and an old creature at once. Yes, he may: he may be partly renewed, which was the very case with those at Corinth. They were doubtless "renewed in the spirit of their mind," or they could not have been so much as "babes in Christ"; yet they had not the whole mind which was in Christ, for they *envied* one another. "But it is said expressly, Old things are passed away: all things are become new!" But we must not so interpret the Apostle's words as to make him contradict himself. And if we will make him consistent with himself, the plain meaning of the words is this: His old judgment concerning justification, holiness,

happiness, indeed concerning the things of God in general, is now passed away: so are his old desires, designs, affections, tempers, and conversation. All these are undeniably become new greatly changed from what they were. And yet, though they are new, they are not wholly new. Still he feels, to his sorrow and shame, remains of the old man, too, manifest taints of his former tempers and affections, though they cannot gain any advantage over him as long as he watches unto prayer.

3. This whole argument, "If he is clean, he is clean"; "if he is holy, he is holy" ... is really no better than playing upon words. ... Propose the sentence entire and it runs thus: "If he is holy *at all*, he is holy *altogether*." That does not follow: every babe in Christ is holy, and yet not altogether so. He is saved from sin; yet not entirely: it *remains* though it does not *reign*. If you think it does not *remain* ... you certainly have not considered the height, and depth, and length, and breadth of the law of God ... and that *every* ... disconformity to, or deviation from this law *is sin*. Now, is there no disconformity to this in the heart or life of a believer? What may be in an adult Christian, is another question; but what a stranger must he be to human nature who can possibly imagine that this is the case with every babe in Christ!

4. "But believers walk after the Spirit (Rom. viii. 1), and the Spirit of God dwells in them; consequently they are delivered from the guilt, the power, or in one word, the being of sin."

These are coupled together as if they were the same thing. But they are not the same thing. The *guilt* is one thing, the *power* another, and the *being* yet another. That believers are delivered from the *guilt* and *power* of sin we allow; that they are delivered from the *being* of it we deny. ... A man may have the Spirit of God dwelling in him, and may "walk after the Spirit," though he still feels "the flesh lusting against the Spirit."

CLEANSING

5. "But the 'church is the body of Christ' (Col. i. 24); this implies that its members are washed from all filthiness; otherwise it will follow that Christ and Belial are incorporated with each other."

Nay, it will not follow from hence, "Those who are the mystical body of Christ, still feel the flesh lusting against the Spirit," that Christ has any fellowship with the devil; or with that sin which he enables them to resist and overcome.

6. "But are not Christians 'come to the heavenly Jerusalem,' where 'nothing defiled can enter'?" (Heb. xii. 22). Yes; "and to an

innumerable company of angels, and to the spirits of just men made perfect": that is,

> Earth and heaven all agree;
> All is one great family.

And they are likewise holy and undefiled while they "walk after the Spirit"; although sensible there is another principle in them, and that "these are contrary to each other."

7. "But Christians are reconciled to God. Now this could not be, if any of the carnal mind remained; for this is enmity against God: consequently, no reconciliation can be effected but by its total destruction."

We are "reconciled to God through the blood of the cross"; and in that moment ... the corruption of nature, which is enmity with God, is put under our feet; the flesh has no more dominion over us. But it still *exists:* and it is still in its nature enmity with God, lusting against His Spirit.

8. "But 'they that are Christ's have crucified the flesh with its affections and lusts'" (Gal. v. 24). They have so; yet it remains in them still and often struggles to break from the cross. "Nay, but they have 'put off the old man with his deeds'" (Col. iii. 9). They have; and, in the sense above described, "old things are passed away; all things are become new." ". . . To say all in one word, 'Christ gave himself for the church that it might be holy and without blemish'" (Eph. v. 25, 27). And so it will be in the end: but it never was yet from the beginning to this day.

9. "But let experience speak: all who are justified do at that time find an absolute freedom from all sin." That I doubt: but, if they do, do they find it ever after? Else you gain nothing. "If they do not, it is their own fault." That remains to be proved.

10. "But in the very nature of things, can a man have pride in him and not be proud; anger, and yet not be angry?"

A man may have *pride* in him, may think of himself in some particulars above what he ought to think ... and yet not be a proud man in his general character. He may have *anger* in him, yea, and a strong propensity to furious anger, without *giving way* to it. "But can anger and pride be in that heart where *only* meekness and humility are felt?" No: but *some* pride and anger may be in that heart where there is much humility and meekness.

"It avails not to say, these tempers are there, but they do not *reign.*

For sin cannot, in any kind or degree, exist where it does not reign; for *guilt* and *power* are essential properties of sin. Therefore, where one of them is, all must be."

Strange indeed! "Sin cannot, in any kind or degree, *exist* where it does not *reign*." Absolutely contrary this to all experience, all Scripture, all common sense. Resentment of an affront is sin; it is ... disconformity to the law of love. This has existed in me a thousand times. Yet it did not, and does not *reign*. "But *guilt* and *power* are essential properties of sin; therefore, where one is, all must be." No: in the instance before us, if the resentment I feel is not yielded to, even for a moment, there is no guilt at all, no condemnation from God upon that account. And in this case, it has no *power*: though it "lusteth against the Spirit," it cannot prevail. Here, therefore, as in ten thousand instances, there is sin without either *guilt* or *power.*

11. "But the supposing [that sin remains] in a believer is pregnant with every thing frightful and discouraging. It implies the contending with a power that has the possession of our strength; maintains his usurpation of our hearts; and there prosecutes the war in defiance of our Redeemer." Not so: The supposing sin is in us, does not imply that it has the possession of our strength; no more than a man crucified has the possession of those that crucify him. As little does it imply, that "sin maintains its usurpation of our hearts." The usurper is dethroned. He remains indeed where he once reigned; but remains *in chains*. So that he does, in some sense, "prosecute the war," yet he grows weaker and weaker; while the believer goes on from strength to strength, conquering and to conquer.

12. "I am not satisfied yet: he that hath sin in him is a slave to sin. Therefore, you suppose a man to be justified while he is a slave to sin. Now if you allow men may be justified while they have pride, anger, or unbelief in them; nay, if you aver, these are (at least for a time) in all that are justified; what wonder that we have so many proud, angry, unbelieving believers?"

I do not suppose any man who is justified is a slave to sin: yet I do suppose sin remains (at least for a time) in all that are justified.

"But, if sin remains in a believer, he is a sinful man: if pride, for instance, then he is proud; if self-will, then he is self-willed; if unbelief, then he is an unbeliever; consequently, no believer at all. How then does he differ from unbelievers, from unregenerate men?" This is still mere playing upon words. It means no more than, if there is sin, pride, self-will in him, then there is sin, pride, self-will. And this nobody can deny. In that sense then he is proud, or self-willed. But he is not proud or self-willed in the same sense that unbelievers are, that is, *governed* by pride or self-will. Herein he differs from unregenerate men. They *obey* sin; he does not. Flesh is in them both; but they *walk after the flesh;* he *walks after the Spirit.*

"But how can *unbelief* be in a believer?" That word has two meanings. It means either no faith, or little faith; either the *absence* of faith, or the *weakness* of it. In the former sense, unbelief is not in a believer; in the latter, it is in all babes. Their faith is commonly mixed with doubt or fear, that is, in the latter sense, with unbelief. "Why are ye fearful (says our Lord), oh ye of little faith?" Again, "Oh thou of little faith, wherefore didst thou doubt?" You see here was *unbelief* in *believers;* little faith and much unbelief.

13. "But this doctrine, That sin remains in a believer; that a man may be in the favour of God while he has sin in his heart; certainly tends to encourage men in sin." Understand the proposition right, and no such consequence follows. A man may be in God's favour though he feel sin; but not if he *yields* to it. *Having sin* does not forfeit the favour of God; *giving way to sin* does. Though the flesh in you "lust against the Spirit," you may still be a child of God; but if you "walk after the flesh," you are a child of the devil. Now this doctrine does not encourage to *obey* sin but to resist it with all your might.

V.

1. The sum of all is this: There are in every person, even after he is justified, two contrary principles, nature and grace, termed by St. Paul, the *flesh* and the *Spirit.* Hence, although even babes in Christ are *sanctified,* yet it is only in part. In a degree, according to the measure of their faith, they are spiritual; yet, in a degree they are carnal. Accordingly, believers are continually exhorted to watch against the flesh, as well as the world and the devil. And to this agrees the constant experience of the children of God. While they feel this witness in themselves, they feel a will not wholly resigned to the will of God. They know they are in Him; and yet find a heart ready to depart from Him, a proneness to evil in many instances, and a backwardness to that which is good. The contrary doctrine is wholly new . . . and it is attended with the most fatal consequences. It cuts off all watching against our evil nature, against the Delilah which we are told is gone, though she is still lying in our bosom. It tears away the shield of weak

believers, deprives them of their faith, and so leaves them exposed to all the assaults of the world, the flesh, and the devil.

2. Let us, therefore, hold fast the sound doctrine "once delivered to the saints," and delivered down by them, with the written word, to all succeeding generations; that although we are renewed, cleansed, purified, sanctified, the moment we truly believe in Christ, yet we are not then renewed, cleansed, purified altogether; but the flesh, the evil nature still *remains* (though subdued), and wars against the Spirit. So much the more let us use all diligence in "fighting the good fight of faith." So much the more earnestly let us "watch and pray" against the enemy within. The more carefully let us take to ourselves, and "put on the whole armour of God"; that, although "we wrestle" both "with flesh and blood, and with principalities, and powers, and wicked spirits in high places," we "may be able to withstand in the evil day, and having done all, to stand."

The Scripture Way of Salvation
1765

This sermon represents Wesley at his best. Outler asserts dogmatically: "If the Wesleyan theology had to be judged by a single essay, this one would do as well as any and better than most."[22] Richard S. Taylor writes of the sermon: "It has long been a favorite with Wesleyan preachers and scholars. To my mind this is Wesley's clearest summary of his doctrine of full salvation; an anthology which is majoring on holiness could hardly be complete without it."[23]

Agar Beet wrote:

> It is . . . a compact statement of Wesley's mature thought about the great doctrines that inspired the Methodist Revival; it is of more practical value than all the other sermons put together.
>
> He asserts again and again that, as we are justified by faith, so we are sanctified by faith; and very forcibly describes this saving faith. He also urged his readers to accept here and now this great salvation.[24]

---

22. Albert C. Outler, *John Wesley* (New York: Oxford University Press, 1964), 271.
23. R. S. Taylor, Letter 11/13/81.
24. *SS*, 2:443.

Seedbeds of the Sermon

Like so many good insights, this sermon came out of Wesley's experiences—one exhilarating and one exhausting.

During the month of February 1760 there occurred a gracious visitation of the Holy Ghost in Otley, Yorkshire, in which a number of believers professed cleansing from all sin. Wesley describes it as the beginning of "that glorious work of sanctification" which soon spread throughout the northeast, moved southward to London, spread to different parts of England and Ireland.

The "glorious work" continued for over four years. Many people professed to have experienced "so deep and universal a change as it had not before entered their hearts to conceive.... Now, whether we call this destruction or suspension of sin, it is a glorious work of God ... as we never saw in these kingdoms before."[25] To John Wesley this was truly a Pentecostal visitation in which persons were indeed sanctified as frequently as many had been justified in the earlier years of the Revival.[26] He did not hesitate to declare: "The peculiar work of this season has been what Paul calls the perfecting of the saints."[27]

In the London area, however, there arose a subversive movement under the influence of two of Wesley's preachers, Thomas Maxfield and George Bell. Bell first became fanatical, claiming miraculous powers and asserting a state of perfection rendering him infallible, untemptable, and of superior spirituality.

To begin with, Maxfield simply sided with Bell. Before long, however, he became captain of the deceived company. Gathering a fairly large group around him he became for a time a severe critic of Wesley and his teaching. In time many of the Bell-Maxfield followers returned to the Wesley fold. Bell, however, was so wildly fanatical and extravagant that Wesley felt compelled to expel him from the Society.

The whole sad affair was a sore and heavy burden on Wesley. Maxfield separated voluntarily from Wesley, but things sweetened somewhat with the passage of time. In Wesley's *Journal* for February 2, 1783, we read: "Mr. Maxfield continuing ill, I preached this afternoon at his chapel. Prejudice seems now dying away: God grant it may never revive."[28]

---

25. *JJW*, 5:40-41.
26. The remarkable story should be read in *JJW*, 4:498-532.
27. *JJW*, 5:41.
28. *JJW*, 6:389-90.

Out of these circumstances came the enlightening correspondence below from Wesley. At a slightly later date he published *The Scriptural Way of Salvation*. If we regard this sermon as "Wesley's clearest summary of his doctrine of full salvation," we should ponder also his answers to those who made extravagant claims with regard to entire sanctification and Christian perfection. Therefore we reproduce Wesley's letter to Thomas Maxfield in chronological relation to the sermon.

Letter to Thomas Maxfield

Fri. October 29, 1762. I left Bristol, and the next day came to London. Monday, November 1, I went down to Canterbury. Here I seriously reflected on some late occurrences; and, after weighing the matter thoroughly, wrote as follows:

"Without any preface or ceremony, which is needless between you and me, I will simply and plainly tell what I dislike in your doctrine, spirit, or outward behaviour. When I say yours, I include brothers Bell and Owen, and those who are most closely connected with them.

"1. I like your doctrine of Perfection, or pure love; love excluding sin; your insisting that it is merely by faith; that consequently it is instantaneous (though preceded and followed by a gradual work), and that it may be now at this instant.

"But I dislike your supposing man may be as perfect as an angel; that he can be absolutely perfect; that he can be infallible, or above being tempted; or that the moment he is pure in heart he cannot fall from it.

"I dislike the saying this was not known or taught among us till within two or three years. I grant you did not know it. You have over and over denied instantaneous sanctification to me; but I have known and taught it (and so has my brother as our writings show) above these twenty years.

"I dislike your directly or indirectly depreciating justification; saying a justified person is not in Christ, is not born of God, is not a new creature, has not a new heart, is not sanctified, not a temple of the Holy Ghost; or that he cannot please God, or cannot grow in grace.

"I dislike your saying that one saved from sin needs nothing more than looking to Jesus; needs not to hear or think of anything else;

believe, believe, is enough; that he needs no self-examination, no times of private prayer; needs not mind little or outward things; and that he cannot be taught by any person who is not in the same state.

"I dislike your affirming that justified persons in general persecute them that are saved from sin [sanctified wholly]; that they have persecuted you on this account; and that for two years past you have been more persecuted by the two brothers than ever you were by the world in all your life.

"2. As to your spirit, I like your confidence in God and your zeal for the salvation of souls.

"But I dislike something which has the appearance of pride, or overvaluing yourselves and undervaluing others; particularly the Preachers; thinking not only that they are blind and that they are not sent of God, but even that they are dead; dead to God and walking in the way of hell; that they are going one way, you another; that they have no life in them. Your speaking of yourselves as though you were the only men who knew and taught the Gospel; and as if, not only the Clergy, but all the Methodists besides were in utter darkness.

"I dislike something that has the appearance of enthusiasm, overvaluing feelings and inward impressions; mistaking the mere work of imagination for the voice of the Spirit; expecting the end without the means; and undervaluing reason, knowledge, and wisdom in general.

"I dislike something that has the appearance of Antinomianism, not magnifying the Law, and making it honourable; not enough valuing tenderness of conscience and exact watchfulness in order thereto, using faith rather as contradistinguished from holiness than as productive of it.

"But what I most of all dislike is your littleness of love to your brethren, to your own society; your want of union of heart with them, and bowels of mercies toward them; your want of meekness, gentleness, longsuffering; your impatience of contradiction; your counting every man your enemy that reproves or admonishes you in love; your bigotry, and narrowness of spirit, loving in a manner only those that love you; your censoriousness, proneness to think hardly of all who do not exactly agree with you; in one word, your divisive spirit. Indeed I do not believe that any of you either design or desire a separation; but you do not enough fear, abhor, and detest it, shuddering at the very thought: And all the preceding tempers tend to it and gradually prepare you for it. Observe, I tell you before. God grant you may immediately and affectionately take the warning!

"3. As to your outward behaviour, I like the general tenor of your life devoted to God and spent in doing good.

"But I dislike your slighting any, the very least Rules of the Bands of [our] society; and your doing anything that tends to hinder others from exactly observing them. Therefore, I dislike your appointing such meetings as hinder others from attending either the public preaching or their class or band; or any other meeting which the Rules of the society or their office requires them to attend.

"I dislike your spending so much time in several meetings, as many that attend can ill spare from the other duties of their calling unless they omit either the preaching or their class or band. This naturally tends to dissolve our society, by cutting the sinews of it.

"As to your more public meetings, I like the praying fervently and

The Wesley Centenary statue at Ciry Road, London

largely for all the blessings of God; and I know much good has been done hereby and hope much more will be done.

"But I dislike several things therein: 1. The singing, or speaking, or praying of several at once. 2. The praying to the Son of God only, or more than to the Father. 3. The using improper expressions in prayer; sometimes too bold, if not irreverent; sometimes too pompous and magnificent, extolling yourselves rather than God, and telling Him what you are, not what you want. 4. Using poor, flat, bald hymns. 5. The never kneeling in prayer. 6. Your using postures or gestures highly indecent. 7. Your screaming, even so as to make the words unintelligible. 8. Your affirming people will be justified or sanctified just now. 9. The affirming they are when they are not. 10. The bidding them say, 'I believe.' 11. The bitterly condemning any that oppose, calling them wolves, etc.; and pronouncing them hypocrites or not justified.

"Read this calmly and impartially before the Lord in prayer: So shall the evil cease and the good remain; and you will then be more than ever united to

"Your affectionate brother,
John Wesley."

THE SCRIPTURE WAY OF SALVATION

Ye are saved through faith (Eph. ii. 8).

1. Nothing can be more intricate, complex, and hard to be understood than religion as it has been often described. And this is not only true concerning the religion of the heathens, even many of the wisest of them, but concerning the religion of those also who were, in some sense, Christians; yea, and men of great name in the Christian world; men who seemed to be pillars thereof. Yet how easy to be understood, how plain and simple a thing is the genuine religion of Jesus Christ; provided only that we take it in its native form, just as it is described in the oracles of God! It is exactly suited by the wise Creator and Governor of the world to the weak understanding and narrow capacity of man in his present state. How observable is this, both with regard to the end it proposes, and the means to attain that end! The end is, in one word, salvation; the means to attain it, faith.

2. It is easily discerned that these two little words: I mean faith and salvation, include the substance of all the Bible, the marrow, as it

were, of the whole Scripture. So much the more should we take all possible care to avoid all mistake concerning them, and to form a true and accurate judgment concerning both the one and the other.

3. Let us then seriously inquire:
   I. What is salvation?
   II. What is that faith whereby we are saved? And,
   III. How are we saved by it?

I.

1. And, first, let us inquire: What is salvation? The salvation which is here spoken of is not what is frequently understood by that word—the going to heaven, eternal happiness. It is not the soul's going to paradise, termed by our Lord, "Abraham's bosom." It is not a blessing which lies on the other side of death; or, as we usually speak, in the other world. The very words of the text itself put this beyond all question: *"ye are saved."* It is not something at a distance; it is a present thing; a blessing which, through the free mercy of God, ye are now in possession of. Nay, the words may be rendered, and that with equal propriety, "Ye have been saved." So that the salvation which is here spoken of might be extended to the entire work of God from the first dawning of grace in the soul till it is consummated in glory.

2. If we take this in its utmost extent, it will include all that is wrought in the soul by what is frequently termed natural conscience, but more properly, preventing [prevenient] grace—all the drawings of the Father; the desires after God which, if we yield to them, increase more and more—all that light wherewith the Son of God "enlighteneth every one that cometh into the world"; showing every man "to do justly, to love mercy, and to walk humbly with his God"—all the convictions which His Spirit from time to time works in every child of man; although it is true the generality of men stifle them as soon as possible, and after awhile forget, or at least deny that they ever had them at all.

3. But we are at present concerned only with that salvation which the apostle is directly speaking of. And this consists of two general parts, justification and sanctification.

Justification is another word for pardon. It is the forgiveness of all our sins; and, what is necessarily implied therein, our acceptance with God. The price whereby this hath been procured for us (commonly termed the meritorious cause of our justification) is the blood and righteousness of Christ or, to express it a little more clearly, all that

Christ had done and suffered for us, till He "poured out his soul for the transgressors." The immediate effects of justification are the peace of God, a "peace that passeth all understanding," and a "rejoicing in hope of the glory of God," "with joy unspeakable and full of glory."

4. And at the same time that we are justified, yea, in that very moment, sanctification begins. In that instant we are born again, born from above, born of the Spirit, there is a *real* as well as a *relative* change. We are inwardly renewed by the power of God. We feel "the love of God shed abroad in our heart by the Holy Ghost, which is given unto us," producing love to all mankind, and more especially to the children of God; expelling the love of the world, the love of pleasure, of ease, of honour, of money; together with pride, anger, self-will, and every other evil temper; in a word changing the earthly, sensual, devilish mind, into "the mind which was in Christ Jesus."

5. How naturally do those who experience such a change imagine that all sin is gone; that it is utterly rooted out of their heart and has no more any place therein! How easily do they draw that inference! "I *feel* no sin, therefore, I *have* none; it does not *stir*, therefore, it does not *exist*; it has no *motion*, therefore it has no *being*."

6. But it is seldom long before they are undeceived, finding sin was only suspended, not destroyed. Temptations return and sin revives; showing it was but stunned before, not dead. They now feel two principles in themselves, plainly contrary to each other, "the flesh lusting against the spirit"; nature opposing the grace of God. They cannot deny that, although they still feel power to believe in Christ and love God; and although His "Spirit (still) witnesses with their spirits that they are children of God," yet they feel in themselves sometimes pride or self-will, sometimes anger or unbelief. They find one or more of these frequently *stirring* in their hearts, though not *conquering*; yea, perhaps "thrusting sore at them that they may fall," but the Lord is their help.

CARNALITY

7. How exactly did Macarius, 1,400 years ago describe the present experience of the children of God! "The unskilful (or inexperienced), when grace operates, presently imagine they have no more sin. Whereas they that have discretion cannot deny that even we who have the grace of God may be molested again. For we have often had instances of some among the brethren who have experienced such grace as to affirm that they had no sin in them; and yet, after all, when they thought themselves entirely freed from it, the corruption that lurked within was stirred up anew and they were well nigh burned up."

8. From the time of our being born again, the gradual work of sanctification takes place. We are enabled, "by the spirit, to mortify the deeds of the body," or our evil nature; and as we are more and more dead to sin, we are more and more alive to God. We go on from grace to grace while we are careful to "abstain from all appearance of evil," and are "zealous of good works," as we have opportunity of doing good to all men; while we walk in all His ordinances blameless, therein worshiping Him in spirit and in truth; while we take up our cross and deny ourselves every pleasure that does not lead us to God.

GROWTH

9. It is thus that we wait for entire sanctification; for a full salvation from all our sins—from pride, self-will, anger, unbelief; or, as the apostle expresses it, "go on to perfection." But what is perfection? The word has various senses; here it means perfect love. It is love excluding sin; love filling the heart, taking up the whole capacity of the soul. It is love "rejoicing evermore, praying without ceasing, in everything giving thanks."

PERFECT LOVE

II.

But what is that faith through which we are saved? This is the second point to be considered.

1. Faith, in general, is defined by the apostle. . . . *An evidence,* a divine *evidence and conviction* (the word means both) *of things not seen;* not visible, not perceptible either by sight or by any other of the external senses. It implies both a supernatural *evidence* of God, and of the things of God, a kind of spiritual light exhibited to the soul, and a supernatural *sight* or perception thereof. Accordingly the Scripture speaks of God's giving sometimes light, sometimes a power of discerning it. So St. Paul, "God, who commanded light to shine out of darkness, hath shined in our hearts to give us the light of the knowledge of the glory of God in the face of Jesus Christ." And elsewhere the same Apostle speaks of "the eyes of" our "understanding being opened." By this twofold operation of the Holy Spirit, having the eyes of our soul both *opened* and *enlightened,* we see the things which the natural "eye hath not seen, neither the ear heard."

We have a prospect of the invisible things of God; we see the *spiritual world* which is all around about us, and yet no more discerned by our natural faculties than if it had no being; and we see the *eternal world* piercing through the veil which hangs between time and eternity. Clouds and darkness then rest upon it no more, but we already see the glory which shall be revealed.

2. Taking the word in a more particular sense, faith is a divine evidence and conviction, not only that "God was in Christ, reconciling the world unto himself," but also that Christ loved me, and gave himself for me. It is by this faith (whether we term it the essence, or rather a property thereof) that we receive Christ; that we receive Him in all His offices, as our Prophet, Priest, and King. It is by this that He is "made of God unto us wisdom and righteousness, and sanctification, and redemption."

3. "But is this the *faith of assurance* or *faith of adherence?*" The Scripture mentions no such distinction. The apostle says, "There is one faith, and one hope of our calling"; one Christian, saving faith; "as there is one Lord" in whom we believe, and "one God and Father of us all." And it is certain this necessarily implies an *assurance* (which is here only another word for *evidence,* it being hard to tell the difference between them) that Christ loved me, and gave himself for me. For "he that believeth," with the true living faith, "hath the witness in himself"; "The Spirit witnesses with his spirit, that he is a child of God." Because he is a son, God hath sent forth the Spirit of His Son into his heart, crying, "Abba, Father"; giving him assurance that he is so, and a childlike confidence in Him. But let it be observed that, in the very nature of the thing, the assurance goes before the confidence. For a man cannot have a childlike confidence in God till he knows he is a child of God. Therefore confidence, trust, reliance, adherence, or whatever else it may be called, is not the first, as some have supposed, but the second branch or act of faith.

4. It is by this faith we are saved, justified, and sanctified; taking that word in its highest sense. But how are we justified and sanctified by faith? This is our third head of inquiry. And this being the main point in question, and a point of no ordinary importance, it will not be improper to give it a more distinct and particular consideration.

III.

1. And, first, How are we justified by faith? In what sense is this to be understood? I answer, faith is the *condition* and the *only condition* of justification. It is the *condition:* none is justified but he that believes; without faith no man is justified. And it is the *only condition:* this alone is sufficient for justification. Everyone that believes is justi-

fied, whatever else he has or has not. In other words, no man is justified till he believes; every man when he believes is justified.

2. "But does not God command us to repent also? Yea, and to 'bring forth fruits meet for repentance'? To cease, for instance, from doing evil, and learn to do well? And is not both the one and the other of the utmost necessity, insomuch that if we willingly neglect either, we cannot reasonably expect to be justified at all? But if this be so, how can it be said that faith is the only condition of justification?"

God does undoubtedly command us both to repent and to bring forth fruits meet for repentance; which if we willingly neglect we cannot reasonably expect to be justified at all; therefore both repentance and fruits meet for repentance are in some sense necessary to justification. But they are not necessary in the *same sense* with faith, nor in the *same degree*. Not in the same degree; for those fruits are necessary *conditionally;* if there be time and opportunity for them. Otherwise a man may be justified without them, as was the *thief* upon the cross . . . but he cannot be justified without faith; this is impossible. Likewise, let a man have ever so much repentance, or ever so many of the fruits meet for repentance, yet all this does not at all avail; he is not justified till he believes. But the moment he believes with or without those fruits, yea, with more or less repentance, he is justified; not in the *same sense;* for repentance and its fruits are only *remotely* necessary—necessary in order to faith; whereas faith is *immediately* and *directly* necessary to justification. It remains that faith is the only condition which is *immediately* and *proximately* necessary to justification.

3. "But do you believe we are sanctified by faith? We know you believe that we are justified by faith; but do not you believe, and accordingly teach, that we are sanctified by our works?" So it

FAITH

has been roundly and vehemently affirmed for these five and twenty years; but I have constantly declared just the contrary; and that in all manner of ways. I have continually testified in private and in public that we are sanctified as well as justified by faith. And indeed the one of those great truths does exceedingly illustrate the other. Exactly as we are justified by faith, so we are sanctified by faith. Faith is the condition, and the only condition of sanctification exactly as it is of justification. It is the *condition;* none is sanctified but he that believes; without faith no man is sanctified. And it is the *only condition;* this alone is sufficient for sanctification. Everyone that believes is sanctified, whatever else he has or has not. In other words, no man is sanctified till he believes; every man when he believes is sanctified.

4. "But is there not a repentance consequent upon as well as a repentance previous to justification? And is it not incumbent on all that are justified to be 'zealous of good works'? Yea, are not these so necessary that if a man willingly neglect them he cannot reasonably expect that he shall ever be sanctified in the full sense; that is, perfected in love? Nay, can he grow at all in grace, in the loving knowledge of our Lord Jesus Christ? Yea, can he retain the grace which God has already given him? Can he continue in the faith which he has received, or in the favour of God? Do you not yourself allow all this and continually assert it? But, if this be so, how can it be said that faith is the only condition of sanctification?"

5. I do allow all this and continually maintain it as the truth of God. I allow there is a repentance consequent upon as well as a repentance previous to justification. It is incumbent on all that are justified to be zealous of good works. And these are so necessary that if a man willingly neglect them he cannot reasonably expect that he shall ever be sanctified; he cannot grow in grace, in the image of God, the mind which was in Christ Jesus; nay, he cannot retain the grace he has received, he cannot continue in faith or in the favour of God.

What is the inference we must draw herefrom? Why, that both repentance, rightly understood, and the practice of all good works, works of piety as well as works of mercy (now properly so called, since they spring from faith), are in some sense necessary to sanctification.

6. I say repentance rightly understood; for this must not be confounded with the former repentance. The repentance consequent upon justification is widely different from that which is antecedent to it. This implies no guilt, no sense of condemnation, no consciousness of the wrath of God. It does not suppose any doubt of the favour of God, or any "fear that hath torment." It is properly a conviction, wrought by the Holy Ghost, of the *sin* which still remains in our heart; of the *phronama sarkas, the carnal mind,* which "does still *remain* (as our church speaks) even in them that are regenerate"; although it does no longer *reign,* it has not now dominion over them. It is a conviction of our proneness to evil, of a heart bent to backsliding, of the still continuing tendency of the flesh to lust against the Spirit. Sometimes, unless we continually watch and pray, it lusteth to pride, sometimes to anger, sometimes to love of the world, love of honour, or love of pleasure more than of God. It is a conviction of the tendency of our

heart to self-will, to atheism or idolatry, and, above all, to unbelief, whereby, in a thousand ways and under a thousand pretenses, we are ever departing more or less from the living God.

7. With this conviction of the sin remaining in our hearts, there is joined a clear conviction of the sin remaining in our lives; still *cleaving* to all our words and actions. In the best of these we now discern a mixture of evil, either in the spirit, the matter, or the manner of them, something that could not endure the righteous judgment of God, were He extreme to mark what is done amiss. Where we least suspect it, we find a taint of pride or self-will, of unbelief or idolatry; so that we are now more ashamed of our best duties than formerly of our worst sins; and hence we can but feel that these are so far from having anything meritorious in them, yea, so far from being able to stand in sight of the divine justice, that for those also we should be guilty before God, were it not for the blood of the covenant.

8. Experience shows that, together with the conviction of sin *remaining* in our hearts and *cleaving* to all our words and actions, as well as the guilt which on account thereof we should incur, were we not continually sprinkled with the atoning blood, one thing more is implied in this repentance, viz: a conviction of our helplessness, of our utter inability to think one good thought, or to form one good desire; and much more to speak one word aright, or to perform one good action, but through His free, almighty grace, first preventing us and then accompanying us every moment.

ATONEMENT

9. "But what good works are those, the practice of which you affirm to be necessary to sanctification?" First, all works of piety, such as public prayer, family prayer, and praying in our closets, receiving the supper of the Lord, searching the Scriptures, by hearing, reading, meditating, and using such measures of fasting or abstinence as our bodily health allows.

10. Secondly, all works of mercy, whether they relate to the bodies or souls of men, such as feeding the hungry, clothing the naked, entertaining the stranger, visiting those that are in prison, or sick, or variously afflicted; such as the endeavouring to instruct the ignorant, to awaken the stupid sinner, to quicken the lukewarm, to confirm the wavering, to comfort the feeble-minded, to succour the tempted, or contribute in any manner to the saving of souls from death. This is the repentance, and these the "fruits meet for repentance," which are necessary to full sanctification. This is the way wherein God hath appointed His children to wait for complete salvation.

11. Hence may appear the extreme mischievousness of that seemingly innocent opinion: that there is no sin in a believer; that all sin is destroyed, root and branch, the moment a man is justified. By totally preventing that repentance, it quite blocks up the way to sanctification; there is no place for repentance in him who believes there is no sin in his life or heart; consequently, there is no place for his being perfected in love, to which that repentance is indispensably necessary.

12. Hence, it may likewise appear that there is no possible danger in *thus* expecting full salvation. For suppose we were mistaken; suppose no such blessing ever was, or can be attained; yet we lose nothing; nay, that every expectation quickens us in using all the talents which God has given us; yea, in improving them all, so that when our Lord cometh, He will receive His own with increase.

13. But to return. Though it be allowed that both this repentance and its fruits are necessary to full salvation, yet they are not necessary either in the same sense with faith, or in the same degree; not in the *same degree*—for these fruits are necessary *conditionally*, if there be time and opportunity for them; otherwise, a man may be sanctified without them. But he cannot be sanctified without faith. Likewise, let a man have ever so much of this repentance, or ever so many good works, yet all this does not avail; he is not sanctified until he believes; but the moment he believes, with, or without those fruits, yea, with more or less of this repentance, he is sanctified. Not in the *same sense*—for this repentance and these fruits are only *remotely* necessary—necessary in order to the continuance of his faith, as well as the increase of it; whereas faith is *immediately* and *directly* necessary to sanctification. It remains, that faith is the only condition which is *immediately* and *proximately* necessary to sanctification.

14. "But what is that faith whereby we are sanctified, saved from sin, and perfected in love?" It is a divine evidence and conviction, first, **SCRIPTURAL** that God hath promised it in the Holy Scripture. Till we are thoroughly satisfied of this, there is no moving one step farther. And one would imagine there needed not one word more to satisfy a reasonable man of this than the ancient promise, "Then will I circumcise thy heart and the heart of thy seed, to love the Lord thy God with all thy heart, and with all thy soul, and with all thy mind." How clearly does this express the being perfected in love! How strongly imply the being saved from all sin! For as long as love takes up the whole heart, what room is there for sin therein?

15. It is a divine evidence and conviction, secondly, that what

God hath promised He is able to perform. Admitting, therefore, that "with men it is impossible" to "bring a clean thing out of an unclean," to purify the heart from all sin, and to fill it with all holiness; yet this creates no difficulty in the case, seeing "with God all things are possible." And surely no one ever imagined it was possible to any power less than that of the Almighty! But if God speaks, it shall be done. God saith, "Let there be light; and there" is "light"!

16. It is, thirdly, a divine evidence and conviction that He is able and willing to do it now. And why not? Is not a moment to Him the same as a thousand years? He cannot want more time to accomplish whatever is His will. And He cannot want or stay for any more *worthiness* or *fitness* in the persons He is pleased to honour. We may therefore boldly say, at any one point of time, "Now is the day of salvation!" "Today, if ye will hear his voice, harden not your hearts." "Behold, all things are now ready, come unto the marriage!"

17. To this confidence, that God is both able and willing to sanctify us now, there needs to be added one thing more—a divine evidence and conviction that He doeth it. In that hour it is done; God says to the inmost soul, "According to thy faith be it unto thee!" Then the soul is pure from every spot of sin; it is clean "from all unrighteousness." The believer then experiences the deep meaning of these solemn words, "If we walk in the light as he is in the light, we have fellowship one with another, and the blood of Jesus Christ his Son cleanseth us from all sin."

ASSURANCE

18. "But does God work this great work in the soul gradually or instantaneously?" Perhaps it may be gradually wrought in some; I mean in this sense: they do not advert to the particular moment wherein sin ceases to be. But it is infinitely desirable, were it the will of God, that it should be done instantaneously; that the Lord should destroy sin "by the breath of his mouth," in a moment, in the twinkling of an eye. And so He generally does; a plain fact, of which there is evidence enough to satisfy any unprejudiced person. *Thou*, therefore, look for it every moment! Look for it in the way above described; in all those *good works* whereunto thou art "created anew in Christ Jesus." There is then no danger; you can be no worse, if you are no better, for that expectation. For were you to be disappointed of your hope, still you lose nothing. But you shall not be disappointed of your hope; it will come and will not tarry. Look for it, then, every day, every hour, every moment! Why not this hour, this moment? Certainly you may look for it *now*, if you believe it is by faith. And by this token, you

may surely know whether you seek it by faith or by works. If by works, you want something to be done *first, before* you are sanctified. You think I must *be* or *do* thus or thus. Then you are seeking it by works unto this day. If you are seeking it by faith, you may expect it *as you are;* and if as you are, then expect it *now.* It is of importance to observe that there is an inseparable connection between these three points, expect it *by faith,* expect it *as you are,* expect it *now!* To deny one of them is to deny them all. Do *you* believe we are sanctified by faith? Be true, then, to your principle; and look for the blessing just as you are, neither better nor worse; as a poor sinner that has still nothing to pay, nothing to plead, but Christ *died.* And if you look for it as you are, then expect it *now.* Stay for nothing; why should you? Christ is ready; and He is all you want. He is waiting for you; He is at the door! Let your inmost soul cry out:

FAITH

> *Come in, come in, thou heavenly Guest!*
> *Nor hence again remove;*
> *But sup with me, and let the feast*
> *Be everlasting love.*

The Repentance of Believers
1767 (Abridged)

This sermon logically and experientially follows "Sin in Believers." We place it here out of sequence because of chronology. It was prepared in Ireland in April 1767 and published in London the following year.

The sermon is constructed in three parts. Part two could well stand alone as a remarkably plain and concise statement of entire sanctification by faith in the blood of Jesus Christ the Son of God. Part three persuasively explains the conditions prerequisite to complete heart cleansing.

No Wesley sermon searches the Christian soul more deeply. It is a humbling but healing word that can hardly be read without sincere heart searching.

THE REPENTANCE OF BELIEVERS

Repent ye, and believe the Gospel (Mark i. 15).

1. It is generally supposed that repentance and faith are only the gate of religion; that they are necessary only at the beginning of our Christian course, when we are setting out in the way to the kingdom....

2. This is undoubtedly true, that there is a repentance and a faith, which are more especially necessary at the beginning: a repentance which is a conviction of our utter sinfulness, and guiltiness, and helplessness; and which precedes our receiving that kingdom of God which our Lord observes is "within us"; and a faith whereby we receive that kingdom, even "righteousness, and peace, and joy in the Holy Ghost."

3. But ... there is also a repentance and a faith ... which are requisite after we have "believed the gospel"; yea, and in every subsequent stage of our Christian course, or we cannot "run the race which is set before us." And this repentance and faith are full as necessary in order to our *continuance* and *growth* in grace as the former faith and repentance were in order to our *entering* into the kingdom of God.

But in what sense are we to repent and believe, after we are justified? This is an important question, and worthy of being considered with the utmost attention.

I.

And first, in what sense are we to repent?

1. Repentance frequently means an inward change, a change of mind from sin to holiness. But we now speak of it in a quite different sense, as it is one kind of self-knowledge, the knowing ourselves sinners, yea, guilty, helpless sinners, even though we know we are children of God.

2. ... When we first find redemption in the blood of Jesus ... it is natural to suppose that we are no longer sinners, that all our sins are not only covered but destroyed. As we do not then feel any evil in our hearts, we readily imagine none is there. Nay, some well-meaning men have imagined this not only at that time but ever after; having persuaded themselves that when they were justified they were entirely sanctified.... These sincerely believe, and earnestly maintain, that all

sin is destroyed when we are justified; and that there is no sin in the heart of a believer; but that it is altogether clean from that moment. But though we readily acknowledge, "He that believeth is born of God," and "he that is born of God doth not commit sin"; yet we cannot allow that he does not *feel* it within; it does not *reign,* but it does remain. And a conviction of the sin which *remains* in our heart, is one great branch of the repentance we are now speaking of.

3. For it is seldom long before he who imagined all sin was gone, feels there is still *pride* in his heart. He is convinced both that in many respects he has thought of himself more highly than he ought to think, and that he has taken to himself the praise of something he had received, and gloried in it as though he had not received it; and yet he knows he is in the favour of God. He cannot, and ought not, "to cast away his confidence." "The Spirit" still "witnesses with" his "spirit, that he is a child of God."

4. Nor is it long before he feels *self-will* in his heart; even a will contrary to the will of God. A will every man must inevitably have as long as he has an understanding. This is an essential part of human nature, indeed of the nature of every intelligent being. Our blessed Lord himself had a will as a man; otherwise He had not been a man. But His human will was invariably subject to the will of His Father. At all times, and on all occasions, even in the deepest affliction, He could say, "Not as I will, but as thou wilt." But this is not the case at all times, even with a true believer in Christ. He frequently finds his will more or less exalting itself against the will of God. He wills something because it is pleasing to nature, which is not pleasing to God; and he is averse from something because it is painful to nature, which is the will of God concerning him. . . .

5. Now self-will, as well as pride, is a species of *idolatry;* and both are directly contrary to the love of God. The same observation may be made concerning the *"love of the world."* But this likewise even true believers are liable to feel in themselves; and every one of them does feel it, more or less, sooner or later, in one branch or another. . . . In process of time he will feel again, though perhaps only for a few moments, either "the desire of the flesh," or "the desire of the eye," or "the pride of life." If he does not continually watch and pray, he may find *lust* reviving. . . . He may feel the assaults of *inordinate affection;* a strong propensity to "love the creature more than the Creator"; whether it be a child, a parent, a husband or wife, or "the friend that is as his own soul." . . .

6. If he does not keep himself every moment, he will again feel *the desire of the eye;* the desire of gratifying his imagination with something great, or beautiful, or uncommon. . . . How hard is it, even for those who know in whom they have believed, to conquer but one branch of the desire of the eye, curiosity; constantly to trample it under their feet; to desire nothing, merely because it is new!

7. And how hard is it even for the children of God wholly to conquer the *pride of life!* St. John seems to mean by this nearly the same with what the world terms the sense of honour. This is no other than a desire of, and delight in, "the honour that cometh of men"; a desire and love of praise; and, which is always joined with it, a proportionable *fear of dispraise.* Nearly allied to this is *evil shame;* the being ashamed of that wherein we ought to glory. And this is seldom divided from the *fear of man,* which brings a thousand snares upon the soul. . . .

8. And do we not feel other tempers which are as contrary to the love of our neighbour as these are to the love of God? The love of our neighbour "thinketh no evil." Do not we find any thing of the kind? Do we never find any *jealousies,* any *evil surmisings,* any groundless or unreasonable suspicions? He that is clear in these respects, let him cast the first stone at his neighbour. Who does not sometimes feel other tempers or inward motions, which he knows are contrary to brotherly love? If nothing of *malice, hatred,* or *bitterness,* is there no touch of *envy?* Particularly toward those who enjoy some real or supposed good which we desire but cannot attain? Do we never find any degree of *resentment,* when we are injured or affronted; especially by those whom we peculiarly loved, and whom we had most laboured to help or oblige? Does injustice or ingratitude never excite in us any desire of *revenge?* Any desire of returning evil for evil, instead of "overcoming evil with good"? . . .

CARNALITY

9. *Covetousness,* in every kind and degree, is certainly as contrary to this as to the love of God; whether the *love of money,* which is too frequently "the root of all evil"; or a desire of *having more,* or increasing in substance. And how few, even of the real children of God, are entirely free from both! . . .

10. It is their experiencing this, which has inclined so many serious persons to understand the latter part of the seventh chapter to the Romans, not of them that are "under the law," that are convinced of sin, which is undoubtedly the meaning of the apostle, but of them that are "under grace"; that are "justified freely through the redemption

that is in Christ." And it is most certain, they are thus far right: there does still *remain,* even in them that are justified, a *mind* which is in some measure *carnal.* . . . A *heart bent to backsliding,* still ever ready to "depart from the living God"; in propensity to pride, self-will, anger, revenge, love of the world, yea, and all evil; a root of bitterness, which, if the restraint were taken off for a moment, would instantly spring up; yea, such a depth of corruption, as, without clear light from God, we cannot possibly conceive. And a conviction of all this sin *remaining in their hearts,* is the repentance which belongs to them that are justified.

11. But we should likewise be convinced, that as sin remains in our hearts, so it *cleaves* to all our words and actions. Indeed it is to be feared, that many of our words are more than mixed with sin; that they are sinful altogether; for such undoubtedly is all *uncharitable conversation;* all of which does not spring from brotherly love; all of which does not agree with that golden rule, "What ye would that others should do to you, even so do unto them." Of this kind is all backbiting, all tale-bearing, all whispering, all evil speaking, that is, repeating the faults of absent persons; for none would have others repeat his faults when he is absent. Now how few are there, even among believers, who are in no degree guilty of this; who steadily observe the good old rule, "Of the dead and the absent—nothing but good!" And suppose they do, do they likewise abstain from *unprofitable conversation?* Yet all this is unquestionably sinful, and "grieves the Holy Spirit of God": yea, and "for every idle word that men shall speak, they shall give an account in the day of judgment."

12. But let it be supposed that they continually "watch and pray," and so do "not enter into this temptation"; that they constantly set a watch before their mouth and keep the door of their lips; suppose they exercise themselves herein, that *all* their "conversation may be in grace, seasoned with salt, and meet to minister grace to the hearers"; yet do they not daily slide into useless discourse, notwithstanding all their caution? And even when they endeavour to speak for God, are their words pure, free from unholy mixtures? Do they find nothing wrong in their very *intention?* . . . When they are reproving sin, do they feel no anger or unkind temper to the sinner? When they are instructing the ignorant, do they not find any pride, any self-preference? When they are comforting the afflicted or provoking one another to love and to good works, do they never perceive any inward self-commendation; *"Now you have spoke well!"* Or any vanity, a desire that others should think so, and esteem them on the account?

In some or all of these respects, how much sin cleaves to the best *conversation* even of believers? The conviction of which is another branch of the repentance which belongs to them that are justified.

13. And how much sin, if their conscience is thoroughly awake, may they find cleaving to *their actions* also? Nay, are there not many of these, which, though they are such as the world would not condemn, yet cannot be commended, no, nor excused, if we judge by the word of God? Are there not many of their actions which they themselves know are not to the glory of God? Many, wherein they did not even aim at this; which were undertaken with an eye to God? And of those that were, are there not many wherein their eye is not singly fixed on God? Wherein they are doing their own will, at least as much as His; and seeking to please themselves as much, if not more, than to please God! And while they are endeavouring to do good to their neighbour, do they not feel wrong tempers of various kinds? . . . So that they are now more ashamed of their best duties than they were once of their worst sins.

14. Again: How many *sins of omission* are they chargeable with? We know the words of the apostle, "To him that knoweth to do good, and doeth it not, to him it is sin." But do they not know a thousand instances wherein they might have done good, to enemies, to strangers, to their brethren, either with regard to their bodies or their souls and they did it not? How many omissions have they been guilty of in their duty toward God! . . .

15. But, besides these outward omissions, may they not find in themselves *inward defects* without number? Defects of every kind: they have not the love, the fear, the confidence, they ought to have toward God. They have not the love which is due to their neighbour, to every child of man; no, nor even that which is due to their brethren, to every child of God, whether those that are at a distance from them or those with whom they are immediately connected. They have no holy temper in the degree they ought; they are defective in everything. . . .

16. A conviction of their *guiltiness* is another branch of that repentance which belongs to the children of God. But this is cautiously to be understood and in a peculiar sense. For it is certain, "there is no condemnation to them that are in Christ Jesus," that believe in Him, and, on the power of that faith, "walk not after the flesh, but after the Spirit." Yet can they no more bear the strict justice of God now than before they believed. This pronounces them to be

still *worthy of death* on all the preceding accounts. And it would absolutely condemn them thereto, were it not for the atoning blood. . . .

17. A conviction of their *utter helplessness* is yet another branch of this repentance. I mean hereby two things: First, that they are no more able now of *themselves* to think one good thought, to form one good desire, to speak one good word, or do one good work, than before they were justified; that they have still no kind or degree of strength of their own; no power either to do good or resist evil; no ability to conquer or even withstand the world, the devil, or their own evil nature. They can, it is certain, do all these things; but it is not by their own strength. . . .

18. By this helplessness I mean, secondly, an absolute inability to deliver ourselves from that guiltiness or desert of punishment whereof we are still conscious; and an inability to remove, by all the grace we have, . . . either the pride, self-will, love of the world, anger, and general proneness to depart from God, which we experimentally know to *remain* in the heart, even of them that are regenerate; or the evil which, in spite of all our endeavours, cleaves to all our words and actions. . . .

19. If any man is not satisfied of this, if any believes that whoever is justified is able to remove these sins out of his heart and life, let him make the experiment. Let him try whether, by the grace he has already received, he can expel pride, self-will, or inbred sin in general.

GRACE

Let him try, whether he can cleanse his words and actions from all mixture of evil; whether he can avoid all uncharitable and unprofitable conversation, with all the sins of omission; and, lastly, whether he can supply the numberless defects which he still finds in himself. Let him not be discouraged by one or two experiments, but repeat the trial again and again; and the longer he tries the more deeply will he be convinced of his utter helplessness in all these respects.

20. Indeed this is so evident a truth, that well nigh all the children of God scattered abroad, however they differ in other points, yet generally agree in this; that although we may, "by the Spirit, mortify the deeds of the body"; resist and conquer both outward and inward sin; although we may *weaken* our enemies day by day; yet we cannot *drive them out*. By all the grace which is given at justification we cannot extirpate them. Though we watch and pray ever so much, we cannot wholly cleanse either our hearts or hands. Most sure we cannot till it shall please our Lord to speak to our hearts

SECOND BLESSING

again, to speak the second time, Be clean: and then

only the leprosy is cleansed. Then only the evil root, the carnal mind is destroyed; and inbred sin subsists no more. But if there be no such second change, if there be no instantaneous deliverance after justification, if there be *none but* a gradual work of God . . . then we must be content, as well as we can, to remain full of sin till death; and, if so, we must remain guilty till death, continually *deserving* punishment. For it is impossible the guilt, or desert of punishment, should be removed from us, as long as all this sin remains in our heart and cleaves to our words and actions. Nay, in rigorous justice, all we think, and speak, and act continually increases it.

II.

1. In this sense we are to *repent,* after we are justified. And till we do so we can go no farther. For, till we are sensible of our disease, it admits of no cure. But, supposing we do thus repent, then are we called to "believe the gospel."

2. And this also is to be understood in a peculiar sense, different from that wherein we believed in order to justification. Believe the glad tidings of great salvation, which God hath prepared for all people. Believe that he who is "the brightness of his Father's glory, the express image of his person," is "able to save unto the uttermost all that come unto God through him." He is able to save you from all the sin that still remains in your heart. He is able to save you from all the sin that cleaves to all your words and actions. He is able to save you from sins of omission, and to supply whatever is wanting in you. It is true, this is impossible with man; but with God-man all things are possible. . . . But this He has done: He has promised it over and over in the strongest terms. He has given us these "exceeding great and precious promises," both in the Old and New Testament. So we read in the law, in the most ancient part of the oracles of God, "The Lord thy God will circumcise thy heart . . . to love the Lord thy God with all thy heart, and with all thy soul" (Deut. xxx. 6). So in the Psalms, "He shall redeem Israel (the Israel of God) from all his sins." So in the prophet: "Then will I sprinkle clean water upon you and ye shall be clean: from all your filthiness and from all your idols will I cleanse you. And I will put my Spirit within you, and ye shall keep my judgments and do them. I will also save you from all your uncleannesses" (Ezek. xxxvi. 25, etc.). So likewise in the New Testament: "Blessed be the Lord God of Israel, for he hath visited and redeemed his people, and hath raised up a horn of salvation for us—to perform the oath which he sware to

our father Abraham, that he would grant unto us, that we, being delivered out of the hands of our enemies, should serve him without fear, in holiness and righteousness before him, all the days of our life" (Luke i. 68).

3. You have therefore good reason to believe He is not only able but *willing* to do this; to cleanse you from all your filthiness of flesh and spirit; to "save you from all your uncleannesses." This is the thing which you now long for; this is the faith which you now particularly need, namely, that the Great Physician, the Lover of my soul, is willing to make me clean. But is He willing to do this tomorrow or today? Let Him answer for himself. "To day, if ye will hear" my "voice, harden not your hearts." If you put it off till tomorrow, you harden your hearts; you refuse to hear His voice. Believe therefore that He is willing to save you *today*. He is willing to save you *now*. "Behold, now is the accepted time." He now saith, "Be thou clean!" Only believe; and you also will immediately find, "All things are possible to him that believeth."

CLEANSING

4. Continue to believe in Him that loved thee and gave himself for thee; that bore all thy sins in His own body on the tree; and He saveth thee from all condemnation, by His blood continually applied. Thus it is that we continue in a justified state. And when we go on "from faith to faith," when we have faith to be cleansed from indwelling sin, to be saved from all our uncleannesses, we are likewise saved from all that *guilt,* that *desert* of punishment, which we felt before. So that then we may say not only,

> *Every moment, Lord, I* want
> *The merit of Thy death!*

but, likewise, in the full assurance of faith,

> *Every moment, Lord, I* have
> *The merit of Thy death!*

For, by that faith in His life, death, and intercession for us, renewed from moment to moment, we are every whit clean, and there is not only now no condemnation for us, but no such desert of punishment as was before, the Lord cleansing both our hearts and lives.

5. By the same faith we feel the power of Christ every moment resting upon us, whereby alone we are what we are; whereby we are enabled to continue in spiritual life, and without which, notwithstanding all our present holiness, we should be devils the next mo-

ment. But as long as we retain our faith in Him, we "draw water out of the wells of salvation." Leaning on our beloved, even Christ in us the hope of glory, who dwelleth in our hearts by faith, who likewise is ever interceding for us at the right hand of God, we receive help from Him to think, and speak, and act what is acceptable in His sight. Thus does He "prevent" them that believe, in all their "doings, and further them with his continual help," so that all their designs, conversations, and actions are "begun, continued, and ended in him." Thus doth He "cleanse the thoughts of their hearts by the inspiration of his Holy Spirit, that they may perfectly love him and worthily magnify his holy name."

6. Thus it is, that in the children of God, repentance and faith exactly answer each other. By repentance we feel the sin remaining in our hearts and cleaving to our words and actions: by faith we receive the power of God in Christ, purifying our hearts and cleansing our hands. By repentance we are still sensible that we deserve punishment for all our tempers, and words, and actions: by faith we are conscious that our Advocate with the Father is continually pleading for us and thereby continually turning aside all condemnation and punishment from us. By repentance we have an abiding conviction that there is no help in us: by faith we receive not only mercy, "but grace to help in" *every* "time of need." Repentance disclaims the very possibility of any other help: faith accepts all the help we stand in need of, from Him that hath all power in heaven and earth. Repentance says, "Without him I can do nothing." Faith says, "I can do all things through Christ strengthening me." Through Him I can not only overcome, but expel all the enemies of my soul. Through Him I can "love the Lord my God with all my heart, mind, soul, and strength"; yea, and "walk in holiness and righteousness before him all the days of my life."

FAITH

III.

1. From what has been said, we may easily learn the mischievousness of that opinion, that we are *wholly* sanctified when we are justified; that our hearts are then cleansed from all sin. It is true, we are then delivered, as was observed before, from the dominion of outward sin; and, at the same time, the power of inward sin is so broken that we need no longer follow or be led by it: but it is by no means true that inward sin is then totally destroyed; that the root of pride, self-will, anger, love of the world, is then taken out of the heart; or that the carnal mind and the heart bent to backsliding are entirely

extirpated.... If, therefore, we think we are quite made whole already there is no room to seek any farther healing. On this supposition it is absurd to expect a farther deliverance from sin, whether gradual or instantaneous.

2. On the contrary, a deep conviction that we are not yet whole; that our hearts are not fully purified; that there is yet in us a "carnal mind," which is still in its nature "enmity against God"; that a whole body of sin remains in our heart, weakened indeed, but not destroyed; shows beyond all possibility of doubt the absolute necessity of a farther change. We allow that at the very moment of justification we are *born again:* in that instant we experience that inward change from "darkness into marvelous light"; from the image of the brute and the devil, into the image of God; from the earthly, sensual, devilish mind, to the mind which was in Christ Jesus.

But are we then *entirely* changed? Are we *wholly* transformed into the image of Him that created us? Far from it: we still retain a depth of sin: and it is the consciousness of this which constrains us to groan for a full deliverance to Him that is mighty to save. Hence it is, **HUNGER** that those believers who are not convinced of the deep corruption of their hearts, or but slightly, and as it were notionally convinced, have little concern about *entire sanctification*. They may possibly hold the opinion that such a thing is to be either at death or some time, they know not when, before it. But they have no great uneasiness for the want of it, and no great hunger or thirst after it. They cannot until they know themselves better, until they repent in the sense above described, until God unveils the inbred monster's face and shows them the real state of their souls. Then only when they feel the burden will they groan for deliverance from it. Then, and not until then, will they cry out in the agony of their soul:

> *Break off the yoke of inbred sin,*
> *And fully set my spirit free!*
> *I cannot rest, till pure within;*
> *Till I am wholly lost in Thee!*

3. We may learn from hence, secondly, that a deep conviction of our *demerit* after we are accepted ... is absolutely necessary in order to our seeing the true value of the atoning blood; in order to our feeling that we need this as much after we are justified as ever we did before. Without this conviction we cannot but account the blood of the covenant *as a common thing,* something of which we have not now

any great need, seeing all our past sins are blotted out. Yea, but if both our hearts and lives are thus unclean, there is a kind of guilt which we are contracting every moment and which, of consequence, would every moment expose us to fresh condemnation but that

> He ever lives above,
> For us to intercede,
> His all-atoning love,
> His precious blood to plead.

It is this repentance, and the faith intimately connected with it, which is expressed in those strong lines:

> I sin in every breath I draw,
> Nor do Thy will, nor keep Thy law,
> On earth, as angels do above:
> But still the fountain open stands,
> Washes my feet, my heart, my hands,
> Till I am perfected in love.

4. We may observe, thirdly, a deep conviction of our utter *helplessness*, of our total inability to retain anything we have received. We are not able to deliver ourselves from the world of iniquity remaining both in our hearts and lives. This teaches us truly to live upon Christ by faith, not only as our Priest, but as our King. Hereby we are brought to "magnify him," indeed; to "give him all the glory of his grace"; to make Him a whole Christ, an entire Saviour; and truly "to set the crown upon his head." . . . Then His almighty grace having abolished "every high thing which exalted itself against him," every temper, and thought, and word, and work, "is brought to the obedience of Christ."

GRACE

On Perfection
1788

This sermon represents Wesley's most matured thinking on entire sanctification. It was written in 1788 when Wesley was nearing the end of his long life.

Forty-seven years earlier he had preached another sermon on the same subject under the title "Christian Perfection," but using a different scripture, namely Phil. 3:12. The sermons are quite similar but the later one has a greater pungency. Perhaps the more forceful language of Heb. 6:1 explains this distinction. At any rate, this sermon presents the ripened convictions of the aged preacher. It reflects the experience of half a century of preaching, counseling, and pondering this area of doctrine, experience, and testimony.

The earlier sermon remains the standard sermon on the subject for Methodists, but the present editor has opted for the later sermon on the ground of its being Wesley's most developed presentation of the subject.

Here, then, is the mature Wesley, preacher of Christian perfection, laying his message clearly and unequivocally before all men; and willingly examining in love the objections to that message.

Charles Wesley's hymn, "The Promise of the Spirit," appended to the earlier sermon in the 1742 republication, is retained in this version of the 1788 sermon.

Editor's Outline

I. Distinctions that must be made
   A. This perfection must be distinguished from
      1. Angelic
      2. Adamic
      3. Intellectual perfection
   B. This perfection must be distinguished from
      1. Perfection of emotion
      2. Perfection of performance

II. Descriptions and definitions
   A. It is perfection in holy love
   B. It is perfection of intention
   C. It is perfection of the harvest of the indwelling Spirit
   D. It is perfection of holiness of heart
   E. It is blamelessness of moral character
   F. It is entire devotement to God
   G. It is life as spiritual worship
   H. It is full salvation from inward and outward sin

III. Objections and replies
   A. "It is not scriptural"
   B. "It is not possible"
   C. "There are no witnesses"

D. "It does not last"
   E. "I never met one"
IV. Expostulation. Why should any child of God object to:
   A. Loving God with all human parts and powers?
   B. Having "the mind that was in Christ Jesus"?
   C. Expecting the harvest of the indwelling Spirit?
   D. Being kept blameless by the power of God?
   E. Living the whole of life as a "living sacrifice"?
   F. Maintaining that all sin is inconsistent with life in the Spirit?

On Perfection

Let us go on unto perfection (Heb. vi. 1).

The whole sentence runs thus: "Therefore, leaving the principles of the doctrine of Christ, let us go on unto perfection: not laying again the foundation of repentance from dead works, and of faith towards God," which he had just before termed "the first principles of the oracles of God," and "meat fit for babes"; for such as have just tasted that the Lord is gracious.

That the doing of this is a point of the utmost importance, the apostle intimates in the next words: "This will we do, if God permit. For it is impossible for those who were once enlightened, and have tasted of the good word of God, and the powers of the world to come, and have fallen away, to renew them again to repentance." As if he had said, If we do not "go on to perfection," we are in the utmost danger of "falling away." And if we do fall away, it is "impossible [that is, exceeding hard] to renew us again to repentance."

In order to make this very important Scripture as easy to be understood as possible, I shall endeavour,
   I. To show what perfection is
   II. To answer some objections to it, and
   III. To expostulate a little with the opposers of it.

I. I will endeavour to show what perfection is.

   1. And first, I do not conceive the perfection here spoken of to be the perfection of angels. As those glorious beings never "left their first estate," never declined from their original perfection; all their native faculties are unimpaired; their understanding, in particular, is

still a lamp of light; their apprehension of all things clear and distinct, and their judgment always true. Hence, though their knowledge is limited (for they are creatures), though they are ignorant of innumerable things, yet they are not liable to mistake; their knowledge is perfect in its kind. And as their affections are constantly guided by their unerring understanding, so that all their actions are suitable thereto, so they do, every moment, not their own will but the good and acceptable will of God.

Therefore it is not possible for man, whose understanding is darkened, to whom mistake is as natural as ignorance, . . . it is not possible, I say, for man always to think right, to apprehend things distinctly, and to judge truly of them. In consequence thereof, his affections, depending on his understanding, are variously disordered; and his words and actions are influenced, more or less, by the disorder both of his understanding and affections. It follows that no man, while in the body, can possibly attain to angelic perfection.

2. Neither can any man, while he is in a corruptible body, attain to Adamic perfection. Adam, before his fall, was undoubtedly as pure, as free from sin as even the holy angels. In like manner, his understanding was as clear as theirs, and his affections as regular. In virtue of this, as he always judged right, so he was able always to speak and act right. But since man rebelled against God, the case is widely different with him. He is no longer able to avoid falling into innumerable mistakes; consequently, he cannot always avoid wrong affections; neither can he always think, speak, and act right. Therefore man, in his present state, can no more attain Adamic than angelic perfection.

3. The highest perfection which man can attain, while the soul dwells in the body, does not exclude ignorance, and error, and a thousand other infirmities. Now from wrong judgments, wrong words and actions will often necessarily flow; and in some cases wrong affections also may spring from the same source. I may judge wrong of you; I may think more or less highly of you than I ought to think; and this mistake in my judgment may not only occasion something wrong in my behaviour, but it may have a still deeper effect; it may occasion something wrong in my affection. From a wrong apprehension, I may love and esteem you either more or less than I ought. Nor can I be freed from a liableness to such a mistake while I remain in a corruptible body. A thousand infirmities, in consequence of this, will attend my spirit till it returns to God who gave it. And in numberless instances it

comes short of doing the will of God, as Adam in paradise. Hence the best of men may say from the heart:

> Every moment, Lord, I need
> The merit of Thy death

for innumerable violations of the Adamic as well as the angelic law. It is well, therefore, for us, that we are not now under these, but under the law of love. "Love is [now] the fulfilling of the law," which is given to fallen man. This is now, with respect to us, "the perfect law." But even against this, through the present weakness of our understanding, we are continually liable to transgress. Therefore, every man living needs the blood of atonement, or he could not stand before God.

4. What is then the perfection of which man is capable, while he dwells in a corruptible body? It is the complying with that kind command, "My son, give me thy heart." It is the "loving the Lord his God with all his heart, and with all his soul, and with all his mind." **PERFECT LOVE** This is the sum of Christian perfection: it is all comprised in that one word, love. The first branch of it is the love of God; and as he that loves God loves his brother also, it is inseparably connected with the second, "Thou shalt love thy neighbour as thyself." Thou shalt love every man as thy own soul, as Christ loved us. "On these two commandments hang all the law and the prophets"; these contain the whole of Christian perfection.

5. Another view of this is given us in those words of the great apostle, "Let this mind be in you, which was also in Christ Jesus." For **CHRISTLIKENESS** although this immediately and directly refers to the humility of our Lord, yet it may be taken in a far more extensive sense so as to include the whole disposition of His mind, all His affections, all His tempers, both toward God and man. Now it is certain that as there was no evil affection in Him, so no good affection or temper was wanting. So that "whatsoever things are holy, whatsoever things are lovely," are all included in "the mind that was in Christ Jesus."

6. St. Paul, when writing to the Galatians, places perfection in yet another view. It is the one undivided *fruit of the Spirit,* which he describes thus: "The fruit of the Spirit is love, joy, peace, longsuffering, gentleness, goodness, fidelity" (so the word should be translated here), "meekness, temperance." What a glorious constellation of grace is here! Now suppose all these things to be knit together in one, to be united together in the soul of a believer, this is Christian perfection.

7. Again, he writes to the Christians at Ephesus of "putting on the new man which is created after God in righteousness and true holiness"; and to the Colossians, of "the new man renewed after the image of him that created him"; plainly referring to the words in Genesis, chap. i. 27, "So God created man in his own image." Now the moral image of God consists (as the apostle observes) "in righteousness and true holiness." By sin this is totally destroyed. And we never can recover it, till we are "created anew in Christ Jesus." And this is perfection.

8. St. Peter expresses it in a still different manner, though to the same effect. "As he that hath called you is holy, so be ye holy in all manner of conversation" (1 Pet. i. 15). According to this apostle, then, perfection is another name for universal holiness; inward and outward righteousness: holiness of life arising from holiness of heart.

9. If any expressions can be stronger than these, they are those of St. Paul to the Thessalonians, 1 Epistle v. 23: "The God of peace himself sanctify you wholly; and may the whole of you, the spirit, the soul, and the body [this is the literal translation], be preserved blameless unto the coming of our Lord Jesus Christ."

10. We cannot show this sanctification in a more excellent way than by complying with that exhortation of the apostle: "I beseech you, brethren, by the mercies of God, that ye present your bodies" (yourselves, your souls and bodies; a part put for the whole, by a common figure of speech) "a living sacrifice unto God"; to whom ye were consecrated many years ago in baptism. When what was then devoted is actually presented to God, then the man of God is perfect.

11. To the same effect St. Peter says, 1 Epistle ii. 5: "Ye are a holy priesthood, to offer up spiritual sacrifices acceptable to God, through Jesus Christ." But what sacrifices shall we offer now, seeing the Jewish dispensation is at an end? If you have truly presented yourselves to God, you offer up to Him continually all your thoughts, and words, and actions through the Son of His love, as a sacrifice of praise and thanksgiving.

12. Thus you experience that He whose name is called Jesus, does not bear that name in vain; that He does, in fact, "save his people from their sins"; the root, as well as the branches. And this salvation from sin, from all sin, is another description of perfection, though indeed it expresses only the least, the lowest branch of it, only the negative part of the great salvation.

II. I propose, in the second place, to answer some objections to this scriptural account of perfection.

1. One common objection to it is that there is no promise of it in the word of God. If this were so, we must give it up; we should have no foundation to build upon: for the promises of God are the only sure foundation of our hope. But surely there is a very clear and full promise that we shall all love the Lord our God with all our hearts. So we read Deut. xxx. 6: "Then will I circumcise thy heart, and the heart of thy seed, to love the Lord thy God with all thy heart and with all thy soul." Equally express is the word of our Lord, which is no less a promise though in the form of a command, Matt. xxii. 37: "Thou shalt love the Lord thy God with all thy heart, and with all thy soul, and with all thy mind." No words can be more strong than these; no promise can be more express. In like manner, "Thou shalt love thy neighbour as thyself" is as express a promise as a command.

2. And, indeed, that general unlimited promise which runs through the whole gospel dispensation, "I will put my laws in their minds, and write them in their hearts," turns all the commands into promises; and consequently that among the rest, "Let this mind be in you which was also in Christ Jesus." The command here is equivalent to a promise, and gives us full reason to expect that He will work in us what He requires of us.

3. With regard to the fruit of the Spirit, the apostle in affirming, "The fruit of the Spirit is love, joy, peace, long suffering, gentleness, goodness, fidelity, meekness, temperance," does, in effect, affirm that the Holy Spirit actually works love, and these other tempers, in those that are led by Him. So that here, also, we have firm ground to tread upon; this scripture likewise being equivalent to a promise, and assuring us that all these shall be wrought in us provided we are led by the Spirit.

4. And when the apostle says to the Ephesians, chap. iv. 21-24: "Ye have been taught, as the truth is in Jesus," to be "renewed in the spirit of your mind, and to put on the new man which is created after God"; that is, after the image of God, "in righteousness and true holiness"; He leaves us no room to doubt but God will thus "renew us in the spirit of our mind" and "create us anew" in the image of God, wherein we were at first created; otherwise it could not be said that this is "the truth as it is in Jesus."

5. The command of God given by St. Peter: "Be ye holy, as he that hath called you is holy, in all manner of conversation," implies a

promise that we shall be thus holy, if we are not wanting to ourselves. Nothing can be wanting on God's part; as He has called us to holiness, He is undoubtedly willing, as well as able, to work this holiness in us. For He cannot mock His helpless creatures, calling us to receive what He never intends to give. That He does call us thereto is undeniable; therefore, He will give it if we are not disobedient to the heavenly calling.

6. The prayer of St. Paul for the Thessalonians, that God would "sanctify them throughout," and "that the whole of them, the spirit, the soul, and the body, might be preserved blameless," will undoubtedly be heard in behalf of all the children of God, as well as those at Thessalonica. Hereby, therefore, all Christians are encouraged to expect the same blessing from "the God of peace," namely, that they also shall be "sanctified throughout, in spirit, soul, and body"; and that "the whole of them shall be preserved blameless unto the coming of our Lord Jesus Christ."

FOR ALL CHRISTIANS

7. But the great question is, whether there is any promise in Scripture that we shall be *saved from sin?* Undoubtedly there is. Such is that promise, Ps. cxxx. 8, "He shall redeem Israel from all his sins"; exactly answerable to these words of the angel, "He shall save his people from their sins." And surely "he is able to save to the uttermost, them that come unto God through him." Such is that glorious promise given through the prophet Ezekiel, chap. xxxvi. 25-27: "Then will I sprinkle clean water upon you, and ye shall be clean: from all your filthiness, and from all your idols, will I cleanse you. A new heart also will I give you, and a new spirit will I put within you: and I will take away the stony heart out of your flesh, and I will give you a heart of flesh. And I will put my Spirit within you, and cause you to walk in my statutes, and ye shall keep my judgments, and do them." Such (to mention no more) is that pronounced by Zacharias, Luke i. 73-75: "The oath which he sware to our father Abraham, that he would grant unto us, being delivered out of the hands of our enemies [and such, doubtless, are all our sins], to serve him without fear, in holiness and righteousness before him, all the days of our life." The last part of this promise is peculiarly worthy of our observation. Lest any should say, "True, we shall be saved from our sins when we die"; that clause is remarkably added, as if on purpose to obviate this pretense, *all the days of our life*. With what modesty, then, can anyone affirm, "that none shall enjoy this liberty *till death*"?

8. "But," say some, "this cannot be the meaning of the words, for

the thing is impossible." It is impossible to men; but the things impossible with men are possible with God. "Nay, but this is impossible in its own nature; for it implies a contradiction, that a man should be saved from all sin while he is in a sinful body."

There is a great deal of force in this objection. And perhaps we must allow most of what you contend for. We have already allowed, that while we are in the body we cannot be wholly free from mistake. Notwithstanding all our care, we shall still be liable to judge wrong in many instances. And a mistake in judgment will very frequently occasion a mistake in practice. Nay, a wrong judgment may occasion something in the temper or passions which is not strictly right. It may occasion needless fear or ill-grounded hope; unreasonable love or unreasonable aversion. But all this is no way inconsistent with the perfection above described.

9. You say, "Yes, it is inconsistent with the last article [no. 8, above], it cannot consist with salvation from sin." I answer, it will perfectly well consist with salvation from sin, according to that definition of sin (which I apprehend to be the scriptural definition of it), *a voluntary transgression of a known law.* "Nay, but all transgressions of the law of God, whether voluntary or involuntary, are sin; for St. John says, All *sin is a transgression of the law.*" True, but he does not say, *All transgression of the law is sin.* This I deny; let him prove it that can.

To say the truth, this is a mere strife of words. You say, "None is saved from sin in *your* sense of the word"; but I do not admit of that sense, because the word is never so taken in the Scripture. And you cannot destroy the possibility of being saved from sin, in *my* sense of the word. And this is the sense wherein the word sin is over and over taken in Scripture.

"But surely we cannot be saved from sin while we dwell in a *sinful body.*" A *sinful body?* I pray observe how deeply ambiguous, how equivocal this expression is! But there is no authority for it in Scripture; the word *sinful body* is never found there. And as it is totally unscriptural, so it is palpably absurd. For no *body,* or matter of any kind, can be *sinful;* spirits alone are capable of sin. Pray, in what part of the body should sin lodge? It cannot lodge in the skin, nor in the muscles, or nerves, or veins, or arteries; it cannot be in the bones, any more than in the hair or nails. Only the soul can be the seat of sin.

10. "But does not St. Paul himself say, 'They that are in the flesh cannot please God'?" I am afraid the sound of these words has deceived many unwary souls who have been told these words, *they that*

are in the flesh, mean the same as they that are in the body. No; nothing less. *The flesh,* in this text, no more means the body than it does the soul. Abel, Enoch, Abraham; yea, all that cloud of witnesses recited by St. Paul in the eleventh of Hebrews, did actually please God while they were in the body, as he himself testifies. The expression, therefore, here means neither more nor less than they that are unbelievers; they that are in their natural state; they that are without God in the world.

11. But let us attend to the reason of the thing. Why cannot the Almighty sanctify the soul while it is in the body? Cannot He sanctify *you* while you are in this house as well as in the open air? Can the walls of brick or stone hinder Him? No more can these walls of flesh and blood hinder Him for a moment from sanctifying you throughout. He can just as easily save you from all sin in the body as out of the body.

"But has He promised thus to save us from sin while we are in the body?" Undoubtedly He has; for a promise is implied in every commandment of God; consequently in that, "Thou shalt love the Lord thy God with all thy heart, and with all thy soul, and with all thy mind." For this and every other commandment is given, not to the dead, but to the living. It is expressed in the words above recited, that we should "walk in holiness before him all the days of our life."

I have dwelt the longer on this because it is the grand argument of those that oppose salvation from sin; and also, because it has not been so frequently and so fully answered; whereas the arguments taken from Scripture have been answered a hundred times over.

12. But a still more plausible objection remains, taken from experience; which is, that "there are no living witnesses of this salvation from sin." In answer to this,

(1) I allow that there are not many. Even in this sense, there are *not many fathers.* Such is our hardness of heart; such our slowness to believe what both the prophets and apostles have spoke, that there are few, exceeding few true witnesses of the great salvation.

(2) I allow that there are false witnesses who either deceive their own souls and speak of things they know not, or "speak lies in hypocrisy." And I have frequently wondered that we have not more of both sorts. It is nothing strange that men of warm imaginations should deceive themselves in this matter. Many do the same with regard to justification; they imagine they are justified and are not. But though many imagine it falsely, yet there are some that are truly justified. And

thus, though many imagine they are sanctified and are not, yet there are some that are really sanctified.

(3) I allow that some who once enjoyed full salvation have now totally lost it. They once walked in glorious liberty, giving God their whole heart, "rejoicing evermore, praying without ceasing, and in every thing giving thanks." But it is past. They now are shorn of their strength and become like other men. Yet, perhaps, they do not give up their confidence; they still have a sense of His pardoning love. But even this is frequently assaulted by doubts and fears so that they hold it with a trembling hand.

13. "Nay, this," say some pious and sensible men, "is the very thing which we contend for. We grant it may please God to make some of His children, for a time, unspeakably holy and happy. We will not deny that they may enjoy all the holiness and happiness which you speak of. But it is only *for a time;* God never designed that it should continue to their lives' end. Consequently, sin is only suspended; it is not destroyed."

This you affirm. But it is a thing of so deep importance that it cannot be allowed without clear and cogent proof. And where is the proof? We know that, in general, "the gifts and calling of God are without repentance." He does not repent of any gifts which He hath bestowed upon the children of men. And how does the contrary appear, with regard to this particular gift of God? Why should we imagine that He will make an exception with respect to the most precious of all His gifts on this side of heaven? Is He not as able to give it us always as to give it once? As able to give it for fifty years as for one day? And how can it be proved that He is not willing to continue this, His loving kindness?

How is this supposition that He is not willing consistent with the positive assertion of the apostle who, after exhorting the Christians at Thessalonica, and in them all Christians in all ages, to "rejoice evermore, pray without ceasing, and in every thing give thanks," immediately adds (as if on purpose to answer those who denied, not the *power,* but the *will* of God to work in them), "For this is the will of God concerning you in Christ Jesus"? Nay, and it is remarkable that after He had delivered that glorious promise (such it properly is) in the twenty-third verse, "The very God of peace shall sanctify you wholly, and the whole of you" (so it is in the original); "the spirit, the soul, and the body, shall be preserved blameless unto the coming of the Lord Jesus Christ," he adds again, "Faithful is he that hath called you, who also will do it." He *will* not only sanctify you wholly, but will preserve you in that state until He comes to receive you unto himself.

14. Agreeably to this is the plain matter of fact. Several persons have enjoyed this blessing without any interruption for many years; several enjoy it at this day; and not a few have enjoyed it unto their death, as they have declared with their latest breath, calmly witnessing that God saved them from all sin, till their spirit returned to God.

15. As to the whole of the objections taken from experience, I desire it may be observed farther; either the persons objected to, have attained Christian perfection, or they have not. If they have not, whatever objections are brought against them strike wide of the mark. For they are not the persons we are talking of; therefore, whatever they are or do is beside the question. But if they have attained it, if they answer the description given under the nine preceding articles, no reasonable objection can lie against them. They are superior to all censure. And "every tongue that riseth up against them will they utterly condemn."

16. "But I never saw one," continues the objector, "that answered my idea of perfection." It may be so. And it is probable (as I observed elsewhere) you never will. For your idea includes abundantly too much; even freedom from these infirmities which are not separable from spirit that is connected with flesh and blood. But if you keep to the account that is given above, and allow for the weakness of human understanding, you may see, at this day, undeniable instances of genuine, scriptural perfection.

III. It only remains, in the third place, to expostulate a little with the opposers of this perfection.

1. Now permit me to ask, why are you so angry with those who profess to have attained this? and so mad (I cannot give it any softer title) against Christian perfection—against the most glorious gift which God ever gave to the children of men upon earth? View it in every one of the preceding points of light, and see what it contains that is either odious or terrible; that is calculated to excite either hatred or fear in any reasonable creature.

What rational objection can you have to the loving the Lord your God with all your heart? Why should you be afraid of it? Would it do you any hurt? Would it lessen your happiness, either in this world or the world to come? And why should you be unwilling that others should give Him their whole heart? Or that they should love their neighbours as themselves, yea, "As Christ hath loved us"? Is this detestable? Is it the proper object of hated? Or is it the most amiable thing under the sun? Is it proper to move terror? Is it not rather desirable in the highest degree?

2. Why are you so averse to having in you the whole "mind which was in Christ Jesus"—all the affections, all the tempers and dispositions, which were in Him while He dwelt among men? Why should you be afraid of this? Would it be any worse for you, were God to work in you this very hour all the mind that was in Him? If not, why should you hinder others from seeking this blessing? Or be displeased at those who think they have attained it? Is anything more lovely? Anything more to be desired by every child of man?

CHRISTLIKENESS

3. Why are you averse to having the whole "fruit of the Spirit"—"love, joy, peace, longsuffering, meekness, gentleness, fidelity, goodness, temperance"? Why should you be afraid of having all these planted in your inmost soul? As "against these there is no law," so there cannot be any reasonable objection. Surely nothing is more desirable than that all these tempers should take deep root in your heart; nay, in the hearts of all that name the name of Christ; yea, of all the inhabitants of the earth.

4. What reasons have you to be afraid of or to entertain any aversion to the being "renewed in the [whole] image of him that created you"? Is not this more desirable than anything under heaven? Is it not consummately amiable? What can you wish for in comparison of this, either for your own soul or for those for whom you entertain the strongest and tenderest affection? And when you enjoy this, what remains but to be "changed from glory to glory, by the Spirit of the Lord?"

5. Why should you be averse to universal holiness?—the same thing under another name. Why should you entertain any prejudices against this, or look upon it with apprehension? Whether you understand by that term, the being inwardly conformed to the whole image and will of God; or an outward behaviour in every point suitable to that conformity. Can you conceive anything more amiable than this? Anything more desirable? Set prejudice aside, and surely you will desire to see it diffused over all the earth.

6. Is perfection (to vary the expression) the being "sanctified throughout, in spirit, soul, and body"? What lover of God and man can be averse to this, or entertain frightful apprehensions of it? Is it not, in your best moments, your desire to be all of a

HUNGER

piece?—all consistent with yourself?—all faith, all meekness, all love? And suppose you were once possessed of this glorious liberty, would not you wish to continue therein?—to be preserved "blameless unto the coming of our Lord Jesus Christ"?

7. For what cause should you that are the children of God be averse to, or afraid of, presenting yourselves, your souls and bodies, as a living sacrifice, holy, acceptable to God?—to God your Creator, your Redeemer, your Sanctifier? Can anything be more desirable than this entire self-dedication to Him? And is it not your wish that all mankind should unite in this "reasonable service"? Surely no one can be averse to this, without being an enemy to all mankind.

CONSECRATION

8. And why should you be afraid of, or averse to, what is naturally implied in this, namely, the offering up all your thoughts, and words, and actions, as a spiritual sacrifice to God, acceptable to Him through the blood and intercession of His well-beloved Son? Surely you cannot deny that this is good and profitable to men as well as pleasing to God. Should you not then devoutly pray that both you and all mankind may thus worship Him in spirit and in truth?

9. Suffer me to ask one question more. Why should any man of reason and religion be either afraid of or averse to salvation from all sin? Is not sin the greatest evil on this side of hell? And if so, does it not naturally follow that an entire deliverance from it is one of the greatest blessings this side of heaven? How earnestly, then, should it be prayed for by all the children of God! By sin I mean, *a voluntary transgression of a known law.* Are you averse to being delivered from this? Are you afraid of such a deliverance? Do you then love sin, that you are so unwilling to part with it? Surely no. You do not love either the devil or his works. You rather wish to be totally delivered from them, to have sin rooted out both of your life and heart.

CLEANSING

10. I have frequently observed, and not without surprise, that the opposers of perfection are more vehement against it when it is placed in this view than in any other whatsoever. They will allow all you say of the love of God and man, of the mind which was in Christ, of the fruit of the Spirit, of the image of God, of universal holiness, of entire self-dedication, of sanctification in spirit, soul, and body; yea, and of the offering up of all our thoughts, words, and actions, as a sacrifice to God; all this they will allow, so we will allow a sin, a little sin, to remain in us till death.

11. Pray compare this with that remarkable passage in John Bunyan's "Holy War." "When Immanuel," says he, "had driven Diabolus and all his forces out of the city of Man-soul, Diabolus preferred a petition to Immanuel that he might have only a small part of the city. When this was rejected, he begged to have only a little room within the walls." But Immanuel answered, "He should have no place in it at all, no, not to rest the sole of his foot."

Had not the good old man forgot himself? Did not the force of truth so prevail over him here as utterly to overturn his own system? To assert perfection in the clearest manner? For if this is not salvation from sin, I cannot tell what is.

12. "No," says a great man, "this is the error of errors; I hate it from my heart. I pursue it through all the world with fire and sword." Nay, why so vehement? Do you seriously think there is no error under heaven equal to this? Here is something which I cannot understand. Why are those that oppose salvation from sin (few excepted) so eager—I had almost said, furious? Are you fighting *pro aris et focis!* For God and your country? for all you have in the world? for all that is near and dear unto you? for your liberty? your life? In God's name, why are you so fond of sin? What good has it ever done you? What good is it ever likely to do you, either in this world or in the world to come?

And why are you so violent against those that hope for deliverance from it? Have patience with us, if we are in error; yea, suffer us to enjoy our error. If we should not attain it, the very expectation of this deliverance gives us present comfort; yea, and ministers strength to resist those enemies which we expect to conquer. If you could persuade us to despair of that victory, we should give over the contest. Now "we are saved by hope"; from this very hope a degree of salvation springs. Be not angry with those who are *felices errore suo;* happy in their mistake. Else, be their opinion right or wrong, your temper is undeniably sinful. Bear then with *us*, as we do with *you*, and see whether the Lord will not deliver us! Whether He is not able, yea, and willing, "to save them to the uttermost that come unto God through him."

On Patience
1788 (Abridged)

This sermon was written in 1788, less than three years before Wesley's death. In it he gives us a most thorough and beautiful presentation of the work of the Holy Spirit in purifying the believer's heart and cleansing him from all unrighteousness. He makes his supreme point the instantaneousness of this deliverance from sin in the crisis work of entire sanctification, asserting that he has found it so all over England and Ireland.

This is one of those sermons that Tyerman describes as an expression of Wesley's concept of perfect love: a concept that he held firmly over the ups and downs, evil report and good, for upwards of a half century. It is an exposition of the fullness of peace, joy, hope, and love that the Lord intends to be the possession of all of His people.

ON PATIENCE

Let patience have its perfect work, that ye may be perfect and entire, wanting nothing (James i. 4).

1. "My brethren," says the apostle in the preceding verse, "count it all joy when ye fall into divers temptations." At first view this may appear a strange direction; seeing most temptations are "for the present, not joyous, but grievous." Nevertheless ye know by your own experience that "the trial of your faith worketh patience"; and if "patience have its proper work, ye shall be perfect and entire, wanting nothing."

2. It is not to any particular person, or church, that the apostle gives this instruction; but to all who are partakers of like precious faith and are seeking after that common salvation. For as long as any of us are upon earth, we are in the region of temptation. He who came into the world to save His people from their sins, did not come to save them from temptation. He himself "knew no sin"; yet while He was in this vale of tears, "he suffered, being tempted"; and herein also, "left us an example, that we should tread in his steps." We are liable to a thousand temptations, from the corruptible body variously affecting

the soul. The soul itself, encompassed as it is with infirmities, exposes us to ten thousand more. And how many are the temptations which we meet with even from the good men . . . with whom we are called to converse from day to day? . . . Add to this, that the most dangerous of our enemies are not those that assault us openly. No:

> Angels our march oppose,
> Who still in strength excel.
> Our secret, sworn, eternal foes,
> Countless, invisible!

For is not our "adversary the devil, as a roaring lion," with all his infernal legions, still going "about seeking whom he may devour"? . . . But instead of counting this a loss, as unbelievers would do, "count it all joy; knowing that the trial of your faith," even when it is "tried as by fire," "worketh patience." But "let patience have its perfect work, and ye shall be perfect and entire, wanting nothing."

3. But what is *patience?* We do not now speak of a heathen virtue; neither of a natural indolence; but of a gracious temper, wrought in the heart of a believer by the power of the Holy Ghost. It is a disposition to suffer whatever pleases God, in the manner and for the time that pleases Him. We thereby hold the middle way, neither . . . *despising* our sufferings, *making little* of them, passing over them lightly, as if they were owing to chance, or second causes; nor, on the other hand . . . *affected too much, unnerved, dissolved, sinking under them.* We may observe, the proper object of patience is suffering, either in body or mind. Patience . . . is not apathy or insensibility. It is at the utmost distance from . . . fretfulness or dejection. The patient believer is preserved from falling into either of these extremes by considering, Who is the author of all his suffering? Even God his Father. What is the *motive* of His *giving us* to suffer? Not so properly His justice as His love. And what is the *end* of it? Our "profit, that we may be partakers of his holiness."

4. Very nearly related to patience is *meekness:* if it be not rather a species of it. For may it not be defined, patience of injuries; particularly affronts, reproach, or unjust censure? This teaches not to return evil for evil, or railing for railing; but contrariwise blessing. Our blessed Lord himself seems to place peculiar value upon this temper. This He peculiarly calls us to "learn of him, if we would find rest for our souls."

5. But what may we understand by the *work of patience?* "Let

patience have its perfect work." It seems to mean, let it have its full fruit or effect. And what is the fruit which the Spirit of God is accustomed to produce hereby in the heart of a believer? One immediate fruit of patience is peace: a sweet tranquility of mind; a serenity of spirit which can never be found unless where patience reigns. And this peace often rises into joy. Even in the midst of various temptations those that are enabled "in patience to possess their souls," can witness not only quietness of spirit, but triumph and exultation....

6. How lively is the account which the apostle Peter gives, not only of the peace and joy, but of the hope and love which God works in patient sufferers, "who are kept by the power of God through faith unto salvation!" Indeed he appears herein to have an eye to this very passage of St. James: "Though ye are grieved for a season with manifold temptations ... that the trial of your faith ... may be found to praise, and honour, and glory, at the revelation of Jesus Christ: whom, having not seen, ye love: in whom, though now ye see him not, yet believing, ye rejoice with joy unspeakable and full of glory." See here the peace, the joy, and the love, which through the mighty power of God are the fruit or "work of patience"!

7. And as peace, hope, joy, and love are the fruits of patience, both springing from and confirmed by it, so is also rational, genuine *courage,* which indeed cannot subsist without patience. The brutal courage, or rather fierceness of a lion may probably spring from impatience; but true fortitude, the courage of a man, springs from just the contrary temper. Christian *zeal* is likewise confirmed and increased by patience, and so is *activity* in every good work: the same Spirit ... making us equally willing to do and suffer the whole will of God.

8. But what is the *perfect work* of patience? Is it anything less than the "perfect love of God," constraining us to love every soul of man, "even as Christ loved us"? Is it not the whole of religion, the whole "mind which was also in Christ Jesus"? Is it not "the renewal of our soul in the image of God after the likeness of him that created us"? And is not the fruit of this the constant resignation of ourselves, body and spirit, to God; entirely giving up all we are, all we have, and all we love, as a holy sacrifice, acceptable unto God through the Son of His love? ...

9. But how does this work differ from that gracious work which is wrought in every believer when he first finds redemption in the blood of Jesus, even the remission of his sins? Many persons that are

not only upright of heart, but that fear, nay, and love God, have not spoken warily upon this head, not according to the oracles of God. They have spoken of the work of sanctification, taking the word in its full sense, as if it were quite of another kind, as if it differed entirely from that which is wrought in justification. But this is a great and dangerous mistake and has a natural tendency to make us undervalue that glorious work of God which was wrought in us when we were justified: whereas in that moment when we are justified freely by His grace, when we are accepted through the beloved, we are born again, born from above, born of the Spirit. And there is as great a change wrought in our souls when we are born of the Spirit as was wrought in our bodies when we were born of a woman. There is in that hour a general change from inward sinfulness to inward holiness. . . . The earthly, sensual, devilish mind, gives place to the "mind that was in Christ Jesus."

CHRISTLIKENESS

10. "Well, but what more than this can be implied in entire sanctification?" It does not imply any new *kind* of holiness: let no man imagine this. From the moment we are justified till we give up our spirits to God, love is the fulfilling of the law; of the whole evangelical law, which took the place of the Adamic law when the first promise of "the seed of the woman" was made. Love is the sum of Christian sanctification; it is the one *kind* of holiness, which is found only in various *degrees* in the believers who are distinguished by St. John into "little children, young men, and fathers." The difference between one and the other properly lies in the degree of love. And herein there is as great a difference in the spiritual as in the natural sense between fathers, young men, and babes.

Everyone that is born of God, though he be as yet only a "babe in Christ," has the love of God in his heart; the love of his neighbour, together with lowliness, meekness, and resignation. But all of these are then in a low degree in proportion to the degree of his faith. The faith of a babe in Christ is weak, generally mingled with doubts or fears; with doubts, whether he has not deceived himself; or fear, that he shall not endure to the end. . . . In the same proportion as he grows in faith, he grows in holiness; he increases in love, lowliness, meekness, in every part of the image of God; till it pleases God after he is thoroughly convinced of inbred sin, of the total corruption of his nature, to take it all away; to purify his heart and cleanse him from all unrighteousness; to fulfill that promise which He made first to His ancient people, and in them to the Israel of God in all ages: "I will

GROWTH

circumcise thy heart, and the heart of thy seed, to love the Lord thy God with all thy heart, and with all thy soul."

It is not easy to conceive what a difference there is between that which he experiences now and that which he experienced before. Till this universal change was wrought in his soul, all his holiness was *mixed*.... His whole soul is now consistent with itself; there is no jarring string. All his passions flow in a continual stream with an even tenor to God. To him that is entered into his rest, you may truly say,

WHOLENESS

> *Calm thou ever art within,*
> *All unruffled, all serene!*

There is no mixture of any contrary affections: all is peace and harmony after. Being filled with love, there is no more interruption of it than of the beating of his heart; and continual love bringing continual joy in the Lord, he rejoices evermore. He converses continually with the God whom he loves, unto whom in everything he gives thanks. And as he now loves God with all his heart, and with all his soul, and with all his mind, and with all his strength; so Jesus now reigns alone in his heart the Lord of every motion there.

11. But it may be inquired, In what manner does God work this entire, this universal change in the soul of a believer? ... Does He work it gradually, by slow degrees; or instantaneously in a moment? ... Be the change instantaneous or gradual, see that you never rest till it is wrought in your own soul, if you desire to dwell with God in glory.

12. This premised, in order to throw what light I can upon this interesting question, I will simply relate what I have seen myself in the course of many years. Four or five and forty years ago, when I had no distinct views of what the apostle meant by exhorting us to "leave the principles of the doctrine of Christ, and go on to perfection," two or three persons in London whom I knew to be truly sincere desired to give me an account of their experience. It appeared exceeding strange, being different from any that I had heard before: but exactly similar to the preceding account of entire sanctification. The next year, two or three more persons in Bristol and two or three in Kingswood, coming to me severally, gave me exactly the same account of their experience.

A few years after, I desired all those in London who made the same profession to come to me all together at the Foundery, that I might be thoroughly satisfied. I desired that man of God, Thomas Walsh, to give us the meeting there. When we met, first one of us and then the other asked them the most searching questions we could devise. They answered every one without hesitation and with the utmost simplicity so that we were fully persuaded they did not deceive themselves. In the years 1759, 1760, 1761, and 1762, their numbers multiplied exceedingly, not only in London and Bristol but in various parts of Ireland as well as England.

Not trusting to the testimony of others, I carefully examined most of these myself; and in London alone, I found six hundred and fifty-two members of our society who were exceeding clear in their experience, and of whose testimony I could see no reason to doubt. I believe no year has passed since that time, wherein God has not wrought the same work in many others; but sometimes in one part of England or Ireland, sometimes in another, as "the wind bloweth where it listeth"; and every one of these . . . has declared that his deliverance from sin was *instantaneous;* that the change was wrought in a moment.

Had half of these, or one third, or one in twenty, declared it was *gradually* wrought in *them,* I should have believed this with regard to *them* and thought that *some* were gradually sanctified and some instantaneously. But I have not found in so long a space of time a single person speaking thus; all who believe they are sanctified declare with one voice that the change was wrought in a moment. I cannot but believe that sanctification is commonly, if not always, an *instantaneous* work.

SECOND BLESSING

13. But however that question be decided, whether sanctification in the full sense of the word be wrought instantaneously or gradually, how may we attain to it? . . . What shall we do, that this work of God may be wrought in us? "This is the work of God, that ye believe on him whom he hath sent." On this one work all the others depend. Believe on the Lord Jesus Christ and all His wisdom, and power, and faithfulness, are engaged on thy side. In this, as in all other instances, "by grace we are saved through faith." Sanctification too is "not of works, lest any man should boast." "It is the gift of God," and is to be received by plain, simple faith.

Suppose you are now labouring to "abstain from all appearance of evil," "zealous of good works," and walking diligently and carefully in all the ordinances of God; there is then only one point remaining: the voice of God to your soul is, "Believe, and be saved." First, believe that God has *promised* to save you from all sin and to fill you with all holiness; secondly, believe that He is *able* thus "to save to

FAITH

the uttermost all that come unto God through him"; thirdly, believe that He is *willing*, as well as able, to save *you* to the uttermost; to purify you from all sin and fill up all your heart with love. Believe, fourthly, that He is not only able but willing to do it *now!* Not when you come to die; not at any distant time; not tomorrow, but *today.* He will then enable you to believe, *it is done,* according to His word: and then "patience shall have its perfect work, that ye may be perfect and entire, wanting nothing."

14. Ye shall then be perfect. . . . Ye shall be wholly delivered from every evil work; from every evil word; from every sinful thought; yea, from every evil desire, passion, temper; from all inbred corruption, from all remains of the carnal mind, from the body of sin; and ye shall be renewed in the spirit of your mind in every right temper, after the image of Him that created you in righteousness and true holiness. Ye shall be *entire* . . . (the same word which the apostle uses to the Christians in Thessalonica). This seems to refer, not so much to the kind as to the degree of holiness, as if he had said, "Ye shall enjoy as high a degree of holiness as is consistent with your present state of pilgrimage," and ye shall *want nothing;* the Lord being your Shepherd, your Father, your Redeemer, your Sanctifier, your God, and your All, will *feed* you with the bread of heaven and give you meat enough. He will lead you forth beside the waters of comfort and keep you every moment: so that loving Him with all your heart (which is the sum of all perfection), you will "rejoice evermore, pray without ceasing, and in every thing give thanks," till "an abundant entrance is ministered unto you into his everlasting kingdom!"

The More Excellent Way
1788 (Excerpts)

Wesley opened this sermon with a brief statement on the extraordinary gifts of the Holy Ghost, the subject of Paul in the earlier context of Wesley's text. Having indicated the use of these gifts in the apostolic days and their seeming disuse after the third or fourth century, Wesley declares his intention to preach about the ordinary gifts of the Holy Ghost that make Christians "to be more useful in their generation."

He deals briefly with the qualities listed by Paul in 1 Cor. 13:1-3, especially persuasive speech, knowledge, and faith. "These gifts we may innocently desire, but there is a more excellent way."

The way of love; of loving all men for God's sake; of humble, gentle, patient love, is that which the apostle so admirably describes in the ensuing chapter and without which all eloquence, all knowledge, all faith, all works, and all sufferings, are of no more value in the sight of God than sounding brass or a rumbling cymbal; and are not of the least avail towards our eternal salvation.

Without this, all we know, all we believe, all we do, all we suffer, will profit us nothing in the great day of accounts.

But at this point Wesley declares he will take the text in a different manner and describe "two orders of Christians."

The printed portion of the sermon here picks up at point 5 following the preamble.

THE MORE EXCELLENT WAY

Covet earnestly the best gifts: And yet I show unto you a more excellent way (1 Cor. xii. 31).

5. It is the observation of an ancient writer that there have been from the beginning two orders of Christians. The one lived an innocent life, conforming in all things not sinful to the customs and fashions of the world; doing many good works, abstaining from gross evils and attending all the ordinances of God. They endeavoured, in general, to have a conscience void of offence in their behaviour, but did not aim at any particular strictness, being in most things like their neighbours.

The other Christians not only abstained from all appearance of evil, were zealous of good works in every kind and attended all the ordinances of God, but likewise used all diligence to attain the whole mind that was in Christ, and laboured to walk in every point as their beloved Master. In order to [do] this they walked in a constant course of universal self-denial, trampling on every pleasure which they were not divinely conscious prepared them for taking pleasure in God. They took up their cross daily. They strove, they agonized without intermission, to enter in at the strait gate.

This one thing they did, they spared no pains to arrive at the summit of Christian holiness; "leaving the first principles of the doctrine of Christ to go on to perfection," to "know all that love of God which passeth knowledge, and to be filled with all the fulness of God."

6. From long experience and observation I am inclined to think that whoever finds redemption in the blood of Jesus, whoever is justified, has then the choice of walking in the higher or the lower path. I believe the Holy Spirit at that time sets before him the "more excellent way," and incites him to walk therein; to choose the narrowest path in the narrow way; to aspire after the heights and depths of holiness, after the entire image of God. But if he does not accept this offer, he insensibly declines into the lower order of Christians. He still goes on in what may be called a good way, serving God in his degree, and finds mercy in the close of life, through the blood of the covenant.

FOR ALL CHRISTIANS

7. I would be far from quenching the smoking flax, from discouraging those that serve God in a low degree. But I could not wish them to stop here; I would encourage them to come up higher, without thundering hell and damnation in their ears. Without condemning the way wherein they were, telling them it is the way that leads to destruction, I will endeavour to point out to them what is, in every respect, "a more excellent way."

8. Let it be well remembered, I do not affirm that all who do not walk in this way are in the high road to hell. But this much I must affirm, they will not have so high a place in heaven as they would have had if they had chosen the better part. And will this be a small loss, the having so many fewer stars in your crown of glory? Will it be a little thing to have a lower place than you might have had in the kingdom of your Father? Certainly there will be no sorrow in heaven; there all tears will be wiped from our eyes; but if it were possible grief could enter there, we should grieve at that irreparable loss. Irreparable then, but not now. Now, by the grace of God, we may choose the "more excellent way." . . .

VI. 6. Who, then, is a wise man and endued with knowledge among you? Let him resolve this day, this hour, this moment, the Lord assisting him to choose in all the preceding particulars the "more excellent way." And let him steadily keep it both with regard to sleep, prayer, work, food, conversation, and diversions; and particularly with regard to the employment of that important talent, money. Let *your* heart answer to the call of God, "From this moment, God being my helper, I will lay up no more treasure upon earth: this one thing I will do, I will lay up treasure in heaven; I will render unto God the things that are God's: I will give Him all my goods and all my heart!"

On the Wedding Garment
1790 (Abridged)

In the course of this sermon completed by Wesley at Madeley in 1790, he dismisses various opinions set out by other expositors as to what the wedding garment represents. He rejects proper observance of the sacrament of the Lord's Supper as being the wedding garment in the story; he rejects also the opinion that it is the righteousness of Christ. He unhesitatingly declares his confidence in the merit of Christ, but insists upon steering clear of "Antinomian jargon." The wedding garment is defined here as "personal holiness" through the cleansing of the blood of the Lamb.

On the Wedding Garment

How camest thou in hither not having a wedding garment? (Matt. xxii. 12).

1. In the verses preceding the text we read, "After these things, Jesus spake to them again in parables, and said, A certain king made a supper for his son. And when the king came in to see the guests, he saw one who had not on a wedding garment. And he saith unto him, Friend, how camest thou in hither not having a wedding garment? And he was speechless. Then said the king to the servants, Bind him hand and foot, and cast him into outer darkness; there shall be weeping and gnashing of teeth." . . .

8. Is there any expression similar to this of the "wedding garment" to be found in Holy Scripture? In the Revelation we find mention made of linen, white and clean, which is "the righteousness of the saints." And this, too, many vehemently contend, means the righteousness of Christ. But how, then, are we to reconcile this with that passage in the seventh chapter, "They have washed their robes, and made them white in the blood of the Lamb"? Will they say, "The righteousness of Christ was washed and made white in the blood of Christ"? Away with such Antinomian jargon! Is not the plain meaning this: It was from the atoning blood that the very righteousness of the saints derived its value and acceptableness with God?

9. In the nineteenth chapter of the Revelation, at the ninth verse,

there is an expression which comes much nearer to this: "The wedding supper of the Lamb." There is a near resemblance between this and the marriage feast mentioned in the parable. Yet they are not altogether the same: there is a clear difference between them. The supper mentioned in the parable belongs to the Church Militant; that mentioned in the Revelation to the Church Triumphant. The one, to the kingdom of God on earth; the other, to the kingdom of God in heaven. Accordingly, in the former, there may be found those who have not a "wedding garment." But there will be none such to be found in the latter. No, not "in that great multitude which no man can number, out of every kindred, and tongue, and people, and nation." They will all be "kings and priests unto God, and shall reign with him for ever and ever."

10. Does not that expression, "The righteousness of the saints," point out what is the "wedding garment" in the parable? It is the "holiness without which no man shall see the Lord." The righteousness of Christ is doubtless necessary for any soul that enters into glory. But so is personal holiness, too, for every child of man. But it is highly needful to be observed, that they are necessary in different respects. The former is necessary to *entitle* us to heaven; the latter to *qualify* us for it. Without the righteousness of Christ we could have no *claim* to glory; without holiness we could have no *fitness* for it. By the former we become members of Christ, children of God, and heirs of the kingdom of heaven. By the latter, "we are made meet to be partakers of the inheritance of the saints in light."

11. From the very time that the Son of God delivered the weighty truth to the children of men, That all who had not the "wedding garment" would be "cast into outer darkness, where are weeping and gnashing of teeth," the enemy of souls has been labouring to obscure it, that they might still seek death in the error of their life; and many ways has he tried to disguise the holiness without which we cannot be saved. How many things have been palmed, even upon the Christian world, in the place of this! Some of these are utterly contrary thereto, and subversive of it. Some were no ways connected with or related to it, but useless and insignificant trifles. Others might be deemed to be some part of it, but by no means the whole. It may be of use to enumerate some of them, lest ye should be ignorant of Satan's devices. . . .

15. When things of an indifferent nature are represented as necessary to salvation, it is a folly of the same kind, though not the same

magnitude. Indeed, it is not a little sin to represent as necessary to salvation such as going of pilgrimages or anything that is not expressly enjoined in the Holy Scripture. Among these we may undoubtedly rank orthodoxy, or right opinions. We know, indeed, that wrong opinions in religion naturally lead to wrong tempers, or wrong practices; and that, consequently, it is our bounden duty to pray that we may have a right judgment in all things. But still a man may judge as accurately as the devil, and yet be as wicked as he.

16. Something more excusable are they who imagine holiness to consist in things that are only a part of it (that is, when they are connected with the rest; otherwise they are no part of it at all).... And how exceeding common is this! How many take holiness and harmlessness to mean one and the same thing? Whereas were a man as harmless as a post, he might be as far from holiness as heaven from earth....

17. What, then, is that holiness which is the true wedding garment, the only qualification for glory? "In Christ Jesus" (that is, according to the Christian institution, whatever be the case of the heathen world) "neither circumcision availeth any thing, nor uncircumcision; but a new creation," the renewal of the soul "in the image of God wherein it was created." In "Christ Jesus neither circumcision availeth any thing, nor uncircumcision, but faith which worketh by love." It first, through the energy of God, worketh love to God and all mankind; and, by this love, every holy and heavenly temper. In particular, lowliness, meekness, gentleness, temperance, and long suffering. "It is neither circumcision"—the attending on all the Christian ordinances—"nor uncircumcision"—the fulfilling of all heathen morality—but "the keeping the commandments of God"; particularly those, "Thou shalt love the Lord thy God with all thy heart, and thy neighbour as thyself." In a word, holiness is the having "the mind that was in Christ," and the "walking as Christ walked."

CHRISTLIKENESS

18. Such has been my judgment for these threescore years, without any material alteration. Only about fifty years ago I had a clearer view than before of justification by faith; and in this, from that very hour, I never varied, no, not a hair's breadth.... I am now on the borders of the grave; but, by the grace of God, I still witness the same confession. Indeed, some have supposed that when I began to declare, "By grace ye are saved through faith," I retracted what I had before maintained: "Without holiness no man shall see the Lord." But it is an

entire mistake: these scriptures well consist with each other; the meaning of the former being plainly this: By faith we are saved from sin, and made holy. The imagination that faith *supersedes* holiness is the marrow of Antinomianism.

19. The sum of all is this: The God of love is willing to save all the souls that He has made. This He has proclaimed to them in His word, together with the terms of salvation, revealed by the Son of His love, who gave His own life that they that believe in Him might have everlasting life. And for these He has prepared a kingdom, from the foundation of the world. But He will not force them to accept of it; He leaves them in the hands of their own counsel. He saith, "Behold, I set before you life and death, blessing and cursing; choose life, that ye may live." Choose holiness, by My grace; which is the way, the only way to everlasting life. He cries aloud, be holy, and be happy; happy in this world, and happy in the world to come. "Holiness becometh his house for ever!" This is the wedding garment of all that are called to "the marriage of the Lamb." Clothed in this, they will not be found naked: "They have washed their robes and made them white in the blood of the Lamb." But as to all those who appear in the last day without the wedding garment, the Judge will say, "Cast them into outer darkness: there shall be weeping and gnashing of teeth."

FOR ALL CHRISTIANS

3

A PLAIN ACCOUNT OF CHRISTIAN PERFECTION

First Tract on Christian Perfection
Sermon on Christian Perfection (1741)
Holiness in the Hymns
Methodist Conferences
Scriptural Proofs
Teachings of Charles Wesley
Thoughts on Christian Perfection
Helping Seekers After Holiness
Danger of Fanaticism
Plain Questions of a Plain Man
Jane Cooper's Testimony
Further Thoughts on Christian Perfection
Advice for the Entirely Sanctified
Recommended Reflections
Eleven Propositions on Perfection
Summary
An Earnest Appeal to the Children of God

A commemorative tablet in London
honoring the Wesley brothers

3 A Plain Account of Christian Perfection (1765)

The doctrine of Christian perfection was John Wesley's principal doctrinal concern for all of his adult life. The renewal of the divine image in man, the imitation of Christ, holy living and holy dying, these were the obsessions of his soul. His high Anglican upbringing and his youthful years amid churchly connections probably influenced him to place a high value on the life lived in conformity to "the Christian's Pattern."

But he did not hastily reach those conclusions that became the main strands of his teaching on Christian perfection. We learn of his progress from different writings and many references, but there are two documents that most clearly outline and summarize the formulation of the doctrine and experience. These documents were both produced in 1765. There is Wesley's remarkable letter to John Newton in which he writes "the main point between you and me is Perfection" and goes on to ask, "But how came this opinion into my mind?" He then proceeds to summarize his pilgrimage through Jeremy Taylor, Thomas à Kempis, and William Law.[1] There is also *A Plain Account of Christian Perfection,* the first six paragraphs of which amplify the summary given to John Newton.[2]

Outler says: "Wesley asserted that his doctrine of Christian Perfection had been the creative focus of his understanding of the Christian life from his first conversion to 'serious' religion in 1725, and that it had continued as such without substantial alteration."[3]

In 1725 perfection was his quest. His sermon preached in 1733 titled "The Circumcision of the Heart" had this as its principal theme. It was his deepest longing and prayer in 1738. We should not forget the eagerness with which he listened to Arvid Gradin that year. Gradin's witness about the experience of perfect rest of soul in the atoning blood of Jesus Christ powerfully impressed seeker John.

Wesley's preaching and teaching on Christian perfection brought him considerable criticism. Tyerman writes:

---

1. *LJW,* 4:296-300.
2. *WW,* 11:366-446.
3. Outler, *John Wesley,* 251.

He had to enforce and to defend his doctrine of Christian perfection, a doctrine imperfectly understood and bitterly assailed. Hence the publication of a small 12 mo. volume of 162 pages entitled A *Plain Account of Christian Perfection,* as believed and taught by the Rev. Wm. John Wesley, from the year 1725 to the year 1765.[4]

Wesley had given the doctrine continuous and deep meditation. He had not only preached and taught it, but he had also written about it in his journals, sermons, letters, and essays. He continued to do so for 28 years after the publication of A *Plain Account.* Indeed, the little book, appearing first in 1765 called for a second edition in 1766, and six editions were published before the death of its author in 1791.[5]

It is Wesley's *Apologia for Christian Perfection;* the record of his personal quest under holy guides and divine guidance; the truth as Wesley saw it taught in Scripture, and verified and attested to by numerous individuals. Here by the question-and-answer method he turns over every stone he sees or can suppose; he exhausts language to plainly present the grand depositum God had lodged with the people called Methodists.

It is notable that Wesley makes use of his brother Charles' hymns to support and illustrate his theme. He also uses his own translation of German hymns. Here, indeed, poetry becomes the handmaid of piety, and theology becomes both speculative and practical.

Conference after conference during Wesley's lifetime devoted a great deal of attention to the matter of Christian perfection. Wesley also interviewed scores of persons who were witnessing to the experience of love made perfect. He questioned them closely as one responsible for protecting them from self-deception, fanaticism, and mysticism.

It is true there were some minor differences between the three early writers on the theme—John Wesley, Charles Wesley, and John Fletcher. But the differences were minor in the light of the great ultimate fact of complete cleansing from all sin and renewal in the moral image of God.

---

4. Luke Tyerman, *The Life and Times of the Rev. John Wesley,* M.A. (New York: Harper and Bros., 1872), 2:593.

5. An editor's footnote at the bottom of the opening page of the "tract" reads in part as follows: "This tract underwent several revisions and enlargements during his life-time. . . . The last revision appears to have been made in the year 1777, and since that period, this date has been generally continued on the title-page of the several editions of the pamphlet."

John and Charles discuss whether the work is instantaneous, as John believed and taught; or whether it is sometimes gradual but completed in this life, as Charles inclined to believe.

Both John Wesley and John Fletcher gave attention to the possibility of the cleansing of the heart in the experience of death, but it was firmly rejected. Love made perfect in a "second blessing properly so-called" was the grand forte and distinctive message of the people called Methodists.

Within *A Plain Account* Wesley included portions of another tract, *The Character of a Methodist,* which is descriptive of the ideal Christian walk. This ideal, as R. Newton Flew so aptly put it, is "possible in grace."

The text selected for this reprinting of *A Plain Account* is that authorized by the Wesleyan Conference Office, London, 1892, under the title below.

We here present a slightly condensed version, but the arrangement and the material are Wesley's own. Headings have been inserted to help guide the reader through the text. As elsewhere in this volume, cut-in heads identify doctrinal concepts widely heard in holiness teaching of the 20th century.

Wesley's system of numbering his paragraphs has been retained. Omitted numbers and ellipses will alert the reader to abridgement. Those interested in determining what was omitted may consult *The Works of John Wesley,* Vol. XI, 366-446.

A Plain Account of Christian Perfection

*As Believed and Taught
by the Reverend Mr. John Wesley
from the Year 1725 to the Year 1777*

Roots of Faith and Doctrine

1. What I purpose in the following papers is to give a plain and distinct account of the steps by which I was led during a course of many years to embrace the doctrine of Christian perfection. This I owe to the serious part of mankind, those who desire to know all "the truth as it is in Jesus." And these only are concerned in questions of this kind. To these I would nakedly declare the thing as it is, endeavouring all along to show, from one period to another, both what I thought and why I thought so.

2. In the year 1725, being in the twenty-third year of my age, I met with Bishop Taylor's *Rule and Exercises of Holy Living and Dying.* In reading several parts of this book, I was exceedingly affected; that part in particular which relates to purity of intention. Instantly I resolved to dedicate all my life to God, all my thoughts, my words, and actions; being thoroughly convinced there was no medium; but that every part of my life (not some only) must either be a sacrifice to God, or myself, that is, in effect, to the devil.

Can any serious person doubt of this, or find a medium between serving God and serving the devil?

3. In the year 1726, I met with Kempis's *Christian's Pattern.* The nature and extent of inward religion, the religion of the heart, now appeared to me in a stronger light than ever it had done before. I saw that giving even all my life to God (supposing it possible to do this and go no farther) would profit me nothing unless I gave my heart, yea, all my heart to Him.

I saw that "simplicity of intention, and purity of affection," one design in all we speak or do, and one desire ruling all our tempers, are indeed "the wings of the soul," without which she can never ascend to the mount of God.

4. A year or two after, Mr. Law's *Christian Perfection* and *Serious Call* were put into my hands. These convinced me more than ever of the absolute impossibility of being half a Christian; and I determined, through His grace (the absolute necessity of which I was deeply sensible of), to be all devoted to God, to give Him all my soul, my body, and my substance.

Will any considerate man say that this is carrying matters too far? or that anything less is due to Him who has given himself for us than to give Him ourselves, all we have, and all we are?

5. In the year 1729 I began not only to read, but to study the Bible as the one, the only standard of truth and the only model of pure religion. Hence I saw in a clearer and clearer light the indispensable necessity of having "the mind which was in Christ," and of "walking as Christ also walked"; even of having not some part only, but all the mind which was in Him; and of walking as He walked, not only in many or in most respects, but in all things. And this was the light wherein at this time I generally considered religion as a uniform following of Christ, an entire inward and outward conformity to our Master. Nor was I afraid of anything more than of bending this rule to

the experience of myself or of other men; of allowing myself in any the least disconformity to our grand Examplar.

6. On January 1, 1733, I preached before the university in St. Mary's Church on "The Circumcision of the Heart"; an account of which I gave in these words: "It is that habitual disposition of soul which in the sacred writings is termed holiness; and which directly implies the being cleansed from sin, 'from all filthiness both of flesh and spirit'; and, by consequence, the being endued with those virtues which were in Christ Jesus; the being so 'renewed in the image of our mind,' as to be 'perfect as our Father in heaven is perfect.'" . . .

It may be observed, this sermon was composed the first of all my writings which have been published. This was the view of religion I then had, which even then I scrupled not to term *perfection*. This is the view I have of it now, without any material addition or diminution. And what is there here which any man of understanding who believes in the Bible can object to? What can he deny without flatly contradicting the Scripture? What retrench, without taking from the Word of God?

7. In the same sentiment did my brother and I remain (with all those young gentlemen in derision termed *Methodists*) till we embarked for America in the latter end of 1735. It was the next year while I was at Savannah that I wrote the following lines:

> *Is there a thing beneath the sun,*
>   *That strives with Thee my heart to share?*
> *Ah! tear it thence, and reign alone,*
>   *The Lord of every motion there!*

In the beginning of the year 1738, as I was returning from thence, the cry of my heart was,

> *O grant that nothing in my soul*
>   *May dwell, but Thy pure love alone!*
> *O may Thy love possess me whole,*
>   *My joy, my treasure, and my crown.*
> *Strange fires far from my heart remove—*
>   *My every act, word, thought, be love!*

I never heard that anyone objected to this. And, indeed, who can object? Is not this the language, not only of every believer but of everyone that is truly awakened? But what have I written to this day which is either stronger or plainer?

8. In August following, I had a long conversation with Arvid Gradin in Germany. After he had given me an account of his experience, I desired him to give me in writing a definition of "the full assurance of faith," which he did in the following words:

> Repose in the blood of Christ; a firm confidence in God, and persuasion of His favour; the highest tranquillity, serenity, and peace of mind, with a deliverance from every fleshly desire, and a cessation of all, even inward sins.

This was the first account I ever heard from any living man of what I had before learned myself from the oracles of God, and had been praying for (with the little company of my friends) and expecting for several years.

9. In 1739 my brother and I published a volume of *Hymns and Sacred Poems*. In many of these we declared our sentiments strongly and explicitly. So, page 24,

> Turn the full stream of nature's tide;
> Let all our actions tend
> To Thee, their source; Thy love the guide,
> Thy glory be the end.
>
> Earth then a scale to heaven shall be;
> Sense shall point out the road;
> The creatures all shall lead to Thee,
> And all we taste be God.

Again,

> Lord, arm me with Thy Spirit's might,
> Since I am call'd by Thy great name
> In Thee my wand'ring thoughts unite,
> Of all my works be Thou the aim;
> Thy love attend me all my days,
> And my sole business be Thy praise. (p. 122)

Again,

> Eager for Thee I ask and pant,
> So strong the principle Divine,
> Carries me out with sweet constraint,
> Till all my hallow'd soul be Thine;
> Plunged in the Godhead's deepest sea,
> And lost in Thine immensity! (p. 125)

Once more,

> *Heavenly Adam, life Divine,*
> *Change my nature into Thine;*
> *Move and spread throughout my soul,*
> *Actuate and fill the whole.* (p. 153) . . .

First Tract on Christian Perfection

The Character of a Methodist

10. The first tract I ever wrote expressly on this subject was published in the latter end of this year. That none might be prejudiced before they read it, I gave it the indifferent title of "The Character of a Methodist." In this I described a perfect Christian, placing in the front, "Not as though I had already attained." Part of it I subjoin without any alteration:[6]

"A Methodist is one who loves the Lord his God with all his heart, with all his soul, with all his mind, and with all his strength. God is the joy of his heart and the desire of his soul, which is continually crying, 'Whom have I in heaven but Thee? and there is none upon earth whom I desire besides Thee.' My God and my all! 'Thou art the strength of my heart, and my portion forever.' He is therefore happy in God; yea, always happy, as having in him a well of water springing up into everlasting life, and overflowing his soul with peace and joy. Perfect love having now cast out fear, he rejoices evermore. Yea, his joy is full and all his bones cry out, 'Blessed be the God and Father of our Lord Jesus Christ, who, according to his abundant mercy, hath begotten me again unto a living hope of an inheritance incorruptible and undefiled, reserved in heaven for me.'

"And he who hath this hope, thus full of immortality, in everything giveth thanks, as knowing this (whatsoever it is) is the will of God in Christ Jesus concerning him. From Him, therefore, he cheerfully receives all, saying, 'Good is the will of the Lord'; and whether He giveth or taketh away, equally blessing the name of the Lord. Whether in ease or pain, whether in sickness or health, whether in life or death, he giveth thanks from the ground of the heart to Him who orders it for good; into whose hands he hath wholly committed his body and soul, 'as into the hands of a faithful Creator.' He is, therefore, anx-

---

6. For the entire tract, see *WW*, 8:339-47.

iously 'careful for nothing,' as having 'cast all his care on him that careth for him'; and 'in all things' resting on Him, after 'making' his 'request known to him with thanksgiving.'

"For, indeed, he 'prays without ceasing'; at all times the language of his heart is this, 'Unto Thee is my mouth, though without a voice; and my silence speaketh unto Thee.' His heart is lifted up to God at all times, and in all places. In this he is never hindered, much less interrupted, by any person or thing. In retirement or company, in leisure, business, or conversation, his heart is ever with the Lord. Whether he lie down or rise up, 'God is in all his thoughts'; he walks with God continually, having the loving eye of his soul fixed on Him, and everywhere 'seeing him that is invisible.'

"And loving God, he 'loves his neighbours as himself'; he loves every man as his own soul. He loves his enemies, yea, and the enemies of God. And if it be not in his power to 'do good to them that hate' him, yet he ceases not to 'pray for them,' though they spurn his love, and still 'despitefully use him, and persecute him.'

"For he is 'pure in heart.' Love has purified his heart from envy, malice, wrath, and every unkind temper. It has cleansed him from pride, whereof 'only cometh contention'; and he hath now 'put on bowels of mercies, kindness, humbleness of mind, meekness, longsuffering.' And, indeed, all possible ground for contention, on his part, is cut off. For none can take from him what he desires, seeing he 'loves not the world, nor any of the things of the world'; but 'all his desire is unto God and to the remembrance of his name.'

"Agreeable to this his one desire is the one design of his life; namely, 'to do not his own will but the will of him that sent him.' His one intention at all times and in all places is not to please himself but Him whom his soul loveth. He hath a single eye; and because his 'eye is single, his whole body is full of light. The whole is light, as when the bright shining of a candle doth enlighten the house.' God reigns alone; all that is in the soul is 'holiness to the Lord.' There is not a motion in his heart but is according to His will. Every thought that arises points to Him and is in 'obedience to the law of Christ.'

"And the tree is known by its fruits. For, as he loves God, so he 'keeps his commandments'; not only some, or most of them, but all, from the least to the greatest. He is not content to 'keep the whole law and offend in one point,' but has in all points 'a conscience void of offense toward God and toward man.' Whatever God has forbidden, he avoids; whatever God has enjoined, he does. 'He runs the way of God's commandments,' now He hath set his heart at liberty. It is his glory and joy so to do; it is his daily crown of rejoicing to 'do all the will of God on earth as it is done in heaven.'

"All the commandments of God he accordingly keeps, and that with all his might; for his obedience is in proportion to his love, the source from whence it flows. And, therefore, loving God with all his heart, he serves Him with all his strength; he continually presents his soul and 'body a living sacrifice, holy, acceptable to God'; entirely and without reserve devoting himself, all he has, all he is, to His glory. All the talents he has, he constantly employs according to his Master's will; every power and faculty of his soul, every member of his body.

"By consequence, 'whatsoever he doeth, it is all to the glory of God.' In all his employments of every kind, he not only aims at this, which is implied in having a single eye, but actually attains it; his business and his refreshments, as well as his prayers, all serve to this great end. Whether he 'sit in the house, or walk by the way,' whether he lie down or rise up, he is promoting, in all he speaks or does, the one business of his life. Whether he put on his apparel, or labour, or eat and drink, or divert himself from too wasting labour, it all tends to advance the glory of God, by peace and good will among men. His one invariable rule is this: 'Whatsoever ye do, in word or deed, do it all in the name of the Lord Jesus, giving thanks to God, even the Father through him.'

"Nor do the customs of the world at all hinder his 'running the race which is set before him.' He cannot, therefore, 'lay up treasures upon earth,' no more than he can take fire into his bosom. He cannot speak evil of his neighbour, any more than he can lie either for God or man. He cannot utter an unkind word of anyone; for love keeps the door of his lips. He cannot 'speak idle words; no corrupt conversation' ever 'comes out of his mouth'; as is all that is not 'good to the use of edifying,' not fit to 'minister grace to the hearers.' But 'whatsoever things are pure, whatsoever things are lovely, whatsoever things are' justly 'of good report,' he thinks, speaks, and acts, 'adorning the doctrine of God our Saviour in all things.'"

These are the very words wherein I largely declared, for the first time, my sentiments of Christian perfection. . . . And it is the same which, by the grace of God, I have continued to teach from that time till now. . . .

Sermon on Christian Perfection (1741)

12. I think it was in the latter end of the year 1740 that I had a conversation with Dr. Gibson, then bishop of London, at Whitehall. He asked me what I meant by perfection. I told him without any disguise or reserve. When I ceased speaking he said, "Mr. Wesley, if this be all you mean, publish it to all the world. If anyone then can confute what you say, he may have free leave." I answered, "My lord, I will"; and accordingly wrote and published the sermon on Christian perfection.[7]

In this I endeavoured to show, (1) In what sense Christians are not, (2) In what sense they are, perfect.

"(1) In what sense they are not. They are not perfect in knowledge. They are not free from ignorance, no, nor from mistake. We are no more to expect any living man to be infallible, than to be omniscient. They are not free from infirmities, such as weakness or slowness of understanding, irregular quickness or heaviness of imagination. Such in another kind are impropriety of language, ungracefulness of pronunciation; to which one might add a thousand nameless defects, either in conversation or behavior. From such infirmities as these none are perfectly freed till their spirits return to God; neither can we expect till then to be wholly freed from temptation; for 'the servant is not above his master.' But neither in this sense is there any absolute perfection on earth. There is no perfection of degrees, none which does not admit of a continual increase.

"(2) In what sense then are they perfect? Observe, we are not now speaking of babes in Christ but adult Christians. But even babes in Christ are so far perfect as not to commit sin. This St. John affirms expressly; and it cannot be disproved by the examples of the Old Testament. . . .

"The privileges of Christians are in no wise to be measured by what the Old Testament records concerning those who were under the Jewish dispensation; seeing the fulness of time is now come, the Holy Ghost is now given, the great salvation of God is now brought to men by the revelation of Jesus Christ. The kingdom of heaven is now set up on earth, concerning which the Spirit of God declared of old time (so far is David from being the pattern or standard of Christian

---

7. Only excerpts of this sermon are used by Wesley in *Plain Account*. In a later sermon on the same subject, the views of the mature Wesley appear in "On Perfection" (1788), which is reproduced in its entirety in this volume (see previous chapter).

perfection), 'He that is feeble among them, at that day, shall be as David, and the house of David shall be as the angel of the Lord before them' (Zech. xii. 8).

"But the Apostles themselves committed sin; Peter by dissembling, Paul by his sharp contention with Barnabas. Suppose they did, will you argue thus: 'If two of the Apostles once committed sin, then all other Christians in all ages do and must commit sin as long as they live?' Nay, God forbid we should thus speak. No necessity of sin was laid upon them; the grace of God was surely sufficient for them. And it is sufficient for us at this day.

"But St. James says, 'In many things we offend all.' True: but who are the persons here spoken of? Why, those many masters or teachers whom God had not sent; not the Apostle himself, nor any real Christian. That in the word *we,* used by a figure of speech, common in all other as well as the inspired writings, the Apostle could not possibly include himself, or any other true believer, appears, first, from the ninth verse, 'Therewith bless we God, and therewith curse we men.' Surely not we Apostles! not we believers! Secondly, from the words preceding the text: 'My brethren, be not many masters,' or teachers, 'knowing that we shall receive the great condemnation. For in many things we offend all.' *We!* Who? Not the Apostles nor true believers, but they who were to 'receive the greater condemnation,' because of those many offenses. Nay, thirdly, the verse itself proves that 'we offend all,' cannot be spoken either of all men or all Christians. For in it immediately follows the mention of a man who 'offends not,' as the *we* first mentioned did; from whom therefore he is professedly contradistinguished, and pronounced a 'perfect man.'

"But St. John himself says, 'If we say we have no sin, we deceive ourselves'; and, 'If we say we have not sinned, we make him a liar and his word is not in us.'

"I answer, (1) The tenth verse fixes the sense of the eighth: 'If we say we have no sin,' in the former, being explained by, 'If we say we have not sinned,' in the latter verse. (2) The point under consideration is not whether we have or have not sinned, heretofore; and neither of these verses asserts that we do sin or commit sin now. (3) The ninth verse explains both the eighth and tenth: 'If we confess our sins, he is faithful and just to forgive us our sins, and to cleanse us from all unrighteousness.' As if He had said, 'I have before affirmed, The blood of Christ cleanseth from all sin.' And no man can say, 'I need it not; I have no sin to be cleansed from.' 'If we say, we have no sin,' that 'we have not sinned, we deceive ourselves,' and make God a liar: but, 'if we confess our sins, he is faithful and just,' not only 'to forgive us our sins,' but also 'to cleanse us from all unrighteousness,' that we may 'go and sin no more.' In conformity, therefore, both to the doctrine of St. John and the whole tenor of the New Testament, we fix this conclusion: A Christian is so far perfect, as not to commit sin.

"This is the glorious privilege of every Christian, yea, though he be but a babe in Christ. But it is only of grown Christians it can be affirmed, they are in such a sense perfect, as, secondly, to be freed from evil thoughts and evil tempers. First from evil or sinful thoughts. Indeed, whence should they spring? 'Out of the heart of man,' if at all, 'proceed evil thoughts.' If, therefore, the heart be no longer evil, then evil thoughts no longer proceed out of it: for 'a good tree cannot bring forth evil fruit.'

"And as they are freed from evil thoughts, so likewise from evil tempers. Every one of these can say, with St. Paul, 'I am crucified with Christ; nevertheless I live; yet not I, but Christ liveth in me'; words that manifestly describe a deliverance from inward as well as from outward sin. This is expressed both negatively, 'I live not,' my evil nature, the body of sin is destroyed; and positively, 'Christ liveth in me,' and, therefore, all that is holy, and just, and good. Indeed, both these, 'Christ liveth in me,' and 'I live not,' are inseparably connected. For what communion hath light with darkness, or Christ with Belial?

"He therefore, who liveth in these Christians hath 'purified their hearts by faith'; insomuch that everyone that has Christ in him, 'the hope of glory, purifieth himself even as he is pure.' He is purified from pride, for Christ was lowly in heart; he is pure from desire and self-will, for Christ desired only to do the will of the Father; and he is pure from anger, in the common sense of the word, for Christ was meek and gentle. I say, *in the common sense of the word;* for He is angry at sin, while He is grieved for the sinner. He feels a displacency at every offense against God, but only tender compassion to the offender.

CHRISTLIKENESS

"Thus doth Jesus save His people from their sins; not only from outward sins, but from the sins of their hearts. 'True,' say some, 'but not till death, not in this world.' Nay, St. John says, 'Herein is our love made perfect, that we may have boldness in the day of judgment; because as He is so are we in this world.' The Apostle here, beyond all contradiction, speaks of himself and other living Christians, of whom he flatly affirms that not only at or after death, but 'in this world' they are 'as their Master.'

"Exactly agreeable to this are his words in the first chapter: 'God is light, and in him is no darkness at all. If we walk in the light, as he is in the light, we have fellowship one with another, and the blood of Jesus Christ his Son cleanseth us from all sin.' And again: 'If we confess our sins, he is faithful and just to forgive us our sins, and to cleanse us from all unrighteousness.' Now it is evident the Apostle here speaks of a deliverance wrought in this world: for he saith not, The blood of Christ *will* cleanse (at the hour of death, or in the day of judgment), but it 'cleanseth,' at the time present, us living Christians 'from all sin.' And it is equally evident that if *any* sin remain, we are not cleansed from all sin. If *any* unrighteousness remain in the soul, it is not cleansed from all unrighteousness. Neither let any say that this relates to justification only, or the cleansing us from the guilt of sin: first, because this is confounding together what the Apostle clearly distinguishes, who mentions, first, 'to forgive us our sins,' and then 'to cleanse us from all unrighteousness." Secondly, because this is asserting justification by works in the strongest sense possible; it is making all inward as well as all outward holiness necessarily previous to justification. For if the cleansing here spoken of is no other than the cleansing us from the guilt of sin, then we are not cleansed from guilt, that is, not justified, unless on condition of walking 'in the light, as he is in the light.' It remains, then, that Christians are saved in this world from all sin, from all unrighteousness; that they are now in such a sense perfect, as not to commit sin, and to be free from evil thoughts and evil tempers." . . .

Holiness in the Hymns

13. Not long after, I think in the spring, 1741, we published a second volume of hymns. As the doctrine was still much misunderstood and consequently misrepresented, I judged it needful to explain yet farther upon the head (Christian Perfection). . . .

Here I cannot but remark (1) That this [the preface to the second volume of hymns] is the strongest account we ever gave of Christian perfection, indeed, too strong in more than one particular as is observed in the notes annexed. (2) That there is nothing which we have since advanced upon the subject, either in verse or prose, which is not either directly or indirectly contained in this preface. So that whether our present doctrine be right or wrong, it is, however, the same which we taught from the beginning.

14. I need not give additional proofs of this, by multiplying quotations from the volume itself. It may suffice to cite part of one hymn only, the last in that volume:

> *Lord, I believe a rest remains,*
>   *To all Thy people known;*
> *A rest where pure enjoyment reigns,*
>   *And Thou art loved alone;*
>
> *A rest where all our soul's desire*
>   *Is fixed on things above;*
> *Where doubt and pain and fear expire,*
>   *Cast out by perfect love.*
>
> *From every evil motion freed,*
>   *(The Son hath made us free,)*
> *On all the powers of hell we tread,*
>   *In glorious liberty.*
>
> *Safe in the way of life, above*
>   *Death, earth, and hell we rise;*
> *We find, when perfected in love,*
>   *Our long-sought paradise.*
>
> *Oh, that I now the rest might know,*
>   *Believe and enter in!*
> *Now, Saviour, now the power bestow,*
>   *And let me cease from sin!*
>
> *Remove this hardness from my heart,*
>   *This unbelief remove;*
> *To me the rest of faith impart,*
>   *The sabbath of Thy love.*
>
> *Come, O my Saviour, come away!*
>   *Into my soul descend!*
> *No longer from Thy creature stay,*
>   *My author and my end.*

> *The bliss Thou hast for me prepared,*
> *No longer be delayed:*
> *Come, my exceeding great reward,*
> *For whom I first was made.*
>
> *Come Father, Son, and Holy Ghost,*
> *And seal me Thine abode!*
> *Let all I am in Thee be lost;*
> *Let all be lost in God!*

Can anything be more clear than, (1) That here, also, is as full and high a salvation as we have ever spoken of? (2) That this is spoken of as receivable by mere faith and as hindered only by unbelief? (3) That this faith, and consequently the salvation which it brings, is spoken of as given in an instant? (4) That it is supposed that instant may be now? that we need not stay another moment? that "now," the very "now is the accepted time? now is the day of" this full "salvation"? And, lastly, that if any speak otherwise, he is the person that brings new doctrine among us?

15. About a year after, namely, in the year 1742, we published another volume of hymns. The dispute being now at the height, we spoke upon the head more largely than ever before. Accordingly, abundance of the hymns in this volume treat expressly on this subject. And so does the preface, which, as it is short, it may not be amiss to insert entire:

"(1) Perhaps the general prejudice against Christian perfection may chiefly arise from a misapprehension of the nature of it. . . .

"(2) First. We not only allow, but earnestly contend that there is no perfection in this life which implies any dispensation from attending all the ordinances of God, or from doing good unto all men while we have time, though 'especially unto the household of faith.' We believe that not only the babes in Christ who have newly found redemption in His blood, but those also who are 'grown up into perfect men,' are indispensably obliged, as often as they have opportunity, 'to eat bread and drink wine in remembrance of him,' and to 'search the Scriptures'; by fasting, as well as temperance, to 'keep their bodies under, and bring them into subjection'; and, above all, to pour out their souls in prayer, both secretly and in the great congregation.

"(3) We secondly believe that there is no such perfection in this life as implies an entire deliverance, either from ignorance or mistake

HUMANITY in things not essential to salvation, or from manifold temptations, or from numberless infirmities, wherewith the corruptible body more or less presses down the soul. We cannot find any ground in Scripture to suppose that any inhabitant of a house of clay is wholly exempt either from bodily infirmities or from ignorance of many things; or to imagine any is incapable of mistake or falling into divers temptations.

"(4) But whom, then, do you mean by 'one that is perfect'? We mean one in whom is 'the mind which was in Christ,' and who so 'walketh as Christ walked'; a man 'that hath clean hands and a pure heart,' or that is 'cleansed from all filthiness of flesh and spirit'; one in whom is 'no occasion of stumbling,' and who, accordingly, 'does not commit sin.' To declare this a little more particularly: we understand by that scriptural expression, 'a perfect man,' one in whom God hath fulfilled His faithful word, 'From all your filthiness and from all your idols I will cleanse you: I will also save you from all your uncleannesses.' We understand, hereby, one whom God hath 'sanctified throughout in body, soul, and spirit'; one who 'walketh in the light as he is in the light, in whom is no darkness at all; the blood of Jesus Christ his Son having cleansed him from all sin.'

"(5) This man can now testify to all mankind, 'I am crucified with Christ: nevertheless I live; yet not I, but Christ liveth in me.' He is 'holy as God who called' him 'is holy,' both in heart and 'in all manner of conversation.' He 'loveth the Lord his God with all his heart' and serveth him 'with all his strength.' He 'loveth his neighbour,' every man, 'as himself'; yea, 'as Christ loveth us'; them, in particular, that 'despitefully use him and persecute him, because they know not the Son, neither the Father.' Indeed, his soul is all love, filled with 'bowels of mercies, kindness, meekness, gentleness, long-suffering.' And his life agreeth thereto, full of 'the work of faith, the patience of hope, the labour of love.' 'And whatsoever' he 'doeth either in word or deed,' he 'doeth it all in the name,' in the love and power, 'of the Lord Jesus.' In a word, he doeth 'the will of God on earth as it is done in heaven.'

"(6) This it is to be a perfect man, to be 'sanctified throughout'; even 'to have a heart so all-flaming with the love of God' (to use Archbishop Usher's words), 'as continually to offer up every thought, word, and work, as a spiritual sacrifice, acceptable to God through Christ.' In every thought of our hearts, in every word of our tongues, in every work of our hands, to 'show forth his praise, who hath called us out of darkness into his marvellous light.' O that both we, and all who seek the Lord Jesus in sincerity may thus 'be made perfect in one!' " . . .

16. The hymns concerning it in this volume are too numerous to transcribe. I shall only cite a part of three:

> Saviour from sin, I wait to prove
>   That Jesus is Thy healing name;
> To lose when perfected in love,
>   Whate'er I have, or can, or am;
> I stay me on Thy faithful word,
> "The servant shall be as his Lord."
>
> Answer that gracious end in me
>   For which Thy precious life was given;
> Redeem from all iniquity,
>   Restore, and make me meet for heaven.
> Unless Thou purge my every stain,
> Thy suffering and my faith is vain.
>
> Didst Thou not die, that I might live,
>   No longer to myself but Thee?
> Might body, soul, and spirit give
>   To Him who gave himself for me?
> Come then, my Master and my God,
> Take the dear purchase of Thy blood.
>
> Thy own peculiar servant claim,
>   For Thy own truth and mercy's sake;
> Hallow in me Thy glorious name;
>   Me for Thine own this moment take;
> And change and throughly purify;
> Thine only may I live and die. (p. 80)
>
>
> Chose from the world, if now I stand,
>   Adorn'd with righteousness divine;
> If, brought into the promised land,
>   I justly call the Saviour mine;
>
> The sanctifying Spirit pour,
>   To quench my thirst and wash me clean,

Now, Saviour, let the gracious shower
   Descend, and make me pure from sin.

Purge me from every sinful blot:
   My idols all be cast aside:
Cleanse me from every evil thought,
   From all the filth of self and pride.

The hatred of the carnal mind
   Out of my flesh at once remove:
Give me a tender heart, resign'd,
   And pure, and full of faith and love.

Oh that I now, from sin releas'd,
   Thy word might to the utmost prove,
Enter into Thy promised rest;
   The Canaan of Thy perfect love!

Now let me gain perfection's height!
   Now let me into nothing fall;
Be less than nothing in my sight,
   And feel that Christ is all in all. (p. 258)

Lord, I believe, Thy work of grace
   Is perfect in the soul:
His heart is pure who sees Thy face,
   His spirit is made whole.

From every sickness, by Thy word,
   From every foul disease,
Saved, and to perfect health restored,
   To perfect holiness:

He walks in glorious liberty,
   To sin entirely dead:
The Truth, the Son hath made him free,
   And he is free indeed.

Throughout his soul Thy glories shine,
   His soul is all renew'd,

> And deck'd in righteousness divine,
> And clothed and fill'd with God.
>
> This is the rest, the life, the peace,
> Which all Thy people prove;
> Love is the bond of perfectness,
> And all their soul is love.
>
> O joyful sound of gospel grace!
> Christ shall in me appear;
> I, even I, shall see His face,
> I shall be holy here!
>
> He visits now the house of clay,
> He shapes his future home;
> O wouldst Thou, Lord, on this glad day,
> Into Thy temple come!
>
> Come, O my God, Thyself reveal,
> Fill all this mighty void;
> Thou only canst my spirit fill:
> Come, O my God, my God!
>
> Fulfil, fulfil my large desires,
> Large as infinity!
> Give, give me all my soul requires,
> All, all that is in Thee! (p. 208)

Methodist Conferences

17. On Monday, June 25, 1744, our first conference began; six clergymen and all our preachers being present. The next morning we seriously considered the doctrine of sanctification, or perfection. The questions asked concerning it, and the substances of the answers given were as follows:

"What is it to be sanctified?"

"To be renewed in the image of God, 'in righteousness and true holiness.'"

"What is implied in being a perfect Christian?"

"The loving God with all our heart, and mind, and soul (Deut. vi. 5).

"*Does this imply that all inward sin is taken away?*

"Undoubtedly; or how can we be said to be 'saved from all our uncleannesses'? (Ezek. xxxvi. 29)."

Our second conference began August 1, 1745. The next morning we spoke of sanctification as follows:

"*When does inward sanctification begin?*

"In the moment a man is justified. (Yet sin remains in him, yea, the seed of all sin, till he is sanctified throughout.) From that time a believer gradually dies to sin and grows in grace.

"*Is this ordinarily given till a little before death?*

"It is not, to those who expect it no sooner.

"*But may we expect it sooner?*

"Why not? For, although we grant, (1) that the generality of be-

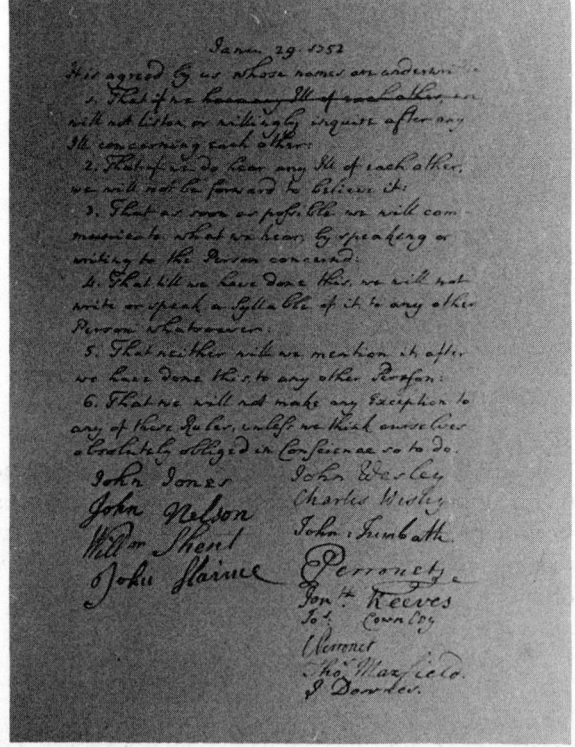

The covenant made among early Methodist preachers

lievers, whom we have hitherto known, were not so sanctified till near death; (2) that few of those to whom St. Paul wrote his Epistles were so at that time; nor, (3) he himself at the time of writing his former Epistles; yet all this does not prove that we may not be so today.

"*In what manner should we preach sanctification?*

PREACHING "Scarce at all to those who are not pressing forward; to those who are, always by way of promise: always drawing rather than driving." . . .

Our fourth conference began on Tuesday, June the 16th, 1747. As several persons were present, who did not believe the doctrine of perfection, we agreed to examine it from the foundation.

In order to do this, it was asked,

"*How much is allowed by our brethren who differ from us with regard to entire sanctification?*

"They grant, (1) That every one must be entirely sanctified in the article of death. (2) That till then, a believer daily grows in grace, comes nearer and nearer to perfection. (3) That we ought to be continually pressing after it, and to exhort all others so to do.

"*What do we allow them?*

"We grant, (1) That many of those who have died in the faith, yea, the greater part of those we have known, were not perfected in love till a little before their death. (2) That the term *sanctified* is continually applied by St. Paul to all that were justified. (3) That by this term alone, he rarely, if ever, means, 'saved from all sin.' (4) That, consequently, it is not proper to use it in that sense without adding the word *wholly, entirely,* or the like. (5) That the inspired writers almost continually speak of, or to, those who were justified, but very rarely of, or to, those who were wholly sanctified.* (6) That, consequently, it behooves us to speak almost continually of the state of justification; but more rarely,** at least in full and explicit terms, concerning entire sanctification.

"*What, then, is the point where we divide?*

"It is this: should we expect to be saved from all sin before the article of death?"

Wesley's Own Footnotes:
  *That is, unto those alone, exclusive of others; but they speak to them, jointly with others, almost continually.
  **More rarely, I allow; but yet in some places very frequently, strongly, and explicitly.

Scriptural Proofs

"*Is there any clear Scripture promise of this, that God will save us from all sin?*

"There is: 'He shall redeem Israel from all his sins' (Ps. cxxx. 8).

SCRIPTURAL

"This is more largely expressed in the prophecy of Ezekiel: 'Then will I sprinkle clean water upon you, and ye shall be clean; from all your filthiness, and from all your idols, will I cleanse you; I will also save you from all your uncleannesses' (xxxvi. 25, 29). No promise can be more clear. And to this the Apostle plainly refers in that exhortation: 'Having these promises, let us cleanse ourselves from all filthiness of flesh and spirit, perfecting holiness in the fear of God' (2 Cor. vii. 1). Equally clear and express is that ancient promise: "The Lord thy God will circumcise thy heart, and the heart of thy seed, to love the Lord thy God with all thy heart and with all thy soul' (Deut. xxx. 6).

"*But does any assertion answerable to this occur in the New Testament?*

"There does, and that laid down in the plainest terms. So 1 John iii. 8: 'For this purpose the Son of God was manifested, that he might destroy the works of the devil'; the works of the devil, without any limitation or restriction; but all sin is the work of the devil. Parallel to which is the assertion of St. Paul: 'Christ loved the Church, and gave himself for it, that he might present it to himself, a glorious Church, not having spot or wrinkle, or any such thing, but that it might be holy and without blemish' (Eph. v. 25-27).

"And to the same effect is his assertion in the eighth of the Romans, verses 3-4: 'God sent his Son, that the righteousness of the law might be fulfilled in us, who walk not after the flesh, but after the Spirit.'

"*Does the New Testament afford any farther ground for expecting to be saved from all sin?*

"Undoubtedly it does; both in those prayers and commands, which are equivalent to the strongest assertions.

"*What prayers do you mean?*

"Prayers for entire sanctification; which, were there no such thing, would be mere mockery of God. Such in particular are, (1) 'Deliver us from evil.' Now, when this is done, when we are delivered from all evil, there can be no sin remaining. (2) 'Neither pray I for these alone, but for them also who shall believe on me through their word; that they all may be one; as thou, Father, art in me, and I in thee, that they also may be one in us; I in them, and thou in me, that they may be made perfect in one' (John xvii. 20-23). (3) 'I bow my knees unto the God and Father of our Lord Jesus Christ, that he would grant you, that ye, being rooted and grounded in love, may be able to comprehend, with all saints, what is the breadth, and length, and depth, and height, and to know the love of Christ, which passeth knowledge; that ye may be filled with all the fulness of God' (Eph. iii. 14, etc.). (4) 'The very God of peace sanctify you wholly. And I pray God, your whole spirit, soul, and body, may be preserved blameless unto the coming of our Lord Jesus Christ' (1 Thess. v. 23).

"*What command is there to the same effect?*

"(1) 'Be ye perfect, as your Father who is in heaven, is perfect' (Matt. v. 48). (2) 'Thou shalt love the Lord thy God with all thy heart, and with all thy soul, and with all thy mind' (Matt. xxii. 37). But if the love of God fill all the heart, there can be no sin therein.

"*But how does it appear that this is to be done before the article of death?*

"(1) From the very nature of a command which is not given to the dead but to the living. Therefore, 'Thou shalt love God with all thy heart,' cannot mean 'Thou shalt do this when thou diest,' but, while thou livest.

"(2) From express texts of Scripture: (i) 'The grace of God, that bringeth salvation, hath appeared to all men; teaching us that, having renounced ungodliness and worldly lusts, we should live soberly, righteously, and godly, in this present world; looking for the glorious appearing of our Lord Jesus Christ, who gave himself for us, that he might redeem us from all iniquity, and purify unto himself a peculiar people, zealous of good works' (Titus ii. 11-14). (ii) 'He hath raised up a horn of salvation for us, to perform the mercy promised to our fathers; the oath which he sware to our father Abraham, that he would grant unto us, that we, being delivered out of the hands of our enemies, should serve him without fear, in holiness and righteousness before him, all the days of our life' (Luke i. 69, etc.).

"*Is there any example in Scripture of persons who had attained to this?*

"Yes; St. John, and all those of whom he says, 'Herein is our love made perfect, that we may have boldness in the day of judgment; because, as he is, so are we in this world' (1 John iv. 17). . . .

"Are we not apt to have a secret distaste to any who say they are saved from all sin?

"It is very possible we may, and that upon several grounds; partly from a concern for the good of souls who may be hurt if these are not what they profess; partly from a kind of implicit envy at those who speak of higher attainments than our own; and partly from our natural slowness and unreadiness of heart to believe the works of God.

"Why may we not continue in the joy of faith till we are perfected in love?

"Why indeed? since holy grief does not quench this joy; since even while we are under the cross, while we deeply partake of the sufferings of Christ, we may rejoice with joy unspeakable."

From these extracts, it undeniably appears, not only what was mine and my brother's judgment, but what was the judgment of all the preachers in connection with us in the years 1744, 45, 46, and 47. Nor do I remember that in any one of these conferences we had one dissenting voice; but whatever doubts any one had when we met, they were all removed before we parted.

Teachings of Charles Wesley

18. In the year 1749, my brother printed two volumes of "Hymns and Sacred Poems." As I did not see these before they were published, there were some things in them which I did not approve of. But I quite approved of the main of the hymns on this head [Christian perfection]; a few verses of which are subjoined:

> Come, Lord, be manifested here,
>   And all the devil's works destroy;
> Now, without sin, in me appear,
>   And fill with everlasting joy;
> Thy beatific face display;
> Thy presence is the perfect day. (Vol. I, p. 203) . . .

> From this inbred sin deliver;
> Let the yoke now be broke;
> Make me Thine forever.

> Partner of Thy perfect nature,
> Let me be now in Thee
> A new, sinless creature. (Vol. II, p. 156)

Turn me, Lord, and turn me now,
To Thy yoke my spirit bow;
Grant me now the pearl to find
Of a meek and quiet mind.

Calm, O calm my troubled breast;
Let me gain that second rest;
From my works for ever cease,
Perfected in holiness. (p. 162)

Come in this accepted hour,
  Bring Thy heavenly kingdom in!
Fill us with the glorious power
  Rooting out the seeds of sin. (p. 168)

Come, Thou dear Lamb, for sinners slain,
  Bring in the cleansing flood:
Apply, to wash out every stain,
  Thine efficacious blood.

O let it sink into our soul
  Deep as the inbred sin;
Make every wounded spirit whole,
  And every leper clean! (p. 171) . . .

Jesus, to Thee we look,
  Till saved from sin's remains,
Reject the inbred tyrant's yoke,
  And cast away his chains.

Our nature shall no more
  O'er us dominion have;
By faith we apprehend the power
  Which shall for ever save. (p. 188)

Jesus, our life, in us appear,
  Who daily die Thy death;
Reveal Thyself the finisher,
  Thy quick'ning Spirit breathe!

> *Unfold the hidden mystery,*
>   *The second gift impart;*
> *Reveal Thy glorious self in me,*
>   *In every waiting heart.* (p. 195) . . .

I have been the more large in these extracts because hence it appears, beyond all possibility of exception, that to this day both my brother and I maintained, (1) That Christian perfection is that love of God and our neighbour, which implies deliverance from all sin. (2) That this is received merely by faith. (3) That it is given instantaneously, in one moment. (4) That we are to expect it, not at death, but every moment; that now is the accepted time, now is the day of this salvation.

Thoughts on Christian Perfection (1759)

19. At the conference in the year 1759 . . . we again largely considered this doctrine; and soon after I published "Thoughts on Christian Perfection," prefaced with the following advertisement:

"The following tract is by no means designed to gratify the curiosity of any man. It is not intended to prove the doctrine at large, in opposition to those who explode and ridicule it; no, nor to answer the numerous objections against it which may be raised even by serious men. All I intend here is simply to declare what are my sentiments on this head; what Christian perfection does, according to my apprehension, include, and what it does not; and to add a few practical observations and directions relative to the subject.

"As these thoughts were at first thrown together by way of question and answer, I let them continue in the same form. They are just the same that I have entertained for about twenty years.

"*What is Christian perfection?*

"The loving God with all our heart, mind, soul, and strength. This implies that no wrong temper, none contrary to love, remains in the soul; and that all the thoughts, words, and actions, are governed by pure love.

"*Do you affirm that this perfection excludes all infirmities, ignorance, and mistake?*

"I continually affirm quite the contrary and always have done so.

"*But how can every thought, word, and work be governed by pure love and the man be subject, at the same time, to ignorance and mistake?*

"I see no contradiction here: 'A man may be filled with pure love and still be liable to mistake.' Indeed, I do not expect to be freed from actual mistakes till this mortal puts on immortality. I believe this to be a natural consequence of the soul's dwelling in flesh and blood. For we cannot now think at all, but by the mediation of those bodily organs which have suffered equally with the rest of our frame. And hence we cannot avoid sometimes thinking wrong, till this corruptible shall have put on incorruption.

HUMANITY

"But we may carry this thought further yet. A mistake in judgment may possibly occasion a mistake in practice. . . . Yet, where every word and action springs from love, such a mistake is not openly a sin. However, it cannot bear the rigor of God's justice, but needs the atoning blood. . . . It follows, that the most perfect have continual need of the merits of Christ, even for their actual transgressions, and may say for themselves as well as for their brethren, 'Forgive us our trespasses.'

ATONEMENT

"This easily accounts for what might otherwise seem to be utterly unaccountable; namely, that those who are not offended when we speak of the highest degree of love, yet will not hear of living without sin. The reason is, they know all men are liable to mistake, and that in practice as well as in judgment. But they do not know, or do not observe, that this is not sin, if love is the sole principle of action.

"*But still, if they live without sin, does not this exclude the necessity of a Mediator? At least, is it not plain that they stand no longer in need of Christ in His priestly office?*

"Far from it. None feel their need of Christ like these; none so entirely depend upon Him. For Christ does not give life to the soul separate from, but in and with himself. Hence His words are equally true of all men in whatsoever state of grace they are: 'As the branch cannot bear fruit of itself, except it abide in the vine; no more can ye, except ye abide in me: without' (or separate from) 'me ye can do nothing.'

"In every state we need Christ in the following respects, (1) Whatever grace we receive, it is a free gift from Him. (2) We receive it as His purchase, merely in consideration of the price He paid. (3) We have this grace, not only from Christ, but in Him. For our perfection is not like that of a tree, which flourishes by the sap derived from its own root, but, as was said before, like that of a branch which, united to the vine, bears fruit; but, severed from it, is dried up and withered. (4) All our blessings, temporal, spiritual, and eternal, depend on His intercession for us, which is one branch of His priestly office, whereof therefore we have always equal need. (5) The best of men still need Christ in His priestly office to atone for their omissions, their shortcomings (as some not improperly speak), their mistakes in judgment and practice, and their defects of various kinds. For these are all deviations from the perfect law and consequently need an atonement. Yet that they are not properly sins we apprehend may appear from the words of St. Paul, 'He that loveth, hath fulfilled the law; for love is the fulfilling of the law' (Rom. xiii. 10). Now, mistakes, and whatever infirmities necessarily flow from the corruptible state of the body, are no way contrary to love; nor therefore, in the Scripture sense, sin.

"To explain myself a little farther on this head: (1) Not only sin, properly so called (that is, a voluntary transgression of a known law), but sin, improperly so called (that is, an involuntary transgression of a divine law, known or unknown), needs the atoning blood. (2) I believe there is no such perfection in this life as excludes these involuntary transgressions which I apprehend to be naturally consequent on the ignorance and mistakes inseparable from mortality. (3) Therefore *sinless perfection* is a phrase I never use, lest I should seem to contradict myself. (4) I believe a person filled with the love of God is still liable to these involuntary transgressions. (5) Such transgressions you may call sins, if you please: I do not, for the reasons above mentioned.

"*What advice would you give to those that do, and those that do not call them so?*

"Let those that do not call them sins never think that themselves or any other persons are in such a state as that they can stand before infinite justice without a Mediator. This must argue either the deepest ignorance or the highest arrogance and presumption.

"Let those who do call them so, beware how they confound these defects with sins, properly so called.

"But how will they avoid it? How will these be distinguished from those if they are all promiscuously called sins?

"I am much afraid, if we should allow any sins to be consistent with perfection, few would confine the idea to those defects concerning which only the assertion could be true.

"*But how can a liableness to mistake consist with perfect love? Is not a person who is perfected in love every moment under its influence? And can any mistake flow from pure love?*

"I answer, (1) Many mistakes may consist with pure love; (2) Some may accidentally flow from it: I mean, love itself may incline us to mistake. The pure love of our neighbour, springing from the love of God, thinketh no evil, believeth and hopeth all things. Now, this very temper, unsuspicious, ready to believe and hope the best of all men, may occasion our thinking some men better than they really are. Here, then, is a manifest mistake, accidentally flowing from pure love.

"*How shall we avoid setting perfection too high or too low?*

"By keeping to the Bible, and setting it just as high as the Scripture does. It is nothing higher and nothing lower than this—the pure love of God and man. . . .

"*Suppose one had attained to this, would you advise him to speak of it?*

"At first perhaps he would scarce be able to refrain, the fire would be so hot within him; his desire to declare the loving-kindness of the Lord, carrying him away like a torrent. But afterward he might; and then it would be advisable, not to speak of it to them that know not God (it is most likely, it would only provoke them to contradict and blaspheme); nor to others, without some particular reason, without some good in view. And then he should have especial care to avoid all appearance of boasting; to speak with the deepest humility and reverence giving all the glory to God.

WITNESSING

"*But would it not be better to be silent; not to speak of it at all?* . . .

"This could not be done with a clear conscience; for undoubtedly he ought to speak. Men do not light a candle to put it under a bushel. . . . Nor does anything under heaven more quicken the desires of those who are justified than to converse with those whom they believe to have experienced a still higher salvation. This places that salvation full in their view, and increases their hunger and thirst after it; an advantage which must have been entirely lost, had the person so saved buried himself in silence. . . .

"*What is reasonable proof? How may we certainly know one that is saved from all sin?*

"We cannot infallibly know one that is thus saved (nor even one that is justified) unless it should please God to endow us with the miraculous discernment of spirits. But we apprehend those would be sufficient proofs to any reasonable man, and such as would leave little room to doubt either the truth or depth of the work: (1) If we had clear evidence of his exemplary behaviour for some time before this supposed change. This would give us reason to believe he would not 'lie for God,' but speak neither more nor less than he felt; (2) If he gave a distinct account of the time and manner wherein the change was wrought, with sound speech which could not be reproved; and, (3) If it appeared that all his subsequent words and actions were holy and unblamable.

"The short of the matter is this: (1) I have abundant reason to believe this person will not lie; (2) He testifies before God, 'I feel no sin, but all love; I pray, rejoice, and give thanks without ceasing; and I have as clear an inward witness that I am fully renewed as that I am justified.' Now, if I have nothing to oppose to this plain testimony, I ought in reason to believe it. . . .

"*But what does the perfect one do more than others? more than the common believers?*

"Perhaps nothing; so may the providence of God have hedged him in by outward circumstances. Perhaps not so much; though he desires and longs to spend and be spent for God; at least not externally: he neither speaks so many words nor does so many works. As neither did our Lord himself speak so many words or do so many, no, nor so great works as some of His Apostles (John xiv. 12). But what then? This is no proof that he has not more grace; and by this God measures the outward work. Hear ye Him: 'Verily, I say unto you, this poor widow has cast in more than them all.' Verily, this poor man, with his few broken words, hath spoken more than them all. Verily, this poor woman that hath given a cup of cold water hath done more than them all. Oh, cease to 'judge according to appearance,' and learn to 'judge righteous judgment!'

"*But is not this a proof against him [that] I feel no power either in his words or prayer?*

"It is not, for perhaps this is your own fault. You are not likely to feel any power therein if any of these hindrances lie in the way: (1) Your own deadness of soul. The dead Pharisees felt no power even in His words who 'spake as never man spake.' (2) The guilt of some unrepented sin lying upon the conscience. (3) Prejudice toward him of any kind. (4) Your not believing that state to be attainable wherein he professes to be. (5) Unreadiness to think or own he has attained it. (6) Overvaluing or idolizing him. (7) Overvaluing yourself and your own judgment. If any of these is the case, what wonder is it that you feel no power in anything he says? But do not others feel it? If they do, your argument falls to the ground. And if they do not, do none of these hindrances lie in their way too? You must be certain of this before you can build any argument thereon; and even then your argument will prove no more than that grace and gifts do not always go together.

"'But he does not come up to my idea of a perfect Christian.' And perhaps no one ever did, or ever will. For your idea may go beyond, or at least beside the scriptural account. It may include more than the Bible includes therein. Scripture perfection is pure love filling the heart and governing all the words and actions. If your idea includes anything more or anything else, it is not scriptural; and then no wonder that a scripturally perfect Christian does not come up to it.

"I fear many stumble on this stumbling-block. They include as many ingredients as they please not according to Scripture but their own imagination in their idea of one that is perfect; and then readily deny anyone to be such who does not answer that imaginary idea.

"The more care should we take to keep the simple, scriptural account continually in our eye. Pure love reigning alone in the heart and life—this is the whole of scriptural perfection.

"*When may a person judge himself to have attained this?*

"When, after having been convinced of inbred sin, by a far deeper and clearer conviction than that he experienced before justification, and after having experienced a gradual mortification of it, he experiences a total death to sin and an entire renewal in the love and image of God, so as to rejoice evermore, to pray without ceasing, and in everything to give thanks. Not that 'to feel all love and no sin' is a sufficient proof. Several have experienced this for a time before their souls were fully renewed. None, therefore, ought to believe that the work is done, till there is added the testimony of the Spirit, witnessing his entire sanctification as clearly as his justification.

ASSURANCE

"*But whence is it, that some imagine they are thus sanctified, when in reality they are not?*

"It is hence; they do not judge by all the preceding marks, but either by part of them, or by others that are ambiguous. But I know no instance of a person attending to them all and yet deceived in this matter. I believe there can be none in the world. If a man be deeply and fully convinced, after justification, of inbred sin; if he then experience a gradual mortification of sin, and afterward an entire renewal in the image of God; if to this change, immensely greater than that wrought when he was justified, be added a clear, direct witness of the renewal; I judge it as impossible this man should be deceived herein, as that God should lie. And if one whom I know to be a man of veracity testify these things to me, I ought not without some sufficient reason to reject his testimony.

"Is this death to sin, and renewal in love, gradual or instantaneous?

"A man may be dying for some time; yet he does not, properly speaking, die till the soul is separated from the body; and in that instant he lives the life of eternity. In like manner, he may be dying to sin for some time; yet he is not dead to sin till sin is separated from his soul; and in that instant he lives the full life of love. And as the change undergone when the body dies is of a different kind, and is infinitely greater than any we had known before, yea, such as till then, it is impossible to conceive; so the change wrought when the soul dies to sin is of a different kind, and infinitely greater than any before, and than any can conceive, till he experiences it. Yet he still grows in grace, in the knowledge of Christ, in the love and image of God; and will do so, not only till death, but to all eternity.

SECOND BLESSING

"How are we to wait for this change?

"Not in careless indifference, or indolent inactivity; but in vigorous, universal obedience, in a zealous keeping of all the commandments, in watchfulness and painfulness, in denying ourselves, and taking up our cross daily; as well as in earnest prayer and fasting, and a close attendance on all the ordinances of God. And if any man dream of attaining it any other way (yea, or of keeping it when it is attained, when he has received it even in the largest measure), he deceiveth his own soul. It is true, we receive it by simple faith; but God does not, will not, give that faith unless we seek it with all diligence, in the way which He hath ordained.

"This consideration may satisfy those who enquire, why so few have received the blessing. Enquire how many are seeking it in this way and you have a sufficient answer.

"Prayer especially is wanting. Who continues instant therein? Who wrestles with God for this very thing? So, 'ye have not, because ye ask amiss' namely, that you may be renewed before you die. *Before you die!* Will that content you? Nay, but ask that it may be done now; today, while it is called today. Do not call this 'setting God a time.' Certainly today is His time as well as tomorrow. Make haste, man, make haste! Let

> *Thy soul break out in strong desire*
> *The perfect bliss to prove;*
> *Thy longing heart be all on fire*
> *To be dissolved in love!*

"But may we not continue in peace and joy till we are perfected in love?

"Certainly we may; for the kingdom of God is not divided against itself; therefore, let not believers be discouraged from 'rejoicing in the Lord always.' And yet we may be sensibly pained at the sinful nature that still remains in us. It is good for us to have a piercing sense of this, and a vehement desire to be delivered from it. But this should only incite us the more zealously to fly every moment to our strong Helper, the more earnestly to 'press forward to the mark, the prize of our high calling in Christ Jesus.' And when the sense of our sin most abounds, the sense of His love should much more abound.

Helping Seekers After Holiness

"*How should we treat those who think they have attained?*

"Examine them candidly, and exhort them to pray fervently that God would show them all that is in their hearts. The most earnest exhortations to abound in every grace, and the strongest cautions to avoid all evil, are given throughout the New Testament, to those who are in the highest state of grace. But this should be done with the utmost tenderness; and without any harshness, sternness, or sourness. We should carefully avoid the very appearance of anger, unkindness, or contempt. . . . If they are faithful to the grace given, they are in no danger of perishing thereby; no, not if they remain in that mistake till their spirit is returning to God.

"*But what hurt can it do to deal harshly with them?*

"Either they are mistaken or they are not. If they are, it may destroy their souls. This is nothing impossible, no, nor improbable. . . . If they are not mistaken, it may grieve those whom God has not grieved, and do much hurt unto our own souls. For, undoubtedly, he that toucheth them toucheth, as it were, the apple of God's eye. If they are indeed full of His Spirit, to behave unkindly or contemptuously to them, is doing no little despite to the Spirit of grace. . . . Are we qualified for the office? Can we pronounce, in all cases, how far infirmity reaches? What may and what may not be resolved into it? What may in all circumstances, and what may not consist with perfect love? Can we precisely determine how it will influence the look, the gesture, the tone of the voice? If we can, doubtless we are 'the men, and wisdom shall die with us.'

"*But if they are displeased at our not believing them, is not this a full proof against them?*

"According as that displeasure is. If they are angry, it is a proof against them; if they are grieved, it is not. They ought to be grieved, if we disbelieve a real work of God, and thereby deprive ourselves of the advantage we might have received from it. And we may easily mistake this grief for anger as the outward expressions of both are much alike.

"*But is it not well to find out those who fancy they have attained when they have not?*

"It is well to do it by mild, loving examination. But it is not well to triumph even over these. It is extremely wrong, if we find such an instance to rejoice as if we had found great spoils. Ought we not rather to grieve, to be deeply concerned, to let our eyes run down with tears? Here is one who seemed to be a living proof of God's power to save to the uttermost; but, alas! it is not as we hoped. He is weighed in the balance and found wanting! And is this a matter of joy? Ought we not to rejoice a thousand times more, if we can find nothing but pure love? . . .

"*But what does it signify whether any have attained it or no, seeing so many scriptures witness for it?*

"If I were convinced that none in England had attained what has been so clearly and strongly preached by such a number of preachers, in so many places, and for so long a time, I should be clearly convinced that we had all mistaken the meaning of those scriptures; and, therefore, for the time to come, I too must teach that 'sin will remain till death.'"

Danger of Fanaticism

20. In the year 1762 there was a great increase of the work of God in London. Many who had hitherto cared for none of these things were deeply convinced of their lost estate; many found redemption in the blood of Christ; not a few backsliders were healed; and a considerable number of persons believed that God had saved them from all sin. Easily foreseeing that Satan would be endeavouring to sow tares among the wheat, I took much pains to apprize them of the danger, particularly with regard to pride and enthusiasm.[8] And while I stayed in town, I had reason to hope they continued both humble and sober-minded. But almost as soon as I was gone, enthusiasm broke in. Two or three began to take their own imaginations for impressions

---

8. Wesley, and others in the 18th century, used the term *enthusiasm* to mean what we describe as "fanaticism."

from God, and thence to suppose that they should never die; and these, labouring to bring others into the same opinion, occasioned much noise and confusion.

Soon after, the same persons, with a few more, ran into other extravagances; fancying they could not be tempted; that they should feel no more pain; and that they had the gift of prophecy, and of discerning of spirits. At my return to London, in autumn, some of them stood reproved; but others were got above instruction. Meantime, a flood of reproach came upon me almost from every quarter; from themselves, because I was checking them on all occasions; and from others, because they said I did not check them. However, the hand of the Lord was not stayed, but more and more sinners were convinced; while some were almost daily converted to God, and others enabled to love Him with all their heart.

21. About this time, a friend at some distance from London wrote to me as follows:

"Be not over alarmed that Satan sows tares among the wheat of Christ. It ever has been so, especially on any remarkable outpouring of His Spirit; and ever will be so till he is chained up for a thousand years. Till then he will always ape and endeavour to counteract the work of the Spirit of Christ.

"One melancholy effect of this has been that a world who is always asleep in the arms of the evil one has ridiculed every work of the Holy Spirit.

"But what can real Christians do? Why, if they would act worthy of themselves, they should (1) Pray that every deluded soul may be delivered; (2) Endeavour to reclaim them in the spirit of meekness; and, lastly, take the utmost care, both by prayer and watchfulness, that the delusion of others may not lessen their zeal in seeking after that universal holiness of soul, body, and spirit, 'without which no man shall see the Lord.'" . . .

Plain Questions of a Plain Man

23. [In answer to those who taught that Christian perfection was not obtainable in this life, Wesley posed these rhetorical questions. To consider the question suggests the true answer.]

"(1) Has there not been a larger measure of the Holy Spirit given under the gospel, than under the Jewish dispensation? If not, in what sense was the Spirit not given before Christ was glorified? (John vii. 39).

"(2) Was that 'glory which followed the sufferings of Christ' (1 Pet. i. 11), an external glory, or an internal, viz., the glory of holiness?

"(3) Has God anywhere in Scripture commanded us more than He has promised to us?

"(4) Are the promises of God respecting holiness to be fulfilled in this life, or only in the next?

"(5) Is a Christian under any other laws than those which God promises to 'write in our hearts'? (Jer. xxxi. 31, etc.; Heb. viii. 10).

"(6) In what sense is 'the righteousness of the law fulfilled in those who walk not after the flesh, but after the Spirit'? (Rom. vii. 4).

"(7) Is it impossible for anyone in this life to 'love God with all his heart, and mind, and soul, and strength'? And is the Christian under any law which is not fulfilled in this love?

"(8) Does the soul's going out of the body effect its purification from indwelling sin?

"(9) If so, is it not something else, not 'the blood of Christ, which cleanseth' it 'from all sin'?

"(10) If his blood cleanseth us from all sin, while the soul and body are united, is it not in this life?

"(11) If when that union ceases, is it not in the next? And is not this too late?

"(12) If in the article of death; what situation is the soul in when it is neither in the body nor out of it?

"(13) Has Christ anywhere taught us to pray for what He never designs to give?

"(14) Has He not taught us to pray, 'Thy will be done on earth, as it is done in heaven'? And is it not done perfectly in heaven?

"(15) If so, has He not taught us to pray for perfection on earth? Does He not then design to give it?

"(16) Did not St. Paul pray according to the will of God, when he prayed that the Thessalonians might be 'sanctified wholly, and preserved' (in this world, not the next, unless he was praying for the dead) 'blameless in body, soul, and spirit, unto the coming of Jesus Christ'?

"(17) Do you sincerely desire to be freed from indwelling sin in this life?

"(18) If you do, did not God give you that desire?

"(19) If so, did He not give it you to mock you, since it is impossible it should ever be fulfilled?

"(20) If you have not sincerity enough even to desire it, are you not disputing about matters too high for you?

"(21) Do you ever pray God to 'cleanse the thoughts of your heart, that' you 'may perfectly love Him'?

"(22) If you neither desire what you ask, nor believe it attainable, pray you not as a fool prayeth?

"God help thee to consider these questions calmly and impartially!"

Jane Cooper's Testimony

[At this point Wesley inserts the personal testimony of Jane Cooper who had been convicted of her inbred sin under Wesley's preaching.]

24. In the latter end of this year, God called to himself that burning and shining light, Jane Cooper. As she was both a living and a dying witness of Christian perfection, it will not be at all foreign to the subject to add a short account of her death[9] with one of her own letters containing a plain and artless relation of the manner wherein it pleased God to work that great change in her soul.

"May 2, 1761

"I believe while memory remains in me gratitude will continue. From the time you preached on Gal. v. 5, I saw clearly the true state of my soul. That sermon described my heart and what it wanted to be, namely, truly happy. You read Mr. M—'s letter, and it described the religion which I desired. From that time the prize appeared in view, and I was enabled to follow hard after it. I was kept watching unto prayer, sometimes in much distress, at other times in patient expectation of the blessing. For some days before you left London my soul was stayed on a promise I had applied to me in prayer: 'The Lord whom ye seek shall suddenly come to his temple.' I believed He would, and that He would sit there as a refiner's fire.

HUNGER

"The Tuesday after you went I thought I could not sleep unless He fulfilled His word that night. I never knew as I did then the force of these words: 'Be still, and know that I am God.' I became nothing before Him, and enjoyed perfect calmness in my soul. I knew not whether He had destroyed my sin, but I desired to know that I might praise Him. Yet I soon found the return of unbelief and groaned, being burdened.

"On Wednesday I went to London and sought the Lord without ceasing. I promised if He would save me from sin I would praise Him.

---

9. Only her testimony is included here.

I could part with all things, so I might win Christ. But I found all these pleas to be nothing worth; and that if He saved me, it must be freely for His own name's sake.

"On Thursday I was so much tempted that I thought of destroying myself or never conversing more with the people of God; and yet I had no doubt of His pardoning love, but

> 'Twas worse than death my God to love,
> And not my God alone.

"On Friday my distress was deepened. I endeavoured to pray, and could not. I went to Mrs. D—, who prayed for me and told me it was the death of nature.... I returned that night and found Mrs. G—. She prayed for me; and the predestinarian had no plea but 'Lord, thou art no respecter of persons.' He proved He was not by blessing me. I was in a moment enabled to lay hold of Jesus Christ and found salvation by simple faith. He assured me, the Lord, the King, was in the midst of me, and that I should see evil no more. I now blessed Him who had visited and redeemed me, and was become my 'wisdom, righteousness, sanctification, and redemption.'

"I saw Jesus altogether lovely; and knew He was mine in all His offices. And, glory be to Him, He now reigns in my heart without a rival. I find no will but His. I feel no pride; nor any affection but what is placed on Him. I know it is by faith I stand; and that watching unto prayer must be the guard of faith. I am happy in God this moment, and I believe for the next. I have often read the chapter you mention (1 Cor. xiii), and compared my heart and life with it. In so doing I feel my shortcomings and the need I have of the atoning blood. Yet I dare not say I do not feel a measure of the love there described, though I am not all I shall be. I desire to be lost in that 'love which passeth knowledge.' I see 'the just shall live by faith,' and unto me, who am less than the least of all saints is this grace given." ...

ASSURANCE

Farther Thoughts on Christian Perfection (1762)

25. The next year, the number of those who believed they were saved from sin still increasing, I judged it needful to publish, chiefly for their use, "Farther Thoughts on Christian Perfection."

"(1) *How is 'Christ the end of the law for righteousness to every one that believeth?'* (Rom. x. 4).

"In order to understand this, you must understand what law is here spoken of; and this, I apprehend is, (1) The Mosaic law, the whole

Mosaic dispensation; which St. Paul continually speaks of as one though containing three parts: the political, moral, and ceremonial. (2) The Adamic law, that given to Adam in innocence, properly called 'the law of works.' This is in substance the same with the angelic law, being common to angels and men. It required that man should use to the glory of God all the powers with which he was created. Now, he was created free from any defect, either in his understanding or his affections. His body was then no clog to the mind; it did not hinder his apprehending all things clearly, judging truly concerning them, and reasoning justly if he reasoned at all.

"Consequently, this law, proportioned to his original powers, required that he should always think, always speak, and always act precisely right, in every point whatever. He was well able so to do: and God could not but require the service he was able to pay.

"But Adam fell; and his incorruptible body became corruptible; and ever since it is a clog to the soul and hinders its operations. Hence, at present, no child of man can at all times apprehend clearly or judge truly. And where either the judgment or apprehension is wrong, it is impossible to reason justly. Therefore, it is as natural for a man to mistake as to breathe; and he can no more live without the one than without the other: consequently no man is able to perform the service which the Adamic law requires.

"And no man is obliged to perform it; God does not require it of any man: for Christ is the end of the Adamic as well as the Mosaic law. By His death He hath put an end to both; He hath abolished both the one and the other, with regard to man; and the obligation to observe either the one or the other is vanished away. Nor is any man living bound to observe the Adamic more than the Mosaic law. (I mean, it is not the condition either of present or future salvation.)

"In the room of this, Christ hath established another, namely, the law of faith. Not every one that doeth, but every one that believeth, now receiveth righteousness in the full sense of the word; that is, he is justified, sanctified, and glorified.

"(2) *Are we then dead to the law?*

"We are 'dead to the law, by the body of Christ' given for us; (Rom. vii. 4) to the Adamic as well as Mosaic law. We are wholly freed therefrom by His death; that law expiring with Him.

"(3) *How, then, are we 'not without law to God, but under the law to Christ'?* (1 Cor. ix. 21).

"We are without that law; but it does not follow that we are without any law; for God hath established another law in its place, even the law of faith; and we are all under this law to God and to Christ; both our Creator and our Redeemer require us to observe it.

"(4) *Is love the fulfilling of this law?*

"Unquestionably it is. The whole law under which we now are is fulfilled by love (Rom. xiii. 9-10). Faith working or animated by love is all that God now requires of man. He has substituted, not sincerity, but love in the room of angelic perfection.

"(5) *How is 'love the end of the commandment'?* (1 Tim. i. 5).

"It is the end of every commandment of God. It is the point aimed at by the whole and every part of the Christian institution. The foundation is faith, purifying the heart; the end love, preserving a good conscience.

"(6) *What love is this?*

"The loving the Lord our God with all our heart, mind, soul, and strength; and the loving our neighbour, every man as ourselves, as our own souls.

"(7) *What are the fruits or properties of this love?*

"St. Paul informs us at large, love is long-suffering. It suffers all the weaknesses of the children of God, all the wickedness of the children of the world; and that not for a little time only, but as long as God pleases. In all, it sees the hand of God, and willingly submits thereto. Meantime, it is kind. In all, and after all, it suffers, it is soft, mild, tender, benign. 'Love envieth not'; it excludes every kind and degree of envy out of the heart; 'love acteth not rashly,' in a violent, headstrong manner, nor passes any rash or severe judgment: it 'doth not behave itself indecently'; is not rude, does not act out of character: 'seeketh not her own' ease, pleasure, honor, or profit; 'is not provoked'; expels all anger from the heart: 'thinketh no evil'; casteth out all jealousy, suspiciousness, and readiness to believe evil: 'rejoiceth not in iniquity'; yea, weeps at the sin or folly of its bitterest enemies: 'but rejoiceth in the truth'; in the holiness and happiness of every child of man. 'Love covereth all things,' speaks evil of no man; 'believeth all things,' that tend to the advantage of another's character. It 'hopeth all things,' whatever may extenuate the faults which cannot be denied; and it 'endureth all things,' which God can permit, or men and devils inflict. This is 'the law of Christ, the perfect law, the law of liberty.'

ATTITUDES

"And this distinction between the 'law of faith' (or love) and 'the law of works,' is neither a subtle nor an unnecessary distinction. It is plain, easy, and intelligible to any common understanding. And it is absolutely necessary to prevent a thousand doubts and fears, even in those who do 'walk in love.'

"(8) *But do we not 'in many things offend all,' yea, the best of us, even against this law?*

"In one sense we do not, while all our tempers, and thoughts, and words, and works spring from love. But in another we do and shall do, more or less, as long as we remain in the body. For neither love nor the 'unction of the Holy One' makes us infallible. Therefore, through unavoidable defect of understanding, we cannot but mistake in many things. And these mistakes will frequently occasion something wrong, both in our temper, and words, and actions. From mistaking his character, we may love a person less than he really deserves. And by the same mistake we are unavoidably led to speak or act with regard to that person in such a manner as is contrary to this law in some or other of the preceding instances.

"(9) *Do we not then need Christ, even on thus account?*

"The holiest of men still need Christ, as their Prophet, as 'the light of the world.' For He does not give them light, but from moment to moment; the instant He withdraws, all is darkness. They still need Christ as their King; for God does not give them a stock of holiness. But unless they receive a supply every moment, nothing but unholiness would remain. They still need Christ as their Priest to make atonement for their holy things. Even perfect holiness is acceptable to God only through Jesus Christ.

"(10) *May not, then, the very best of men adopt the dying martyr's confession: 'I am in myself nothing but sin, darkness, hell; but thou art my light, my holiness, my heaven'?*

"Not exactly. But the best of men say, 'Thou art my light, my holiness, my heaven. Through my union with Thee, I am full of light, of holiness, and happiness. But if I were left to myself, I should be nothing but sin, darkness, hell.'

"But to proceed: The best of men need Christ as their Priest, their Atonement, their Advocate with the Father; not only as

ATONEMENT

the continuance of their every blessing depends on His death and intercession, but on account of their coming short of the law of love. For every man living does so. You who feel all love, compare yourselves with the preceding description. Weigh yourselves in this balance, and see if you are not wanting in many particulars.

"(11) *But if all this be consistent with Christian perfection, that* perfection is not freedom from all sin; seeing 'sin is the transgression of the law': and the perfect transgress the very law they are under. Besides, they need the atonement of Christ; and He is the atonement of nothing but sin. Is, then, the term 'sinless perfection,' proper?

"It is not worth disputing about. But observe in what sense the persons in question need the atonement of Christ. They do not need Him to reconcile them to God afresh; for they are reconciled. They do not need Him to restore the favor of God, but to continue it. He does not procure pardon for them anew, but 'ever liveth to make intercession for them'; and 'by one offering he hath perfected forever them that are sanctified' (Heb. x. 14).

"For want of duly considering this, some deny that they need the atonement of Christ. Indeed, exceeding few; I do not remember to have found five of them in England. Of the two, I would sooner give up perfection. But we need not give up either one or the other. The perfection I hold, 'Love rejoicing evermore, praying without ceasing, and in everything giving thanks,' is well consistent with it; if any hold a perfection which is not, they must look to it.

"(12) *Does the Christian perfection imply any more than sincerity?*

"Not if you mean by that word, love filling the heart, expelling pride, anger, desire, self-will; rejoicing evermore, praying without ceasing, and in everything giving thanks. But I doubt few use sincerity in this sense. Therefore, I think the old word is best.

"A person may be sincere who has all his natural tempers, pride, anger, lust, self-will. But he is not perfect until his heart is cleansed from these and all its other corruptions.

"To clear this point a little farther: I know many that love God with all their heart. He is their one desire, their one delight, and they are continually happy in Him. They love their neighbour as themselves. They feel as sincere, fervent, constant a desire for the happiness of every man, good or bad, friend or enemy, as for their own. They rejoice evermore, pray without ceasing, and in everything give thanks. Their souls are continually streaming up to God, in holy joy, prayer, and praise. This is a point of fact; and this is plain, sound, scriptural experience.

PERFECT LOVE

"But even these souls dwell in a shattered body, and are so pressed down thereby that they cannot always exert themselves as they would by thinking, speaking, and acting precisely right. For want of better bodily organs, they must at times think,

HUMANITY

speak, or act wrong; not, indeed, through a defect of love, but through a defect of knowledge. And while this is the case, notwithstanding that defect, and its consequences, they fulfill the law of love.

"Yet, as even in this case, there is not a full conformity to the perfect law, so the most perfect do, on this very account, need the blood of atonement, and may properly for themselves as well as for their brethren say, 'Forgive us our trespasses.'

"(13) *But if Christ has put an end to that law, what need of any atonement for their transgressing it?*

"Observe in what sense He has put an end to it and the difficulty vanishes. Were it not for the abiding merit of His death and His continual intercession for us, the law would condemn us still. These, therefore, we still need for every transgression of it.

"(14) *But can one that is saved from sin be tempted?*

"Yes; for Christ was tempted.

"(15) *However what you call temptation, I call the corruption of my heart. And how will you distinguish one from the other?*

"In some cases, it is impossible to distinguish, without the direct witness of the Spirit. But in general, one may distinguish thus:

"One commends me. Here is a temptation to pride. But instantly my soul is humbled before God. And I feel no pride; of which I am as sure, as that pride is not humility.

"A man strikes me. Here is a temptation to anger. But my heart overflows with love. And I feel no anger at all; of which I can be as sure as that love and anger are not the same.

"A woman solicits me. Here is a temptation to lust. But in an instant I shrink back. And I feel no desire or lust at all; of which I can be as sure as that my hand is cold or hot.

"Thus it is, if I am tempted by a present object; and it is the same if when it is absent the devil recalls a commendation, an injury, or a woman to my mind. In the instant the soul repels the temptation and remains filled with pure love.

"And the difference is still plainer when I compare my present state with my past wherein I felt temptation and corruption too.

"(16) *But how do you know that you are sanctified, saved from your inbred corruption?*

"I can know it no otherwise than I know that I am justified. 'Hereby know we that we are of God,' in either sense 'by the Spirit that he hath given us.'

"We know it by the witness and by the fruit of the Spirit. And first, by the witness. As when we were justified the Spirit bore witness with our spirit that our sins were forgiven, so, when we were sanctified, He bore witness that they were taken away. Indeed, the witness of sanctification is not always clear at first (as neither is that of justification); neither is it afterward always the same, but like that of justification, sometimes stronger and sometimes fainter. Yea, and sometimes it is withdrawn. Yet, in general, the latter testimony of the Spirit is both as clear and as steady as the former. . . .

ASSURANCE

"(19) *But what scripture makes mention of any such thing, or gives any reason to expect it?*

"That scripture, 'We have received, not the spirit that is of the world, but the Spirit which is of God; that we may know the things which are freely given us of God' (1 Cor. ii. 12).

"Now surely sanctification is one of 'the things which are freely given us of God.' And no possible reason can be assigned why this should be excepted when the Apostle says, 'We receive the Spirit' for this very end, 'that we may know the things which are thus 'freely given us.'

"Is not the same thing implied in that well-known scripture, 'The Spirit itself witnesses with our spirit, that we are the children of God'? (Rom. viii. 16). Does He witness this only to those who are children of God in the lowest sense? Nay, but to those also who are such in the highest sense. And does He not witness that they are such in the highest sense? What reason have we to doubt it?

"What if a man were to affirm (as, indeed, many do) that this witness belongs only to the highest class of Christians? Would not you answer, 'The Apostle makes no restriction; therefore, doubtless it belongs to all the children of God'? And will not the same answer hold, if any affirm that it belongs only to the lowest class?

"Consider likewise 1 John v. 19: 'We know that we are of God.' How? 'By the Spirit that he hath given us.' Nay, 'hereby we know that he abideth in us.' And what ground have we either from Scripture or reason, to exclude the witness any more than the fruit of the Spirit from being here intended? By this, then, also 'we know that we are of God,' and in what sense we are so; whether we are babes, young men, or fathers, we know in the same manner.

"Not that I affirm that all young men, or even fathers, have this testimony every moment. There may be intermissions of the direct testimony that they are thus born of God; but these intermissions are fewer and shorter as they grow up in Christ; and some have the testimony both of their justification and sanctification without any intermission at all; which I presume more might have did they walk humbly and closely with God.

"(20) *May not some of them have a testimony from the Spirit that they shall not finally fall from God?*

"They may. And this persuasion, that neither life nor death shall separate them from Him, far from being hurtful, may in some circumstances be extremely useful. These, therefore, we should in no wise grieve, but earnestly encourage them to 'hold the beginning of their confidence steadfast to the end.'

"(21) *But have any a testimony from the Spirit that they shall never sin?*

"We know not what God may vouchsafe to some particular persons; but we do not find any general state described in Scripture from which a man cannot draw back to sin. If there were any state wherein this was impossible, it would be that of these who are sanctified, who are 'fathers in Christ, who rejoice evermore, pray without ceasing, and in everything give thanks'; but it is not impossible for these to draw back. They who are sanctified yet may fall and perish (Heb. x. 29). Even fathers in Christ need that warning: 'Love not the world' (1 John ii. 15). They who 'rejoice, pray,' and 'give thanks without ceasing,' may, nevertheless, 'quench the Spirit' (1 Thess. v. 16, etc.). Nay, even they who are 'sealed unto the day of redemption' may yet 'grieve the Holy Spirit of God' (Eph. iv. 30).

"Although, therefore, God may give such a witness to some particular persons, yet it is not to be expected by Christians in general, there being no scripture whereon to ground such an expectation.

"(22) *By what 'fruit of the Spirit' may we 'know that we are of God,' even in the highest sense?*

"By love, joy, peace, always abiding; by invariable long-suffering, patience, resignation; by gentleness, triumphing over all provocation; by goodness, mildness, sweetness, tenderness of spirit; by fidelity, simplicity, godly sincerity; by meekness, calmness, evenness of spirit; by temperance, not only in food and sleep, but in all things natural and spiritual.

"(23) *But what great matter is there in this? Have we not all this when we are justified?*

"What! total resignation to the will of God, without any mixture of self-will? gentleness, without any touch of anger even the moment we are provoked? love to God, without the least love to the creature, but in and for God, excluding all pride? love to man, excluding all envy, all jealousy, and rash judging? meekness, keeping the whole soul inviolably calm? and temperance in all things? Deny that any ever came up to this, if you please; but do not say all who are justified do.

"(24) *But some who are newly justified do. What, then, will we say to these?*

"If they really do, I will say they are sanctified; saved from sin in that moment; and that they never need lose what God has given, or feel sin any more.

"But certainly this is an exempt [unusual] case. It is otherwise with the generality of those that are justified: they feel in themselves more or less pride, anger, self-will, a heart bent to backsliding. And till they have gradually mortified these, they are not fully renewed in love.

"(25) *But is not this the case of all that are justified? Do they not gradually die to sin and grow in grace, till at, or perhaps a little before death, God perfects them in love?*

"I believe this is the case of most, but not all. God usually gives a considerable time for men to receive light, to grow in grace, to do and suffer His will before they are either justified or sanctified; but He does not invariably adhere to this; sometimes He 'cuts short his work'; He does the work of many years in a few weeks; perhaps in a week, a day, an hour. He justifies or sanctifies both those who have done or suffered nothing, and who have not had time for a gradual growth either in light or grace. And 'may He not do what He will with His own? Is thine eye evil, because He is good?'

"It need not, therefore, be affirmed over and over and proved by forty texts of Scripture, either that most men are perfected in love at last, that there is a gradual work of God in the soul, or that, generally speaking, it is a long time, even many years, before sin is destroyed. All this we know: but we know likewise, that God may, with man's good leave, 'cut short his work,' in whatever degree He pleases, and do the usual work of many years in a moment. He does so in many instances; and yet there is a gradual work, both before and after that moment; so that one may affirm the work is gradual; another, it is instantaneous, without any manner of contradiction.

"(26) *Does St. Paul mean any more by being 'sealed with the Spirit,' than being 'renewed in love'?*

"Perhaps in one place (2 Cor. i. 22), he does not mean so much; but in another (Eph. i. 13), he seems to include both the fruit and the witness; and that in a higher degree than we experience even when we are first 'renewed in love'; God 'sealed us with the Spirit of promise' by giving us 'the full assurance of hope'; such a confidence of receiving all the promises of God as excludes the possibility of doubting; with that Holy Spirit by universal holiness stamping the whole image of God on our hearts.

"(27) *But how can those who are thus sealed, 'grieve the Holy Spirit of God'?*

"St. Paul tells you very particularly, (1) By such conversation as is not profitable, not to the use of edifying, not apt to minister grace to the hearers. (2) By relapsing into bitterness or want of kindness. (3) By wrath, lasting displeasure, or want of tender-heartedness. (4) By anger, however soon it is over; want of instantly forgiving one another. (5) By clamor or bawling, loud, harsh, rough speaking. (6) By evil speaking, whispering, tale-bearing; needlessly mentioning the fault of an absent person, though in ever so soft a manner.

"(28) *What do you think of those in London, who seem to have been lately 'renewed in love'?*

"There is something very peculiar in the experience of the greater part of them. One would expect that a believer should first be filled with love, and thereby emptied of sin; whereas these were emptied of sin first, and then filled with love. Perhaps it pleased God to work in this manner, to make His work more plain and undeniable; and to distinguish it more clearly from that overflowing love which is often felt even in a justified state.

"It seems likewise most agreeable to the great promise: 'From all your filthiness I will cleanse you; a new heart also will I give you, and a new spirit will I put within you' (Ezek. xxxvi. 25-26).

"But I do not think of them all alike; there is a wide difference between some of them and others. I think most of them with whom I have spoken have much faith, love, joy, and peace. Some of these I believe are renewed in love and have the direct witness of it; and they manifest the fruit above described in all their words and actions. Now, let any man call this what he will, it is what I call perfection. . . .

"(29) *Can those who are perfect grow in grace?*

"Undoubtedly they can; and that not only while they are in the body, but to all eternity.

"(30) *Can they fall from it?*

"I am well assured they can; matter of fact puts this beyond dispute. Formerly we thought one saved from sin could not fall; now we know the contrary. We are surrounded with instances of those who lately experienced all that I mean by perfection. They had both the fruit of the Spirit and the witness; but they have now lost both. Neither does anyone stand by virtue of anything that is implied in the nature of the state. There is no such height or strength of holiness as it is impossible to fall from. If there be any that cannot fall, this wholly depends on the promise of God.

"(31) *Can those who fall from this state recover it?*

"Why not? We have many instances of this also. Nay, it is an exceeding common thing for persons to lose it more than once before they are established therein.

"It is therefore to guard them who are saved from sin, from every occasion of stumbling that I give the following advices. But first I shall speak plainly concerning the work itself.

"I esteem this late work to be of God; probably the greatest now upon earth. Yet, like all others, this also is mixed with much human frailty. But these weaknesses are far less than might have been expected; and ought to have been joyfully borne by all that loved and followed after righteousness. That there have been a few weak, warm-headed men is no reproach to the work itself, no just ground for accusing a multitude of sober-minded men who are patterns of strict holiness. Yet (just the contrary to what ought to have been) the opposition is great; the helps few. Hereby many are hindered from seeking faith and holiness by the false zeal of others; and some who at first began to run well are turned out of the way.

Advice for the Entirely Sanctified[10]

"(32) *What is the first advice you would give them?*"

1. *Watch and Pray*

"Watch and pray continually against pride. If God has cast it out, see that it enter no more: it is full as dangerous as desire. And you may slide back into it unawares; especially if you think there is no danger of it. 'Nay, but I ascribe all I have to God.' So you may and be proud nevertheless. For it is pride not only to ascribe anything we have to ourselves but to think we have what we really have not. . . . So you ascribe all the knowledge you have to God; and in this respect you are humble. But if you think you have more than you really have; or if you

---

10. The extravagant claims of some professors of perfection moved Wesley to publish these cautions later as a separate pamphlet, probably in 1762.

think you are so taught of God as no longer to need man's teaching; pride lieth at the door. . . .

"Do not therefore say to any who would advise or reprove you, 'You are blind; you cannot teach me.' Do not say, 'This is your wisdom, your carnal reason'; but calmly weigh the thing before God.

"Always remember, much grace does not imply much light. These do not always go together. As there may be much light where there is but little love, so there may be much love where there is little light. The heart has more heat than the eye; yet it cannot see. And God has wisely tempered the members of the body together that none may say to another, 'I have no need of thee.'

"To imagine none can teach you but those who are themselves saved from sin is a very great and dangerous mistake. Give not place to it for a moment; it would lead you into a thousand other mistakes, and that irrecoverably. No; dominion is not founded in grace, as the madmen of the last age talked. Obey and regard 'them that are over you in the Lord,' and do not think you know better than them. Know their place and your own; always remembering much love does not imply much light.

"The not observing this has led some into many mistakes, and into the appearance, at least, of pride. Oh, beware of the appearance, and the thing! Let 'there be in you that lowly mind which was in Christ Jesus.' And 'be ye likewise clothed with humility.' Let it not only fill, but cover you all over. Let modesty and self-diffidence appear in all your words and actions. Let all you speak and do show that you are little, and base, and mean, and vile in your own eyes.

"As one instance of this, be always ready to own any fault you have been in. If you have at any time thought, spoken, or acted wrong, be not backward to acknowledge it. Never dream that this will hurt the cause of God; no, it will further it. Be, therefore, open and frank when you are taxed with anything; do not seek either to evade or disguise it; but let it appear just as it is, and you will thereby not hinder but adorn the gospel.

"(33) *What is the second advice you would give them?*"

2. *Beware of Fanaticism*

"Beware of that daughter of pride, enthusiasm [fanaticism]. Oh, keep at the utmost distance from it! Give no place to a heated imagination."

a. Test your impressions. "Do not hastily ascribe things to God. Do not easily suppose dreams, voices, impressions, visions, or revelations to be from God. They may be from Him. They may be from nature. They may be from the devil. Therefore, 'believe not every spirit, but try the spirits whether they be of God.' Try all things by the written word, and let all bow down before it. You are in danger of enthusiasm every hour if you depart ever so little from Scripture; yea, or from the plain, literal meaning of any text taken in connection with the context. And so you are, if you despise or lightly esteem reason, knowledge, or human learning; every one of which is an excellent gift of God, and may serve the noblest purposes.

"I advise you, never to use the words, wisdom, reason, or knowledge, by way of reproach. On the contrary, pray that you yourself may abound in them more and more. If you mean worldly wisdom, useless knowledge, false reasoning, say so; and throw away the chaff, but not the wheat."

b. Use the means of grace. "One general inlet to enthusiasm is, expecting the end without the means; the expecting knowledge, for instance, without searching the Scriptures and consulting the children of God; the expecting spiritual strength without constant prayer and steady watchfulness; the expecting any blessing without hearing the word of God at every opportunity.

"Some have been ignorant of this device of Satan. They have left off searching the Scripture. They said, 'God writes all the Scriptures on my heart. Therefore, I have no need to read it.' Others thought they had not so much need of hearing and so grew slack in attending the morning preaching. Oh, take warning, you who are concerned herein! You have listened to the voice of a stranger. Fly back to Christ, and keep in the good old way which was 'once delivered to the saints'; the way that even a heathen bore testimony of: 'That the Christians rose early every day to sing hymns to Christ as God.'

"The very desire of 'growing in grace' may sometimes be an inlet of enthusiasm. As it continually leads us to seek new grace, it may lead us unawares to seek something else new beside new degrees of love to God and man. So it has led some to seek and fancy they had received gifts of a new kind after a new heart, as (1) The loving God with all our mind; (2) With all our soul; (3) With all our strength; (4) Oneness with God; (5) Oneness with Christ; (6) Having our life hid with Christ in God; (7) Being dead with Christ; (8) Rising with Him; (9) The sitting with Him in heavenly places; (10) The being taken up into His throne; (11) The being in the New Jerusalem; (12) The seeing the tabernacle of

God come down among men; (13) The being dead to all works; (14) The not being liable to death, pain, grief, or temptation."

c. Use Scripture wisely. "One ground of many of these mistakes is the taking every fresh, strong application of any of these scriptures to the heart to be a gift of a new kind; not knowing that several of these scriptures are not fulfilled yet; that most of the others are fulfilled when we are justified; the rest, the moment we are sanctified. It remains only to experience them in higher degrees. This is all we have to expect."

d. Manifest love. "Another ground of these and a thousand mistakes, is the not considering deeply that love is the highest gift of God; humble, gentle, patient love; that all visions, revelations, manifestations whatever are little things compared to love; and that all the gifts above mentioned are either the same with, or infinitely inferior to it.

"It were well you should be thoroughly sensible of this—the 'heaven of heavens is love.' There is nothing higher in religion; there is, in effect, nothing else; if you look for anything but more love, you are looking wide of the mark, you are getting out of the royal way. And when you are asking others, 'Have you received this or that blessing?' If you mean anything but more love, you mean wrong; you are leading them out of the way and putting them upon a false scent. Settle it then in your heart that from the moment God has saved you from all sin you are to aim at nothing more but more of that love described in the thirteenth of First Corinthians. You can go no higher than this till you are carried into Abraham's bosom.

"I say yet again, beware of enthusiasm. Such is the imagining you have the gift of prophesying or discerning of spirits, which I do not believe one of you has; no nor ever had yet. Beware of judging people to be either right or wrong by your own feelings. This is no scriptural way of judging. Oh, keep close to 'the law and to the testimony'!

"(34) *What is the third?*"

3. Beware of Faith Without Works

"Beware of Antinomianism; 'making void the law,' or any part of it, 'through faith.' Enthusiasm naturally leads to this; indeed, they can scarcely be separated. This may steal upon you in a thousand forms so that you cannot be too watchful against it. Take heed of everything, whether in principle or practice, which has any tendency thereto. Even that great truth that 'Christ is the end of the law,' may betray us into it, if we do not consider that He has adopted every point of the moral law and grafted it into the law of love. Beware of thinking, 'Because I am filled with love I need not have so much holiness. Because I pray always, therefore I need no set time for private prayer. Because I watch always, therefore I need no particular self-examination.' Let us 'magnify the law, the whole written word, 'and make it honorable.' Let this be our voice: "I prize Thy commandments above gold or precious stones. Oh, what love have I unto Thy law! all the day long is my study in it. . . .

"Beware of bigotry. Let not your love or beneficence be confined to Methodists, so-called only; much less to that very small part of them who seem to be renewed in love; or to those who believe yours and their report. Oh, make not this your Shibboleth! . . .

"Beware of self-indulgence; yea, and making a virtue of it, laughing at self-denial and taking up the cross daily at fasting or abstinence.

"Beware of censoriousness; thinking or calling them that any ways oppose you whether in judgment or practice, blind, dead, fallen, or 'enemies to the work.' Once more, beware of Solifidianism; crying nothing but 'Believe, believe!' and condemning those as ignorant or legal who speak in a more scriptural way. At certain seasons, indeed, it may be right to treat of nothing but of repentance, or merely of faith, or altogether of holiness; but in general, our call is to declare the whole counsel of God and to prophesy according to the analogy of faith. The written word treats of the whole and every particular branch of righteousness, descending to its minutest branches; as to be sober, courteous, diligent, patient, to honor all men. So, likewise, the Holy Spirit works the same in our hearts not merely creating desires after holiness in general but strongly inclining us to every particular grace, leading us to every individual part of 'whatsoever is lovely.' And this with the greatest propriety: for as 'by works faith is made perfect,' so the completing or destroying the work of faith, and enjoying the favor or suffering the displeasure of God, greatly depends on every single act of obedience or disobedience.

"(35) *What is the fourth?*"
4. Be Zealous of Good Works

"Beware of sins of omission; lose no opportunity of doing good in any kind. Be zealous of good works; willingly omit no work, either of piety or mercy. Do all the good you possibly can to the bodies and souls of men. Particularly, 'thou shalt in any wise reprove thy neighbor and not suffer sin upon him.' Be active. Give no place to indolence or sloth; give no occasion to say, 'Ye are idle, ye are idle.' Many will say so still; but let your whole spirit and behavior refute the slander. Be always employed; lose no shred of time; gather up the fragments that nothing be lost. And whatsoever thy hand findeth to do, do it with all thy might. Be 'slow to speak' and wary in speaking. 'In a multitude of words there wanteth not sin.' Do not talk much; neither long at a time. Few can converse profitably above an hour. Keep at the utmost distance from pious chit-chat, from religious gossiping.

"(36) What is the fifth?"

5. *Desire God Only*

"Beware of desiring anything but God. Now you desire nothing else; every other desire is driven out; see that none enter again. 'Keep thyself pure'; let your 'eye' remain 'single, and your whole body shall be full of light.' . . . O stand fast in the liberty wherewith Christ hath made you free!

"Be patterns to all of denying yourselves and taking up your cross daily. Let them see that you make no account of any pleasure which does not bring you nearer to God, nor regard any pain which does; that you simply aim at pleasing Him, whether by doing or suffering; that the constant language of your heart with regard to pleasure or pain, honor or dishonor, riches or poverty, is,

> *All's alike to me, so I*
> *In my Lord may live and die!*

"(37) What is the sixth?"

6. *Beware of Division*

"Beware of schism, of making a rent in the Church of Christ. Inward disunion, the members ceasing to have a reciprocal love 'one for another' (1 Cor. xii. 25), is the very root of all contention and every outward separation. Beware of everything tending thereto. Beware of a dividing spirit; shun whatever has the least aspect that way. Therefore, say not 'I am of Paul, or of Apollos'; the very thing which occasioned the schism at Corinth. . . . All this tends to breed or foment division, to disunite those whom God hath joined. Do not despise or run down any preacher; do not exalt anyone above the rest, lest you hurt both him and the cause of God. On the other hand, do not bear hard upon any by reason of some incoherency or inaccuracy of expression; no, nor for some mistakes, were they really such.

"Suffer not one thought of separating from your brethren

whether their opinions agree with yours or not. Do not dream that any man sins in not believing you, in not taking your word; or that this or that opinion is essential to the work, and both must stand or fall together. Beware of impatience of contradiction. Do not condemn or think hardly of those who cannot see just as you see, or who judge it their duty to contradict you whether in a great thing or a small. I fear some of us have thought hardly of others merely because they contradicted what we affirmed. All this tends to division; and by everything of this kind we are teaching them an evil lesson against ourselves.

"O beware of touchiness, of testiness, not bearing to be spoken to; starting at the least word; and flying from those who do not implicitly receive mine or another's sayings!

"Expect contradiction and opposition, together with crosses of various kinds. Consider the words of St. Paul: 'To you it is given, in the behalf of Christ'—for His sake, as a fruit of His death and intercession for you—'not only to believe but also to suffer for his sake' (Phil. i. 29). *It is given!* God gives you this opposition or reproach; it is a fresh token of His love. And will you disown the Giver; or spurn His gift and count it a misfortune? Will you not rather say, 'Father, the hour is come that Thou shouldest be glorified; now Thou givest Thy child to suffer something for Thee; do with me according to Thy will?' Know that these things, far from being hindrances to the work of God, or to your soul, unless by your own fault, are not only unavoidable in the course of providence, but profitable, yea, necessary for you. Therefore, receive them from God (not from chance), with willingness, with thankfulness. Receive them from men with humility, meekness, yieldingness, gentleness, sweetness. Why should not even your outward appearance and manner be soft? . . .

"Beware of tempting others to separate from you. Give no offense which can possibly be avoided; see that your practice be in all things suitable to your profession, adorning the doctrine of God our Savior. Be particularly careful in speaking of yourself. You may not, indeed, deny the work of God; but speak of it when you are called thereto, in the most inoffensive manner possible. Avoid all magnificent, pompous words; indeed, you need give it no general name; neither perfection, sanctification, the second blessing, nor the having attained. Rather speak of the particulars which God has wrought for you. You may say, 'At such a time, I felt a change which I am not able to express; and since that time, I have not felt pride, or self-will, or anger, or unbelief; nor any thing but a fulness of love to

WITNESSING

God and to all mankind.' And answer any other plain question that is asked with modesty and simplicity.

"And if any of you should at any time fall from what you now are, if you should again feel pride or unbelief or any temper from which you are now delivered; do not deny, do not hide, do not disguise it at all, at the peril of your soul. At all events, go to one in whom you can confide and speak just what you feel. God will enable him to speak a word in season which shall be health to your soul. And surely He will again lift up your head and cause the bones that have been broken to rejoice.

"(38) *What is the last advice that you would give them?*"
7. *Be an Example to the Saints*

"Be exemplary in all things; particularly in outward things (as in dress), in little things, in the laying out of your money (avoiding every needless expense), in deep, steady seriousness, and in the solidity and usefulness of all your conversation. So shall you be 'a light shining in a dark place.' So shall you daily 'grow in grace' till 'an entrance be ministered unto you abundantly into the everlasting kingdom of our Lord Jesus Christ.'

Recommended Reflections

"Most of the preceding advices are strongly enforced in the following reflections which I recommend to your deep and frequent consideration, next to the Holy Scriptures:

"(1) *The sea is an excellent figure of the fulness of God and that of the blessed Spirit.* For as the rivers all return into the sea; so the bodies, the souls, and the good works of the righteous, return into God to live there in His eternal repose.

"Although all the graces of God depend on His mere bounty, yet is He pleased generally to attach them to the prayers, the instructions, and the holiness of those with whom we are. By strong, though invisible attractions, He draws some souls through their intercourse with others.

"The sympathies formed by grace far surpass those formed by nature.

"The truly devout show that passions as naturally flow from true as from false love, so deeply sensible are they of the goods and evils of those whom they love for God's sake. But this can only be comprehended by those who understand the language of love.

"The bottom of the soul may be in repose even while we are in many outward troubles; just as the bottom of the sea is calm while the surface is strongly agitated.

"The best helps to growth in grace are the ill-usage, the affronts, and the losses which befall us. We should receive them with all thankfulness, as preferable to all others, were it only on this account—that our will has no part therein.

"The readiest way to escape from our sufferings is to be willing they should endure as long as God pleases.

"If we suffer persecution and affliction in a right manner, we attain a larger measure of conformity to Christ by a due improvement of one of these occasions, than we could have done merely by imitating His mercy in abundance of good works.

"One of the greatest evidences of God's love to those that love Him is to send them afflictions with grace to bear them.

"Even in the greatest afflictions we ought to testify to God that, in receiving them from His hand, we feel pleasure in the midst of the pain from being afflicted by Him who loves us and whom we love.

"The readiest way which God takes to draw a man to himself is to afflict him in that he loves most and with good reason; and to cause this affliction to arise from some good action done with a single eye; because nothing can more clearly show him the emptiness of what is most lovely and desirable in the world.

"(2) *True resignation consists in a thorough conformity to the whole will of God,* who wills and does all (excepting sin) which comes to pass in the world. In order to do this we have only to embrace all events, good and bad, as His will.

"In the greatest afflictions which can befall the just, either from heaven or earth, they remain immovable in peace and perfectly submissive to God by an inward, loving regard to Him, uniting in one all the powers of their souls.

"We ought quietly to suffer whatever befalls us, to bear the defects of others and our own, to confess them to God in secret prayer, or with groans which cannot be uttered; but never to speak a sharp or peevish word, nor to murmur or repine but thoroughly willing that God should treat you in the manner that pleases Him. We are His lambs, and therefore ought to be ready to suffer, even to the death, without complaining.

"We are to bear with those we cannot amend, and to be content with offering them to God. This is true resignation. And since He has borne our infirmities we may well bear those of each other for His sake.

"To abandon all, to strip one's self of all in order to seek and to follow Jesus Christ naked to Bethlehem where He was born; naked to the hall where He was scourged; and naked to Calvary where He died on the cross, is so great a mercy that neither the thing, nor the knowledge of it is given to any but through faith in the Son of God.

"(3) *There is no love of God without patience, and no patience without lowliness and sweetness of spirit.*

"Humility and patience are the surest proofs of the increase of love.

"Humility alone unites patience with love, without which it is impossible to draw profit from suffering, or indeed, to avoid complaint especially when we think we have given no occasion for what men make us suffer.

"True humility is a kind of self-annihilation, and this is the centre of all virtues.

"A soul returned to God ought to be attentive to everything which is said to him on the head of salvation, with a desire to profit thereby.

"Of the sins which God has pardoned, let nothing remain but a deeper humility in the heart and a stricter regulation in our words, in our actions, and in our sufferings.

"(4) *The bearing of men, and suffering evils in meekness and silence is the sum of a Christian life.*

"God is the first object of our love: its next office is to bear the defects of others. And we should begin the practice of this amidst our own household.

"We should chiefly exercise our love toward them who most shock either our way of thinking, or our temper, or our knowledge, or the desire we have that others should be as virtuous as we wish to be ourselves.

"(5) *God hardly gives His Spirit even to those whom He has established in grace, if they do not pray for it on all occasions, not only once but many times.*

"God does nothing but in answer to prayer; and even they who have been converted to God, without praying for it themselves (which is exceeding rare), were not without the prayers of others. Every new victory which a soul gains is the effect of a new prayer.

"On every occasion of uneasiness we should retire to prayer that we may give place to the grace and light of God and then form our resolutions without being in any pain about what success they may have.

"In the greatest temptations, a single look to Christ and the barely pronouncing His name suffices to overcome the wicked one, so it be done with confidence and calmness of spirit.

"God's command to 'pray without ceasing' is founded on the necessity we have of His grace to preserve the life of God in the soul, which can no more subsist one moment without it than the body can without air.

"Whether we think of, or speak to God, whether we act or suffer for Him, all is prayer when we have no other object than His love and the desire of pleasing Him.

"All that a Christian does, even in eating and sleeping, is prayer when it is done in simplicity, according to the order of God, without either adding to or diminishing from it by his own choice.

"Prayer continues in the desire of the heart, though the understanding be employed on outward things.

"In souls filled with love, the desire to please God is a continual prayer.

"As the furious hate which the devil bears us is termed the roaring of a lion, so our vehement love may be termed crying after God.

"God only requires of His adult children that their hearts be truly purified, and that they offer Him continually the wishes and vows that naturally spring from perfect love. For these desires, being the genuine fruits of love, are the most perfect prayers that can spring from it.

"(6) *It is scarce conceivable how straight the way is wherein God leads them that follow Him; and how dependent on Him we must be unless we are wanting in our faithfulness to Him.*

"It is hardly credible of how great consequence before God the smallest things are; and what great inconveniences sometimes follow those which appear to be light faults.

"As a very little dust will disorder a clock, and the least sand will obscure our sight, so the least grain of sin which is upon the heart will hinder its right motion toward God.

"We ought to be in the church as the saints are in heaven, and in the house as the holiest men are in the church; doing our work in the house as we pray in the church; worshiping God from the ground of the heart.

"We should be continually laboring to cut off all the useless things that surround us: and God usually retrenches the superfluities of our souls in the same proportion as we do those of our bodies.

"The best means of resisting the devil is to destroy whatever of the world remains in us in order to raise for God, upon its ruins, a building all of love. Then shall we begin, in this fleeting life, to love God as we shall love Him in eternity.

"We scarce conceive how easy it is to rob God of His due, in our friendship with the most virtuous persons, until they are torn from us by death. But if this loss produce lasting sorrow, that is a clear proof that we had before two treasures between which we divided our heart.

"(7) *If after having renounced all, we do not watch incessantly and beseech God to accompany our vigilance with His, we shall be again entangled and overcome.*

"As the most dangerous winds may enter at little openings, so the devil never enters more dangerously than by little unobserved incidents which seem to be nothing; yet insensibly open the heart to great temptations.

"It is good to renew ourselves from time to time by closely examining the state of our souls, as if we had never done it before; for nothing tends more to the full assurance of faith than to keep ourselves by this means in humility and the exercise of all good works.

"To continual watchfulness and prayer ought to be added continual employment. For grace fills a vacuum as well as nature; and the devil fills whatever God does not fill.

"There is no faithfulness like that which ought to be between a guide of souls and the person directed by Him. They ought continually to regard each other in God, and closely to examine themselves whether all their thoughts are pure and all their words directed with Christian discretion. Other affairs are only the things of men; but these are peculiarly the things of God.

"(8) *The words of St. Paul, 'No man can call Jesus Lord, but by the Holy Ghost,' show us the necessity of eyeing God in our good works, and even in our minutest thoughts;* knowing that none are pleasing to Him but those which He forms in us and with us. From hence we learn that we cannot serve Him unless He use our tongue, hands, and heart to do by himself and His Spirit whatever He would have us to do.

"If we were not utterly impotent, our good works would be our own property; whereas now they belong wholly to God because they proceed from Him and His grace: while raising our works, and making them all divine, He honors himself in us through them.

"One of the principal rules of religion is to lose no occasion of serving God. And, since He is invisible to our eyes, we are to serve Him in our neighbor; which He receives as if done to himself in person standing visibly before us.

"God does not love men that are inconstant, nor good works that are intermitted. Nothing is pleasing to Him, but what has a resemblance of His own immutability.

"A constant attention to the work which God entrusts us with is a mark of solid piety.

"Love fasts when it can, and as much as it can. It leads to all the ordinances of God and employs itself in all the outward works whereof it is capable. It flies as it were, like Elijah over the plain to find God upon His holy mountain.

"God is so great that He communicates greatness to the least thing that is done for His service.

"Happy are they who are sick, yea, or lose their life for having done a good work.

"God frequently conceals the part which His children have in the conversion of other souls. Yet one may boldly say that person who long groans before Him for the conversion of another, whenever that soul is converted to God, is one of the chief causes of it.

"Charity cannot be practiced right unless first we exercise it the moment God gives the occasion; and secondly, retire the instant after to offer it to God by humble thanksgiving. And this for three reasons: First, to render Him what we have received from Him. The second, to avoid the dangerous temptation which springs from the very goodness of these works. And the third, to unite ourselves to God in whom the soul expands itself in prayer with all the graces we have received and the good works we have done to draw from Him new strength against the bad effects which these very works may produce in us. . . . The true means to be filled anew with the riches of grace is thus to strip ourselves of it; and without this it is extremely difficult not to grow faint in the practice of good works.

"Good works do not receive their last perfection till they, as it were, lose themselves in God. This is a kind of death to them, resembling that of our bodies which will not attain their highest life, their immortality, till they lose themselves in the glory of our souls, or rather of God, wherewith they shall be filled. And it is only what they had of earthly and mortal, which good works lose by this spiritual death.

"Fire is the symbol of love; and the love of God is the principle and the end of all our good works. But truth surpasses figure; and the fire of divine love has this advantage over material fire, that it can reascend to its source and raise thither with it all the good works which it produces. And by this means it prevents their being corrupted by pride, vanity, or any evil mixture. But this cannot be done otherwise than by making these good works in a spiritual manner die in God by a deep gratitude which plunges the soul in Him as in an abyss, with all that it is, and all the grace and works for which it is indebted to Him; a gratitude whereby the soul seems to empty itself of them, that they may return to their source as rivers seem willing to empty themselves when they pour themselves with all their waters into the sea.

"When we have received any favor from God, we ought to retire, if not into our closets, into our hearts, and say, 'I come, Lord, to restore to Thee what Thou hast given; and I freely relinquish it to enter again into my own nothingness. For what is the most perfect creature in heaven or earth in Thy presence but a void capable of being filled with Thee and by Thee; as the air which is void and dark is capable of being filled with the light of the sun who withdraws it every day to restore it the next, there being nothing in the air that either appropriates this light or resists it? O give me the same facility of receiving and restoring Thy grace and good works! I say, *Thine;* for I acknowledge the root from which they spring is in Thee, and not in me.'"

Eleven Propositions on Perfection

26. In the year 1764, upon a review of the whole subject, I wrote down the sum of what I had observed in the following short propositions:

"(1) There is such a thing as perfection; for it is again and again mentioned in Scripture.

"(2) It is not so early as justification, for justified persons are to 'go on unto perfection' (Heb. vi. 1).

"(3) It is not so late as death; for St. Paul speaks of living men that were perfect (Phil. iii. 15).

"(4) It is not absolute. Absolute perfection belongs not to man, nor to angels, but to God alone.

"(5) It does not make a man infallible; none is infallible while he remains in the body.

"(6) Is it sinless? It is not worth while to contend for a term. It is 'salvation from sin.'

"(7) It is 'perfect love' (1 John iv. 18). This is the essence of it; its properties, or inseparable fruits, are rejoicing evermore, praying without ceasing, and in every thing giving thanks (1 Thess. v. 16, etc.).

"(8) It is improvable. It is so far from lying in an indivisible point, from being incapable of increase, that one perfected in love may grow in grace far swifter than he did before.

"(9) It is amissible, capable of being lost; of which we have numerous instances. But we were not thoroughly convinced of this till five or six years ago.

"(10) It is constantly both preceded and followed by a gradual work.

"(11) But is it in itself instantaneous or not? In examining this, let us go on step by step.

"An instantaneous change has been wrought in some believers. None can deny this.

"Since that change, they enjoy perfect love; they feel this, and this alone; they 'rejoice evermore, pray without ceasing, and in everything give thanks.' Now this is all that I mean by perfection; therefore, these are witnesses of the perfection which I preach.

"'But in some, this change was not instantaneous.' They did not perceive the instant when it was wrought. It is often difficult to perceive the instant when a man dies; yet there is an instant in which life ceases. And if even sin ceases, there must be a last moment of its existence and a first moment of our deliverance from it.

"'But if they have this love now, they will lose it.' They may; but they need not. And whether they do or no, they have it now; they now experience what we teach. They now are all love; they now rejoice, pray, and praise without ceasing.

"'However sin is only suspended in them; it is not destroyed.' Call it which you please. They are all love today; and they take no thought for the morrow.

"'But this doctrine has been much abused.' So has that of justification by faith. But that is no reason for giving up either this or any other scriptural doctrine. 'When you wash your child,' as one speaks, 'throw away the water; but do not throw away the child.'

"'But those who think they are saved from sin, say they have no need of the merits of Christ.' They say just the contrary. Their language is:

> Every moment, Lord, I want
> The merit of thy death!

They never before had so deep, so unspeakable a conviction of the need of Christ in all of His offices as they have now. "Therefore, all our Preachers should make a point of preaching perfection to believers, constantly, strongly and explicitly; and all believers should mind this one thing and continually agonize for it."

PREACHING

Summary

27. I have now done what I proposed. I have given a plain and simple account of the manner wherein I first received the doctrine of perfection, and the sense wherein I received and wherein I do receive and teach it to this day. I have declared the whole and every part of what I mean by that scriptural expression. I have drawn the picture of it at full length without either disguise or covering.

And I would now ask any impartial person, what is there so frightful therein? Whence is all this outcry, which, for these twenty years and upwards, has been made throughout the kingdom; as if all Christianity were destroyed and all religion torn up by the roots? Why is it that the very name of perfection has been cast out of the mouths of Christians; yea, exploded and abhorred as if it contained the most pernicious heresy? . . .

"This is Mr. Wesley's doctrine! He preaches perfection!" He does; yet this is not his doctrine any more than it is yours or any one's else that is a minister of Christ. For it is His doctrine, peculiarly, emphatically His; it is the doctrine of Jesus Christ. Those are His words, not mine: "Ye shall therefore be perfect, as your Father who is in heaven is perfect." And who says ye shall not; or at least not till your soul is separated from the body?

SCRIPTURAL

It is the doctrine of St. Paul, the doctrine of St. James, of St. Peter, and St. John; and no otherwise Mr. Wesley's than as it is the doctrine of everyone who preaches the pure and the whole gospel. I tell you as plain as I can speak where and when I found this. I found it in the oracles of God, in the Old and New Testament; when I read them with no other view or desire, but to save my own soul. But whosoever this doctrine is, I pray you, what harm is there in it?

Look at it again; survey it on every side, and that with the closest attention. In one view, it is purity of intention, dedicating all the life to God. It is the giving God all our heart; it is one desire and design ruling all our tempers. It is the devoting, not a part, but all our soul, body, and substance to God. In another view, it is all the mind which was in Christ enabling us to walk as Christ walked. It is the circumcision of the heart from all filthiness, all inward as well as outward pollution. It is a renewal of the heart in the whole image of God, the full likeness of Him that created it. In yet another, it is the loving God with all our heart and our neighbor as ourselves. Now take it in which of these views you please (for there is no material difference), and this is the whole and sole perfection, as a train of writings prove to a demonstration, which I have believed and taught for these forty years, from the year 1725 to the year 1765.

An Earnest Appeal to the Children of God

28. Now let this perfection appear in its native form, and who can speak one word against it? Will any dare to speak against loving the Lord our God with all our heart and our neighbor as ourselves? against a renewal of heart, not only in part, but in the whole image of God? Who is he that will open his mouth against being cleansed from all pollution both of flesh and spirit; or against having all the mind that was in Christ, and walking in all things as Christ walked? What man who calls himself a Christian has the hardiness to object to the devoting, not a part, but all our soul, body, and substance to God? What serious man would oppose the giving God all our heart and the having one desire ruling all our tempers? I say again, let this Christian perfection appear in its own shape and who will fight against it? It must be disguised before it can be opposed. It must be covered with a bearskin first, or even the wild beasts of the people will scarce be induced to worry it.

But whatever these do, let not the children of God any longer fight against the image of God. Let not the members of Christ say anything against the whole mind that was in Christ. Let not those who are alive to God oppose the dedicating all our life to Him. Why should you who have His love shed abroad in your heart withstand the giving Him all your heart? Does not all that is within you cry out, "Oh, who that loves can love enough?" What pity that those who desire and design to please Him should have any other design or desire! Much more that they should dread as a fatal delusion, yea, abhor as an abomination to God, the having this one desire and design ruling every temper!

Why should devout men be afraid of devoting all their soul, body, and substance to God? Why should those who love Christ count it a damnable error to think we may have all the mind that was in Him? We allow, we contend that we are justified freely through the righteousness and the blood of Christ.

And why are you so hot against us because we expect likewise to be sanctified wholly through His Spirit? We look for no favor either from the open servants of sin or from those who have only the form of religion. But how long will you who worship God in spirit, who are "circumcised with the circumcision not made with hands," set your battle in array against those who seek an entire circumcision of heart, who thirst to be cleansed from all filthiness of flesh and spirit and to perfect holiness in the fear of God?

Are we your enemies because we look for a full deliverance from the carnal mind which is enmity against God? Nay, we are your brethren, your fellow-laborers in the vineyard of our Lord, your companions in the kingdom and patience of Jesus. Although this we confess (if we are fools therein, yet as fools bear with us), we expect to love God with all our heart, and our neighbor as ourselves. Yea, we do believe that He will in this world so "cleanse the thoughts of our hearts by the inspiration of His Holy Spirit that we shall perfectly love Him, and worthily magnify His holy name."

4

EXPOSITIONS, HYMNS, LETTERS, AND TREATISES

Notes on the Old and New Testaments
John Wesley and His Bible
Preface to Notes on the Old Testament
Two Excerpts from Notes on the Old Testament
Notes on the New Testament
Excerpts from Notes upon the New Testament

Holiness in the Hymns
Hymns Adapted from Others
John Wesley's Own Hymns
The Poetical Works of John and Charles Wesley
Preface to Volume 2
*A Collection of Hymns
for the Use of the People Called Methodists*
Contents
Preface
John Wesley's Rules for Singing

The Letters of John Wesley
To Charles Wesley
Correspondence with Others

Appeals to Men of Reason and Religion
On Living Without Sin
A Farther Appeal to Men of Reason and Religion

Social Implications of Entire Sanctification
Christian Religion Is a Social Religion
A Plain Account of the People Called Methodists
God's Advocate: A Plea for Real Holiness

4 Expositions, Hymns, Letters, and Treatises

Notes on the Old and New Testaments

JOHN WESLEY AND HIS BIBLE

Wesley firmly believed and proclaimed the sufficiency of the Scriptures. Perhaps it was natural that this should be so, considering his upbringing in a Bible-loving home, his earliest experience of education under mother-tutor Susanna, and the orthodox evangelical churchmanship of father Samuel with his almost endless versifying of scripture.

Long before his conversion Wesley proclaimed and defended the sufficiency of the Scriptures. About 1728 he preached his sermon "On Corrupting the Word of God." In this he warned against "introducing into it human mixtures" either errors or fancies, mixing it with false interpretations, or "by taking from it—anything of spirit or substance." To Wesley the sincere preacher is one who preaches "the genuine unmixed word of God and that only" and have "taken the known phrases in their common obvious sense, and when they were less known, explained scripture by scripture."[1]

From this stance Wesley never departed, even under criticism and pressure from clerics such as Rev. Mr. Potter who appears to have been disturbed by Wesley's emphasis upon the action of the Holy Spirit in inspiring, strengthening, and comforting the believer in order that he may persevere in the gospel way.[2]

To Wesley the ministry of the Holy Spirit was necessary "to enlighten the understanding and to rectify the will."[3] His concept of the sufficiency of Scripture was thus held in close association with his understanding of the ministry of the Spirit in interpreting and applying scriptural truth to the humble-hearted Christian.

---

1. *WW*, VII: 468-73.
2. *LJW*, 4:43.
3. Ibid.

EXPLANATORY NOTES

UPON

The New Testament.

BY

JOHN WESLEY, M.A.

Late Fellow of *Lincoln College, Oxford.*

32995

LONDON,
Printed by WILLIAM BOWYER. MDCCLV.

First edition title page of Wesley's "Notes"

Else, be the Scriptures ever so complete, they will not save your soul. How then can you imagine that it (the inspiration of the Spirit) is unnecessary, and that the "supposed need of it is injurious to the written Word"?

This was the heart of his own method of Bible study, as appears from his preface to the *Standard Sermons*. Submitting to the ministry of the Holy Spirit was also his counsel to his lay preachers: "'God's holy inspiration both in order to think the things that be good' and also 'perfectly to love Him and worthily to magnify His holy name.'"[4]

With such a high view of Scripture it is understandable why Wesley should be so careful to provide guidance for "the people called Methodists" in their reading and preaching of the Bible. He provided *Explanatory Notes upon the Old Testament*,[5] in which he acknowledges having extracted some of the material from Matthew Henry (d. 1714) for whom he had a high regard but with reservations. He extracts much more from Matthew Poole (d. 1679).

The extracts that follow are intended to be examples of Wesley's comments on one or two scriptures from which he presented his message of full redemption.

Preface to Notes on the Old Testament

Every thinking man will now easily discern my design in the following sheets. It is not to write sermons, essays, or set discourses, upon any part of Scripture. It is not to draw inferences from the text, or to shew what doctrines may be proved thereby. It is this: to give the direct, literal meaning. . . . I design only, like the hand of a dial, to point every man to this; not to take up his mind with something else, how excellent soever; but to keep his eye fixed upon the naked Bible, that he may read and hear it with understanding. . . . It is not my design to write a book, which a man may read separate from the Bible; but barely to assist those who fear God. . . . by shewing the natural sense of every part in as few and plain words as I can. And I am not without hopes that the following *Notes* may in some measure answer this end, not barely to unlettered and ignorant men, but also to men of education and learning (although it is true, neither these nor the *Notes on the New Testament* were principally designed for them). . . .

---

4. *LJW*, 4:44. There is also in this letter a beautiful claim by Wesley that his preachers are "holy and acceptable to God" (44-45).

5. (Bristol: William Pine, 1765). The *Old Testament Notes*, came "about ten years" (J. W.) after those on the New.

This is the way to understand the things of God: "Meditate thereon day and night"; so shall you attain to the best knowledge, even to "know the only true God, and Jesus Christ whom he hath sent." And this knowledge will lead you to "love the Lord your God with all your heart, and with all your soul, and with all your mind, and with all your strength." Will there not then be all "that mind in you which was also in Christ Jesus"? And in consequence of this, while you joyfully experience all the holy tempers described in this book, you will likewise be outwardly "holy as he that hath called you is holy, in all manner of conversation."[6]

Wesley concludes his Preface by suggesting a method of reading the Scriptures:

If you desire to read the Scriptures in such a manner as may most effectually answer this end, would it not be advisable, (1) To set apart a little time, if you can, every morning and evening for that purpose? (2) At each time, if you have leisure, to read a chapter out of the Old, and one out of the New Testament: if you cannot do this, to take a single chapter, or a part of one? (3) To read this with a single eye, to know the whole will of God, and a fixed resolution to do it? (4) In order to know His will you should have a constant eye to the analogy of faith: the connection and harmony there is between those grand fundamental doctrines, original sin, justification by faith, the new birth, inward and outward holiness. (5) Serious and earnest prayer should be constantly used, before we consult the oracles of God, seeing [that] "Scripture can only be understood through the same Spirit whereby it was given." Our reading should likewise be clothed with prayer, that what we read may be written on our hearts. (6) It might also be of use, if while we read, we were frequently to pause and examine ourselves by what we read, both with regard to our hearts and lives. This would furnish us with matter of praise, where we found God had enabled us to conform to his blessed will; and matter of humiliation and prayer, where we were conscious of having fallen short. And whatever light you then receive should be used to the utmost, and that immediately. Let there be no delay. Whatever you resolve begin to execute the first moment you can. So shall you find this word to be indeed the power of God unto present and eternal salvation.[7]

---

6. "Preface to *Explanatory Notes upon the Old Testament*," iii-ix.
7. Ibid., ix.

Two Excerpts from Notes on the Old Testament
Ezek. 36:25-29

Wesley makes use of this scripture at least four times in *A Plain Account of Christian Perfection,* and no doubt he could have used it for his great sermon "The Circumcision of the Heart," but he did not do so. His notes are worthy of our attention.

Verse 25. *Sprinkle*—This signifies both the blood of Christ sprinkled on their conscience to take away their guilt, as the water of purification was sprinkled to take away their ceremonial uncleanness, and the grace of the Spirit sprinkled on the conscience to purify it from all corrupt inclination and disposition.

Verse 26. *A new heart*—A new frame of soul changed from sinful to holy, from carnal to spiritual. A heart in which the law of God is written (Jer. xxxi. 33). A new heart in which the grace of God is victorious and turns it from all sin to God. *A new spirit*—A new holy frame in the spirit of man, which is given to him, not wrought by his own power. *The stony*—The senseless unfeeling. *Out of your flesh*—Out of you. *Of flesh*—That is, quite of another temper, harkening to God's law, trembling at His threats, moulded into compliance with His whole will. *To forbear*—Do, be, or suffer what God will, receiving the impress of God as soft wax receives the impress of the seal.

Verse 27. *My Spirit*—The Holy Spirit of God, which is given to and dwelleth in all true believers. *And cause you*—Sweetly, powerfully, and yet without compulsion; for our spirits, framed by God's Spirit to a disposition suitable to His holiness, readily concurs. *Ye shall keep*—Be willing, and able to keep the judgments, and to walk in the statutes of God, which is, to live in all holiness.

Verse 28. *And I will be your God*—This is the topstone of a believer's happiness.

Verse 29. *I will also save you*—I will continue to save you. *From all your uncleanness*—Salvation from all uncleanness includes justification, entire sanctification, and meetness for glory.

Psalm 51

Verse 5. *I was shapen in iniquity*—Nor is this the only sin which I have reason to bewail before thee; for this filthy stream leads me to a corrupt fountain: and upon a review of my heart, I find, that this heinous crime was the proper fruit of my vile nature, which ever was and still is ready to commit ten thousand sins as occasion offers.

Verse 6. *Truth*—Uprightness of heart; and this may be added; as an aggravation of the sinfulness of original corruption, because it is contrary to the holy nature and will of God, which requires rectitude of heart: and, as an aggravation of the actual sin, that it was committed against that knowledge, which God had wrote on his heart.

Verse 7. *Hyssop*—As lepers are by the appointment purified by the use of hyssop and other things, so do Thou cleanse me, a leprous and polluted creature, by Thy grace, and by that blood of Christ which is signified by those ceremonial usages.

Verse 8. *Joy*—By Thy Spirit seal the pardon of my sins on my conscience; which will fill me with joy.

Verse 10. *Create*—Work in me a holy frame of heart, whereby my inward filth may be removed. *Right*—Heb. firm or constant, that my resolution may be fixed and unmoveable. *Spirit*—Temper or disposition of soul.

Verse 12. *The joy*—The comfortable sense of Thy saving grace, promised and vouchsafed to me, both for my present and everlasting salvation. *Free*—Or ingenuous, liberal, princely; which he seems to oppose to his own base, illiberal, disingenuous, and servile spirit which he had discovered in his wicked practice: a spirit which may free me from the bondage of sin, and enable me cheerfully to run the way of God's precepts.

Verse 15. *My lips*—Which are shut with shame and grief.

Verse 16. *Not sacrifice*—This is not to be understood absolutely, [but] with respect to David's crimes which were not to be expiated by any sacrifice.

Verse 17. *A broken*—This is of more value than many sacrifices.

NOTES ON THE NEW TESTAMENT

It was upon Wesley's *Explanatory Notes upon the New Testament* that the message of the Methodist preachers more heavily depended as an indispensable part of the Wesley standards of doctrine and preaching.

The preparation of these *Notes* arose from Wesley's feeling that he was soon to die, coupled with his profound desire to help his lay preachers understand and preach the gospel of the New Testament. He began the *Notes* on January 6, 1754, and completed them in September 1755. In this work he was greatly assisted by brother Charles who was a highly competent Greek scholar. It must be noted that Wesley acknowledged and introduced the *Notes* as more of a compilation than an original production. He wrote: "I once designed to write down barely what occurred to my own mind, consulting none but the inspired writers. But no sooner was I acquainted with that great light of the Christian world, Bengelius, lately gone to his reward, than I changed my design."[8]

Thus the *Notes* make extensive use of Bengel's *Gnomon*, but Wesley also used the writings of Heylin, Guise, and Doddridge. Thus the work is really a collection of the finest comments Wesley knew or could find, based on his own translation and heavily salted with his own insights. They contain nothing contrary to or critical of Wesley's personal beliefs, hence their place among the Wesley standard works.

The *Notes* were not prepared for scholars or specialists, but for uneducated, devoted people, especially for that noble army of Methodist lay preachers whom Wesley knew would "lift up their hearts to the Father of lights" if "anything appeared dark or intricate."

The editor believes that the following extracts are notes made by Wesley personally and that they provide some of the guidance given to his preachers in preparing their sermons on Christian holiness. He did not himself build his doctrine of Christian perfection merely on proof texts but on the total biblical revelation. The whole warp and woof of the Scripture, its objective and content go into the presentation. There are, however, passages used more frequently than others. Most of these are New Testament passages although Ezekiel 36 is often employed, and some of Wesley's other Old Testament notes are forceful and pointed.

EXCERPTS FROM NOTES UPON THE NEW TESTAMENT

Wesley preached often from the Sermon on the Mount: almost a third of his standard sermons are based on it. For example:

Matt. 5:8. *The pure in heart*—The sanctified; they who love God with all their hearts. *They shall see God*—In all things here; hereafter in glory.

Matt. 5:48. *Therefore ye shall be perfect, as your Father who is in heaven is perfect*—So the original runs, referring to all that holiness which is described in the foregoing verses, which our Lord in the beginning of the chapter recommends as happiness, and in the close of it as perfection.

And how wise and gracious is this, to sum up, and as it were seal,

---

8. *WN*, 4.

all His commandments with a promise; even the proper promise of the gospel, that He will "put" those "laws in our minds, and write them in our hearts!" He well knew how ready our unbelief would be to cry out, This is impossible! and therefore stakes upon it all the power, truth, and faithfulness of Him to whom all things are possible.

Matt. 6:1. In the foregoing chapter our Lord particularly described the nature of inward holiness. In this He describes that purity of intention without which none of our outward actions are holy. This chapter contains four parts: (1) The right intention and manner in giving alms (vv. 1-4); (2) The right intention, manner, form, and prerequisites of prayer (vv. 5-15); (3) The right intention and manner of fasting (vv. 16-18); (4) The necessity of a pure intention in all things, unmixed either with the desire of riches or worldly care and fear of want (vv. 19-34).

This verse is a general caution against vain glory in any of our good works: all these are here summed up together in the comprehensive word *righteousness*. This general caution our Lord applies in the sequel to the three principal branches of it; relating to our neighbor (vv. 1-4); to God (vv. 5-6); and to ourselves (vv. 16-18).

Matt. 6:10. *Thy will be done on earth as it is in heaven*—May all the inhabitants of the earth do Thy will as willingly as the holy angels! May these do it continually even as they, without any interruption of their willing service; yea, and perfectly as they! Mayest Thou, O Spirit of grace, through the blood of the everlasting covenant, make them perfect in every good work to do Thy will, and work in them all that is well-pleasing in Thy sight!

As we might expect, Wesley scrutinizes and analyzes Paul's Epistles, sometimes almost to the point of crumbling the verses, but never losing sight of the great "despositum"—holiness of heart and life.

Rom. 6:6. *Our old man*—Coeval with our being, and as old as the Fall; our evil nature; a strong and beautiful expression for that entire depravity and corruption which by nature spreads itself over the whole man, leaving no part uninfected. This in a believer is crucified with Christ, mortified, gradually killed, by virtue of our union with Him. *That the body of sin*—All evil tempers, words, and actions, which are the "members" of the "old man" (Col. iii. 5), *might be destroyed.*

Rom. 8:3. *For what the law*—Of Moses. *Could not do, in that it was weak through the flesh*—Incapable of conquering our evil nature. If it could, God needed not to have *sent his own Son in the likeness of* *sinful flesh*—We with our sinful flesh were devoted to death. But God, sending His own Son in the likeness of sinful flesh, though pure from sin, *condemned* that *sin* which was *in* our *flesh;* gave sentence, that sin should be destroyed and the believer wholly delivered from it.

Rom. 8:29. *Whom he foreknew, he also predestinated conformable to the image of his Son.* Here the apostle declares who those are whom He foreknew and predestinated to glory; namely, those who are comformable to the image of His Son. This is the mark of those who are foreknown and will be glorified (2 Tim. ii. 19; Phil. iii. 10, 21).

Rom. 8:30. *Them he*—In due time. *Called*—By His gospel and His Spirit. *And whom he called*—When obedient to the heavenly calling (Acts xxvi. 19). *He also justified*—Forgave and accepted. *And whom he justified*—Provided they "continued in his goodness' (Rom. xi. 22), He in the end *glorified*—St. Paul does not affirm, either here or in any other part of the writings that precisely the same number of men are called, justified, and glorified. He does not deny that a believer may fall away and be cut off between his special calling and his glorification (Rom. xi. 22). Neither does he deny that many are called who never are justified. He only affirms that this is the method whereby God leads us step by step toward heaven. *He glorified*—He speaks as one looking back from the goal upon the race of faith. Indeed grace, as it is glory begun, is both an earnest and a foretaste of eternal glory.

1 Thess. 5:23. *And may the God of peace sanctify you*—By the peace He works in you, which is a great means of sanctification. *Wholly*—The word signifies *wholly and perfectly;* every part and all that concerns you; all that is of or about you. *And may the whole of you, the spirit and the soul and the body*—Just before he said *you;* now he denominated them from their spiritual state. *The spirit*—Gal. vi. 8; wishing that it may be preserved *whole and entire:* then from their natural state, the *soul and the body* (for these two make up the whole nature of man, Matt. x. 28); wishing it *may be preserved blameless till the coming of Christ.* To explain this a little further: of the three here mentioned, only the two last are the natural constituent parts of man. The first is adventitious, and the supernatural gift of God to be found in Christians only. That man cannot possibly consist of three parts appears hence: The soul is either matter or not matter: there is no medium. But if it is matter, it is part of the body: if not matter, it coincides with the spirit.

1 Thess. 5:24. *Who also will do it*—Unless you quench the Spirit.

Heb. 12:14. *And holiness*—The not following after *all* holiness is the direct way to fall into sin of every kind.

Heb. 12:24. *And to the blood of sprinkling*—To all the virtue of His precious blood shed for you, whereby you are sprinkled from an evil conscience. This blood of sprinkling was the foundation of our Lord's mediatorial office. Here the gradation is at the highest point.

Heb. 13:20-25. *The everlasting covenant*—The Christian covenant, which is not temporary like the Jewish but designed to remain forever. By the application of that *blood,* by which this covenant was established may He make you in every respect, inwardly and outwardly holy!

Wesley's preaching style was molded by his desire to be as plain to the understanding as the apostle John in his first Epistle.

> "If any man speak," in the name of God, "let him speak as the oracles of God"; and if he would imitate any part of these above the rest, let it be the First Epistle of St. John. This is the style, the most excellent style, for every gospel preacher. And let him aim at no more ornament than he finds in that sentence, which is the sum of the whole gospel, "We love him, because he first loved us."[9]

Consequently it is not surprising that Wesley uses the First Epistle of John more frequently than any other New Testament book in preaching the message of Christian perfection. The following extracts are from the *Notes,* but Wesley also uses the Apostle's first letter in sermons, journal, and letters; indeed the Epistle is one of his chief biblical warrants for the doctrine of perfect love, not as an ideal only but as a realizable experience. "Holiness was not merely imputed but imparted. God could do more than forgive sin: He could destroy it. Asked for his scriptural authority, he was never more ready to proffer any part of it than he was ready to proffer what he found in the First Epistle of John."[10]

1 John 1:1. *That which we have seen and heard*—Of Him and from Him. *Declare we to you*—For this end. *That ye also may have fellowship with us*—May enjoy the same fellowship which we enjoy. *And truly our fellowship*—Whereby He is in us and we in Him. *Is with*

---

9. Preface to the second edition of Wesley's sermons. See *WJ,* 5:29, 137; 7:232.

10. W. E. Sangster, *The Path to Perfection* (London: Hodder and Stoughton, 1943), 49. Sangster also points out that "A full third of the texts on which Wesley chiefly relies for his doctrine of Christian perfection are taken from the First Epistle of John" (Ibid., 48).

the Father and with the Son—Of the Holy Ghost he speaks afterwards.

Verse 5. *And this is* the sum of *the message which we have heard of him*—The Son of God. *That God is light*—The light of wisdom, love, holiness, glory. What light is to the natural eye, that God is to the spiritual eye. *And in him is no darkness at all*—No contrary principle. He is pure, unmixed light.

Verse 6. *If we say*—Either with our tongue, or in our heart, if we endeavor to persuade either ourselves or others. *We have fellowship with him,* while we *walk,* inwardly or outwardly, *in darkness*—In sin of any kind. *We do not the truth*—Our actions prove that the truth is not in us.

Verse 7. *But if we walk in the light*—In all holiness. *As God is* (a deeper word than *walk,* and more worthy of God) *in the light,* then we may truly say, *we have fellowship one with another*—we who have seen, and you who have not seen, do alike enjoy that fellowship with God. The imitation of God being the only sure proof of our having fellowship with Him. *And the blood of Jesus Christ his Son*—With the grace purchased thereby. *Cleanseth us from all sin*—Both original and actual, taking away all the guilt and all the power.

Verse 8. *If we say*—Any child of man, before his blood has cleansed us. *We have no sin*—To be cleansed from, instead of *confessing our sins,* verse 9, *the truth is not in us*—Neither in our mouth nor in our heart.

Verse 9. But *if* with a penitent and believing heart, *we confess our sins, he is faithful*—Because He had promised this blessing, by the unanimous voice of all His prophets. *Just*—Surely then He will punish. No; for this very reason He will pardon. This may seem strange; but upon the evangelical principle of atonement and redemption, it is undoubtedly true; because, when the debt is paid or the purchase made, it is the part of equity to cancel the bond and consign over the purchased possession. *Both to forgive us our sins*—To take away all the guilt of them. *And to cleanse us from all unrighteousness*—To purify our souls from every kind and every degree of it. . . .

1 John 2:1. . . . *I write these things to you, that ye may not sin*—Thus he guards them beforehand against abusing the doctrine of reconciliation. All the words, institutions, and judgments of God are leveled against sin, either that it may not be committed or that it may be abolished. *But if any one sin*—Let him not lie in sin, despairing of help. *We have an advocate*—We have for our Advocate, not a mean person, but Him of whom it was said, "This is my beloved Son." Not a guilty person, who stands in need of pardon for himself; but *Jesus Christ the righteous;* not a mere petitioner, who relies purely upon liberality, but one that has merited, fully merited, whatever He asks.

Verse 2. *And he is the propitiation*—The atoning sacrifice by which the wrath of God is appeased. *For our sins*—Who believe. *And not for ours only, but also for the sins of the whole world*—Just as wide as sin extends, the propitiation extends also.

Verse 6. *He that saith he abideth in him*—Which implies a durable state; a constant, lasting knowledge of, and communion with, Him. *Ought himself*—Otherwise they are vain words. *So to walk, even as he walked*—In the world. *As he,* are words that frequently occur in this Epistle. Believers having their hearts full of Him, easily supply His name.

Verse 10. *He that loveth his brother*—For Christ's sake. *Abideth in the light*—Of God. *And there is no occasion of stumbling in him*—Whereas he that hates his brother is an occasion of stumbling to himself. He stumbles against himself, and against all things within and without; while he that loves his brother has a free, disencumbered journey.

Verse 11. *He that hateth his brother*—And he must hate, if he does not love him: there is no medium. *Is in darkness*—In sin, perplexity, entanglement. He *walketh in darkness, and knoweth not* that he is in the high road to hell.

1 John 3:4. *Whosoever committeth sin*—Thereby transgresseth the holy, just, and good law of God, and so sets his authority at nought; for this is implied in the very nature of sin.

Verse 5. *And ye know that he*—Christ. *Was manifested*—That He came into the world for this very purpose. *To take away our sins*—To destroy them all, root and branch, and leave none remaining. *And in him is no sin*—So that He could not suffer on His own account, but to make us as himself.

Verse 6. *Whosoever abideth in* communion with *him,* by loving faith, *sinneth not*—While he so abideth. *Whosoever sinneth* certainly *seeth him not*—The loving eye of his soul is not then fixed upon God; *neither* doth he then experimentally *know him*—Whatever he did in time past.

Verse 7. *Let no one deceive you*—Let none persuade you that any man is righteous but he that uniformly *practices righteousness;* he alone *is righteous,* after the example of his Lord.

Verse 8. *He that committeth sin is* a child *of the devil; sinneth from the beginning*—That is, was the first sinner in the universe and has continued to sin ever since. *The Son of God was manifested to destroy the works of the devil*—All sin. And will He not perform this in all that trust in Him?

Verse 9. *Whosoever is born of God*—By living faith, whereby God is continually breathing spiritual life into his soul, and his soul is continually breathing out love and prayer to God, *doth not commit sin. For* the divine *seed* of loving faith *abideth in him; and* so long as it doth, *he cannot sin because he is born of God*—Is inwardly and universally changed.

Verse 21. *If our heart condemn us not*—If our conscience, duly enlightened by the word and Spirit of God, and comparing all our thoughts, words, and works with that word, pronounce that they agree therewith. *Then have we confidence toward God*—Not only our consciousness of His favour continues and increases, but we have a full persuasion, that *whatsoever we ask we* shall *receive of him.*

Verse 24. *And he that keepeth his commandments*—That thus believes and loves. *Abideth in him, and God in him: and hereby we know that he abideth in us, by the Spirit which he hath given us*—Which witnesses with our spirits that we are His children, and brings forth His fruits of peace, love, holiness.

1 John 4:7 *Let us love one another*—From the doctrine he has just been defending he draws this exhortation. It is by the Spirit that the love of God is shed abroad in our hearts. *Every one that* truly *loveth* God and his neighbor *is born of God.*

Verse 8. *God is love*—This little sentence brought St. John more sweetness, even in the time he was writing it, than the whole world can bring. God is often styled holy, righteous, wise; but not holiness, righteousness, or wisdom in the abstract, as He is said to be love; intimating that this is His darling, His reigning attribute, the attribute that sheds an amiable glory on all His other perfections.

Verse 12. *If we love one another, God abideth in us*—This is treated of, verses 13-16. *And his love is perfected*—Has its full effect.

Verse 14. *And* in consequence of this *we have seen and testify that the Father sent the Son*—These are the foundation and the criteria of our abiding in God and God in us—the communion of the Spirit and the confession of the Son. . . .

Verse 16. *And we know and believe*—By the same Spirit, *the love that God hath to us.*

Verse 17. *Hereby*—That is, by this communion with God. *Is our love made perfect; that we may*—That is, so that we shall *have boldness in the day of judgment*—When all the stout-hearted shall tremble. *Because as he*—Christ. *Is*—All love. *So are we*—Who are fathers in Christ, *even in this world.*

Verse 18. *There is no fear in love*—No slavish fear can be where love reigns. *But perfect,* adult *love casteth out* slavish *fear; because such fear hath torment*—And so is inconsistent with the happiness of love. A natural man has neither fear nor love; one that is awakened, fear without love; a babe in Christ, love and fear; a father in Christ, love without fear.

Verse 19. *We love him, because he first loved us*—This is the sum of all religion, the genuine model of Christianity. None can say more: why should anyone say less, or less intelligibly?

1 John 5:5 *Who is he that overcometh the world*—That is superior to all worldly care, desire, fear? Every believer, and none else. The seventh verse (usually so reckoned) is a brief recapitulation of all which has been before advanced concerning the Father, the Son, and the Spirit. It is cited, in conjunction with the sixth and eighth, by Tertullian, Cyprian, and an uninterrupted train of Fathers. And, indeed, what the sun is in the world, what the heart is in a man, what the needle is in the mariner's compass, this verse is in the Epistle. . . .

Verse 6. *And it is the Spirit who* likewise *testifieth*—Of Jesus Christ, namely, by Moses and all the prophets, by John the Baptist, by all the apostles, and in all the writings of the New Testament. And against His testimony there can be no exception, *because the Spirit is truth*—The very God of truth. . . .

Verse 8. *And there are three that testify in heaven. . . . The Father*—Who clearly testified of the Son, both at His baptism and at His transfiguration. *The Word*—Who testified of himself on many occasions, while He was on earth; and again, with still greater solemnity, after His ascension into heaven (Rev. i. 5; xix. 13). *And the Spirit*—Whose testimony was added chiefly after His glorification (1 John ii. 27; John xv. 26; Acts v. 32; Rom. viii. 16). *And these three are one*—Even as those two, the Father and the Son, are one (John x. 30). Nothing can separate the Spirit from the Father and the Son. If He were not one with the Father and the Son, the apostle ought to have said, *The Father and the Word,* who are one, *and the Spirit, are two.* But this is contrary to the whole tenor of revelation. It remains that *these three are one.* They are one in essence, in knowledge, in will, and in their testimony.

Verse 15. *We have*—Faith anticipates the blessings. *The petitions which we asked of him*—Even before the event. And when the event comes, we know it comes in answer to our prayer. . . .

Verse 17. *All* deviation from perfect holiness is sin; but all sin is not unpardonable.

Verse 18. Yet this gives us no encouragement to sin: on the contrary, it is an indisputable truth, *he that is born of God*—That sees and loves God. *Sinneth not*—So long as that loving faith abides in him, he neither speaks nor does anything which God hath forbidden. He *keepeth himself*—Watching unto prayer. *And,* while he does this, *the wicked one toucheth him not*—So as to hurt him.

Verse 19. *We know that we are* children *of God*—By the witness and the fruit of His Spirit (1 John iii. 24). . . .

Verse 20. *And we know*—By all these infallible proofs. *That the Son of God is come*—Into the world. *And he hath given us* a spiritual *understanding, that we may know him, the true one*—"The faithful and true witness." *And we are in the true one*—As branches in the vine, even in Jesus Christ, the eternal Son of God. *This* Jesus *is* the only living and true God, together with the Father and the Spirit, and the original fountain of *eternal life.* So the beginning and the end of the epistle agree.

Verse 21. *Keep yourselves from idols*—From . . . every inward idol; from loving, desiring, fearing anything more than God. Seek all help and defense from evil, all happiness in the true God alone.

Holiness in the Hymns

John Wesley had much more to do with hymns than might be supposed from the immense publicity given to the gift and skills of his brother Charles.

John was a gifted hymnwriter in his own right, and a very splendid translator of hymns, chiefly German. He began his study of the German language on the voyage to Georgia,[11] and his work has given us several meaningful and singable translations.

John's hymns lack that glorious liberty and life of the hymns of Charles who had the aptitude to handle all the stops of the redeemed spirit. Nevertheless John's studied craftmanship with words coupled to his controlled sentimentality imparted height, depth, and intensity to his hymns whether translations or originals. Probably 20 of John's hymns are still being included in British and American compilations, about two-thirds of the 30 or more that he wrote.

It is an almost impossible task to separate the hymns of the brothers with any great certainty as to which brother actually wrote a particular hymn. We know of John's admission that "but a few" of those contained in *A Collection of Hymns for the Use of the People Called Methodists* are his own work. But we know also that the inclusions from Charles were edited by John and thus reflect his teaching. In *A Plain Account of Christian Perfection,* Wesley writes concerning the 1742 hymnbook: "The hymns concerning it (Christian Perfection) in this volume are too numerous to transcribe. I shall only cite a part of three of them" (Par. 16). He then goes on to quote from Charles Wesley's hymn beginning

> *Saviour from sin, I wait to prove*
> *That Jesus is Thy healing name;*
> *To lose, when perfected in love,*
> *Whate'er I have, or can, or am:*
> *I stay me on Thy faithful word:*
> *The servant shall be as his Lord.*

This hymn is followed by another that includes these four stanzas:

---

11. *JJW,* 1:110 (diary).

The Sanctifying Spirit pour,
  To quench my thirst and wash me clean,
Now, Saviour, let the gracious shower
  Descend, and make me pure from sin.

Purge me from every sinful blot;
  My idols all be cast aside;
Cleanse me from every evil thought,
  From all the filth of self and pride.

The hatred of the carnal mind
  Out of my flesh at once remove;
Give me a tender heart, resigned,
  And pure, and full of faith and love.

Now let me gain perfection's height!
  Now let me into nothing fall;
Be less than nothing in my sight,
  And feel that Christ is all in all.

And another:

Lord, I believe Thy work of grace
  Is perfect in the soul:
His heart is pure who sees Thy face,
  His spirit is made whole

From every sickness by Thy word,
  From every foul disease,
Saved, and to perfect health restored,
  To perfect holiness.

This is the rest, the life, the peace,
  Which all Thy people prove;
Love is the bond of perfectness,
  And all their soul is love.

O joyful sound of gospel grace!
  Christ shall in me appear;
I, even I, shall see His face,
  I shall be holy here!

Eight years later, referring to Charles Wesley's two volumes of *Hymns and Sacred Poems,* John writes: "As I did not see these before they were published, there were some things in them which I did not approve of. But I quite approved of the main hymns on this head: a few verses of which are subjoined."[12]

The verses include:

> *From this inbred sin deliver;*
> *Let the yoke now be broke;*
> *Make me Thine forever.*
>
> *Come in this accepted hour,*
>   *Bring Thy heavenly kingdom in:*
> *Fill us with the glorious power,*
>   *Rooting out the seeds of sin.*
>
> *Apply to wash out every stain*
> *Thine efficacious blood.*
>   *O let it sink into our soul*
> *Deep as the inbred sin;*
>   *Make every wounded spirit whole,*
> *And every leper clean!*

John's compositions reflect his piety and were used chiefly as prayers for the blessing of perfect love, and as hymns of worship. They breathe the fragrance of the beauty of holiness, and are in accord with the rest of Wesley's teaching on Christian perfection.

HYMNS ADAPTED FROM OTHERS

The following selections contain specimens of John's original hymns; also hymns he altered from other writers, translations of German hymns, and one of his translations from the French.

On the Descent of the Holy Ghost at Pentecost

From Henry More, 1614-87; altered by J. W.

The original has 15 verses: The entire hymn may be read in the *Poetical Works.*[13]

---

12. *Plain Account of Christian Perfection, WW,* 11:391 (Par. 18).
13. *PWJCW,* 1:165-66.

Father, if justly, still we claim
  To us and ours the promise made,
To us be graciously the same,
  And crown with living fire our head.

Our claim admit, and from above
  Of holiness the Spirit shower,
Of wise discernment, humble love,
  And zeal, and unity, and power.

The Spirit of convincing speech,
  Of power demonstrative, impart,
Such as may every conscience reach,
  And sound the unbelieving heart.

The Spirit of refining fire,
  Searching the inmost of the mind,
To purge all fierce and foul desire,
  And kindle life more pure and kind.

The Spirit of faith, in this Thy day,
  To break the power of cancelled sin,
Tread down its strength, o'erturn its sway,
  And still the conquest more than win.

The Spirit breathe of inward life,
  Which in our hearts Thy laws may write;
Then grief expires, and pain, and strife;
  Tis nature all, and all delight.

Grant this, O holy God, and true!
  The ancient seers Thou didst inspire:
To us perform the promise due;
  Descend, and crown us now with fire.

God with Us

From the German of Nicolas von Zinzendorf

Eternal depth of Love Divine,
  In Jesus, God-with-us, displayed,
How bright Thy beaming mercies shine!
  How wide Thy healing streams are spread!

With whom dost Thou delight to dwell?
  Sinners, a vile, a thankless race.
O God! what tongue aright can tell
  How vast Thy love, how great Thy grace!

The dictates of Thy sovereign will
  With joy our grateful hearts receive:
All Thy delight in us fulfill:
  Lo! all we are to Thee we give,
To Thy sure love, Thy tender care,
  Our flesh, soul, spirit we resign.
O! fix Thy sacred presence there,
  And seal the "abode forever Thine."

O King of Glory, Thy rich grace
  Our short desires surpasses far!
Yea, even our crimes, though numberless,
  Less numerous than Thy mercies are.
Still on Thee, Father, may we rest,
  Still may we pant Thy Son to know!
Thy Spirit still breathe into our breast
  Fountain of peace and joy below!

Oft have we seen Thy mighty power
  Since from the world Thou mad'st us free;
Still may we praise Thee more and more,
  Our hearts more firmly knit to Thee!
Still Lord Thy saving health display,
  And arm our souls with heavenly zeal:
So, fearless shall we urge our way
  Through all the powers of earth and hell!

Living by Christ

From the German of Paul Gerhardt (1606-76)

Jesus, Thy boundless love to me
  No thought can reach, no tongue declare:
O, knit my thankful heart to Thee,
  And reign without a rival there.
Thine wholly, Thine alone I am:
Be Thou alone my constant flame.

O, grant that nothing in my soul
   May dwell, but Thy pure love alone:
O, may that love possess me whole,
   My joy, my treasure, and my crown.
Strange fires far from my soul remove,
My every act, word, thought, be love.

Unwearied may I this pursue,
   Dauntless to the high prize aspire;
Hourly within my breast renew
   This holy flame, this heavenly fire;
And day and night be all my care
To guard this sacred treasure there.

My Saviour, Thou Thy love to me
   In want, in pain, in shame, hast show'd;
For me on the accursed tree
   Thou pouredst forth Thy guiltless blood;
Thy wounds upon my heart impress,
Nor ought shall the loved stamp efface.

O, draw me, Saviour, after Thee;
   So shall I run and never tire;
With gracious words still comfort me;
   Be Thou my hope, my sole desire.
Free me from every weight; nor fear
Nor sin can come, if Thou art here.

What in Thy love possess I not?
   My Star by night, my Sun by day:
My Spring of Life when parched by drought,
   My Wine to cheer, my Bread to stay
My Strength, my Shield, my safe Abode
My Robe before the throne of God!

In suffering be Thy love my peace,
   In weakness be Thy love my power;
And when the storms of life shall cease,
   Jesus, in that important hour,
In death as life be Thou my guide
And save me, who for me hast died.

Renouncing All for Christ

From the French of Madame de Bourignon (1616-80)

Come, Saviour Jesu, from above
　Assist me with Thy heavenly grace,
Withdraw my heart from worldly love,
　And for Thyself prepare the place.

O, let Thy sacred presence fill
　And set my longing spirit free,
Which pants to have no other will
　But night and day to feast on Thee.

Henceforth may no profane delight
　Divide this consecrated soul;
Possess it Thou, who hast the right,
　As Lord and Master of the whole.

Wealth, honour, pleasure, or what else
　This short-enduring world can give
Tempt as you will, my heart repels,
　To Christ alone resolved to live.

Thee I can love, and Thee alone,
　With holy peace, and inward bliss;
To find Thou tak'st me for Thine own,
　O, what a happiness is this!

Nor heaven nor earth do I desire,
　But Thy pure love within my breast:
This, this I always will require,
　And freely give up all the rest.

Redemption Found

Abridged by Wesley from the German of Johanne Andreas Rothe (1688-1758)

Now I have found the ground wherein
　Sure my soul's anchor may remain,
The wounds of Jesus, for my sin
　Before the world's foundation slain;

Whose mercy shall unshaken stay,
When heaven and earth are fled away.

O Love, Thou bottomless abyss!
  My sins are swallowed up in Thee,
Cover'd is my unrighteousness,
  Nor spot of guilt remains in me,
While Jesus' blood through earth and skies,
Mercy, free, boundless mercy, cries.

With faith I plunge me in this sea;
  Here is my hope, my joy, my rest;
Hither when hell assails, I flee
  I look into my Saviour's breast!
Away sad doubt, and anxious fear!
Mercy is all that's written there!

Though waves and storms go o'er my head,
  Though strength, and health, and friends be gone,
Though joys be withered all and dead,
  Though every comfort be withdrawn,
On this my steadfast soul relies,
Father, Thy mercy never dies.

Fix'd on this ground will I remain,
  Though my heart fail, and flesh decay;
This anchor shall my soul sustain,
  When earth's foundations melt away;
Mercy's full power I then shall prove,
Loved with an everlasting love.

Praise for Redemption

From the German of L. A. Gotter (1661-1735)

  Through Thy rich grace, in Jesus' blood
    Blessing, redemption, life we find.
  Our souls wash'd in this cleansing flood,
    No stain of guilt remains behind.
  Who can Thy mercy's stores express?
  Unfathomable, numberless!

Now hast Thou given us through Thy Son,
   The power of living faith to see;
Unconquerable faith, alone
   That gains o'er all the victory;
Faith which nor earth nor hell can move,
Unblamable in perfect love.

Thine is what'er we are: Thy grace
   In Christ created us anew,
To sing Thy never-ceasing praise,
   Thy unexhausted love to show;
And, arm'd with Thy great Spirit's aid,
Blameless in all Thy paths to tread.

Yea, Father, our's through Him Thou art,
   For so is Thy eternal will!
O, live, more reign within my heart,
   My soul, with all Thy fulness fill:
My heart, my all I yield to Thee:
Jesus be all in all to me!

The Confidence of Love

From the German of Johann Scheffler (1626-1677); translated by John Wesley; condensed from seven stanzas, and title supplied by the editor.

Thee will I love my Strength, my Tower,
   Thee will I love my joy, my crown,
Thee will I love with all my power.
   In all Thy works, and Thee alone.
Thee will I love till the pure fire
Fill all my soul with chaste desire.

I thank Thee, uncreated Sun,
   That Thy bright beams on me have shined;
I thank Thee who hast overthrown
   My foes, and healed my wounded mind;
I thank Thee whose enlivening voice
Bids my freed heart in Thee rejoice.

Uphold me in the doubtful race
   Nor suffer me again to stray;

Strengthen my feet with steady pace
  Still to press forward in Thy way.
My soul and flesh, O Lord of might,
Fill, satiate with Thy heavenly light.

Thee will I love, my joy, my crown;
  Thee will I love, my Lord, my God.
Thee will I live, beneath Thy frown
  Or smile, Thy sceptre, or Thy rod.
What though my flesh and heart decay?
Thee shall I love in endless day!

JOHN WESLEY'S OWN HYMNS
Hymn to the Holy Ghost
by John Wesley

Come, Holy Ghost, all-quickening fire
  Come, and in me delight to rest!
Drawn by the lure of strong desire,
  O, come, and consecrate my breast:
The temple of my soul prepare
And fix Thy sacred presence there!

Eager for Thee I ask and pant,
  So strong the principle Divine
Carries me out with sweet constraint,
  Till all my hallowed soul be Thine;
Plunged in the Godhead's deepest sea,
And lost in Thy immensity.

Come, then, my God, mark out Thy heir,
  Of heaven a larger earnest give,
With clearer light Thy witness bear,
  More sensibly within me live;
Let all my powers Thy entrance feel,
And deeper stamp Thyself the seal!

Hymn to God the Sanctifier
by John Wesley

Come, Holy Ghost, all-quickening fire,
Come, and my hallow'd heart inspire

> Sprinkled with the atoning blood:
>   Now to my soul Thyself reveal;
>   Thy mighty working let me feel
>   And know that I am born of God.
>
> Let earth no more my heart divide;
> With Christ may I be crucified
> To Thee with my whole soul aspire:
>   Dead to the world, with all its toys,
>   Its idle pomp, and fading joys,
> Be Thou alone my one desire.
>
> My will be swallowed up in Thee;
> Light in Thy light still may I see,
> Beholding Thee with open face;
>   Call'd the full power of faith to prove,
>   Let all my hallow'd heart be love,
> And all my spotless life be praise.
>
> Come, Holy Ghost, all-quickening fire,
> My consecrated heart inspire,
> Sprinkled with the atoning blood:
>   Still to my soul Thyself reveal,
>   Thy mighty working may I feel
> And know that I am one with God!

The Poetical Works of John and Charles Wesley

Preface to Volume 2

This preface deals specifically with the doctrine and experience of "that glorious liberty from the bondage of corruption which is the privilege of the children of God." In this presentation we give it as it stands in the Osborn edition of *The Poetical Works*.[14]

We must remember, however, that it is one of Wesley's earlier statements, although he was satisfied with it as commented upon in his *Plain Account* (Par. 13).

---

14. Ibid., 2:195-204.

Dr. Timothy Smith writes: "It is so complete and so crystal clear as to both the moment and the process of entire sanctification, and so thoroughly scriptural as well as experiential, as to be in my judgment, his very best short 'tract.'"[15]

1. By grace, saith St. Paul, ye are saved through faith. And it is indeed a great salvation which they have received who truly believe on the name of the Son of God. It is such as eye hath not seen, nor ear heard, neither hath it entered into the heart of man to conceive, until God hath revealed it by His Spirit, which alone showeth these deep things of God.

2. Of this salvation the prophets inquired diligently, searching what manner of time the Spirit which was in them did signify, when it testified beforehand the sufferings of Christ, and the glory that should follow; even that glorious liberty from the bondage of corruption which should then be given to the children of God. Much more doth it behoove us diligently to inquire after this prize of our high calling, and earnestly to hope for the grace which is brought unto us by the revelation of Jesus Christ.

3. Some faint description of this gracious gift of God is attempted in a few of the following verses. But the greater part of them relate to the way, rather than the end; either showing (so far as has fallen under our observation) the successive conquests of grace, and the gradual process of the work of God in the soul; or pointing out the chief hindrances in the way at which many have stumbled and fallen.

4. This great gift of God, the salvation of our souls, which is begun on earth but perfected in heaven, is no other than the image of God fresh stamped upon our hearts. It is a renewal in the spirit of our minds after the likeness of Him that created us. It is a salvation from sin and doubt and fear: from fear; for, being justified freely, they who believe have peace with God through Jesus Christ our Lord, and rejoice in hope of the glory of God; from doubt: for the Spirit of God beareth witness with their spirit that they are the children of God; and from sin: for being now made free from sin they are become the servants of righteousness.

5. God hath now laid the axe to the root of the tree, purifying their hearts by faith, and cleansing all the thoughs of their hearts by the inspiration of His Holy Spirit. Having this hope, that they shall soon see God as He is, they purify themselves even as He is pure; and

---

15. Letter dated December 24, 1981.

are holy as He which hath called them is holy in all manner of conversation. Not that they have already attained all they shall attain, either are already (in this sense) perfect. But they daily go on from strength to strength: beholding now as in a glass the glory of the Lord, they are changed into the same image, from glory to glory, as by the Spirit of the Lord.

6. And where the Spirit of the Lord is, there is liberty; such liberty from the law of sin and death as the children of this world will not believe, though a man declare it unto them. The Son hath made them free, and they are free indeed: insomuch that St. John lays it down as a first principle among true believers. We know that whosoever is born of God sinneth not: but he that is begotten of God keepeth himself and that wicked one toucheth him not. And again, Whosoever abideth in Him (in Christ) sinneth not. And yet again, Whosoever is born of God doth not commit sin. For his seed remaineth in him, and he cannot sin because he is born of God.

7. The Son hath made them free, who are thus born of God, from that great root of sin and bitterness, pride. They feel that all their sufficiency is of God; that it is He alone who is in all their thoughts and worketh in them both to will and to do of His good pleasure. They feel that it is not they who speak, but the Spirit of their Father which speaketh in them; He doeth the works. So that God is to them all in all, and they are as nothing in His sight.

They are free from self-will; as desiring, no, not for one moment (for perfect love casteth out all desire), but the holy and perfect will of God; not supplies in want; not ease in pain;[16] not life or death, or any creature; but continually crying in their inmost soul, "Father, Thy will be done." They are freed from evil thoughts, so that they cannot enter into them; no, not for one instant. Aforetime, when an evil thought came in they looked up and it vanished away. But now it does not come in; there being no room for this in a soul which is full of God.

They are freed from wanderings in prayer. Whensoever they pour out their hearts in a more immediate manner before God, they have no

---

16. "This is too strong," wrote Wesley later. "Our Lord himself desired ease in pain. He asked for it, only with resignation: 'Not as I will,' I desire, 'but as Thou wilt.'"
In this section there are several expressions Wesley was afterwards convinced could not be justified as in harmony with the statements of Scripture or the facts of Christian experience. The corrections and qualifications with which he wished them to be received are here inserted from his *Plain Account of Christian Perfection* (*WW*, 11:379-80, footnotes).

thought of anything past,[17] or absent, or to come, but of God alone; to whom their whole souls flow in one even stream and in whom they are swallowed up. In times past they had wandering thoughts dart in which yet fled away like smoke. But now that smoke does not rise at all, but they continually see Him which is invisible. They are freed from all darkness, having no fear, no doubt, either as to their state in general or as to any particular action:[18] for their eye being single, their whole body is full of light.

Whatsoever is needful, they are taught of God. They have an unction from the Holy One which abideth in them and teacheth them every hour what they shall do and what they shall speak.[19] Nor have they therefore any need to reason concerning it;[20] for they see the way straight before them. The Lamb is their light, and they simply follow Him whithersoever He goeth. Hence also they are, in one sense, freed from temptations; for though numberless temptations fly about them, yet they wound them not, they trouble them not,[21] they have no place in them. At all times their soul is even and calm; their heart is steadfast and unmovable; their peace, flowing as a river, passeth all understanding and they rejoice with joy unspeakable and full of glory. For they are sealed by the Spirit unto the day of redemption; having the witness in themselves that there is laid up for them a crown of righteousness which the Lord shall give them in that day;[22] and being fully persuaded through the Holy Ghost that neither death nor life, nor things present, nor things to come, nor height, nor depth, nor any other creature, shall be able to separate them from the love of God, which is in Christ Jesus, their Lord.

8. Not that every one is a child of the devil (as some have rashly asserted, who know not what they speak, nor whereof they affirm) till he is, in this full sense, born of God.[23] On the contrary, whosoever he be, who hath a sure trust and a confidence in God, that through the

---

17. "This is far too strong," wrote Wesley again. "See the sermon 'On Wandering Thoughts'" (Ibid., 379).

18. "Frequently this is the case; but only for a time" (Ibid., 379).

19. "For a time it may be so; but not always" (Ibid., 379).

20. "Sometimes they have no need; at other times they have" (Ibid., 379).

21. "Sometimes they do not; at other times they do, and that grievously" (Ibid., 380).

22. "Not all who are saved from sin; many of them have not attained it yet" (Ibid., 380).

23. "Sanctified." MS. correction.

merits of Christ his sins are forgiven, and he reconciled to the favour of God; he is a child of God, and, if he abide in Him, an heir of all the great and precious promises. Neither ought he in any wise to cast away his confidence or to deny the faith he hath received, because it is weak, because hitherto it is only as a grain of mustard seed; or because it is tried with fire, so that his soul is in heaviness through manifold temptations. For though the heir, as long as he is a child, differeth nothing from a servant, yet is he lord of all. God doth not despise the day of small things; the day of fears, and doubts, and clouds: but if there be first a willing mind, pressing toward the mark of the prize of our high calling, it is accepted (for the present) according to what a man hath, and not according to what he hath not.

9. Neither therefore dare we affirm (as some have done) that this full salvation is at once given to true believers. There is indeed an instantaneous (as well as a gradual) work of God in the souls of His children; and there wants not, we know, a cloud of witnesses who have received in one moment either a clear sense of the forgiveness of their sins or the abiding witness of the Holy Spirit. But we do not know a single instance, in any place, of a person's receiving in one and the same moment remission of sins the abiding witness of the Spirit and a new, a clean heart.

SECOND BLESSING

10. Indeed how God may work, we cannot tell; but the general manner wherein He does work is this. Those who once trusted in themselves that they were righteous, who were rich and had need of nothing are, by the Spirit of God applying His word, convinced that they are poor and naked. All the things that they have done are brought to their remembrance and set in array before them; so that they see the wrath of God hanging over their heads and feel they deserve the damnation of hell. In their trouble they cry unto the Lord, and He shows He hath taken away their sins and opens the kingdom of heaven in their hearts, even righteousness, and peace, and joy in the Holy Ghost. Fear and sorrow and pain are fled away and sin hath no more dominion over them. Knowing they are justified freely through faith in His blood they have peace with God through Jesus Christ; they rejoice in hope of the glory of God, and the love of God is shed abroad in their hearts.

11. In this peace they remain for days, or weeks, or months, and commonly suppose they shall not know war any more till some of their old enemies, their bosom sins, or the sin which did most easily beset them (perhaps anger or desire), assault them again and thrust

sore at them, that they may fall. Then arises fear that they shall not endure to the end; and often doubt whether God has not forgotten them, or whether they did not deceive themselves in thinking their sins were forgiven and that they were children of God.

Under these clouds, especially if they reason with the devil, or are received to doubtful disputations, they go mourning all the day long, even as a father mourneth for his only son whom he loveth. But it is seldom long before their Lord answers for himself, sending them the Holy Ghost to comfort them, to bear witness continually with their spirit that they are the children of God. And then they are indeed meek, and gentle, and teachable, even as little children. Their stony heart was broken in pieces before they received remission of sins, yet it continued hard; but now it is melted down, it is soft, tender, and susceptible of any impression.

And now first do they see the ground of their heart; which God would not before disclose unto them, lest the flesh should fail before Him, and the spirit which He had made. Now they see all the hidden abominations there; the depths of pride, self-will, and hell. Yet having the witness in themselves, "Thou art an heir of God, a joint heir with Christ; thou shalt inherit the new heavens and the new earth wherein dwelleth righteousness, their spirit rejoiced in God their Saviour, even in the midst of this fiery trial which continually heightens both the strong sense they then have of their inability to help themselves and the inexpressible hunger they feel after a full renewal in His image, in righteousness and all true holiness.

Then God is mindful of the desire of them that fear Him: He remembers His holy covenant, and He giveth them a single eye and a clean heart. He stamps upon them His own image and superscription: He createth them anew in Christ Jesus: He cometh unto them with His Son and His blessed Spirit, and, fixing His abode in their souls, bringeth them into the rest which remaineth for the people of God.

A Collection of Hymns for the Use of the People Called Methodists

Wesley wanted *A Collection of Hymns for the Use of the People Called Methodists,* as edited and published by himself, in 1780, to stand beside his *Standard Sermons* and his *Notes upon the New Testament* as a valid test and statement of Methodist doctrine, worship, and experience.

Add the *contents* page to the *preface* and the point is beyond dispute.

Contents

Exhorting Sinners to Return to God
Describing the Pleasantness of Religion
Describing the Goodness of God
Describing Judgment
Describing Heaven
Praying for a Blessing
Describing Formal Religion
Describing Inward Religion
For Mourners Convinced of Sin
For Persons Convinced of Backsliding
For Backsliders Recovered
For Believers Rejoicing
For Believers Fighting
For Believers Praying
For Believers Watching
For Believers Working
For Believers Suffering
For Believers Seeking for Full Redemption
For Believers Saved
For Believers Interceding for the World
For the Society Meeting
For the Society Giving Thanks
For the Society Parting
Additional Hymns
    on Divine Worship
    on the Death of Christ
    on the Lord's Supper
    on the Resurrection and Ascension of Christ
    Miscellaneous Hymns
Supplement
    Hymns of Adoration
    The Experience and Privileges of Believers
    The Kingdom of Christ

On the Incarnation and Sufferings of Christ
Time, Death, Judgment, and the Future State

Preface

1. For many years I have been importuned to publish such a Hymn Book as might be generally used in all our congregations throughout Great Britain and Ireland. I have hitherto withstood the importunity, as I believed such a publication was needless, considering the various hymn books which my brother and I have published within these forty years last past; so that it may be doubted whether any religious community in the world has a greater variety of them....

3. But it has been answered . . . What we want is a collection not too large, that it may be cheap and portable; not too small, that it may contain a sufficient variety for all ordinary occasions.

4. Such a hymn book you have now before you. It is not so large as to be either cumbersome or expensive: and it is large enough to contain such a variety of hymns as will not soon be worn threadbare. It is large enough to contain all the important truths of our most holy religion, whether speculative or practical; yea to illustrate them all, and to prove them both by Scripture and reason. And this is done in a regular order. The Hymns are not carelessly jumbled together, but carefully ranged under proper heads, according to the experience of real Christians. So that this book is, in effect, a little body of experimental and practical divinity.

5. As but a small part of these hymns is of my own composing, I do not think it inconsistent with modesty to declare that I am persuaded no such hymn book as this has yet been published in the English language. In what other publication of the kind have you so distinct and full an account of scriptural Christianity? such a declaration of the heights and depths of religion, speculative and practical? so strong cautions against the most plausible errors; particularly those that are now most prevalent? and so clear directions for making your calling and election sure; for perfecting holiness in the fear of God?

6. May I be permitted to add a few words with regard to the poetry? . . . (1) In these hymns there is no doggeral; no botches; nothing put in to patch up the rhyme: no feeble expletives. (2) Here is nothing turgid or bombast, on the one hand or low and creeping on the other. (3) Here are no cant expressions; no words without meaning. . . . We talk common sense, both in prose and verse, and use no

word but in a fixed and determinate sense. (4) Here are, allow me to say, both the purity, the strength, and the elegance of the English language....

8. But to return. That which is of infinitely more moment than the spirit of poetry, is the spirit of piety. And I trust, all persons of real judgment will find this breathing through the whole collection. It is in this view chiefly that I would recommend it to every truly pious reader as a means of raising or quickening the spirit of devotion; of confirming his faith; of enlivening his hope and of kindling and increasing his love to God and man. When poetry thus keeps its place, as the handmaid of piety, it shall attain, not a poor perishable wreath, but a crown that fadeth not away.

John Wesley

London,
October 20, 1779.

John Wesley's Rules for Singing

I. Learn these tunes before you learn any others; afterwards learn as many as you please.

II. Sing them exactly as they are printed here, without altering or mending them at all; and if you have learned to sing them otherwise, unlearn it as soon as you can.

III. Sing all. See that you join with the congregation as frequently as you can. Let not a slight degree of weakness or weariness hinder you. If it is a cross to you, take it up, and you will find it a blessing.

IV. Sing lustily and with a good courage. Beware of singing as if you were half dead, or half asleep; but lift up your voice with strength. Be no more afraid of your voice now, nor more ashamed of its being heard than when you sung the songs of Satan.

V. Sing modestly. Do not bawl, so as to be heard above or distinct from the rest of the congregation, that you may not destroy the harmony; but strive to unite your voices together so as to make one clear melodious sound.

VI. Sing in time. Whatever time is sung be sure to keep with it. Do not run before nor stay behind it; but attend close to the leading voices and move therewith as exactly as you can; and take care not to sing too slow. This drawling way naturally steals on all who are lazy; and it is high time to drive it out from us and sing all our tunes just as quick as we did at first.

VII. Above all sing spiritually. Have an eye to God in every word you sing. Aim at pleasing Him more than yourself or any other creature. In order to do this attend strictly to the sense of what you sing, and see that your heart is not carried away with the sound, but offered to God continually; so shall your singing be such as the Lord will approve here and reward you when He cometh in the clouds of heaven.

* * *

The Letters of John Wesley

As with the Puritans, so with John Wesley, his *Journal* was his confessional. But his *Letters* constitute his counseling room.

John wrote about as many letters as his brother Charles wrote hymns, probably close to 7,000. His famous contemporary, Voltaire, may have written five times as many letters as Wesley, and Horace Walpole as many as Wesley. But neither Voltaire nor Walpole had so little leisure in which to write; neither had they so much wise and good counsel to offer, nor so many and such a varied multitude of correspondents. It almost seems as though John Wesley had been born with ink in his veins and a pen for a forefinger!

Although scores of Wesley's letters have disappeared, an astonishingly large number have been diligently collected, carefully kept, and avidly read. These, as Outler has written, contain partial self-portraits "drawn against the background of a specific circumstance or crisis" almost always bearing on the great matter of the Revival and personal spiritual problems or renewal in the recipient. Seldom does Wesley close a letter without offering healthy counsel and direction.

From these letters we have selected a number that deal with the doctrine and experience of entire sanctification or perfect love.

To Charles Wesley

It is well known that the Wesley brothers had their differences as to the true nature of Christian perfection. John held firmly to the belief that it is to be obtained by faith, in an instant, and is consistent with human frailties. On the issue of human frailty, Charles was aiming at an absolute ideal without qualifications. John told Charles plainly that he was setting perfection too high. The occasion was this couplet written by Charles:

When I feel it fixed within
I shall have no power to sin.

John's constant accent was *Now is the time.* He once put it in a letter to Mrs. Mary Fletcher: "How soon can you be a partaker of sanctification? Now, in an instant, in a moment of time." It was a clear and distinct act of God, to be followed by unceasing spiritual growth.

Charles blew hot and cold in his opinion of the "when" of entire sanctification. But if they frequently debated the timing of total deliverance from all sin they were firmly one on the fact of it. Sin must go! Jesus Christ must be central and supreme in every Christian heart.

Excessive and fanatical claims were being made by a few London Society members; they were making the teaching of entire sanctification "a byword and a hissing elsewhere" but Wesley will not allow the counterfeit to destroy the real. He wrote:

May 25, 1764

Dear Brother,

 . . . The frightful stories wrote from London had made all our preachers in the north afraid even to mutter about perfection; and, of course, the people on all sides were grown good Calvinists in that point. It is what I foresaw from the beginning; that the devil would strive by Thomas Maxfield and company to drive perfection out of the kingdom.

O let you and I hold fast whereunto we have attained; and let our yea be yea, and our nay nay! I feel the want of some about me that are all faith and love. No man was more profitable to me than George Bell, while he was simple of heart. O for heat and light united!

July 9, 1766

To Charles,

I shall judge of the Bands at Kingswood when I am there. They have not met tolerably for these dozen years.

Miss Lewen gave me a chaise and a pair of horses. You are a long time in getting to London; therefore, I hope you will do much good there. Yes, says William; "Mr. Charles will stop their prating in the Bands at London, as he has done at Bristol." I believe not. I believe you will rather encourage them to speak humbly and modestly the words of truth and soberness. Great good has flowed and will flow therefrom. Let your "knowledge direct, not quench, the fire." That has been done too much already. I trust you will now raise, not depress their hopes. One word more: Concerning setting perfection **HUMANITY** too high. That perfection which I believe, I can boldly preach; because I think I see five hundred witnesses of it. Of that perfection which you preach, you think, you do not see any witness at all. Why, then, you must have far more courage than me or you could not persist in preaching it. I wonder you do not, in this article, fall in plumb with Mr. Whitefield. For do not you, as well as he, ask, "Where are the perfect ones? I verily believe there are none upon earth; none dwelling in the body." I cordially assent to his opinion, that there is no such perfection here as you describe; at least, I never met with an instance of it; and I doubt I never shall. Therefore I still think to set perfection so high is effectually to renounce it.

London, January 27, 1767

Dear Brother,

Some thoughts occurred to my mind this morning which I believe it may be useful to set down: the rather because it may be a means of our understanding each other clearly; that we may agree as far as ever we can, and then let all the world know it.

I was thinking on Christian perfection with regard to the thing, the manner, and the time.

1. By perfection I mean the humble, gentle, patient love of God and man ruling all the tempers, words, and actions, the **PERFECT LOVE** whole heart by the whole life. I do not include an impossibility of falling from it, either in part or in whole. Therefore I retract several expressions in our hymns which partly express, partly imply, such an impossibility. And I do not contend for the term sinless, though I do not object against it.

Do we agree or differ here? If we differ, wherein?

2. As to the manner. I believe this perfection is always wrought in the soul by faith, by a simple act of faith, consequently in an **FAITH** instant. But I believe in a gradual work both preceding and following that instant.

Do we agree or differ here?

3. As to the time. I believe this instant generally is the instant of death, the moment before the soul leaves the body. But I believe it may be 10, 20, or 40 years before death.

Do we agree or differ here?

I believe it is usually many years after justification, but that it *may be* within five years or five months after it. I know no conclusive argument to the contrary. Do you? If it *must be* many years after justification, I would be glad to know how many.... And how many days or months or even years can you allow to be between perfection and death? How far from justification *must* it be? And how near to death?

SECOND BLESSING

If it be possible, let you and I come to a good understanding, both for our own sakes and for the sake of the people.

February 1767

To Charles,

... The voice of one who truly loves God surely is—

> *'Tis worse than death my God to love*
> *And not my God alone.*

Such an one is certainly "as much athirst for *sanctification* as he once was for justification." You remember this used to be one of *your* constant questions. It is not now. Therefore *you* are altered in your sentiments. And, unless we come to an explanation, we shall inevitably contradict each other. But this ought not to be in any wise, if it can possibly be avoided.

I still think to disbelieve all the *professors* amounts to a *denial of the thing*. For if there be *no living witness* of what we have preached for 20 years, I cannot, dare not preach it any longer. The whole comes to one point—Is there or is there not any instantaneous sanctification between justification and death? I say yes; you (often seem to) say no. What arguments brought you to think so? Perhaps they may convince me too. Nay, there is one question more, if you allow there is such a thing—Can one who has attained it fall? Formerly I thought not; but *you* (with T. Walsh and Jo. Jones) convinced me of my mistake.

IN THIS LIFE

April 1772

Dear Brother,

I meant Mr. Buller. I have not been at Leeds; so I can give you no account of the matter.

I find by long experience it comes exactly to the same point, to tell men they shall be saved from all sin when they die; or to tell them it may be a year hence, or a week hence, or any time but *now*. Our word does not profit, either as to justification or sanctification, unless we can bring them to expect the blessing while we speak.

Correspondence with Others

To Miss Furley

The Wesley brothers thought highly of Dorothy Furley. John counseled her on several occasions. In 1764 she married John Downes, one of Wesley's preachers who died 10 years later while preaching in London. Charles was especially impressed by her bearing in bereavement: "so supported, so calm, so resigned."

St. Ives, September 15, 1762

My Dear Sister,

Whereunto you have attained, hold fast. But expect that greater things are at hand; although our friend talks as if you were not to expect them till the article of death.

Certainly sanctification (in the proper sense) is "an instantaneous power then given, always to cleave to God." Yet this sanctification (at least, in the lower degrees) does not include a power never to think a useless thought, nor ever speak a useless word. I myself believe that such a perfection is inconsistent with living in a corruptible body: For this makes it impossible "always to think right." While we breathe we shall, more or less, mistake. If, therefore, Christian perfection implies this, we must not expect it till after death.

HUMANITY

I want you to be all love. This is the perfection I believe and teach. And this perfection is consistent with a thousand nervous disorders, which that high-strained perfection is not. Indeed, my judgment is, that (in this case particularly) to overdo is to undo; and that to set perfection too high (so high as no man that we ever heard or read of attained) is the most effectual (because unsuspected) way of driving it out of the world.

Take care you are not hurt by anything in the "Short Hymns," contrary to the doctrines you have long received. Peace be with your spirit!

(To Miss Furley as she contemplated marriage.)

My Dear Sister,

1. So far as I know what will make me most holy and most useful, I know what is the will of God.

2. Certainly it is possible for persons to be as devoted to God in a married as in a single state.

3. I believe John Downes is throughly desirous of being wholly devoted to God, and that (if you alter your condition at all) you cannot choose a more proper person. I am, my dear sister,

Your affectionate brother.

Lewisham, December 15, 1763

My Dear Sister,

It has seemed to me, for sometime, that God will not suffer Cornelius Bastable to live at Cork. He may starve there, but he cannot live. The people are not worthy of him.

Salvation from sin is a deeper and higher work than either you or S. Ryan can conceive. But do not imagine (as we are continually prone to do) that it lies in an indivisible point. You experienced a taste of it when you were justified: You since experienced the thing itself, only in a low degree; and God gave you His Spirit, that you might know the things which He had freely given you. Hold fast the beginning of your confidence steadfast unto the end. You are continually apt to throw away what you have for what you want. However, you are right in looking for a farther instantaneous change, as well as a constant gradual one. But it is not good for you to be quite alone. You should converse frequently, as well as freely, with Miss Johnson and any other that is much alive. You have great need of this.

I am, my dear sister,

Your affectionate brother

To Samuel Bardsley

Bolton, April 3, 1772

Dear Sammy,

I am glad you are got into your circuit again. Now put forth all your strength. Never be ashamed of the old Methodist doctrine. Press all believers to go on to perfection. Insist everywhere on **PREACHING** the second blessing as receivable in a moment, and receivable now, by simple faith. Read again the *Plain Account of Christian Perfection*. And strive always to converse in a plain, unaffected manner. I am, dear Sammy,

Yours affectionately

To the Rev. John Newton

(This was a comparatively long letter to the famous minister, now familiar to thousands as the author of "Amazing Grace.")

May 1765

... I think on justification just as I have done any time these seven-and-twenty years, and just as Mr. Calvin does. In this respect I do not differ from him an hair's breadth.

But the main point between you and me is perfection. "This," you say, "has no prevalence in these parts; otherwise I should think it my duty to oppose it with my whole strength—not as an opinion, but as a dangerous mistake, which appears to be subversive of the very foundations of Christian experience, and which has, in fact, given occasion to the most grievous offences." Just so my brother and I reasoned 30 years ago. . . .

But how came this opinion into my mind, I will tell you with all simplicity. In 1725 I met with Bishop Taylor's *Rules of Holy Living and Dying*. I was struck particularly with the chapter upon Intention, and felt a fixed intention to *give myself up to God*. In this I was much confirmed soon after by the *Christian Pattern*, and longed to *give God all my heart*. This is just what I mean by perfection now: I sought after it from that hour.

In 1727 I read Mr. Law's *Christian Perfection* and *Serious Call*, and more explicitly resolved to be *all devoted to God* in body, soul, and spirit. In 1730 I began to be *homo unius libri*, to study (comparatively) no book but the Bible. I then saw in a stronger light than ever before that only one thing is needful, even faith that worketh by the love of God and man, all inward and outward holiness; and I groaned to love God with *all my heart* and to serve Him with *all my strength*.

January 1, 1733, I preached the sermon on the Circumcision of the Heart, which contains all that I now teach concerning salvation from *all sin* and loving God with an *undivided heart*. In the same year I printed (the first time I ventured to print anything) for the use of my pupils *A Collection of Forms of Prayer;* and in this I spoke explicitly of giving 'the whole heart and the whole life to God.' This was then, as it is now, my idea of perfection, though I should have started at the *word*.

In 1735 I preached my farewell sermon at Epworth, in Lincolnshire. In this likewise I spoke with the utmost clearness of having *one design, one desire, one love,* and of pursuing the *one end* of our life in *all* our words and actions.

In January 1738 I expressed my desire in these words:

> O grant that nothing in my soul
> May dwell but Thy pure love alone!
> O may Thy love possess me whole,
> My joy, my treasure, and my crown!
> Strange flames far from my heart remove!
> My every act, word, thought, be love![24]

And I am still persuaded that is what the Lord Jesus hath bought for me with His own blood.

Now, whether *you* desire and expect this blessing or not, is it not an astonishing thing that you or any man living should be disgusted at *me* for expecting it? Is it not more astonishing still "that well nigh all the religious world should be up in arms concerning it," and that they should persuade one another that this hope is 'subversive of the very foundations of Christian experience'? Why, then, whoever retains it cannot possibly have any Christian experience at all! Then my brother, Mr. Fletcher, and I, and 20,000 more, who *seem* both to fear and to love God are in reality children of the devil and in the road to eternal damnation!

In God's name I entreat you make me sensible of this! Show me by plain, strong reasons what dishonour this hope does to Christ, wherein it opposes justification by faith or any fundamental truth of religion. But do not wrest . . . and colour my words as Mr. Hervey (or Cudworth) has done in such a manner that when I look in that glass I do not know my own face! "Shall I call you," says Mr. Hervey, "my father or my friend? For you have been both to me." So I was, and you have as well requited me! It is well my reward is with the Most High. Wishing all happiness to you and yours, I am, dear sir,

Your affectionate brother and servant

To Mrs. Bennis

This lady was first drawn to the Methodists in March 1749, when a Methodist preacher was pressed by a howling mob as he passed her home in Limerick, Ireland. About a month later she became the first member of the Limerick Methodist Society. She was

---

24. Gerhardt's hymn, translated by Wesley (*Hymns and Sacred Poems*, 1739).

converted on June 21 in the Methodist meeting and entirely sanctified on Pentecost Sunday 1762. The Lord spoke to her as she knelt at the Communion table saying, "Be it unto thee according to thy faith." She died in Philadelphia in 1802.

Pembroke, August 23, 1763

My Dear Sister,

You did well to write. This is one of the means which God generally uses to convey either light or comfort. Even while you are writing you will often find relief; frequently while we propose a doubt it is removed.

There is no doubt but what you at first experienced was a real foretaste of the blessing, although you were not properly possessed of it till the Whit Sunday following. But it is very possible to cast away the gift of God, or to lose it by little and little; though I trust this is not the case with you: and yet you may frequently be in heaviness, and may find your love to God not near so warm at some times as it is at others. Many wanderings likewise, and many deficiencies are consistent with pure love; but the thing you mean is the abiding witness of the Spirit touching this very thing. And this you may boldly claim on the warrant of that word, "We have received the Spirit that is of God; that we may know the things which are freely given to us of God." I am, my dear sister,

ASSURANCE

Your affectionate brother

Liverpool, March 31, 1772

My Dear Sister,

You did well to break through and converse with Mrs. Dawson. There is no doubt but she has living faith; but, not having opportunity to converse with believers, she cannot express herself with that clearness that our friends do: cultivate the acquaintance. Now, lay before her by way of promise the whole Christian salvation; she will quickly see the desirableness of it. You may then lend her the *Plain Account of Christian Perfection*. She will not be frightened but rather encouraged at hearing it is possible to attain what her heart longs for. While you are thus feeding God's lambs, He will lead you into rich pastures.

WITNESSING

I do not wonder you should meet with trials: it is by these your faith is made perfect. You will find many things both in your heart and in your life contrary to the perfection of the Adamic law; but it does not follow that they are contrary to the law of love. Let this fill your heart, and it is enough. Still continue active for God. Remember, a talent is entrusted to you; see that you improve it. He does not like a slothful steward.

Your affectionate brother

To Philothea Briggs

Liverpool, March 23, 1772

If useless words or thoughts spring from evil tempers, they are properly evil, otherwise not; but still they are contrary to the *Adamic* law: yet not to the law of love; therefore there is no condemnation for them, but they are a matter of humiliation before God. So are those (seemingly) unbelieving thoughts; although they are not *your own,* and you may boldly say, "Go, go, thou unclean spirit; thou shalt answer for these, and not I."

June 1772

Nothing is sin, strictly speaking, but a voluntary transgression of a known law of God. Therefore every voluntary breach of the law of love is sin; and nothing else, if we speak properly. To strain the matter farther is only to make way for Calvinism. There may be 10,000 wandering thoughts and forgetful intervals without any breach of love, though not without transgressing the Adamic law. But Calvinists would fain confound these together. Let love fill your heart, and it is enough! I am, dear sister,

<small>WHAT SIN IS</small>

Your affectionate brother

To the Bishop of London

In this letter Wesley assumed that Dr. Gibson, the bishop of London, was the author of a pamphlet seriously attacking both the beliefs and the behavior of Wesley and his preachers. Wesley saw that Gibson's widespread influence and authority made it imperative that his charges and complaints be fully answered. Among these was the bishop's complaint against Wesley's perfectionism.

June 11, 1747

The Perfect Man

To the charge of holding "sinless perfection," as your Lordship states it, I might likewise plead not guilty; seeing one ingredient thereof in your Lordship's account is "freedom from temptation." Whereas I believe "there is no such perfection in this life as implies an entire deliverance from manifold temptations." But I will not decline the charge. I will repeat once more my coolest thoughts upon this head; and that in the very terms which I did several years ago, as I presume your Lordship cannot be ignorant:

The Mind of Christ

What, it may be asked, do you mean by "one that is perfect," or, "one that is as his Master"? We mean one in whom is "the mind which was in Christ," and who so "walketh as He walked"; a man that "hath clean hands and a pure heart"; or that is "cleansed from all filthiness of flesh and spirit"; one "in whom there is no occasion of stumbling"; and who, accordingly, "doth not commit sin."

Sanctified Throughout

To declare this a little more particularly: We understand by that scriptural expression, "a perfect man," one in whom God hath fulfilled his faithful word: "From all your filthiness, and from all your idols will I cleanse you. I will also save you from all your uncleanness." We understand hereby, one whom God hath sanctified throughout, even in "body, soul, and spirit;" one who "walketh in the light, as he is in the light," in whom "is no darkness at all; the blood of Jesus Christ his Son" having "cleansed him from all sin."

This man can now testify to all mankind, "I am crucified with Christ; nevertheless I live; yet I live not, but Christ liveth in me." He "is holy, as God who called him is holy," both in life, and "in all manner of conversation."

Perfect Love

He "loveth the Lord his God with all his heart, and serveth him with all his strength." He "loveth his neighbor [every man] as himself"; yea, "as Christ loved us"; them in particular that "despitefully use him and persecute him," because "they know not the Son, neither the Father." Indeed, His soul is all love, filled with "bowels of mercies, kindness, meekness, gentleness, long-suffering." And His life agreeth thereto, full of "the work of faith, the patience of hope, the labour of love." And "whatsoever he doeth, either in word or deed," he doeth "it all in the name," in the love and power, "of the Lord Jesus." In a word he doeth the will of God "on earth, as it is done in heaven."

This is to be "a perfect man," to be "sanctified throughout, created anew in Jesus Christ"; even "to have a heart so all-flaming with the love of God," as continually to offer up every thought, word, and work, as a spiritual sacrifice, acceptable unto God through Christ. In every thought of our hearts, in every word of our tongues, in every work of our hands," to show forth his praise who hath called us out of darkness into his marvellous light." O that both we, and all who seek the Lord Jesus in sincerity, may thus "be made perfect in one"![25]

To Joseph Benson

October 1770

... You judge rightly: Perfect love and Christian liberty are the very same thing; and those two expressions are equally proper, being equally scriptural. "Nay, how can they and you mean the same thing? They say, you insist on holiness in the creature, on good tempers, and sin destroyed." Most surely. And what is Christian liberty but another word for holiness? And where is this liberty or holiness if it is not in the creature? Holiness is the love of God and man, or the mind which was in Christ. Now I trust the love of God is shed abroad in your heart by the Holy Ghost which is given unto you. And if you are holy, is not that mind in you which was also in Christ Jesus?

PERFECT LOVE

And are not the love of God and our neighbour good tempers? And so far as these reign in the soul, are not the opposite tempers, worldly-mindedness, malice, cruelty, revengefulness, destroyed? Indeed, the unclean spirit, though driven out, may return and enter again; nevertheless he was driven out. I use the word "destroyed," because St. Paul does: "Suspended: I cannot find in my Bible." "But they say, you do not consider this as the consequence of the power of Christ dwelling in us." Then what will they not say? My very words are, "none feel their need of Christ like these; none so entirely depend upon Him. For Christ does not give light to the soul separate from, but in and with, himself. Hence His words are equally true of all men, in whatever state of grace they are: 'As the branch cannot bear fruit of itself, except it abide in the vine; no more can ye, except ye abide in me: Without' (or separate from) 'me, ye can do nothing.' For our perfection is not like that of a tree which flourishes by the sap derived from its own root; but like that of a branch which, united to the vine bears fruit; but severed from it is 'dried up and withered.'"

CLEANSING

ATONEMENT

---

25. *WW,* 7:484.

London, December 28, 1770

Dear Joseph,

What a blessing it is, that we can speak freely to each other without either disguise or reserve! So long as we are able to do this we may grow wiser and better every day.

One point I advise you to hold fast and let neither men nor devils tear it from you. You are a child of God; you are justified freely, through the redemption which is in Christ Jesus. Your sins are forgiven! Cast not away that confidence, which hath great recompense of reward.

Now, can any be justified but by faith? None can. Therefore you are a believer; you have faith in Christ; you know the Lord; you can say, "My Lord and my God." And whoever denies this, may as well deny that the sun shines at noonday.

> Yet still ten thousand lusts remain,
> And vex your soul, absolved from sin;
> Still rebel nature strives to reign,
> And you are all unclean, unclean!

This is equally clear and undeniable. And this is not only your experience, but the experience of a thousand believers beside, who yet are sure of God's favour, as of their own existence. To cut off all doubt on this head, I beg you to give another serious reading to those two sermons, "Sin in Believers" and "The Repentance of Believers."

"But is there no help? Is there no deliverance, no salvation from this inbred enemy?" Surely there is; else many great and precious promises must fall to the ground. "I will sprinkle clean water upon you, and ye shall be clean; from all your filthiness and from all your idols will I cleanse you." "I will circumcise thy heart" (from all sin) "to love the Lord thy God with all thy heart, and with all thy soul." This I term sanctification (which is both an instantaneous and a gradual work), or perfection, the being perfected in love, filled with love which still admits of a thousand degrees. But I have no time to throw away in contending for words; especially where the thing is allowed. And you allow the whole thing which I contend for; an entire deliverance from sin, a recovery of the whole image of God, the loving God with all our heart, soul, and strength. And you believe God is able to give you this; yea to give it you in an instant. You trust He will.

O hold fast this also; this blessed hope, which He has wrought in

CLEANSING

your heart! And with all zeal and diligence confirm the brethren. (1) In holding fast that whereto they have attained; namely, the remission of all their sins, by faith in a bleeding Lord; (2) In expecting a second change, whereby they shall be saved from all sin, and perfected in love.

SECOND BLESSING

If they like to call this "receiving the Holy Ghost," they may: Only the phrase, in that sense, is not scriptural, and not quite proper; for they all "receive the Holy Ghost" when they were justified. God then "sent forth the Spirit of his Son into their hearts, crying, Abba, Father."

O Joseph, keep close to the Bible, both as to sentiment and expression! Then there will never be any material difference between you and

Your affectionate brother

London, January 8, 1774

Dear Joseph,

Many persons are in danger of reading too little: You are in danger of reading too much. Wherever you are, take up your cross, and visit all the society from house to house. Do this according to Mr. Baxter's plan, laid down in the Minutes of the Conference. The fruit which will ensue (perhaps in a short time) will abundantly reward your labour. Fruit also we shall have, even in those who have no outward connection with us.

I am glad you "press all believers" to aspire after the full liberty of the children of God. They must not give up their faith in order to do this: Herein you formerly seemed to be in some mistake. Let them go on from faith to faith; from weak faith to that strong faith which not only conquers but casts out sin. Meantime it is certain, many call themselves believers who do not even conquer sin; who are strangers to the whole inward kingdom of God, and void of the whole fruit of the Spirit.

PREACHING

March 1771

To Betsy Briggs

My Dear Betsy,

You have great reason to praise Him who has done great things for you already. What you now want is to come boldly to the throne of grace, that the hunger and thirst after His full image which God has given you may be satisfied.

SEEKING AND FINDING

Full salvation is nigh even at the door. Only believe and it is yours. It is a great blessing that, at your years, you are preserved from seeking happiness in any creature. You need not, seeing Christ is yours! O cleave to Him with your whole heart!

April 1771

TEMPTATION AND WITNESS

Each day will bring just temptation enough, and power enough to conquer it; and, as one says, "temptations with distinct deliverances from them, avail much." The unction of the Holy One is given to believers for this very end—to enable them to distinguish (which otherwise would be impossible) between sin and temptation. And this you will do, not by any general rule, but by listening to Him on all particular occasions, and by your consulting with those that have experience in the ways of God.

Undoubtedly both you and Philothea, and my dear Miss Perronet, are now more particularly called to speak for God. In so doing you must expect to meet with many things which are not pleasing to flesh and blood. But all is well. So much the more will you be comformed to the death of Christ. Go on in His name and in the power of His might. Suffer and conquer all things.

To Rev. Dr. Conyers Middleton

In 1749 there was published by Dr. Conyers Middleton a book attacking the early Christian fathers and what the author described as "the miraculous powers which are supposed to have subsisted in the Church from the earliest ages through several successive centuries."

Wesley felt it necessary to publish a critique of the book. He did so in a letter of abnormal length and vigor, running to almost 80 pages.[26]

There are sections in the long letter that present Wesley's ideal of the Christian life. From these the following extracts are taken; most of them edited or abridged.

A Cameo of a True Christian

VI. I have now finished what I had to say with regard to your book. Yet I think humanity requires me to add a few words concerning

---

26. *WW*, 10:1-79; sections quoted, 67-75.

some points frequently touched upon therein, which perhaps you do not so clearly understand.

We have been long disputing about Christians, about Christianity and the evidence whereby it is supported. But what do these terms mean? Who is a Christian indeed? What is real, genuine Christianity? And what is the surest and most accessible evidence (if I may so speak) whereby I may know that it is of God? May the God of the Christians enable me to speak on these heads in a manner suitable to the importance of them!

Section I

1. I would consider, first, who is a Christian indeed? What does that term properly imply? It has been so long abused, I fear, not only to mean nothing at all, but what was far worse than nothing, to be a cloak for the vilest hypocrisy, for the grossest abominations and immoralities of every kind. It is high time to rescue it out of the hands of wretches that are a reproach to human nature; to show determinately what manner of man he is to whom this name of right belongs.

2. A Christian cannot think of the Author of his being, without abasing himself before Him; without a deep sense of the distance between a worm of earth and Him that sitteth on the circle of the heavens. In His presence he sinks into the dust, knowing himself to be less than nothing in His eye; and being conscious, in a manner words cannot express of his own littleness, ignorance, foolishness. So that he can only cry out from the fulness of his heart, "O God! what is man? What am I?"

3. He has a continual sense of his dependence on the Parent of good for his being, and all the blessings that attend it.... And hence he acquiesces in whatsoever appears to be His will, not only with patience, but with thankfulness. He willingly resigns all he is, all he has, to His wise and gracious disposal. The ruling temper of his heart is the most absolute submission, and the tenderest gratitude to his sovereign Benefactor....

4. And as he has the strongest affection for the Fountain of all good, so he has the firmest confidence in Him; a confidence which neither pleasure nor pain, neither life nor death can shake. But yet this, far from creating sloth or indolence, pushes him on to the most vigorous industry. It causes him to put forth all his strength in obeying Him in whom he confides.

5. Above all, remembering that God is love he is conformed to

PERFECT LOVE the same likeness. He is full of love to his neighbour; of universal love; not confined to one sect or party; not restrained to those who agree with him in opinions, or in outward modes of worship; or to those who are allied to him by blood, or recommended by nearness of place; neither does he love those only that love him or that are endeared to him by intimacy of acquaintance.... His love embraces neighbours and strangers, friends and enemies; yea, not only the good and gentle, but also the froward, the evil and unthankful. For he loves every soul that God has made; every child of man, of whatever place or nation. And yet this universal benevolence does in nowise interfere with a peculiar regard for his relations, friends, and benefactors; a fervent love for his country; and the most endeared affection to all men of integrity, of clear and generous virtue.

6. His love, as to these, so to all mankind, is in itself generous and disinterested; springing from no view of advantage to himself, from no regard to profit or praise; no, nor even the pleasure of loving. This is the daughter, not the parent of his affection. By experience he knows that social love, if it mean the love of our neighbour, is absolutely different from self-love even of the most allowable kind; just as different as the objects at which they point. And yet it is sure that if they are under due regulations, each will give additional force to the other till they mix together never to be divided.

7. And this universal, disinterested love is productive of all right affections.... It makes a Christian rejoice in the virtues of all, and bear a part in their happiness; at the same time that he sympathizes with their pains and compassionates their infirmities. ... It is the parent of generosity, openness, and frankness, void of jealousy and suspicion. It begets candour, and willingness to believe and hope whatever is kind and friendly of every man; and invincible patience, never overcome of evil, but overcoming evil with good.

8. The same love constrains him to converse, not only with a strict regard to truth, but with artless sincerity and genuine simplicity as one in whom there is no guile. And, not content with abstaining from all such expressions as are contrary to justice or truth, he endeavours to refrain from every unloving word, either to a present or of an absent person; in all his conversation aiming at this, either to improve himself in knowledge or virtue, or to make those with whom he converses some way wiser, or better, or happier than they were before.

9. The same love is productive of all right actions. It leads him

into an earnest and steady discharge of all social offices, of whatever is due to relations of every kind; to his friends, to his country, and to any particular community, whereof he is a member. It prevents his willingly hurting or grieving any man. It guides him into a uniform practice of justice and mercy equally extensive with the principle whence it flows. It constrains him to do all possible good, of every possible kind, to all men; and makes him invariably resolved in every circumstance of life to do that, and that only to others, which, supposing he were himself in the same situation, he would desire they should do to him.

10. And as he is easy to others, so he is easy in himself. He is free from the painful swellings of pride, from the flames of anger, from the impetuous gusts of irregular self-will. He is no longer tortured with envy or malice, or with unreasonable and hurtful desire. He is no more enslaved to the pleasures of sense but has the full power both over his mind and body, in a continued cheerful course of sobriety, of temperance and chastity. He knows how to use all things in their place, and yet is superior to them all. He stands above those low pleasures of imagination which captivate vulgar minds, whether arising from what mortals term greatness, or from novelty, or beauty. All these too he can taste and still look upward; still aspire to nobler enjoyments. Neither is he a slave to fame; popular breath affects not him; he stands steady and collected in himself.

ATTITUDES

11. And he who seeks no praise cannot fear dispraise. Censure gives him no uneasiness, being conscious to himself that he would not willingly offend, and that he has the approbation of the Lord of all. He cannot fear want, knowing in whose hand is the earth and the fulness thereof, and that it is impossible for God to withhold from one that fears Him any manner of thing that is good. He cannot fear pain, knowing it will never be sent unless it be for his real advantage; and that then his strength will be proportioned to it as it has always been in times past. He cannot fear death; being able to trust Him he loves with his soul as well as his body; yea, glad to leave the corruptible body in the dust till it is raised incorruptible and immortal. So that, in honour or shame, in abundance or want, in ease or pain, in life or in death, always and in all things he has learned to be content, to be easy, thankful, happy.

12. . . . He is happy in the full assurance he has that [the] Creator and End of all things is a Being of boundless wisdom, of infinite power to execute all the designs of His wisdom, and of no less infinite good-

ness to direct all His power to the advantage of all His creatures. . . . In that immense ocean of all perfections which centre in God from eternity to eternity, is a continual addition to the happiness of a Christian.

13. A farther addition is made thereto. In contemplating even the things that surround him . . . he takes knowledge of the invisible things of God, even His eternal power and wisdom in the things that are seen, the heavens, the earth, the fowls of the air, the lilies of the field. . . . He, as it were, sees the Lord sitting upon His throne and ruling all things well, . . . presiding over the whole universe as over a single person, so watching over every single person as if he were the whole universe. . . . With what triumph of soul, in surveying either the general or particular providence of God, does he observe every line pointing out an hereafter, every scene opening into eternity!

14. He is peculiarly and inexpressibly happy, in the clearest and fullest conviction, "This all-powerful, all-wise, all-gracious Being, this Governor of all, loves me. . . . And I love Him: There is none in heaven but Thee, none on earth that I desire beside Thee! And He has given me to resemble himself; He has stamped His image on my heart. And I live unto Him; I do only His will; I glorify Him with my body and my spirit. And it will not be long before I shall die unto Him; I shall die into the arms of God. And then farewell sin and pain; then it only remains that I should live with Him for ever."

15. This is the plain, naked portraiture of a Christian. But be not prejudiced against him for his name. Forgive his particularities of opinion, and (what you think) superstitious modes of worship. These are circumstances but of small concern, and do not enter into the essence of his character. Cover them with a veil of love, and look at the substance—his tempers, his holiness, his happiness.

HUNGER

Can calm reason conceive either a more amiable or a more desirable character? Is it your own? . . . I ask not what opinion you are of, so you are conscious to yourself, that you are the man whom I have been describing.

Do not you know you ought to be such? Is the Governor of the world well pleased that you are not?

Do you desire it? I would to God that desire may penetrate your inmost soul; and that you may have no rest in your spirit till you are, not only almost, but altogether, a Christian!

Section II

1. The second point to be considered is, What is real, genuine

Christianity? Whether we speak of it as a principle in the soul, or as a scheme or system of doctrine.

Christianity, taken in the latter sense, is that system of doctrine which describes the character above recited, which promises it shall be mine (provided I will not rest till I attain) and which tells me how I may attain it.

2. First. It describes this character in all its parts, and that in the most lively and affecting manner. The main lines of this picture are beautifully drawn in many passages of the Old Testament. These are filled up in the New, retouched and finished with all the art of God.

The same we have in miniature more than once; particularly in the thirteenth chapter of the First Epistle to the Corinthians and in that discourse which St. Matthew records as delivered by our Lord at His entrance upon His public ministry.

3. Secondly. Christianity promises this character shall be mine, if I will not rest till I attain it. This is promised both in the Old Testament and the New. Indeed the New is, in effect, all a promise; seeing every description of the servants of God mentioned therein has the nature of a command; in consequence of those general injunctions: "Be ye followers of me, as I am of Christ" (1 Cor. xi. 1). "Be ye followers of them who through faith and patience inherit the promises" (Heb. vi. 12). And every command has the force of a promise, in virtue of those general promises: "A new heart will I give you, and I will put my Spirit within you, and cause you to walk in my statutes, and ye shall keep my judgments, and do them" (Ezek. xxxv. 26-27). "This is the covenant that I will make after those days, saith the Lord; I will put my laws into their minds, and write them in their hearts" (Heb. viii. 10). Accordingly when it is said, "Thou shalt love the Lord thy God with all thy heart, and with all thy soul, and with all thy mind" (Matt. xxii. 37), it is not only a direction what I shall do, but a promise of what God will do in me; exactly equivalent with what is written elsewhere: "The Lord thy God will circumcise thy heart and the heart of thy seed" (alluding to the custom then in use), "to love the Lord thy God with all thy heart and with all thy soul" (Deut. xxx. 6).

SCRIPTURAL

4. This being observed, it will readily appear to every serious person who reads the New Testament with that care which the importance of the subject demands, that every particular branch of the preceding character is manifestly promised therein; either explicitly, under the very form of a promise, or virtually, under that of description or command.

5. Christianity tells me, in the third place, how I may attain the promise; namely, by faith.

FAITH But what is faith? Not an opinion, no more than it is a form of words; not any number of opinions put together, be they ever so true. A string of opinions is no more Christian faith than a string of beads is Christian holiness.

It is not an assent to any opinion or any number of opinions. A man may assent to three, or three-and-twenty creeds: He may assent to all the Old and New Testament (at least as far as he understands them), and yet have no Christian faith at all.

6. The faith by which the promise is attained is . . . a power wrought by the Almighty in an immortal spirit, inhabiting a house of clay, to see through that veil into the world of spirits, into things invisible and eternal; a power to discern those things which with eyes of flesh and blood no man hath seen or can see, either by reason of their nature, which is not perceivable by these gross senses; or by reason of their distance, as being yet afar off in the bosom of eternity.

7. This is Christian faith in the general notion of it. In its more particular notion, it is a divine evidence or conviction wrought in the heart, that God is reconciled to me through His Son; inseparably joined with a confidence in Him, as a gracious, reconciled Father, as for all things, so especially for all those good things which are invisible and eternal.

To believe is, then, to walk in the light of eternity; and to have a clear sight of, and confidence in, the Most High, reconciled to me through the Son of His love.

8. Now, how highly desirable is such a faith, were it only on its own account! For how little does the wisest of men know of anything more than he can see with his eyes! What clouds and darkness cover the whole scene of things invisible and eternal! What does he know even of himself as to his invisible part? What of his future manner of existence? . . . Poor philosopher Antoninus! with all his wealth, his honour, his power! with all his wisdom and philosophy,

> *What points of knowledge did he gain?*
> *That life is sacred all, and vain!*
> *Sacred, how high, and vain, how low,*
> *He could not tell; but died to know.*

9. "He died to know!" and so must you, unless you are now a partaker of Christian faith. O consider this! Nay, and consider not only

how little you know of the immensity of the things that are beyond sense and time, but how uncertainly do you know even that little! How faintly glimmering a light is that you have! Can you properly be said to know any of these things? Is that knowledge any more than bare conjecture? And the reason is plain. You have no senses suitable to invisible or eternal objects....

10. Is it not so? Let impartial reason speak. Does not every thinking man want a window, not so much in his neighbour's, as in his own breast? He wants an opening there, of whatever kind, that might let in light from eternity....

11. Now these very desiderata faith supplies. It gives a more extensive knowledge of things invisible, showing what eye had not seen, nor ear heard, neither could it before enter into our heart to conceive. And all these it shows in the clearest light, with the fullest certainty and evidence. For it does not leave us to receive our notices of them by mere reflection from the dull glass of sense; but resolves a thousand enigmas of the highest concern by giving faculties suited to things invisible. O who would not wish for such a faith, were it only on these accounts! How much more, if by this I may receive the promise, I may attain all that holiness and happiness!

12. So Christianity tells me; and so I find it, may every real Christian say. I now am assured that these things are so; I experience them in my own breast. What Christianity (considered as a doctrine) promised, is accomplished in my soul. And Christianity, considered as an inward principle, is the completion of all those promises. It is holiness and happiness, the image of God impressed on a created spirit; a fountain of peace and love springing up into everlasting life.

EXPERIENCING IT

Appeals to Men of Reason and Religion

Opposition and persecution were the lot of the Methodists from Oxford days until Methodism was above 40 years old. Indeed the terminal date can be placed as late as 1811 in one part of England.

Literary ridicule, scorn, misrepresentation, and criticism began with an attack upon the Oxford Methodists of the Holy Club in the columns of *Fog's Weekly Journal* in December 1738.[27] On that occasion a powerful pen, commonly believed to have been that of William Law, abundantly answered the criticism; but the attacks continued through the year of Wesley's conversion and on into 1778. Thereafter, as Wesley put it, he became respected and in some circles almost venerated. The number of attacks diminished and finally they died out completely.

Wesley generally responded with dignity and reason when he considered the attack worthy of an answer. His most analytical and impressive polemic, and probably his most sustained writing in defense of the doctrines of Methodism and of the Methodist experience is to be found in the *Appeals*.

These documents are important to a full understanding of Methodism in its primitive setting, especially with reference to a phobia which had overspread English religion in the preceding century. That phobia was the horror of unbridled emotion and fanaticism in religious life. Much of the ecclesiastical opposition to early Methodism may be traced to this source.

Wesley, however, regulated and directed Methodist enthusiasm by giving wonderfully clear counsel on the extraordinary and on the ordinary operations of the Holy Spirit. He admitted the possibility of direct impact and immediate revelation: he patiently listened to boring recitals of spiritual visions and impulses, but because of his emphasis on Scripture and reason he was not sidetracked. He erected doctrinal and organizational barriers by which the early Methodists were prevented from plunging into disastrous excesses.

---

27. D. Dunn Wilson, *Many Waters Cannot Quench* (London: Epworth Press, 1969), 33-34.

Wesley's teaching on the personal Christian experience of the Holy Spirit was safeguarded and reinforced by ethical requirements. "Let no one presume to rest in any supposed witness of the Spirit divorced from the fruit thereof."

The error of Deism in the eighteenth century lay in its claim for the sufficiency of unaided human reason to meet all human needs including soul salvation. That Methodism did not slip off the other end of the plank into the error of divorcing faith and reason was due to John Wesley's crosschecks—Scripture, reason, and experience—in that order. He was a man of sound, sober sense as well as of deep spirituality. He taught the people called Methodists a feeling religion, but also a thinking religion.

The *Appeals* teach us much about the characteristics and peculiarities of the Early Methodists as seen through Wesley's eyes. The orthodox theology and liturgy of the *Prayer Book* are here wedded to Methodist experience and testimony. Here the Rev. John Wesley is the apologist, polemicist, and Methodist preacher on fire for the full salvation of all men everywhere.

There are really four appeals. The first was published in 1743, titled *An Earnest Appeal to Men of Reason and Religion*. About two years later came *A Farther Appeal* in three parts, published separately in 1744 and 1745.

Wesley defined his first *Appeal* as "a short rude sketch of the doctrine we teach. These are our fundamental principles; and we spend our lives in confirming others herein, and in a behavior suitable to them."[28] Wesley was adamant that at no point in Christian Scripture or experience has God made provision for sin in any degree or form. He could have justly called the *Appeals, An Apologia for Methodism*.

On Living Without Sin[29]

51. Bear with me a little longer: My soul is distressed for you. "The god of this world hath blinded your eyes" and you are "seeking death in the error of your life." Because you do not commit gross sin, because you give alms and go to the church and sacrament you imagine that you are serving God; yet, in very deed, you are serving the devil; for you are doing still your own will, not the will of God your Saviour. You are pleasing yourself in all you do. . . .

---

28. *WW*, 2:49.
29. Excerpted from *WW*, 8:20-23.

52. Of you who "have tasted the good work of God, and the powers of the world to come," I would be glad to learn if we have "erred from the faith," or walked contrary to "the truth as it is in Jesus." . . .

53. Perhaps the first thing that now occurs to your mind relates to the doctrine which we teach. You have heard that we say, "Men may live without sin." And have you not heard that the Scripture says the same; we mean, without committing sin? Does not St. Paul say plainly that those who believe "do not continue in sin," that they cannot "live any longer therein"? (Rom. vi. 1-2). Does not St. Peter say, "He that hath suffered in the flesh hath ceased from sin; that he no longer should live to the desires of men but to the will of God"? (1 Pet. iv. 1-2). And does not St. John say expressly, "He that committeth sin is of the devil? For this purpose the Son of God was manifested, that he might destroy the works of the devil. Whosoever is born of God doth not commit sin; for his seed remaineth in him: And he cannot sin, because he is born of God" (1 John iii. 8-9). And again: "We know that whosoever is born of God sinneth not" (v. 18).

CLEANSING

54. You see, then, it is not we that say this, but the Lord. These are not our words, but His. And who is he that replieth against God? Who is able to make God a liar? Surely He will be justified in His saying and clear when He is judged! Can you deny it? Have you not often felt a secret check when you were contradicting this great truth? And how often have you wished for what you were taught to deny? Nay, can you help wishing for it this moment? Do you not now earnestly desire to cease from sin? to commit it no more? Does not your soul pant after this glorious liberty of the sons of God? And what strong reason have you to expect it! Have you not had a foretaste of it already? Do you not remember the time when God first lifted up the light of His countenance upon you? Can it ever be forgotten? the day when the candle of the Lord first shone upon your head?

HUNGER

> *Butter and honey did you eat*
>   *And, lifted up on high,*
> *You saw the clouds beneath your feet,*
>   *And rode upon the sky.*
> *Far, far above all earthly things*
>   *Triumphantly you rode;*
> *You soar'd to heaven on eagles' wings,*
>   *And found and talk'd with God.*

You then had power not to commit sin. You found the apostle's words strictly true, "He that is begotten of God keepeth himself, and that wicked one toucheth him not." But those whom you took to be experienced Christians told you this was only the time of your espousals, this could not last always, you must come down from the mount, and [they] shook your faith. You looked at men more than God, and so became weak and like another man. Whereas, had you then had any to guide you according to the truth of God, had you then heard the doctrine which now you blame, you had never fallen from your steadfastness; but had found that, in this sense also, "the gifts and calling of God are without repentance."

55. Have you not another objection nearly allied to this, namely that we preach perfection? True; but what perfection? The term you cannot object to, because it is scriptural. All the difficulty is to fix the meaning of it according to the word of God. And this we have done again and again, declaring to all the world that Christian perfection does not imply an exemption from ignorance or mistake or infirmities or temptations; but that it does imply the being so crucified with Christ as to be able to testify, "I live not, but Christ liveth in me" (Gal. ii. 20) and hath "purified my heart by faith" (Acts xv. 9). It does imply "the casting down every high thing that exalteth itself against the knowledge of God, and bringing into captivity every thought to the obedience of Christ." It does imply "the being holy, as he that hath called us is holy, in all manner of conversation" (2 Cor. x. 5; 1 Pet. i. 15); and, in a word, "the loving the Lord our God with all our heart, and serving him with all our strength."

CHRISTIAN PERFECTION

56. Now, is it possible for any who believe the Scripture to deny one tittle of this? You cannot. You dare not. You would not for the world. You know it is the pure word of God. And this is the whole of what we (with St. Paul) call perfection; a state of soul devoutly to be wished by all who have tasted of the love of God. O pray for it without ceasing! It is the one thing you want. Come with boldness to the throne of grace; and be assured that when you ask this of God, you shall have the petition you ask of Him. We know indeed that to man, to the natural man, this is impossible. But we know also that as no word is impossible with God, so "all things are possible to him that believeth."

57. For "we are saved by faith." But have you not heard this urged as another objection against us, that we preach salvation by faith

FAITH alone? And does not St. Paul do the same thing? "By grace," saith he, "ye are saved through faith." Can any words be more express? And elsewhere, "Believe in the Lord Jesus, and thou shalt be saved" (Acts xvi. 31).

What we mean by this (if it has not been sufficiently explained already) is that we are saved from our sins only by a confidence in the love of God. As soon as we "behold what manner of love it is which the Father hath bestowed upon us, we love him" (as the apostle observes) "because he first loved us." And then is that commandment written in our heart, "That he who loveth God love his brother also"; from which love of God and man, meekness, humbleness of mind, and all holy tempers spring. Now, these are the very essence of salvation, of Christian salvation, salvation from sin; and from these outward salvation flows, that is, holiness of life and conversation. Well, and are not these things so? If you know in whom you have believed, you need no further witnesses.

A Farther Appeal
to Men of Reason and Religion

Wesley's opening sections of his *Farther Appeal* consist of precise reviews of his observations in the earlier *Appeal*. Having briefly described and defined the nature of justification in relation to good works and to repentance, he declares his concept of salvation.

What Salvation Is

3. By salvation I mean, not barely deliverance from hell, or going to heaven; but a present deliverance from sin, a restoration of the soul to its primitive health, its original purity; a recovery of the divine nature; the renewal of our souls after the image of God, in righteousness and true holiness, in justice, mercy, and truth. This implies all holy and heavenly tempers, and by consequence, all holiness of conversation.

Now if by salvation we mean a present deliverance from sin, we cannot say that holiness is a condition of it, for it is the thing itself. In this sense salvation and holiness are synonymous terms. We must therefore say, "We are saved by faith." Faith is the sole condition of this salvation, for without faith we cannot thus be saved. But whosoever believeth is saved already.[30]

---

30. *WW*, 8:47.

The Ordinary Operations of the Holy Ghost

FOR ALL CHRISTIANS

Wesley has been defending his teaching that all Christians are now to receive the Holy Spirit, saying, "We may all now enjoy, and know that we enjoy, the heavenly direction of God's Spirit." He then defends himself against the criticism that he confuses the extraordinary work of the Holy Ghost—the miraculous gifts such as miracles, knowledge, and prophecy—with the "ordinary gifts of the Spirit of Christ, which if a man have not he is none of his." . . .

22. Therefore, upon the whole, the sense of the primitive Church . . . is, that although some of the scriptures primarily refer to those extraordinary gifts of the Spirit which were given to the apostles and a few other persons in the apostolical age; yet they refer also, in a secondary sense, to those ordinary operations of the Holy Spirit which all the children of God do and will experience, even to the end of the world.[31]

(Wesley then expresses what he means by "the ordinary operations of the Holy Ghost" by borrowing heavily from Bishop Pearson's exposition of the Creed.)

CLEANSING

23. Sanctification being opposed to our corruption, and answering fully to the latitude thereof, whatsoever of holiness and perfection is wanting in our nature must be supplied by the Spirit of God. Wherefore, being by nature . . . totally void of all saving truth, and under an impossibility of knowing the will of God, this "Spirit searcheth all things, yea, even the deep things of God," and revealeth them unto the sons of men, so that thereby the darkness of their understanding is expelled, and they are enlightened with the knowledge of God. The same Spirit which revealeth the object of faith generally to the universal Church, doth also illuminate the understanding of such as believe, that they may receive the truth. For "faith is the gift of God," not only in the object, but also in the act. And this gift is a gift of the Holy Ghost working within us. And as the increase of perfection, so the original of faith is from the Spirit of God, by an internal illumination of the soul.

The second part of the office of the Holy Ghost is the renewing of man in all the parts and faculties of his soul. For our natural corruption consisting in an aversion of our wills, and a depravation of our

---

31. *WW,* Ibid., 99.

affections, an inclination of them to the will of God is wrought within us by the Spirit of God.

The third part of this office is to lead, direct, and govern us in our actions and conversations. "If we live in the Spirit," quickened by His renovation, we must also "walk in the Spirit," following His direction, led by His hand. We are also animated and activated by the Spirit of God who giveth "both to will and to do"; And "as many as are" thus "led by the Spirit of God, are the sons of God" (Rom. viii. 14).

Moreover, that this direction may prove more effectual, we are guided in our prayers by the same Spirit; according to the promise, "I will pour upon the house of David, and upon the inhabitants of Jerusalem, the Spirit of grace and supplication" (Zech. xii. 10). Whereas then "this is the confidence which we have in him, that if we ask anything according to his will, he heareth us"; and whereas "we know not what we should pray for as we ought, the Spirit itself maketh intercession for us with groanings which cannot be uttered"; and "he that searcheth the hearts knoweth what is the mind of the Spirit, because he maketh intercession for the saints, according to the will of God" (Rom. viii. 27).

From which intercession (made for all true Christians) he hath the name of the Paraclete given Him by Christ who said, "I will pray the Father, and he will give you another Paraclete" (John xiv. 16, 26). "For if any man sin, we have a Paraclete with the Father, Jesus Christ the righteous," saith St. John; "who maketh intercession for us," saith St. Paul (Rom. viii. 34). And we have "another Paraclete," saith our Saviour (John xiv. 16); "which also maketh intercession for us," saith St. Paul (Rom. viii. 27). A Paraclete, then, in the notion of the Scriptures, is an intercessor.

It is also the office of the Holy Ghost, to "assure us of the adoption of sons," to create in us a sense of the paternal love of God toward us, to give us an earnest of our everlasting inheritance. "The love of God is shed abroad in our hearts, by the Holy Ghost which is given unto us." "For as many as are led by the Spirit of God, they are the sons of God." "And because we are sons, God hath sent forth the Spirit of his Son into our hearts, crying, Abba, Father." "For we have not received the spirit of bondage again to fear; but we have received the Spirit of adoption, whereby we cry, Abba, Father; the Spirit itself bearing witness with our spirit, that we are the children of God" (vv. 15-16).

ASSURANCE

As, therefore, we are born again by the Spirit and receive from him our regeneration, so we are also by the same Spirit assured of our adoption." Because, being "sons, we are also heirs, heirs of God and joint-heirs with Christ," by the same Spirit we have the pledge, or rather the "earnest of our inheritance." For "he which establisheth us in Christ and hath anointed us, is God; who hath also sealed us, and given us the earnest of his Spirit in our hearts"; So that "we are sealed with that Holy Spirit of promise, which is the earnest of our inheritance." The Spirit of God as given unto us in this life is to be looked upon as an earnest, being part of that reward which is promised; and upon performance of the covenant which God hath made with us, certainly to be received."

(Wesley now amasses a score of quotations and examples from the Homilies, Collects, and Offices of the Church of England.)

25. . . . He died to destroy the rule of the devil in us; and He rose again to send down His Holy Spirit into our hearts.

It is the office of the Holy Ghost to sanctify; which the more it [that is, the more particular manner of His working] is hid from an understanding the more it ought to move all men to wonder at the secret and mighty workings of God's Holy Spirit within us.

It is the Holy Ghost that doth quicken the minds of men, stirring up godly motions in their hearts. Neither doth He think it sufficient inwardly to work the new birth of man, unless He do also dwell and abide in him. "Know ye not," saith St. Paul, "that ye are the temple of God, and that his Spirit dwelleth in you? Know ye not that your bodies are the temple of the Holy Ghost, which is in you?" Again he saith, "Ye are not in the flesh, but in the Spirit." For why? "The Spirit of God dwelleth in you." To this agreeth St. John: "The anointing which ye have received" (he meaneth the Holy Ghost) "abideth in you" (1 John ii. 27). And St. Peter saith the same: "The Spirit of glory and of God resteth upon you."

O what comfort is this to the heart of a true Christian, to think that the Holy Ghost dwelleth in him! "If God be with us," as the apostle saith, "who can be against us?" He giveth patience and joyfulness of heart, in temptation and affliction, and is therefore worthily called "the Comforter" (John xiv. 16). He doth instruct the hearts of the simple in the knowledge of God and His word; therefore He is justly termed "the Spirit of truth" (xvi. 13). And where the Holy Ghost doth instruct and teach, there is no delay at all in learning.

From this passage I learn, *first* that every true Christian now "receives the Holy Ghost" as the Paraclete or Comforter promised by our Lord (John xiv. 16). *Secondly* that every Christian receives him as "the Spirit of truth" (promised John xvi) to "teach him all things." And, *thirdly* that "the anointing," mentioned in the first Epistle of St. John, "abides in every Christian." . . .

26. God give us grace to know these things and to *feel* them in our hearts! This knowledge and *feeling* is not of ourselves. Let us therefore meekly call upon the bountiful Spirit, the Holy Ghost, to inspire us with His presence that we may be able to hear the goodness of God to our salvation. For without His lively inspiration can we not so much as speak the name of the Mediator. "No man can say that Jesus is the Lord, but by the Holy Ghost"; much less should we be able to believe and know these great mysteries that be opened to us by Christ. "But we have received," saith St. Paul, "not the spirit of the world, but the Spirit which is of God"; for this purpose, "that we may know the things which are freely given to us of God."

In the power of the Holy Ghost resteth all ability to *know* God, and to *please* Him. It is He that *purifieth* the mind by His secret working. He *enlighteneth* the heart, to conceive worthy thoughts of Almighty God. He sitteth in the *tongue* of man, to stir him to speak his honour. He only ministereth spiritual strength to the powers of the *soul* and *body*. And if we have any gift whereby we may profit our neighbour, all is wrought by this one and the self-same Spirit.

27. Every proposition which I have anywhere advanced concerning those *operations* of the Holy Ghost, which, I believe, are *common* to all Christians in all ages, is here clearly maintained by our own Church.

Social Implications of Entire Sanctification

Man's most sensitive nerve is often the one connecting heart with hip-pocket or purse; money and its use is very often the acid test of a person's religion. These extracts are presented as a very real part of Wesley's teaching on Christian holiness as a life-style.

Social service was not a mere program to the Wesleys, it was a passion, as much a part of perfect love as heat is part of a fire or fragrance part of a flower. It continued all the way from the days of the Holy Club at Oxford to the final weeks of John's life when the aged evangelist could be seen going from door to door collecting money for the poor.

Giving and receiving good
Twixt the mount and multitude.

It was part of the fabric of the Revival: it was woven into sermons, appeals, letters, essays. Here was a necessary "mark of a Methodist." Love of our neighbor is for Wesley a near synonym for perfect love, and is known only in service to that neighbor. We cite three excerpts to reflect Wesley's understanding of holy living as a life-style.

1. His sermon based on Matt. 5:13-16, "Ye are the salt of the earth."

2. A long letter to Reverend Mr. Perronet, giving *A Plain Account of the People Called Methodists,* and

3. Wesley's address in Dublin, July 2, 1789, just 19 months before his death.

"Holy solitaries is a phrase no more consistent with the gospel than holy adulterers." So wrote Wesley. Genuine holiness of heart cannot be attained nor maintained in isolation but only in community. The holy life is the balanced life; balanced between solitude and society; between hours of devotion and a life of service; the holy person is a saint and a citizen.

John Wesley insisted in countless ways and on numerous occasions that the Bible knows nothing of solitary religion, and Charles Wesley's famous lines nailed down the same truth:

> To serve the present age,
> My calling to fulfill
> O may it all my powers engage,
> To do my Master's will.

Love-filled service to people grows out of obedient love for God.

CHRISTIAN RELIGION IS A SOCIAL RELIGION

Sermon on Matt. 5:13-16, "Ye are the salt of the earth." [32]

1. The beauty of holiness, of that inward man of the heart which is renewed after the image of God, cannot but strike every eye which God hath opened—every enlightened understanding. The ornament of a meek, humble, loving spirit will at least excite the approbation of all those who are capable in any degree of discerning spiritual good and evil. . . .

2. If religion, therefore, were carried no farther than this they could have no doubt concerning it; they should have no objection against pursuing it with the whole ardour of their souls. "But why," say they, "is it clogged with other things? What need of loading it with *doing* and *suffering*? These are what damps the vigour of the soul, and sinks it down to earth again. Is it not enough to 'follow after charity'; to soar upon the wings of love? Will it not suffice to worship God, who is a Spirit, with the spirit of our minds, without encumbering ourselves with outward things, or even thinking of them at all? Is it not better that the whole extent of our thought should be taken up with high and heavenly contemplation; and that instead of busying ourselves at all about externals, we should only commune with God in our hearts?"

3. Many eminent men have spoken thus; have advised us "to cease from all outward action"; wholly to withdraw from the world; to leave the body behind us; to abstract ourselves from all sensible things; to have no concern at all about outward religion, but *to work all virtues in the will*; as the far more excellent way, more perfective of the soul, as well as more acceptable to God.

4. It needed not that any should tell our Lord of this masterpiece of the wisdom from beneath, this fairest of all the devices wherewith Satan hath perverted the ways of the Lord. . . .

---

32. WW, 5:294-310.

I.

1. First. I shall endeavour to show, that Christianity is essentially a social religion; and that to turn it into a solitary religion is indeed to destroy it.

By Christianity I mean that method of worshiping God which is here revealed to man by Jesus Christ. When I say this is essentially a social religion, I mean not only that it cannot subsist so well, but that it cannot subsist at all without society—without living and conversing with other men. . . .

7. This is the great reason why the providence of God has so mingled you together with other men, that whatever grace you have received of God may through you be communicated to others; that every holy temper and word and work of yours may have an influence on them also. By this means a check will in some measure be given to the corruption which is in the world; and a small part at least saved from the general infection and rendered holy and pure before God. . . .

The Light Cannot Be Hid

II.

1. But although we may not wholly separate ourselves from mankind, although it be granted we ought to season them with the religion which God has wrought in our hearts, yet may not this be done insensibly? May we not convey this into others in a secret and almost imperceptible manner, so that scarce any one shall be able to observe how or when it is done?—even as salt conveys its own savour into that which is seasoned thereby, without any noise, and without being liable to any outward observation. . . .

2. Of this plausible reasoning of flesh and blood our Lord was well aware also: And He has given a full answer to it. . . . It is impossible for any that have it, to conceal the religion of Jesus Christ. This our Lord makes plain beyond all contradiction, by a twofold comparison: "Ye are the light of the world: A city set upon a hill cannot be hid." Ye Christians are "the light of the world," with regard both to your tempers and actions. Your holiness makes you as conspicuous as the sun in the midst of heaven. As ye cannot go out of the world, so neither can ye stay in it without appearing to all mankind. Ye may not flee from men; and while ye are among them, it is impossible to hide your lowliness and meekness, and those other dispositions whereby ye aspire to be perfect as your Father which is in heaven is perfect. Love

cannot be hid any more than light; and least of all, when it shines forth in action, when ye exercise yourselves in the labour of love. . . .

4. Sure it is, that a secret, unobserved religion cannot be the religion of Jesus Christ. Whatever religion can be concealed is not Christianity. . . . Never, therefore, let it enter into the heart of him whom God hath renewed in the spirit of his mind, to hide that light, to keep his religion to himself. . . .

Give Your Witness

IV.

1. "Let your light so shine before men, that they may see your good works, and glorify your Father which is in heaven." This is the practical application which our Lord himself makes of the fore-going considerations.

"Let your light so shine": Your lowliness of heart; your gentleness, and meekness of wisdom; your serious, weighty concern for the things of eternity, and sorrow for the sins and miseries of men; your earnest desire of universal holiness, and full happiness in God; your tender goodwill to all mankind, and fervent love to your supreme Benefactor. Endeavor not to conceal this light, wherewith God hath enlightened your soul; but let it shine before men, before all with whom you are, in the whole tenor of your conversation. Let it shine still more eminently in your actions in your doing all possible good to all men; and in your suffering for righteousness' sake, while you "rejoice and are exceeding glad, knowing that great is your reward in heaven."

2. "Let your light so shine before men, that they may see your good works.' . . . Let it be your desire not to conceal it; not to put the light under a bushel. Let it be your care to place it "on a candlestick, that it may give light to all that are in the house." Only take heed, not to seek your own praise herein, not to desire any honour to yourselves. But let it be your sole aim, that all who see your good works may "glorify your Father which is in heaven."

Glorify God

3. Be this your one ultimate end in all things. With this view, be plain, open, undisguised. Let your love be without dissimulation: Why should you hide fair, disinterested love? Let there be no guile found in your mouth: Let your words be the genuine picture of your heart. Let there be no darkness or reservedness in your conversation, no disguise in your behaviour. Leave this to those who have other designs in view;

designs which will not bear the light. Be ye artless and simple to all mankind; that all may see the grace of God which is in you. And although some will harden their hearts, yet others will take knowledge that ye have been with Jesus, and, by returning themselves to the great Bishop of their souls, "glorify your Father which is in heaven."

Live Simply

4. With this one design that men may glorify God in you, go on in His name and in the power of His might. Be not ashamed even to stand alone, so it be in the ways of God. Let the light which is in your heart shine in all good works, both works of piety and works of mercy. And in order to enlarge your ability of doing good, renounce all superfluities. Cut off all unnecessary expense in food, in furniture, in apparel. Be a good steward of every gift of God, even of these his lowest gifts. Cut off all unnecessary expense of time, all needless or useless employments; and "whatsoever thy hand findeth to do, do it with thy might." In a word, be thou full of faith and love; do good; suffer evil. And herein be thou "steadfast, unmovable"; yea, "always abounding in the work of the Lord; forasmuch as thou knowest that thy labour is not in vain in the Lord."

A Plain Account of the People Called Methodists

In this letter to a Mr. Perronet, Wesley gives a graphic account of the social involvement of his leaders and their Societies. It reflects holiness in action within the Societies, and beyond them.[33]

The Sick

XI.

1. It was not long before the Stewards found a great difficulty with regard to the sick. Some were ready to perish before they knew of their illness; and when they did know, it was not in their power (being persons generally employed in trade) to visit them so often as they desired.

2. When I was apprised of this, I laid the case at large before the whole society; showed how impossible it was for the Stewards to attend all that were sick in all parts of the town; desired the Leaders of classes would more carefully inquire, and more constantly inform

---

33. *WW*, 8:248-68. Sections quoted, 263-68.

them, who were sick, and asked, "Who among you is willing, as well as able, to supply this lack of service?"

3. The next morning many willingly offered themselves. I chose six-and-forty of them, whom I judged to be of the most tender, loving spirits; divided the town into 23 parts, and desired 2 of them to visit the sick in each division.

4. It is the business of a visitor of the sick to see every sick person within his district thrice a week. To inquire into the state of their souls, and to advise them as occasion may require. To inquire into their disorders, and procure advice for them. To relieve them, if they are in want. To do anything for them which he (or she) can do. To bring in his accounts weekly to the Stewards. . . .

5. I did not think it needful to give them any particular rules beside these that follow:

(1) Be plain and open in dealing with souls. (2) Be mild, tender, patient. (3) Be cleanly in all you do for the sick. (4) Be not nice [fastidious].

6. We have ever since had great reason to praise God for His continued blessing on this undertaking. Many lives have been saved, many sicknesses healed, much pain and want prevented or removed. Many heavy hearts have been made glad, many mourners comforted: and the visitors have found, from Him whom they serve, a present reward for all their labour.

The Poor

XII.

1. But I was still in pain for many of the poor that were sick; there was so great expense and so little profit. And first I resolved to try whether they might not receive more benefit in the hospitals. Upon the trial, we found there was indeed less expense, but no more good done than before. I then asked the advice of several physicians for them; but still it profited not. I saw the poor people pining away, and several families ruined, and that without remedy.

2. At length I thought of a kind of desperate expedient. "I will prepare, and give them physic [medical aid] myself." For 6 or 7 and 20 years, I had made anatomy and medicine the diversion of my leisure hours; though I never properly studied them, unless for a few months when I was going to America, where I imagined I might be of some

service to those who had no regular physician among them. I applied to it again. I took into my assistance an Apothecary [druggist] and an experienced surgeon [doctor]; resolving at the same time not to go out of my depth, but to leave all difficult and complicated cases to such physician as the patients should choose.

3. I gave notice of this to the society; telling them that all who were ill of chronic distempers (for I did not care to venture upon acute) might, if they pleased, come to me at such a time, and I would give them the best advice I could, and the best medicines I had.

4. Many came: (And so every Friday since.) Among the rest was one William Kirkman, a weaver, near Old Nichol-Street. I asked him "What complaint have you?" "O Sir," said he, "a cough, a very sore cough. I can get no rest day nor night."

I asked, "How long have you had it?" He replied, "About threescore years: It began when I was 11 years old." I was nothing glad that this man should come first, fearing our not curing him might discourage others. However, I looked up to God and said, "Take this three or four times a day. If it does you no good, it will do you no harm." He took it two or three days. His cough was cured and has not returned to this day. . . .

6. In five months, medicines were occasionally given to above 500 persons. Several of these I never saw before; for I did not regard whether they were of the society or not. In that time 71 of these, regularly taking their medicines, and following the regimen prescribed (which three in four would not do), were entirely cured of distempers long thought to be incurable. The whole expense of medicines during this time, was nearly 40 pounds. We continued this ever since, and, by the blessing of God, with more and more success.

The Widows

XIII.

1. But I had for some years observed many who, although not sick, were unable to provide for themselves and had none who took care to provide for them: These were feeble, aged widows. I consulted with the Stewards how they might be relieved. They all agreed if we could keep them in one house it would not only be far less expensive to us but also far more comfortable for them. Indeed we had no money to begin; but we believed He would provide, "who defendeth the cause of the widow." So we took a lease of two little houses near; we fitted them up so as to be warm and clean. We took in as many

widows as we had room for and provided them with things needful for the body; toward the expense of which I set aside first, the weekly contributions of the bands, and then all that was collected at the Lord's Supper. It is true this does not suffice: So that we are considerably in debt on this account also. But we are persuaded it will not always be so; seeing "the earth is the Lord's, and the fulness thereof."

2. In this (commonly called The Poor House) we have now nine widows, one blind woman, two poor children, two upper-servants, a maid and a man. I might add, four or five preachers; for I myself, as well as the other preachers who are in town, diet [dine] with the poor on the same food and at the same table; and we rejoice herein as a comfortable earnest of our eating bread together in our Father's kingdom....

The Children

XIV.

1. Another thing which had given me frequent concern was the case of abundance of children. Some their parents could not afford to put to school: So they remained like "a wild ass's colt." Others were sent to school, and learned at least to read and write; but they learned all kind of vice at the same time: So that it had been better for them to have been without their knowledge than to have bought it at so dear a price.

2. At length I determined to have them taught in my own house, that they might have an opportunity of learning to read, write, and cast accounts (if no more) without being under almost a necessity of learning Heathenism at the same time: And after several unsuccessful trials, I found two such schoolmasters as I wanted; men of honesty and of sufficient knowledge, who had talents for, and their hearts in the work.

3. They have now under their care near 60 children: The parents of some pay for their schooling; but the greater part, being very poor, do not; so that the expense is chiefly defrayed by voluntary contributions. We have of late clothed them too, as many as wanted....

5. A happy change was soon observed in the children, both with regard to their tempers and behaviour. They learned reading, writing, and arithmetic swiftly; and at the same time they were diligently instructed in the sound principles of religion, and earnestly exhorted to fear God and work out their own salvation.

Lending to the Lord

XV.

1. A year or two ago, I observed among many a distress of another kind. They frequently wanted, perhaps in order to carry on their business, a present supply of money. They scrupled to make use of a pawnbroker; but where to borrow it they knew not. I resolved to try if we could not find a remedy for this also. I went in a few days from one end of the town to the other and exhorted those who had this world's goods to assist their needy brethren. Fifty pounds were contributed. This was immediately lodged in the hands of two Stewards; who attended every Tuesday morning in order to lend to those who wanted any small sum not exceeding 20 shillings, to be repaid within three months.

2. It is almost incredible, but it manifestly appears from their accounts that with this inconsiderable sum, 250 have been assisted within the space of one year. . . . If this is not "lending unto the Lord," what is? . . .

3. I think, Sir, now you know all that I know of this people. You see the nature, occasion, and design of whatever is practiced among them. . . .

Sacred to God and the Poor

6. All that is contributed or collected in every place is both received and expended by others; nor have I so much as the "beholding thereof with my eyes." For I look upon all this revenue, be it what it may, as sacred to God and the poor; out of which, if I want anything, I am relieved, even as another poor man. . . .

7. To have "conscience void of offence toward God and toward man" is the desire of,

Reverend and dear Sir,
Your affectionate brother and servant,
John Wesley

God's Advocate: A Plea for Real Holiness

Wesley was not a professional do-gooder. His soul went with his silver. He was a lover of souls who recognized their cheerful habit of living in bodies: bodies that were temples and had to be cared for. To him "healing the hurts of man" was part of loving God with all his heart, soul, mind, and strength.

What follows is a most impassioned argument and plea for reality in living the holy life. It is probably more relevant now than ever before. Wesley wrote and spoke these words[34] just 19 months before 6 poor men bore him in his coffin to the grave just as he had requested, each one of them receiving one sovereign just as he had instructed.

O that God would enable me once more, before I go hence and am no more seen, to lift up my voice like a trumpet to those who *gain* and *save* all they can, but do not *give* all they can! Ye are the men, some of the chief men who continually grieve the Holy Spirit of God, and in a great measure stop His gracious influence from descending on our assemblies. Many of your brethren, beloved of God, have not food to eat; they have not raiment to put on; they have not a place where to lay their head. And why are they thus distressed? Because *you* impiously, injustly, and cruelly detain from them what your Master and theirs lodges in *your* hands on purpose to supply *their* wants!

See that poor member of Christ, pinched with hunger, shivering with cold, half naked! Meantime you have plenty of this world's goods, of meat, drink, and apparel. In the name of God, what are you doing? Do you neither fear God nor regard man? Why do you not deal your bread to the hungry and cover the naked with a garment? Have you laid out in your own costly apparel what would have answered both these intentions? Did God command you so to do? Does He commend you for so doing? Did He entrust you with *His* (not *your*) goods for this end? And does He now say, "Servant of God, well done?"

You well know that He does not. This idle expense has no approbation either from God or your own conscience. But you say you can *afford* it! O be ashamed to take such miserable nonsense into your mouths! Never more utter such stupid cant; such palpable absurdity! Can any steward *afford* to be an arrant knave? To waste his Lord's goods? Can any servant *afford* to lay out his Master's money, any otherwise than his Master appoints him? So far from it, that whoever does this ought to be excluded from a Christian society.

But is it possible to supply all the poor in our society with the necessaries of life? It *was* possible once to do this, in a larger society

---

34. Address in Dublin. *WJ*, 7:515 (fm.); Tyerman, *John Wesley*, 3:636-38; *Methodist Magazine*, 1790, 348-49.

than this. In the first Church at Jerusalem "there was not any among them that lacked; but distribution was made to every one according as he had need." And we have full proof that it may be so still. It is so among the people called Quakers. Yea, and among the Moravians, so called. And why should it not be so with *us?* "Because they are 10 times richer than we." Perhaps 50 times—and yet we are able enough if we were equally willing to do this.

A gentleman (a Methodist) told me some years since, "I shall leave 40,000 pounds among my children." Now, suppose he had left them but 20,000 and given the other 20,000 to God and the poor, would God have said to him, "Thou fool"? And this would have set all the society far above want.

But I will not talk of giving to God, or leaving half your fortune. You might think this to be too high a price for heaven. I will come to lower terms. Are there not a few among you that could give a hundred pounds, perhaps some that could give a thousand, and yet leave your children as much as would help them to work out their own salvation? With 2,000 pounds, and not much less, we could supply the present wants of all our poor, and put them in a way of supplying their own wants for the time to come. Now suppose this could be done, are we clear before God while it is not done? Is not the neglect of it one cause why so many are still sick and weak among you; and that both in soul and in body? that they still grieve the Holy Spirit by preferring the fashions of the world to the commands of God? And I many times doubt whether we preachers are not, in some measure, partakers of their sin. . . .

Self-denial

I am distressed. I know not what to do. I see what I might have done once. I might have said preemptorily and expressly, "Here I am: I and my Bible. I will not, I dare not vary from this book either in great things or small. I have no power to dispense with one jot or tittle of what is contained therein. I am determined to be a Bible Christian, not almost, but altogether." Who will meet me on this ground? Join me on this, or not at all. . . .

Why has Christianity done so little good, even among us? among the Methodists, among them that hear and receive the whole Christian doctrine, and that have Christian discipline added thereto, in the most essential parts of it? Plainly, because we have forgot, or at least not duly attended to those solemn words of our Lord, "If any man will come after me, let him deny himself, and take up his cross daily, and follow me." ... The work of God does go on, and in a surprising manner, notwithstanding this capital defect; but it cannot go on in the same degree as it otherwise would; neither can the word of God have its full effect, unless the hearers of it "deny themselves, and take up their cross daily." ...

Can True Christianity Survive?

But why is self-denial in general so little practiced at present among the Methodists? Why is so exceedingly little of it to be found even in the oldest and largest societies? The more I observe and consider things, the more clearly it appears what is the cause of this. ... The Methodists grow more and more self-indulgent, because they *grow rich.* Although many of them are still deplorably poor; yet many others, in the space of 20, 30, or 40 years, are 20, 30, yea, a hundred times richer than they were when they first entered the society. And it is an observation which admits of few exceptions, that 9 in 10 of these decreased in grace, in the same proportion as they increased in wealth. Indeed, according to the natural tendency of riches, we cannot expect it to be otherwise.

Preventive to Decay

But how astonishing a thing is this! How can we understand it? ... Wherever true Christianity spreads, it must cause diligence and frugality, which, in the natural course of things must beget riches! And riches naturally beget pride, love of the world, and every temper that is destructive of Christianity. Now, if there be no way to prevent this, Christianity is inconsistent with itself, and of consequence cannot stand, cannot continue long among any people; since, wherever it generally prevails it saps its own foundation.

But is there no way to prevent this? to continue Christianity among a people? Allowing that diligence and frugality must produce riches, is there no means to hinder riches from destroying the religion of those that possess them? I can see only one possible way; find out another who can. Do you gain all you can and save all you can? Then you must, in the nature of things, grow rich. Then if you have any desire to escape the damnation of hell, *give* all you can; otherwise I can have no more hope of your salvation than of that of Judas Iscariot.

God Is My Witness

I call God to record upon my soul that I advise no more than I practice. I do, blessed be God, gain, and save, and give all I can. And so, I trust in God, I shall do while the breath of God is in my nostrils. But what then? I count all things but loss for the excellency of the knowledge of Jesus my Lord! Still,

> *I give up every plea beside,*
> *Lord, I am damn'd! but thou hast died!*

Dublin, July 2, 1789

5

WESLEY'S CLOSE ASSOCIATES

Charles Wesley (1707-88)
Doctrinal Hymns
Poetic Expositions of Holiness Scriptures

Adam Clarke LL.D. (1760-1832)
The Grand Office of the Holy Spirit
Perfect, Present Cleansing
The Universal Outpouring of the Holy Spirit
The Corruption of the World Through Lust
Christian Perfection
The Double Benefit of the Gospel

Richard Watson (1781-1833)
The Pure in Heart
Power from on High
The Right State of the Heart

Charles Wesley

5 Wesley's Close Associates

Charles Wesley
(1707-88)

Luke Wiseman described John and Charles Wesley thus:

> Either apart from the other would have done great things; neither without the other could have done a tithe of the work he actually achieved. The brothers had many traits in common, while the deficiencies of the one were in a remarkable manner made up by the qualities of the other. Both were accomplished scholars, able theologians, consummate evangelists. John was a capable commander-in-chief, Charles an intrepid leader of the Cavalry division. . . . John, though not deficient in emotion, was severely logical; Charles, by no means lacking in reasoning power, was strongly swayed by feeling. John must follow principles to their logical conclusion, and with advancing years became more and more liberal; Charles, on the other hand, was not disturbed by the presence of two contrary tendencies, and in later life yielded to his conservative pre-dilections. John became the statesman and organizer of the Methodist movement; Charles its bard.[1]

Charles Wesley gave little evidence of life for 10 days after his birth as he lay wrapped in blankets and cotton wool in the parental bedroom. Born on December 18, 1707, it was early January before he gave evidence of lung-power.

At five years the little fellow started to learn his lessons under mother Susanna in the kitchen college, surrounded by what must have seemed a small army of little girls. By then John was almost 10 and about to leave home for Charterhouse School in London.

In 1716 Charles too was sent to London, not to Charterhouse, but to Westminster School. His courage earned him a bit of a reputation and he became school captain in 1725.

About this time also he chose to be the son of Epworth rather than heir to an earldom when he rejected an adoption offer by Garrett Wesley of Ireland. He might have become a rich country squire and have been lost in the list of aristocracy, but he chose not to be, and unwittingly walked into immortal fame.

---

1. F. L. Wiseman, *Charles Wesley and His Hymns*. Wesley Bi-centenary Manual No. 6 (London: Epworth Press, n.d.), 5 ff.

In 1726 Charles went up to Christ Church College, Oxford University, on a scholarship of about $200 a year. He knew the taste of hunger and the burden of study, but became founder of the Holy Club of Oxford, and leader of the group until the return of big brother John to whom he gratefully relinquished precedence.

From this point there is an intermeshing of the lives of the Wesley brothers that makes it virtually impossible to disentwine them. Clearly John has the ascendancy of personal forcefulness and authority. This was most evident when in 1735 Charles went to Georgia as secretary to the founder of that state, for no other reason than that John was going.

In May 1738 through the persistent witness of the Moravians, particularly Peter Bohler, Charles Wesley found peace of soul through faith in Christ. The immediate agents of his conversion were, first a "poor ignorant mechanic who knows nothing but Christ"; and secondly a book, *Luther's Commentary on Galatians,* especially chapter two, verses 20-21.

That was on Sunday, May 21. And on Wednesday the 24th, John was converted in a meeting room on Aldersgate street.

Like Bunyan's pilgrim who, when his burden of guilt rolled away, "gave three leaps of joy and went on his way singing," Charles Wesley almost immediately began to write a hymn celebrating his conversion. He had written poetry previously, but now Christ's troubadour was tuned up and tuned in to the true source of song. He wrote:

> *Where shall my wondering soul begin*
> *How shall I all to heaven aspire?*
> *A slave redeemed from death and sin,*
> *A brand plucked from eternal fire.*
> *How shall I equal triumphs raise?*
> *Or sing my Great Deliverer's praise?*[2]

This hymn the two brothers sang together in Charles's bedroom when John rushed in to witness on May 24.

After a brief spell as a curate (pastor) in Islington, London, Charles launched into evangelism, partnering John Wesley, George Whitefield, and other Anglican preachers in the battle for the soul and souls of England.

---

2. From *A Collection of Hymns for the Use of the People Called Methodists* (London: John Mason, 1831).

For more than 30 years Charles Wesley was a daring singing cavalier for Christ. He rode his patient little pony as though it were a white charger; writing hymns on horseback, rushing into houses and calling for pencil and paper as the artesian well of rhyme and rhythm poured forth its fullness. Fourteen volumes of poetry, and most of it by Charles! One writer has described the river of verse that flowed through his pen as "the Bible in solution."

He faces wild mobs, endures hardness, and the opposition of ignorant workers and stupid clergymen. He almost thrives on persecution, rushing over the miles to stand by John in the midst of his mob attacks. He is arraigned as a Jacobite traitor, accused of being a Catholic, tried for disturbing the peace. He rips his gown open to bare his breast to the sword point of a soldier who attacks him, and stands bolt upright amid showers of stones and dirt! Jesus Christ never had a more intrepid cavalier in England.

In 1749 he married a Welsh lady, Sally Gwynne. Charles allayed her mother's fears for Sally's insecurity as the wife of a Methodist preacher by having John draw up a contract based on hymn royalties. For some years thereafter he continued to itinerate, but as family responsibilities grew he centered his evangelism on Bristol, adding to it the supervision of the Methodist Societies in that area.

In 1771 he moved with his wife and children to a home in Marylebone in London. Here he and his sons Charles and Samuel made a kind of center of classical music, the boys giving concerts before many famous and talented people.

In London Charles continued both his pastoral work among the London Methodists, and his prison evangelism at Newgate jail which had always claimed a large place in his affections.

Charles Wesley died in London on May 29, 1788. He died as he had lived—a loyal son of the Church of England. As such he left instructions that he was to be buried, not in the Methodist ground at City Road, but in "consecrated ground." Therefore he was interred at Marylebone church yard. This burial ground was destroyed by enemy bombing during the Second World War, and in the research made preparatory to its restoration it was revealed that in fact it had never been episcopally consecrated!

Charles Wesley's obituary appeared in Minutes of the Conference thus:

> Mr. Charles Wesley, who, after spending four score years with much sorrow and pain, quietly retired into Abraham's bosom. He

had no disease; but, after a gradual decay of some months, "The weary wheels of life stood still at last."[3]

Dr. R. Newton Flew wrote in the preface to his lecture, *The Hymns of Charles Wesley:*

> Those Methodists who observe and treasure this part of our tradition know why we say to Christians of other Communions that our Hymnbook is our liturgy, both in public worship and in private prayer. We know that this book is a "little body of experimental and practical divinity," and we admire the method of teaching theology through these hymns. . . . It was a Cambridge historian of genius, one who spoke from outside our tradition, who first praised it in terms which none of us would ever have dared to use, but which we knew were true for us. . . . This little book ranks in Christian literature with the Psalms, the Book of Common Prayer, the Canon of the Mass. In its own way it is perfect, unapproachable, elemental in its perfection. You cannot alter it except to mar it; it is a work of supreme devotional art by a religious genius.[4]

Doctrinal Hymns

No holiness preacher, nor for that part anyone who can read and learn from the printed word, should be without access to and knowledge of the hymns of Charles Wesley.

Every major doctrine of the Christian faith is set to music, and if we desire to know what theology the early Methodists learned—and how they learned it—we must become acquainted with their hymnbook.

The brief selection that follows is limited to those hymns directly contributive to the objectives of the series on *Great Holiness Classics*. All are taken from Osborne's *The Poetical Works of John and Charles Wesley*.

Hymn to God the Sanctifier

This hymn captures the positive note of the fire-cleansed and blood-sprinkled heart powerfully and clearly.

---

3. *JJW*, 7:377.

4. R. Newton Flew, *The Hymns of Charles Wesley: A Study of Their Structure* (London: Epworth Press, 1953).

Come, Holy Ghost, all-quickening fire,
Come, and my hallow'd heart inspire,
    Sprinkled with the atoning blood:
Now to my soul Thyself reveal;
Thy mighty working let me feel,
    And know that I am born of God.

Thy witness with my spirit bear,
That God, my God, inhabits there,
    Thou, with the Father and the Son,
Eternal Light's coeval Beam.
Be Christ in me, and I in Him,
    'Till perfect we are made in one.

When wilt Thou my whole heart subdue?
Come, Lord, and form my soul anew,
    Emptied of pride, self-will, and hell:
Less than the least of all Thy store
Of mercies, I myself abhor:
    All, all my vileness may I feel.

Humble, and teachable, and mild,
O, may I, as a little child,
    My lowly Master's steps pursue:
Be anger to my soul unknown;
Hate, envy, jealousy, be gone!
    In love create Thou all things new.

Let earth no more my heart divide;
With Christ may I be crucified,
    To Thee with my whole soul aspire;
Dead to the world, and all its toys,
Its idle pomp, and fading joys,
    Be Thou alone my one desire.

Be Thou my joy; be Thou my dread;
In battle, cover Thou my head,
    Nor earth nor hell so shall I fear;
So shall I turn my steady face
Want, pain defy, enjoy disgrace,
    Glory in dissolution near.

My will be swallow'd up in Thee:
Light in Thy light still may I see,
  Beholding Thee with opening face;
Call'd the full power of faith to prove,
Let all my hallow'd heart be love,
  And all my spotless life be praise.

Come, Holy Ghost, all-quickening fire,
My consecrated heart inspire,
  Sprinkled with the atoning blood;
Still to my soul Thyself reveal;
Thy mighty working may I feel,
  And know that I am one with God!
        —PWJCW, 1:240-42

Waiting for the Promise

Here is Charles Wesley's counsel to a seeker after inward holiness. He encourages the seeker to cling to the promises of the ever-faithful sanctifying Savior: a magnificent prayer based on and interpreting Ezekiel's mighty words on the new, clean, loving heart.

Drooping soul, shake off thy fears;
  Fearful soul, be strong, be bold;
Tarry till the Lord appears,
  Never, never quit thy hold!
Murmur not at His delay,
  Dare not set thy God a time,
Calmly for His coming stay,
  Leave it, leave it all to Him.

Fainting soul, be bold, be strong;
  Wait the leisure of thy Lord:
Though it seem to tarry long,
  True and faithful is His word.
On His word my soul I cast;
(He cannot himself deny);
Surely it shall speak at last,
  It shall speak, and shall not lie.

Everyone that seeks shall find;
  Every one that asks shall have;

Christ, the Saviour of mankind,
  Willing, able, all to save:
I shall His salvation see;
  I in faith on Jesus call;
I from sin shall be set free,
  Perfect, set free from all.

Lord, my time is in Thine hand;
  Weak and helpless as I am,
Surely Thou canst make me stand:
  I believe in Jesu's name;
Saviour, in temptation Thou,
  Thou hast saved me heretofore;
Thou from sin dost save me now,
  Thou shalt save me evermore.

Wherefore should I doubt the grace
  Which I every moment prove?
Sin and Satan must give place,
  Both must yield to stronger love.
Sin and Satan rage their hour;
  But Thou all-sufficient art,
Thou art infinite in power,
  Thou art greater than my heart.

Gladly therefore will I boast
  Of my soul's infirmities;
I a sinner, helpless, lost,
  I cannot from sinning cease;
Yet the power on me doth rest,
  Now it doth from sin secure;
When it sinks into my breast,
  Pure I am as God is pure.
            —PWJCW, 2:293-95

Pleading the Promise of Sanctification

This remarkable hymn makes Ezek. 36:23-27 come alive for Christians hungering and thirsting after a clean heart: "Then will I sprinkle clean water upon you, and ye shall be clean; from all your filthiness, and from all your idols, will I cleanse you. A new heart also will I give you, and a new spirit will I put within you: and I will take away the stony heart out of your flesh, and I will give you an heart of flesh. And I will put my spirit within you, and cause you to walk in my statutes, and ye shall keep my judgments, and do them."

The poem has frequently been abbreviated but its full force can be felt only when we read the hymn in its entirety.

God of all power, and truth, and grace,
  Which shall from age to age endure,
Whose word, when heaven and earth shall pass,
  Remains, and stands for ever sure:

Calmly to Thee my soul looks up,
  And waits Thy promises to prove,
The object of my steadfast hope,
  The seal of Thine eternal love.

That I Thy mercy may proclaim,
  That all mankind Thy truth may see,
Hallow Thy great and glorious name,
  And perfect holiness in me.

Chose from the world if now I stand
  Adorn'd in righteousness divine,
If brought into the promised land
  I justly call the Saviour mine,

Perform the work Thou hast begun,
  My inmost soul to Thee convert,
Love me, for ever love Thine own,
  And sprinkle with Thy blood my heart.

Thy sanctifying Spirit pour,
  To quench my thirst and wash me clean;
Now, Father, let the gracious shower
  Descend, and make me pure from sin.

Purge me from every sinful blot,
  My idols all be cast aside;
Cleanse me from every evil thought,
  From all the filth of self and pride.

Give me a new a perfect heart,
    From doubt, and fear, and sorrow free;
The mind which was in Christ impart,
    And let my spirit cleave to Thee.

O take this heart of stone away,
    (Thy sway it doth not, cannot own,)
In me no longer let it stay;
    O take away this heart of stone.

The hatred of the carnal mind
    Out of my flesh at once remove;
Give me a tender heart, resign'd,
    And pure, and full of faith and love.

Within me Thy good Spirit place,
    Spirit of health, and love, and power;
Plant in me Thy victorious grace,
    And sin shall never enter more.

Cause me to walk in Christ my Way;
    And I Thy statutes shall fulfil,
In every point Thy law obey,
    And perfectly perform Thy will.

Hast Thou not said, who canst not lie,
    That I Thy law shall keep and do?
Lord, I believe, though men deny;
    They all are false, but Thou art true.

O that I now, from sin released,
    Thy word might to the utmost prove!
Enter into the promised rest,
    The Canaan of Thy perfect love.

There let me ever, ever dwell;
    Be Thou my God, and I will be
Thy servant: O set to Thy seal;
    Give me eternal life in Thee.

From all remaining filth within
    Let me in Thee salvation have;

From actual and from inbred sin
  My ransom'd soul persist to save.

Wash out my deep original stain—
  Tell me no more it cannot be,
Demons or men! The Lamb was slain,
  His blood was all pour'd out for me.

Sprinkle it, Jesu, on my heart!
  One drop of Thine all-cleansing blood
Shall make my sinfulness depart,
  And fill me with the life of God.

Father, supply my every need;
  Sustain the life Thyself hast given:
Call for the never-failing Bread,
  The manna that comes down from heaven.

The gracious fruits of righteousness,
  Thy blessings' unexhausted store,
In me abundantly increase,
  Nor let me ever hunger more.

Let me no more, in deep complaint,
  My leanness, O my leanness! cry;
Alone consumed with pining want,
  Of all my Father's children, I!

The painful thirst, the fond desire,
  Thy joyous presence shall remove,
While my full soul doth still require
  Thy whole eternity of love.

Holy, and true, and righteous Lord,
  I wait to prove Thy perfect will;
Be mindful of Thy gracious word,
  And stamp me with Thy Spirit's seal.

Thy faithful mercies let me find,
  In which Thou causest me to trust;
Give me the meek and lowly mind,
  And lay my spirit in the dust.

Show me how foul my heart hath been,
  When all renew'd by grace I am;
When Thou hast emptied me of sin,
  Show me the fulness of my shame.

Open my faith's interior eye;
  Display Thy glory from above,
And all I am shall sink and die,
  Lost in astonishment and love.

Confound, o'erpower me with Thy grace;
  I would be by myself abhorr'd.
(All might, all majesty, all praise,
  All glory be to Christ my Lord!)

Now let me gain perfection's height;
  Now let me into nothing fall,
Be less than nothing in Thy sight,
  And feel that Christ is all in all.
                          —PWJCW, 2:319-23

One Called Upon to Give Witness to Entire Sanctification

When replying to Bishop Gibson's 1747 criticism of Christian perfection, John Wesley included this hymn. Here are three of its nine stanzas:

I come to testify the grace
My Lord obtain'd for all our race,
  Enough ten thousand worlds to save;
Salvation is in Jesu's name,
Which every soul of man may claim,
  And all that seek the grace, shall have.
Salvation from the power of sin,
Salvation from the root within,
  Salvation into perfect love,
(Thy grace to all hath brought it near,)
And uttermost salvation here,
  Salvation up to heaven above.

> *Thy power and saving grace to show,*
> *A warfare at Thy charge I go,*
>   *Strong in the Lord, and Thy great might,*
> *Gladly take up the hallow'd cross,*
> *And suffering all things for Thy cause,*
>   *Beneath that bloody banner fight.*
> *A spectacle to fiends and men,*
> *To all their fierce or cool disdain*
>   *With calmest pity I submit;*
> *Determined nought to know beside*
> *My Jesus, and Him crucified,*
>   *I tread the world beneath my feet.*
>
> *A faithful witness of Thy grace,*
> *Long may I fill the' allotted space,*
>   *And answer all Thy great design;*
> *Walk in the works by Thee prepared,*
> *And find annex'd the vast reward,*
>   *The crown of righteousness divine.*
> *When I have lived to Thee alone*
> *Pronounce the welcome word, Well done,*
>   *And let me take my place above,*
> *Enter into my Master's joy,*
> *And all eternity employ*
>   *In praise, and ecstasy, and love.*
>   —PWJCW, 5:136

Concerning the Sacrifice of Our Persons

This hymn, selected from *Hymns on the Lord's Supper,* rejoices in the sanctifying grace of the glorious Trinity permeating and possessing the believer's entire personality.

> *Father, Son, and Holy Ghost,*
>   *One in Three, and Three in One.*
> *As by the celestial host*
>   *Let Thy will on earth be done;*
> *Praise by all to Thee be given,*
> *Glorious Lord of earth and heaven!*

Vilest of the fallen race,
  Lo, I answer to Thy call;
Meanest vessel of Thy grace,
  (Grace divinely free for all,)
Lo, I came to do Thy will,
All Thy counsel to fulfil.

If so poor a worm as I
  May to Thy great glory live,
All my actions sanctify,
  All my words and thoughts receive;
Claim me for Thy service, claim
All I have and all I am.

Take my soul and body's powers,
  Take my memory, mind, and will,
All my goods, and all my hours,
  All I know, and all I feel,
All I think, and speak, and do;
Take my heart—but make it new.

Now, O God, Thine own I am,
  Now I give Thee back Thy own,
Freedom, friends, and health, and fame
  Consecrate to Thee alone;
Thine I live, thrice happy I,
Happier still, for Thine I die.

Father, Son, and Holy Ghost,
  One in Three and Three in One,
As by the celestial host
  Let Thy will on earth be done;
Praise by all to Thee be given,
Glorious Lord of earth and heaven.
          —*Hymns on the Lord's Supper,* No. 155, p. 104.

Poetic Expositions of Holiness Scriptures

Charles Wesley tells us that the following verses, taken from his book, *Short Hymns on Select Passages of the Holy Scriptures*, were written while he was disabled for the principal work of the ministry. All titles in this section are the editor's.

The Holy Fire

The fire shall ever be burning upon the altar; it shall never go out (Lev. 6:13).

> O Thou who camest from above,
> The pure celestial fire to 'mpart,
> Kindle a flame of sacred love
> On the mean altar of my heart:
> There let it for Thy glory burn
> With inextinguishable blaze,
> And trembling to its source return,
> In humble prayer, and fervent praise.
>
> Jesus, confirm my heart's desire
> To work, and speak, and think for Thee;
> Still let me guard the holy fire;
> And still stir up Thy gift in me:
> Ready for all Thy perfect will,
> My acts of faith and love repeat,
> Till death Thy endless mercies seal,
> And make my sacrifice complete.
> —PWJCW, 9:58-59

Sin-Consuming Fire

Then the fire of the Lord fell, and consumed the burnt sacrifice, and the wood, and the stones, and the dust, and licked up the water that was in the trench. And when all the people saw it, they fell on their faces: and they said, The Lord, he is the God; the Lord, he is the God (1 Kings 18:38-39).

Without that sin-consuming fire
   The priests of Baal pray in vain,
And teach, as taught by that old liar,
   "Sin cannot be consumed in man!"
      But who Elijah's God believe,
         And wait His coming from above,
      We shall the Holy Ghost receive,
         The Spirit pure, of burning love.

Thou God, that answerest by fire,
   On Thee in Jesu's name we call,
Fulfill our faithful heart's desire,
   And let on us Thy Spirit fall:
      Bound on that altar of Thy Cross
      Our old offending nature lies;
      Now for the honour of Thy cause,
      Come, and consume the sacrifice.

Consume our lusts as rotten wood,
   Consume our stony hearts within
Consume the dust, the serpent's food
   And lick up all the streams of sin.
      Its body totally destroy,
         Thyself the Lord, the God approve,
      And fill our hearts with holy joy,
         And fervent zeal, and perfect love.

O that the fire from heaven might fall,
   Our sins its ready victims find,
Seize on our sins, and burn up all,
   Nor leave the least remains behind!
      Then shall our prostrate souls adore,
         The Lord, He is the God, confess,
      He is the God of saving power
      He is the God of hallowing grace!
            —PWJCW, 9:178-79

Spark of Thy Celestial Flame

I indeed baptize you with water unto repentance: but he that cometh after me is mightier than I. . . . he shall baptize you with the Holy Ghost, and with fire (Matt. 3:11).

Pure baptismal Fire Divine,
  All Thy heavenly powers exert;
In my deepest darkness shine
  Spread Thy warmth throughout my heart.
    Come, seraphic Spirit, come,
      Comforter through Jesus given,
    All my earthly dross consume,
      Fill my soul with love from heaven.

Love in me intensely burn,
  Love mine inmost essence seize,
All into Thy nature turn,
  All into Thy holiness:
    Spark of Thy celestial flame,
      Then my soul shall upward move,
    Trembling on with steady aim,
      Seek, and join its source above.
            —PWJCW, 10:146-47

The Sanctifying Word

Sanctify them through thy truth; thy word is truth (John 17:17).

Through the pure evangelic word
  Thine image, Lord, on us impress,
And speak us after God restored
  In true internal holiness:

Thy word the channel of Thy love
  Through meek and patient faith apply,
And fit us for the joys above,
  And takes us spotless to the sky.
            —PWJCW, 11:64

The Cleansing Holy Spirit

And God, which knowest the hearts, bare them witness, giving them the Holy Ghost, even as he did unto us; and put no difference between us and them, purifying their hearts by faith (Acts 15:8-9).

> The unbelieving heart's unclean
> The faithful heart is purged (from) sin
> > While Christ His blood applies
> Which cleanses us from every stain,
> Sprinkles and washes us again
> > And daily purifies.
>
> Lord if Thou dost my faith approve
> And Thee in some degree I love,
> > My little faith increase;
> So shall I know and love Thee more,
> Till fill'd with all Thy Spirit's power
> > With all Thy holiness.
> > > —PWJCW, 12:299-300

Appropriating Faith

What things soever ye desire, when ye pray, believe that ye receive them, and ye shall have them (Mark 11:24).

> Come then, my God, the promise seal,
> > This mountain-sin remove,
> Now in my gasping soul reveal
> > The virtue of Thy love:
> > > I want Thy life Thy purity,
> > > > Thy righteousness brought in,
> > > I ask, desire, and trust in Thee
> > > > To be redeemed from sin.
>
> Saviour to Thee my soul looks up;
> > My present Saviour Thou;
> In all the confidence of hope
> > I claim the blessing now!
> > > Tis done: Thou dost this moment save,
> > > > Thou dost with pardon bless
> > > Redemption through Thy blood I have,
> > > > And heaven in Thy peace.
>
> Believing all Thy fulness mine
> > Nor earth nor hell I fear,

> Kept by omnipotence divine
> To full salvation here;
> The thing for which I dare believe
> I shall at last obtain,
> And, when Thine image I retrieve
> With Thee in glory reign.
> —PWJCW, 11:45-47

Our Faith and God's Faithfulness

If we confess our sins, he is faithful and just to forgive us our sins, and to cleanse us from all unrighteousness (1 John 1:9).

> Father of my dying Lord,
> To whom I sue for peace,
> Trusting in Thy faithful word,
> Lo! I my sins confess.
> For Thy truth and mercy's sake,
> Grant the blessing which I claim;
> Cast my sins behind Thy back;
> I ask in Jesu's name.
>
> Hast Thou not reversed my doom?
> Thou hast, and I believe:
> Yet I still a sinner come,
> That Thou mayst still forgive;
> Wretched, miserable, blind,
> Poor, and naked, and unclean,
> Still, that I may mercy find,
> I bring Thee nought but sin.
>
> I have always equal need
> Of Thy forgiving love;
> Still do I the promise plead,
> That I Thy truth may prove.
> Just and faithful as Thou art,
> Hear me now my sins confess,
> Hear, and purify my heart
> From all unrighteousness.

Lord, I look to be made clean
    From every sinful blot,
All unrighteousness and sin,
    In deed, and word, and thought;
Evil shall not here abide,
    Sin shall have no place in me,
From the' iniquity of pride
    And self I shall be free.

I shall be redeem'd from all,
    Unless Thy word is vain;
Here recover from my fall,
    My Eden here regain;
Jesus shall His image here
    Perfectly in me restore;
God shall in my flesh appear,
    And sin subsist no more.
        —PWJCW, 2:279-80

Prayer for Perfect Love

O Love Divine, how sweet Thou art!
When shall I find my willing heart
    All taken up by Thee!
I thirst, and faint, and die to prove,
The greatness of redeeming love,
    The love of Christ to me.

Stronger His love than death or hell;
Its riches are unsearchable;
    The first-born sons of light
Desire in vain its depth to see,
They cannot reach the mystery,
    The length, and breadth, and height.

God only knows the love of God;
O that it now were shed abroad
    In this poor stony heart!
For love I sigh, for love I pine:
This only portion, Lord, be mine,
    Be mine this better part.

O that I could for ever sit,
With Mary at the Master's feet!
   Be this my happy choice,
My only care, delight, and bliss,
My joy, my heaven on earth be this
   To hear the Bridegroom's voice.

O that with humbled Peter I
Could weep, believe, and thrice reply
   My faithfulness to prove,
Thou know'st (for all to Thee is known),
Thou know'st, O Lord, and Thou alone,
   Thou know'st that Thee I love.

O that I could with favour'd John
Recline my weary head upon
   The dear Redeemer's breast!
From care, and sin, and sorrow free,
Give me, O Lord, to find in Thee
   My everlasting rest.

Thy only love do I require,
Nothing in earth beneath desire,
   Nothing in heaven above;
Let earth, and heaven, and all things go,
Give me Thy only love to know,
   Give me Thy only love.

—PWJCW, 4:341-42

Prayer for the Coming of the Spirit of Love

Love divine, all loves excelling,
   Joy of heav'n, to earth come down!
Fix in us Thy humble dwelling;
   All Thy faithful mercies crown:
Jesus, Thou art all compassion,
   Pure, unbounded love Thou art,
Visit us with Thy salvation;
   Enter every trembling heart.

Breathe, Oh, breathe Thy loving Spirit
   Into every troubled breast!

Let us all in Thee inherit;
   Let us find that second rest.
Take away our power of sinning;
   Alpha and Omega be,
End of faith as its Beginning;
   Set our hearts at liberty.

Come, Almighty to Deliver,
   Let us all Thy life receive.
Suddenly return, and never,
   Never more Thy temples leave.
Thee we would be always blessing,
   Serve Thee as Thy hosts above,
Pray, and praise Thee without ceasing,
   Glory in Thy perfect love.

Finish then Thy new creation;
   Pure, and spotless let us be.
Let us see Thy great salvation,
   Perfectly restored in Thee.
Changed from glory into glory,
   Till in heaven we take our place,
Till we cast our crowns before Thee,
   Lost in wonder, love, and praise!
        —PWJCW, 4:219-20

The Happiest Place to Be

Tell me, O thou whom my soul loveth, where thou feedest, where thou makest thy flock to rest at noon: for why should I be as one that turneth aside by the flocks of thy companions? (Song of Sol. 1:7).

Thou Shepherd of Israel, and mine,
   The joy and desire of my heart,
For closer communion I pine,
   I long to reside where Thou art;
The pasture I languish to find
   Where all, who their Shepherd obey,
Are fed, on Thy bosom reclined,
   Are screen'd from the heat of the day.

Ah, show me that happiest place,
   That place of Thy people's abode,
Where saints in an ecstasy gaze,
   And hang on a crucified God;
Thy love for a sinner declare,
   Thy passion and death on the tree,
My spirit to Calvary bear,
   To suffer, and triumph, with Thee.

'Tis there with the lambs of Thy flock,
   There only I covet to rest,
To lie at the foot of the Rock,
   Or rise to be hid in Thy breast;
'Tis there I would always abide,
   And never a moment depart,
Conceal'd in the cleft of Thy side,
   Eternally held in Thy heart.
           —PWJCW, 9:362-63

One with Christ

Jesu, we follow Thee,
   In all Thy footsteps tread,
And pant for full conformity
   To our exalted Head;

We would, we would partake
   Thy every state below,
And suffer all things for Thy sake,
   And to Thy glory go.

We in Thy birth are born,
   Sustain Thy grief and loss,
Share in Thy want, and shame, and scorn,
   And die upon Thy cross.

Baptized into Thy death
   We sink into Thy grave,
Till Thou the quickening Spirit breathe,
   And to the utmost save.

Thou said'st, "Where'er I am
  There shall My servant be";
Master, the welcome word we claim,
  And die to live with Thee.

To us who share Thy pain,
  Thy joy shall soon be given,
And we shall in Thy glory reign,
  For Thou art now in heaven.
                —PWJCW, 3:313-14

By Water and by Blood

This, this is He that came
  By water and by blood;
Jesus is our atoning Lamb,
  Our sanctifying God.

See from His wounded side
  The mingled current flow!
The water and the blood, applied,
  Shall wash us white as snow.

The water cannot cleanse
  Before the blood we feel,
To purge the guilt of all our sins,
  And our forgiveness seal.

But both in Jesus join,
  Who speaks our sins forgiven,
And gives the purity divine
  That makes us meet for heaven.
                —PWJCW, 3:267-68

Exuberance of Pentecost

Away with our fears,
Our troubles and tears!
The Spirit is come,
The Witness of Jesus return'd to His home:
The pledge of our Lord

>   To His heaven restored,
>   Is sent from the sky,
>   And tells us our Head is exalted on high.
>
>   Our Advocate there
>   By His blood and His prayer
>   The Gift hath obtain'd.
>   For us He hath pray'd, and the Comforter gain'd:
>   Our glorified Head
>   His Spirit hath shed,
>   With His people to stay,
>   And never again will He take Him away.
>
>   Our heavenly Guide
>   With us shall abide;
>   His comfort impart,
>   And set up His kingdom of love in the heart;
>   The heart that believes
>   His kingdom receives,
>   His power and His peace,
>   His life, and His joy's everlasting increase.
>
>   The Presence Divine
>   Doth inwardly shine,
>   The Shechinah rests
>   On all our assemblies, and glows in our breasts.
>   By day and by night
>   The pillar of light
>   Our steps shall attend,
>   And convoy us safe to our prosperous end.
>
>   Then let us rejoice
>   In heart and in voice,
>   Our Leader pursue,
>   And shout as we travel the wilderness through;
>   With the Spirit remove
>   To Sion above,
>   Triumphant arise,
>   And walk in our God, till we fly to the skies.
>
>   —PWJCW, 4:203-04

Where and How the Life of Love Begins

O Jesus, My Hope,
For me offer'd up,
Who with clamour pursued Thee to Calvary's top,
The blood I have shed
For me let it plead,
And declare, Thou hast died in Thy murderer's stead.

Thy blood, which alone
For sin could atone,
For the' infinite evil I madly have done,
That only can seal
My pardon, and fill
My heart with a power of obeying Thy will.

Come then from above,
The stony remove,
And vanquish my heart with the sense of Thy love:
Thy love on the tree
Display unto me,
And the servant of sin in a moment is free.

Neither passion nor pride
Thy cross can abide,
But melt in the fountain that streams from Thy side:
The wonderful flood
Washes off my foul load,
And purges my conscience, and brings me to God.

Now, now let me know
Its virtue below,
Let it wash me, and I shall be whiter than snow,
Let it hallow my heart,
And throughly convert,
And make me, O Lord, in the world as Thou art.

Each moment applied
My weakness to hide,
Thy blood be upon me, and always abide,
My advocate prove

With the Father above,
And speed me at last to the throne of Thy love.
—PWJCW, 4:365-66

Thanksgiving for the Success of the Gospel

A great many hymns written by Charles Wesley celebrate not only the great work of God in the individual soul, but also what God was doing up and down the country. The hymn that follows captures the spirit of praiseful prayer that marked Charles Wesley as the troubadour of holiness.

All thanks be to God,
Who scatters abroad
Throughout every place,
By the least of His servants His savour of grace!
Who the victory gave,
The praise let Him have,
For the work He hath done,
All honour and glory to Jesus alone.

Our conquering Lord
Hath prosper'd His word,
Hath made it prevail,
And mightily shaken the kingdom of hell.
His arm He hath bared,
And a people prepared,
His glory to show,
And witness the power of His passion below.

He hath open'd a door
To the pentitent poor,
And rescued from sin,
And admitted the harlots and publicans in:
They have heard the glad sound,
They have liberty found
Through the blood of the Lamb,
And plentiful pardon in Jesus' name.

The opposers admire
The hammer and fire,

Which all things o'ercomes,
And breaks the hard rocks, and the mountains consumes.
   With quiet amaze
   They listen and gaze,
   And their weapons resign,
Constrain'd to acknowledge—the work is divine!

   And shall we not sing
   Our Saviour and King?
   Thy witnesses, we
With rapture ascribe our salvation to Thee.
   Thou Jesus hast bless'd,
   And believers increased,
   Who thankfully own,
We freely forgiven through mercy alone.

   Thy Spirit revives
   His work in our lives,
   His wonders of grace,
So mightily wrought in the primitive days.
   O that all men might know
   Thy tokens below,
   Our Saviour confess,
And embrace the glad tidings of pardon and peace!

   Thou Saviour of all,
   Effectually call
   The sinners that stray;
And O let a nation be born in a day!
   Thy sign let them see,
   And flow unto Thee,
   For the oil and the wine,
For the blissful assurance of favour divine.

   Our heathenish land
   Beneath Thy command
   In mercy receive,
And make us a pattern to all that believe:
   Then, then let it spread,

> *Thy knowledge and dread,*
> *Till the earth is o'erflow'd,*
> *And the universe fill'd with the glory of God.*
> —PWJCW, 4:210-12

For the life of Charles Wesley, the world may be grateful. A great many people willingly echo John Fletcher in his note to the author of these hymns:

> I still want a fountain of power, call it what you please, baptism of fire, perfect love, sealing, I contend not for the name ... Help me by your prayer, direction, and example, as you still do by your hymns.[5]

* * *

Adam Clarke, LL.D.
(1760-1832)

If you had been privileged to peep in at the humble schoolroom of John Clarke in Moybeg, Ireland, during the school year 1770 you would probably have gained little hope of John's son, Adam, ever becoming any kind of scholar. He seemed dull and stupid; forgetful enough of his letters to become the butt of ridicule from his classmates.

It seems a mystery that Adam Clarke can be remembered as the author of an eight-volume scripture commentary. He did a great deal of work in linguistics for the British and Foreign Bible Society; was honored as a member of the Royal Irish Academy; awarded the LL.D. degree by the University of Aberdeen; and three times elected by his brethren as president of the Conference of British Methodism.

---

5. Quoted from Dr. Timothy Smith, MS, 41. *Fletcher Volume.* Methodist Archives and Research Center; John Ryland Library, University of Manchester.

Methodism came to Adam Clarke's home parish of Moybeg some time in 1776. The earliest preachers were John Brettel and Thomas Barber. They held meetings first of all in the barn and then in the house of a local farmer. Accompanying some companions planning amusement at the expense of the preacher, Adam attended a service in the barn. But like those of whom the poet wrote, "Some came to scoff but stayed to pray," Adam remained long enough for the services in the house.

Under the influence and preaching of Brettel the young soul of Adam Clarke was deeply probed, but Brettel moved on and Thomas Barber arrived. "With indefatigable diligence," says Adam, "he went though all the country preaching Christ crucified and redemption through His blood."

Encouraged by his parent's acceptance and approval of Barber, young Adam shadowed him everywhere and eventually, after an agonizing sense of guilt and condemnation he heard, or thought he heard, a voice which said, "Try Jesus!" He then and there

> called upon Jesus, and instantly his sorrow was turned into joy.... He felt a sudden transition from darkness to light, from guilt and oppressive fear to confidence and peace.[6]
>
> With this gladness of soul he also received great intellectual enlargement.... He now learned more in a day than formerly he was able to do in one month. His mind became enlarged to take in anything useful.[7]

Adam Clarke joined the Methodist society at Mullica Hill near the city of Coleraine in 1778 and in quick succession was appointed class leader and home missionary. He became a familiar figure around the countryside as he knocked on doors, prayed in homes, and preached in the streets and the country lanes. He preached his first "regular sermon" on June 19, 1782, from the scripture 1 John 5:19: "And we know that we are of God, and the whole world lieth in wickedness."

It was another of Mr. Wesley's helpers who saw the great potential of young Adam Clarke, and on the recommendation of Mr. Bredin, Wesley personally invited Adam to the Methodist school at Kingswood near Bristol. In 1782, therefore, Clarke left home and Ireland.

---

6. J. B. B. Clarke, ed. *An Account of the Infancy, Religious, and Literary Life of Adam Clarke, LL.D., F.A.S.* (New York: D. Appleton and Co., 1833), 92.

7. Adam Clarke, *Christian Theology* (London: Tegg and Son, 1835), 10.

He had little money, and but a scanty wardrobe; but he was carried above the fear of want; he would not ask his parents for help; nor would he intimate to them that he needed any. A few of his own select friends put some money in his purse, and having taken a dutiful and affectionate leave of his parents and friends, he walked to Derry, a journey of upwards of 30 miles in a part of a day, found Mr. Bredin waiting, who had agreed for their passage in a Liverpool trader which was expected to sail the first fair wind.[8]

By this solemn step he had now separated himself from all earthly connections and prospects in his own country; and went on the authority of what he believed to be a divine command, not knowing whither he was going, nor what God intended for him.[9]

About the end of 1782 Adam was called by Mr. Wesley who prayed beautifully for him, placed his hands on Adam's head in benediction and sent him out to itinerate around Wiltshire centering on Bradford.

Clarke kept up his work as an itinerant Methodist preacher from 1782 until 1815. Methodism has never had a more popular itinerant preacher, nor a more learned one. He traveled in most parts of Britain including Guernsey and Ireland, and as far to the north as the Shetland Isles.

Adam married Miss Mary Cooke of Trowbridge in April 1788 and for just more than 42 years Mary Clarke shared her husband's trials and triumphs. Before their marriage Adam made it understood that for him God's work would always come first. But loving God supremely does not mean loving others less, for love is the one thing that grows with the giving. Mary's reply was: "Yes; if I take you, I take you as a minister of Christ, and shall go with you to the ends of the earth."

The Clarkes had 12 children, six girls and six boys. Mary outlived Adam by only four years.

Worn out by preaching, traveling, writing, and administrating, Adam Clarke died in Christian victory in 1826, having made a magnificent contribution to the cause of Methodism as a classical scholar, an antiquarian, a preacher par excellence, a president of the conference, a circuit rider, a holiness expositor, a biographer of the Wesley family, but chiefly as a man who walked with God.

Thus far had come the slowest boy in Moybeg school!

Let these words from Clarke round off this brief profile:

---

8. Clarke, *Adam Clarke*, 128.
9. Ibid., 129.

But go on your way, preaching all our doctrines, but not in a controversial way: and if at any time you may be obliged to repel invective, do it in the meekness of Christ. Our grand doctrines of the witness of the Spirit, and Christian perfection, are opposed to all bad tempers, as well as bad words and works.

Man may be said to be perfect who answers the end for which God made him, and as God requires every man to love Him with all his heart, soul, mind, and strength and his neighbor as himself, then he is a perfect man that does so—he answers the end for which God made him.[10]

The Grand Office of the Holy Spirit[11]

When reconciled to God, and thus brought nigh by the blood of Christ, we receive the gift of the Holy Spirit, which is the fruit of the death, resurrection, and ascension of our Lord. And this Spirit, which is emphatically called the Holy Spirit, because He is not only infinitely holy in His own nature, but His grand office is to make the children of men holy, is given to true believers, not only to "testify with their spirits that they are the children of God," but also to purify their hearts; and thus He transfuses through their souls His own holiness and purity; so that the image of God in which they were created, and which by transgression they had lost, is now restored; and they are, by this holiness, prepared for the enjoyment of eternal blessedness, in perfect union with Him who is the Father and God of glory, and the Fountain of holiness.

GOD'S HOLINESS

The Spirit of Holiness

God promised His Holy Spirit to sanctify and cleanse the heart, so as utterly to destroy all pride, anger, self-will, peevishness, hatred, malice, and every thing contrary to His own holiness.

The very Spirit which is given them, on their believing in Christ Jesus, is the Spirit of holiness; and they can retain this Spirit no longer than they live in the spirit of obedience.

It is the office of the Holy Spirit to witness to the conscience of

---

10. Clarke, *Christian Theology*, 142.
11. Adam Clarke, *Christian Theology*, Dunn edition. Selections systematically arranged by Thomas O. Summers with a life of the author by Samuel Dunn (Nashville: Stevenson Owen, 2nd Rev. American edition, 1857), 162-66. Outlining supplied by the editor.

man the covenant and its conditions, to apply the blood of sprinkling, and to take the things that are Christ's and show them to men; and it is His province to witness to the heart of the believing penitent, that by this shed blood his "conscience is purged from dead works to serve the living God." He is also the sanctifying Spirit; and the Spirit of judgment, and the Spirit of burning; and, as such, He condemns to utter destruction the whole of the carnal mind, and purifies the very thoughts of the heart by His inspiration, enabling the true believer perfectly to love God and worthily to magnify His holy name. And this same Spirit dwelling in the soul of a believer seals him an heir of eternal glory.

The Holy Spirit is called an Advocate, because He transacts the cause of God and Christ with us, explains to us the nature and importance of the great atonement, shows the necessity of it, counsels us to receive it, instructs us how to lay hold on it, vindicates our claim to it, and makes intercessions in us with unutterable groanings.

Our Lord makes intercession for us by negotiating and managing, as our friend and agent, all the affairs pertaining to our salvation. And the Spirit of God maketh intercession for the saints, not by supplication to God in their behalf, but by directing and qualifying their supplications in a proper manner, by His agency and influence upon their hearts; which, according to the gospel scheme, is the peculiar work and office of the Holy Spirit. So that God, who is the Spirit, and who is acquainted with the mind of the Spirit, knows what He means when He leads the saints to express themselves in words, desires, groans, sighs, or tears; in each God reads the language of the Holy Ghost, and prepares the answer according to the request.

Do Not Resist the Spirit

This Spirit is not sent to stocks, stones, or machines, but to human beings endued with rational souls: therefore, it is not to work on them with the irresistible energy which it must exert on inert matter ... but it works upon understanding, will, judgment, conscience, in order to enlighten, convince, and persuade. If, after all, the understanding, the eye of the mind, refuses to behold the light; the will determines to remain obstinate; the judgment purposes to draw false inferences; and the conscience hardens itself against every check and remonstrance; then the Spirit of God is grieved and the sinner is left to reap the fruit of his doings. To force the man to see, feel, repent, believe, and be saved, would be to alter the essential principles of his creation and the nature of mind, and reduce him into the state of a machine. Now man cannot be operated on in this way, because it is contrary to the laws of his creation and nature; nor can the Holy Ghost work on that as a machine which himself has made a free agent.

Man, therefore, may, and generally does, resist the Holy Ghost; and the whole revelation of God bears unequivocal testimony to this most dreadful possibility and most awful truth. It is trifling with the sacred text to say that resisting the Holy Ghost here means "resisting the laws of Moses, the exhortations, threatenings, and promises of the prophets." These, it is true, the uncircumcised ear may resist; but the uncircumcised heart is that alone to which the Spirit that gave the laws, exhortations, promises, speaks; and, as matter resists matter, so spirit resists spirit. These were not only uncircumcised in ear, but uncircumcised also in heart; and, therefore, they resisted the Holy Ghost, not only in His declarations and institutions, but also in His actual energetic operations upon their minds.

Do Not Grieve the Spirit

"Grieve not the Holy Spirit of God," by giving way to any wrong temper, unholy word, or unrighteous action. Even those who have already a measure of the light and life of God, both of which are not only brought in by the Holy Spirit, but maintained by His constant indwelling, may give way to sin, and so grieve this Holy Spirit that it shall withdraw both its light and presence; and, in proportion as it withdraws, then hardness and darkness take place, and, what is still worse, a state of insensibility is the consequence; for the darkness prevents the fallen state from being seen, and hardness prevents it from being felt.

The Spirit of Holy Love

Love is a sovereign preference given to one above all others, present or absent: a concentration of all the thoughts and desires in a single object, which is preferred to all others. Now, apply this definition to the love which God requires of His creatures, and you will have the most correct view of the subject.

Hence, it appears that by this love the soul cleaves to, affectionately admires, and consequently rests in God, supremely pleased and satisfied with Him as its portion. It acts from Him as its Author; for Him, as its Master; and to Him, as its end . . . by it all the powers and faculties of the mind are concentrated in the Lord of the universe . . .

by it the whole man is willingly surrendered to the Most High . . . through it, an identity or sameness of spirit with the Lord is acquired, the person being made a partaker of the divine nature; having the mind in him that was in Christ; and thus dwelling in God, and God in him.

Perfect Love

1. *He loves God with all His heart who loves nothing in comparison to Him,* and nothing but in reference to Him; who is ready to give up, do, or suffer, anything, in order to please and glorify Him; who has in his heart neither love or hatred, hope nor fear, inclination nor aversion, desire nor delight, but as they relate to God, and are regulated by Him. Such a love is merited by that Being who is infinitely perfect, good, wise, powerful, beneficent, and merciful. He merits and requires it from His intelligent creatures; and in fulfilling this duty the soul finds its perfection and felicity; for it rests in the Source of goodness and is penetrated with incessant influences from Him who is the essence and centre of all that is amiable; for his is the God of all grace.

2. *He loves God with all his soul,* with all his life, who is ready to endure all sorts of torments, and to be deprived of all kinds of comforts, rather than dishonour God; he who employs life, with all its comforts and conveniences, to glorify him in, by, and through all; to whom life and death are nothing, but as they come from, and lead to God; who labours to promote the cause of God and truth in the world, denying himself, taking up his cross daily; neither eating, drinking, sleeping, resting, labouring, toiling, but in reference to the glory of God, his own salvation, and that of a lost world.

3. *He loves God with all his mind,* with all his intellect, or understanding, who applies himself only to know God and His holy will; who receives with submission, gratitude, and pleasure, the sacred truths which He has revealed to mankind; who studies neither art nor science, but as far as it is necessary for the service of God, and uses it at all times to promise His glory; who forms no projects nor designs but in reference to God, and to the interests of mankind; who banishes, as much as possible, from his understanding and memory, every idea which has any tendency to defile his soul, or turn it for a moment from the centre of eternal repose.

4. *He uses all his abilities, both natural and acquired, to grow in the grace of God,* and to perform His will in the most acceptable manner: in a word, he who sees God in all things, thinks of him at all

times, having his mind continually fixed upon God; acknowledges Him in all his ways; who begins, continues, and ends all his thoughts, words, and works to the glory of His name; continually planning, scheming, and devising how he may serve God and his generation more effectually; his head, his intellect, going before; his heart, his affections, and desires, coming after.

5. *He loves God with all his strength* who exerts all the powers and faculties of his body and soul in the service of God; who, for the glory of his Maker, spares neither labour nor cost; who sacrifices his body, his health, his time, his ease, for the honour of his divine Master; who employs in his service all his goods, his talents, his power, his credit, authority, and influence; doing what he does with a single eye, a loving heart, and with all his might; in whose conduct is ever seen the work of faith, patience of hope, and labour of love.

O glorious state of him who has given God his whole heart, and in which God ever lives and rules! Glorious state of blessedness upon earth, triumph of the grace of God over sin and Satan! State of holiness and happiness far beyond this description, which comprises an ineffable union and communion between the ever blessed Trinity and the soul of man! O God! let Thy work appear unto Thy servants, and the work of our hands establish upon us! The work of our hands establish Thou it! Amen. Amen.

Love in Control

1. *This love is the spring of all our actions;* it is the motive of our obedience; the principle through which we love God; "we love him because he first loved us"; and we love Him with a love worthy of himself, because it springs from Him: it is His own; and every flame that rises from this pure and vigorous fire must be pleasing in His sight: it consumes what is unholy; refines every passion and appetite; sublimes the whole, and assimilates all to itself.

And we know that this is the love of God: it differs widely from all that is earthly and sensual. The Holy Ghost comes with it; by His energy it is diffused and pervades every part; and by His light we discover what it is, and know the state of grace in which we stand. Thus we are furnished to every good word and work; have produced in us the mind that was in Christ; are enabled to obey the pure law of our God in its spiritual sense, by loving Him with all our heart, soul, mind, and strength, and our neighbour, every son of man, as ourselves. This is, or ought to be, the common experience of every believer.

2. *The love of Christ is opposed to our enmity,* and by it our hatred to God and goodness is overcome. Love conteracts the whole carnal mind, draws out the heart in affectionate attachment to God, and is the incentive to all obedience, as being the fulfilling of the law. Such a person is not obliged to derive the principle of his obedience from anything outward: the moral law is before his eyes; but the love of God, shed abroad in his heart, is the principle by which he obeys it. He performs nothing merely as a duty; he has the law of God written in his heart, and this ever disposes him to do what is right in the sight of his Judge.

If it were not even infallibly true that a life of sin must terminate in endless misery, yet he would abhor the way of the wicked. He has tried the path of disobedience and found it the road to ruin; he now knows the way of righteousness and finds it the path of peace and happiness.

3. *Love is properly the image of God in the soul* for "God is love." By faith we receive from our Maker; by hope we expect a future and eternal goods; but by love we resemble God; and by it alone are we qualified to enjoy heaven and be one with Him throughout eternity. Faith and hope respect ourselves alone; love takes in both God and man. Faith helps, and hope sustains us; but love to God and man makes us obedient and useful.

4. *Love is the means of preserving all other graces;* indeed, properly speaking, it includes them all; and all receive their perfection from it. Love to God and man can never be dispensed with. It is essential to social and religious life; without it no communion can be kept up with God; nor can any man have a preparation for eternal glory whose heart and soul are not deeply imbued with it. Without it there never was true religion, nor ever can be; and it not only is necessary through life, but will exist throughout eternity. What were a state of blessedness if it did not comprehend love to God and to human spirits in the most exquisite, refined, and perfect degrees?

5. *That man is no Christian who is solicitous for his own happiness alone,* and who cares not how the world goes, so that himself be comfortable. How much good is omitted, how many evils caused, how many duties . . . neglected, how many innocent persons deserted, how many good works destroyed, how many truths suppressed, and how many acts of injustice authorized, by those timorous forecasts of what may happen, and those faithless apprehensions concerning the future!

6. *Where is our zeal for God?* Where the sounding of our bowels over the perishing nations who have not yet come under the yoke of the gospel? multitudes of whom are not under the yoke, because they have never heard of it; and they have not heard of it because they who enjoy the blessings of the gospel of Jesus have not felt (or have not obeyed the feeling) the imperious duty of dividing their heavenly bread with those who are famishing with hunger, and giving the water of life to whose who are dying of thirst! How shall they appear in that great day when the conquests of the Lion of the tribe of Judah are ended; when the mediatorial kingdom is delivered up unto the Father; and the Judge of quick and dead sits on the great white throne, and to those on His left say, "I was hungry, and ye gave me no meat; I was thirsty, and ye gave me no drink"?

I say, how shall they appear who have no exertions to tell the lost nations of the earth the necessity for preparing to meet their God; and showing them the means of doing it by affording them the blessings of the gospel of the grace of God? . . .

A religion, the very essence of which is love, cannot suffer at its altars a heart that is revengeful and uncharitable, or which does not use its utmost endeavours to revive love in the heart of another. . . .

7. *If we are not charitable and benevolent, we give the lie to our profession.* If we have not bowels of compassion we have not the love of God in us; if we shut up our bowels against the poor, we shut Christ out of our hearts, and ourselves out of heaven.

CHRISTLIKENESS

Let the person who is called to perform any act of compassion or mercy to the wretched, do it, not grudgingly nor of necessity, but from a spirit of pure benevolence and sympathy.

Works of charity and mercy should be done as much in private as is consistent with the advancement of the glory of God and the effectual relief of the poor.

He whom God has employed in a work of mercy has need to return, by prayer, as speedily to his Maker as he can, lest he should be tempted to value himself on account of that in which he has no merit; for the good that is done upon earth the Lord doeth it alone.

Love heightens the smallest actions, and gives a worth to them, which they cannot possess without it.

Love never supposes that a good action may have a bad motive; gives every man credit for his profession of religion, uprightness, and godly zeal. Nothing is seen in his conduct or in his spirit inconsistent with this profession.

8. *Labour after a compassionate or sympathizing mind.* Let your heart feel for the distressed; enter into their sorrows and bear a part of their burdens. It is a fact, attested by universal experience, that by sympathy a man may receive into his own affectionate feelings a measure of the distress of his friend, and that his friend does find himself relieved in the same proportion as the other has entered into his griefs.

Love Your Enemies

1. *Do not withhold from any man the offices of mercy and kindness.* You have been God's enemy, and yet God fed, clothed, and preserved you alive; do to your enemy as God has done to you. If your enemy be hungry, feed him; if he be thirsty, give him drink; so has God dealt with you. And has not a sense of His goodness and long suffering toward you been the means of melting down your heart into penitential compunction, gratitude, and love toward Him? How know you that a similar conduct toward your enemy may not have the same gracious influence on him toward you? Your kindness may be the means of begetting in him a sense of his guilt; and, from being your fell enemy, he may become your real friend.

He who loves his friends does nothing for God's sake. He who loves for the sake of pleasure, or interest, pays himself.

2. *A mortal enemy is more easily overcome by kindness than by hostility.* Against the latter he arms himself; and all the evil passions of his heart concentrate themselves in opposition to him who is striving to retaliate by violence the injurious acts which he has received from him. But where the injured man is labouring to do him good for his evil; to repay his curses with blessings and prayers, his evil passions have no longer any motive, any incentive; his mind relaxes; the turbulence of his passions is calmed; reason and conscience are permitted to speak; he is disarmed, or, in other words, he finds that he has no use for his weapons; he beholds in the injured man a magnanimous friend, whose mind is superior to all the insults and injuries which he has received, and who is determined never to permit the heavenly principle that influences his soul to bow itself before the miserable, mean, and wretched spirit of revenge.

This amiable man views in his enemy a spirit which he beholds with horror, and he cannot consent to receive into his own bosom a disposition which he sees to be destructive to another; and he knows that as soon as he begins to avenge himself, he places himself on a par with the unprincipled man whose conduct he has so much reason to blame, and whose spirit he has so much cause to abominate. He who avenges himself receives into his own heart all the evil and disgraceful passions by which his enemy is rendered both wretched and contemptible. There is the voice of eternal reason in "Avenge not yourselves: overcome evil with good"; as well as the high authority and command of the living God.

Wicked words and sinful actions may be considered as the overflowings of a heart that is more than full of the spirit of wickedness; and holy words and righteous deeds may be considered as the overflowings of a heart that is filled with the Holy Spirit, and running over with love to God and man.

3. *"Love ye your enemies."* This is the most sublime precept ever delivered to man: a false religion durst not give a precept of this nature, because, without supernatural influence, it must be forever impracticable. In these words of our blessed Lord we see the tenderness, sincerity, extent, disinterestedness, pattern, and issue of the love of God, dwelling in man; a religion which has for its foundation the union of God and man in the same person, and the death of this august Being for His enemies; which consists on earth in a reconciliation of the Creator with His creatures, and which is to subsist in heaven only in the union of the members with the Head: could such a religion as this ever tolerate hatred in the soul of man, even to his most inveterate foes?

The Fear That Perfect Love Casts Out

We are not to suppose that the love of God casts out every kind of fear from the soul; it only casts out that which has torment. A filial fear is consistent with the highest degrees of love; and even **WHOLENESS** necessary to the preservation of that grace. This is properly its guardian; and without this, love would soon degenerate into listlessness or presumptive boldness.

Nor does it cast out that fear which is so necessary to the preservation of life; that fear which leads a man to flee from danger lest his life should be destroyed.

Nor does it cast out that fear which may be engendered by sudden alarm. All these are necessary to our well being. But it destroys, (1) The fear of want; (2) The fear of death; and, (3) The fear of terror of judgment. All these fears bring torment and are inconsistent with this perfect love.

Perfect, Present Cleansing[12]

1. *Can any man expect to be saved from his inward sin in the other world?* None, except such as hold the . . . antiscriptural doctrine of purgatory. "But this deliverance is expected at death." Where is the promise that it shall then be given? There is not one such in the whole Bible! And to believe for a thing essential to our glorification, without any promise to support that faith in reference to the point on which it is exercised, is a desperation that argues as well the absence of true faith as it does of right reason. Multitudes of such persons are continually deploring their want of faith, even where they have the clearest and most explicit promises; and yet, strange to tell, risk their salvation at the hour of death on a deliverance that is nowhere promised in the sacred oracles!

2. *"But it is too great a blessing to be expected."* Nothing is too great for a believer to expect, which God has promised, and Christ has purchased with His blood.

3. *"If I had such a blessing, I should not be able to retain it."* All things are possible to him that believeth. Besides, like all other gifts of God, it comes with a principle of preservation with it; "and upon all thy glory there shall be a defence."

4. *"Such an unfaithful person as I cannot expect it."* Perhaps the infidelity you deplore came through the want of this blessing: and as to worthlessness, no soul under heaven deserves the least of God's mercies. It is not for thy worthiness that He has given thee anything, but for the sake of His Son. You can say, "When I felt myself a sinner, sinking into perdition, I did then flee to the atoning blood, and found pardon."

5. *"But this sanctification is a far greater work."* No; speaking after the manner of men, justification is far greater than sanctification. When thou wert a sinner, ungodly, an enemy in thy mind by wicked works, a child of the devil, an heir of hell, God pardoned thee on thy

---

12. Ibid., 205-9. Editor's title and outlines.

casting thy soul on the merit of the great sacrificial Offering: thy sentence was reversed, thy state was changed, thou wert put among the children, and God's Spirit witnessed with thine that thou wert His child. What a change! and what a blessing!

6. *What then is this complete sanctification?* It is the cleansing by the blood that [which] has not been cleansed; it is washing the soul of a true believer from the remains of sin; it is the making one who is already a child of God more holy, that he may be more happy, more useful in the world, and bring more glory to his Heavenly Father. Great as this work is, how little, humanly speaking, is it when compared with what God has already done for thee! But suppose it were ten thousand times greater, is anything too hard for God? Are not all things possible to him that believes? And does not the blood of Christ cleanse from all unrighteousness? Arise, then, and be baptized with a greater effusion of the Holy Ghost, and wash away thy sin, calling on the name of the Lord.

CLEANSING

7. *In no part of the Scriptures are we directed to seek holiness gradatim.* We are to come to God as well for an instantaneous and complete purification from all sin, as for an instantaneous pardon. Neither the seriatim pardon, nor the gradatim purification, exists in the Bible. It is when the soul is purified from all sin that it can properly grow in grace, and in the knowledge of our Lord Jesus Christ: as the field may be expected to produce a good crop, and all the seed vegetate when the thorns, thistles, briers, and noxious weeds of every kind are grubbed out of it.

8. *From every view of the subject, it appears that the blessing of a clean heart, and the happiness consequent on it, may be obtained in this life;* because here, not in the future world, are we to be saved. Whenever, therefore, such blessings are offered, they may be received: but all the graces and blessings of the gospel are offered at all times; and when they are offered, they may be received. Every sinner is exhorted to turn from the evil of his way, to repent of sin, and supplicate the throne of grace for pardon. In the same moment in which he is commanded to turn, in that moment he may and should return. He does not receive the exhortation to repentance today that he may become a penitent at some future time. Every penitent is exhorted to believe on the Lord Jesus that he may receive remission of sins: he does not, he cannot understand that the blessing thus promised is not to be received today, but at some future time.

9. *In like manner, to every believer the new heart and the right*

spirit are offered in the present moment; that they may, in that moment, be received. For as the work of cleansing and renewing the heart is the work of God, His almighty power can perform it in a moment, in the twinkling of an eye. And as it is this moment our duty to love God with all our heart, and we cannot do this till He cleanse our hearts, consequently He is ready to do it this moment, because He wills that we should in this moment love Him. Therefore we may justly say, "Now is the accepted time, now is the day of salvation." He who in the beginning caused light in a moment to shine out of darkness, can in a moment shine into our hearts and give us to see the light of His glory in the face of Jesus Christ. This moment, therefore, we may be emptied of sin, filled with holiness, and become truly happy.

IN A MOMENT

Such cleansed people never forget the horrible pit and miry clay out of which they have been brought. And can they then be proud? No! they loathe themselves in their own sight. They can never forgive themselves for having sinned against so good a God and so loving a Saviour. And can they undervalue Him by whose blood they were bought and by whose blood they were cleansed? No! That is impossible: they now see Jesus as they ought to see Him; they see Him in His splendour, because they feel Him in His victory and triumph over sin.

10. *To them that thus believe He is precious;* and He was never so precious as now. As to their not needing Him when thus saved from their sins, we may as well say, As soon may the creation not need the sustaining hand of God, because the works are finished! Learn this, that as it requires the same power to sustain creation as to produce it; so it requires the same Jesus who cleansed to keep clean. They feel that it is only through His continued indwelling that they are kept holy, and happy, and useful. Were He to leave them, the original darkness and kingdom of death would soon be restored.

The Universal Outpouring of the Holy Spirit[13]

And it shall come to pass afterward, that I will pour out my spirit upon all flesh; and your sons and your daughters

---

13. *Discourses on Various Subjects* (New York: B. Waugh and T. Mason, 1832), 2:293-94. Editor's title.

shall prophesy, your old men shall dream dreams, your young men shall see visions. . . .

And I will shew wonders in the heavens and in the earth, blood, and fire, and pillars of smoke. . . .

And it shall come to pass, that whosoever shall call on the name of the Lord shall be delivered: for in mount Zion and in Jerusalem shall be deliverance, as the Lord hath said, and in the remnant whom the Lord shall call (Joel 2:28, 30, 32).

Now the glory of the latter days is evidently the revelation of Christ and the universal pouring out of His Spirit: for, as He by the grace of God, tasted death for every man (Heb. ii. 9); and His grace which brings salvation to all men hath appeared (Titus ii. 11); so the *Holy Spirit* was "to convince the world of sin, righteousness, and judgment" (John xvi. 8); to bear witness in the conscience, of what Christ delivered in His discourses; to purify the hearts of men, and make them habitations of God (Eph. ii. 22).

As the disgrace of man in all times, was *sin* and rebellion against God, so the glory of these latter times is the redemption of man from its power, its guilt, and its pollution; so that faith working by love, should fill the whole life with a cheerful obedience. Nor are we in any times, to expect a greater or more efficacious Saviour than *Jesus Christ;* nor a more powerful and energetic Agent, than the *Holy Ghost,* the Spirit of judgment, and the Spirit of burning.

I do not find in any part of the divine Oracles, that there is any reserve of this Spirit in His gifts and graces for some future times; nor do I find from these sacred records, that there is one ray of His light, or spark of His influence, that may not be had now, for all the purposes of salvation from sin here, and glorification hereafter, in as abundant a manner as can be expected, between His present hour, and that in which the angel shall swear by Him who liveth forever and ever, that time shall be no longer.

SCRIPTURAL

I hold also, that those who are absurdly putting off the day of salvation, in expectation of any outpouring of God's Spirit that may not now be had through Christ, by faith and prayer, and rejecting their own mercies, are encompassing themselves with sparks of their own kindling, and shall lie down in sorrow in consequence.

It is truly an astonishing thing that men will prefer hope to enjoyment; and rather content themselves with blessings in prospect than in possession! Thousands in their affections, conversation, and conduct are wandering after an undefined and undefinable period, commonly called a millennial glory, while expectation is paralyzed and prayer and faith restrained in reference to present salvation; and yet none of these can tell what even a day may bring forth; for now we stand on the verge of eternity, and because it is so, now is the accepted time, and now is the day of salvation!

These are the times in which Christ offers to dwell in the hearts of all true believers by faith, that they may be rooted and grounded in love, and prove with all saints, what is the length, and breadth, and depth, and height, and know the love of God that passeth knowledge, and be filled with *all* the *fullness of God!* Is there anything greater than this to be expected or obtained on this side eternity? Can our hearts be more than filled? Can our souls be filled with more than all the fullness of God? These are the days of the Son of man—now is the Holy Spirit given in His plentitude—never were there times more favourable—never were spiritual advantages more numerous—never was the light more abundant—never were the Holy Scriptures more extensively dispersed—and never were their contents better understood. . . .

SEEKING AND FINDING

The whole earth is in the way of being filled with the knowledge of God! Reader, lay these things to heart: now, arise and shake thyself from the dust: we have seen the land, and behold it is very good; and are ye still [hesitating]? Be not slothful to go and to enter to possess the land! Awake, awake; put on thy strength, O Zion; put on thy beautiful garments, O Jerusalem, the Holy City; for henceforth there shall no more come into thee the uncircumcised and the unclean. Death is at the door; but the power of the Lord is present to heal. O Thou, who dwellest between the Cherubim, shine forth! Amen.

The Corruption in the World Through Lust

His divine power hath given unto us all things that pertain unto life and godliness, through the knowledge of him that hath called us to glory and virtue: Whereby are given unto us exceeding great and precious promises: that by these ye might be partakers of the divine nature, having escaped the corruption that is in the world through lust (2 Pet. 1:3-4).

Great and Precious Promises

Clarke is here pressing the point that there are two kinds of promises: first, those which relate to what God has promised to do *for* man; and second, those which relate to what God will do *in* man.

The *Holy Spirit* must be sent from the Father to awaken the consciences of men: convince them of sin, righteousness, and judgment: apply the promise of pardon to the consciences of penitent sinners, and when they have freely accepted Christ crucified for their Saviour, then to testify with their spirits that God, for Christ's sake, has blotted out all that is past, and thus being justified freely through the redemption that is in Christ, and having an entrance into the Holiest by His blood; and by that Spirit, being purified from all unrighteousness, the carnal mind totally destroyed, and the whole image of God restamped upon the soul, they may be fully qualified for, and at last received into an eternal state of glory and happiness. . . .

Sanctification comes through what Christ's spirit does in man.

Those whose faith rests only in the first (what God does *for* man) do not receive the second (what God does *in* man).

Those who do not receive the second (what God does *in* man) cannot see God.

The bare belief of justification through the passion and death of Christ, pardons no man's sins.

The bare belief of sanctification, through His blood, makes no man holy. Pardon must be received into the conscience. Holiness must be received into the heart. This is evident from what the apostle says in the text; which is stated under the following head:

The end to which they are called to be made partakers of the divine nature; and to escape the corruption that is in the world.

The object of all God's promises and dispensations was to bring fallen man back to that state of blessedness in which he was created; and to the image of God which he had lost. This is the sum and substance of the whole gospel and religion of Christ. We have partaken of an earthly, sensual, devilish nature: the design of God is to remove this, and make us partakers of the divine nature; and save us from the corruption in principle and fact which is in the world: and this is termed partakers of *a* divine nature—not *the* divine nature, as if the nature of God were meant; but a divine nature, a holy frame of soul, a holy heart full of pure and righteous tempers, affections, and desires.

The former nature was evil and earthly—this nature is heavenly and divine: one leads to earth and animal enjoyments; the other leads to heaven and pure spiritual blessedness. Of such a nature they are to be such participators as to have fellowship with those who are of such a nature. They are to be made fit companions for the saints in light.

An unholy man cannot enter into heaven; and were he in it, it would be no enjoyment to him, because it is not suited to him. The nature of the resident must be suited to the place of residence. The fishes live not on the elms, and the cattle browse not in the depths of the sea. Hell is for demons and wicked men; heaven for only angels, and spirits of just men made perfect. There is a fellowship among devils, and those who are partakers of a diabolic nature.... And we know that the inhabitants of heaven are brethren with holy souls....

A Warning

Let none of the corrupt—those who through lust are under the influence of the spirit of the world—expect to enter into the kingdom of God. No man's creed, howsoever orthodox, will save him. Devils believe and tremble: and who have more orthodox creeds than they? There is no passport to heaven but Christ in the heart the hope of glory. For in Christ Jesus, circumcision is nothing, and uncircumcision is nothing, but, a new creation—the faith which worketh by love, and purifieth the heart.

We must have a divine nature to go to a divine place. We are called by His glory and virtue, by His glorious power in us as the means, to His own glory as the end. He works virtue, holiness, and purity in us by the energy of His Spirit; and calls us to a future state of blessedness, by glory and virtue as exciting agents. Now this state of salvation is to be expected by those who escape the corruption that is in the world. The word is very emphatic not only having escaped, but who are escaping the corruption that is the world through evil concupiscence, or irregular desire of any kind, and every kind.

FOR ALL CHRISTIANS

God purifies no heart in which sin is indulged. We must escape, and continue to escape: there is a corruption in the world—our adversary the devil, goeth about as a roaring lion, seeking whom he may devour. In every step of our way of probation, there is either an occurring or pursuing corruption—some form of temptation which has not been before seen—or some of those which once having been inmates, have been cast out; and are ever seeking and

CLEANSING

watching for an opportunity to reenter. Hence, we must run, and run on—flee, and continue fleeing; forgetting the things that are behind, and reaching forth unto those that are before; we must press toward the mark for the prize of the high calling of God in Christ Jesus (Phil. iii. 13-14).

An Invitation

1. You also are a subject of that mighty working of the corruption that is in the world through lust, or the principle of irregular and unholy desire.

SEEKING

2. Pray to God deeply to convince you of your fallen state and to give you true repentance.

3. Pray to God earnestly that you may never rest till you have received a clear sense of your acceptance with God through the Son of His love.

4. As He has convinced you that you had a guilty conscience, and needed pardon, pray to Him that He may convince you that you have a fallen nature—also an evil heart—a spirit that lusts to envy; that it must be regenerated and purified from all unrighteousness.

5. Seek this blessing with your whole heart—in all things, by all means, at all times; never lose sight of your necessity and of God's ability to save.

6. Read the "exceeding great and invaluable promises" relative to this point, they are numerous in both Testaments.

7. Do not fear to take the fullest view of *inbred sin*—beg God to lead you by His Spirit into every chamber of your imagination.

8. Having seen your own heart, abhor yourself—you have already received redemption in His blood, the forgiveness of sins—but feel, deeply feel, that you must have the very thoughts of your heart cleansed by the inspiration of His Holy Spirit. Without this you cannot safely rest.

9. While seeking this salvation let no sin, however refined in appearance, have any dominion over you: beware of indulging any easily besetting sin; abstain from every appearance of evil!

10. Strongly exercise the faith you already have. It is as much your duty to strive to believe as it is to strive to pray. Use grace and have grace.

11. Do not give way to discouragement: He who has promised to come will surely come.

12. See that you bring forth the fruits of that faith and love

which you already have, and in the spirit of loving obedience, according to your present means of grace, expect that fullness of God which He has promised: nothing can withstand the conquering blood of Jesus; nothing the sovereign energy of His Almighty Spirit. He will shortly say, "Be clean"—and you shall be clean.

God Is Able, and He Is Willing—Act Now

That God is able thus to cleanse the heart and affections, and purify the soul, can admit of no doubt.

That He wills the happiness of all His intelligent offspring is evident when the infinite excellent and benevolence of His nature is considered.

And that He is thus able, and thus willing at all times, cannot be reasonably disputed; and for proof of these things look at His exceeding great and precious promises.

May not then every believer in Christ Jesus come even now to the throne of grace, and ask mercy and find grace for this and every other time of need? Yes; and what He purifies, He can and will keep pure.

SEEKING Reader, have faith in God. He is more willing to give than thou art to receive; and is wont to give more than thou canst desire. He will therefore save thee to the uttermost. And after having guided thee by His counsel through life, He will receive thee into His everlasting glory.

Then to Him who hath loved us, and washed us from our sins in His own blood, to Him be glory and dominion, forever and ever. Amen.

Christian Perfection[14]

> *To whom God would make known what is the riches of the glory of this mystery among the Gentiles; which is Christ in you, the hope of glory: Whom we preach, warning every man, and teaching every man in all wisdom; that we may present every man perfect in Christ Jesus* (Col. 1:27-28).

---

14. Arranged from the sermon, "Apostolic Preaching," ibid., 3:287 ff. The material is in Clarke's words but has been abbreviated by omission of paragraphs. The headings have been added by the editors.

Adam Clarke insists that Christian perfection is the grand central idea of the work of Christ. This Paul preaches; warning and teaching all who will listen that holiness is not optional but essential. Clarke never wavered on this score, as Wesley Tracy notes:

> Holiness was the major or minor theme of 38 of the 60 sermons, and it was given honorable mention in all of them. Even in sermons in which one might not at first expect holiness to be stressed it emerges as one of the main themes. . . .
>
> Presenting sanctification as part of the whole counsel of God was the great strength of Clarke's preaching on holiness.[15]

Clarke asks, What was the sum and substance of the apostle Paul's teaching "Christ in you the hope of glory"? He answers:

Who Christ Was

This divine Personage was the grand subject of the apostle's preaching; and to preach Him as the Christ or Messiah, he must point out who He was, what He said, what He did, and what was done to Him. Now all this he did amply and faithfully. He represents Him as "the brightness of the Father's glory, and the express image of his person" (Heb. i. 3). "As being God over all and blessed for evermore" (Rom. 9:5). "The blessed and only Potentate" (1 Tim. vi. 15). As the Creator of all things: "For by him were all things created that are in heaven and that are in earth, visible and invisible, whether they be thrones or dominions, or principalities, or powers; all things were created by him and for him, and he is before all things; and by him all things consist" (Col. i. 16-17). And, "In him dwelt all the fulness of the Godhead bodily" (Col. ii. 9).

As to what Christ said, [Paul] shows that he himself was converted to the truth of the gospel by the words of Christ, spoken in a miraculous way to him, when he was going to Damascus. And what concerns us more is that, being converted to the truth, he received a commission, immediately from Christ himself, "to preach among the Gentiles the unsearchable riches of Christ" (Eph. iii. 8), for Christ sent him "to open their eyes, to turn them from darkness to light, from the power of Satan unto God, that they might receive the remission of sins, and an inheritance among them that are sanctified by faith in him" (Acts xxvi. 18).

"We," he says, "preach Christ in you the hope of glory; for with

---

15. Wesley Tracy, *When Adam Clarke Preached, People Listened* (Kansas City: Beacon Hill Press of Kansas City, 1981), 115 ff.

out Christ there is neither glory, nor a hope of glory, for any son of man." Some contend that "in you," should be translated "among you." It means both. He was among them as the object of their faith and hope: He was among them to make their preaching effectual to the salvation of the hearers. The Holy Spirit bearing testimony to every believing heart, He had His residence in them, as an indwelling, sanctifying Comforter.

What Christ Is to Do in Us

Many talk much, indeed well, of what Christ has done for us; but how little is spoken of what He is to do in us. And yet all that He has done for us is in reference to what He is to do in us. He was incarnated, suffered, died, and rose again from the dead; ascended to heaven, and there appears in the presence of God for us. These were all saving, atoning, and mediating acts for us; that He might reconcile us to God; that He might blot out our sin; that He might purge our consciences from dead works; that He might bind the strong man armed—take away the armour in which he trusted—wash the polluted heart, destroy every foul and abominable desire, all tormenting and unholy tempers; that He might make the heart His throne, fill the soul with His light, power, and life; and in a word, destroy the works of the devil.

These are done in us, without which we cannot be saved unto eternal life; but these acts done in us are consequent on the acts done for us; for had He not been incarnated, suffered and died in our stead, we could not receive either pardon or holiness; and did He not cleanse and purify our hearts, we could not enter into the place where all is purity. Nothing is purified by death: nothing in the grave: nothing in heaven.

All the work must be done in the soul on earth, that is necessary to prepare it for heaven.

Apostolic Preaching

Thus did Paul preach Christ, and thus did Christ dwell in the people under Paul's preaching.

And wherever Christ is preached in the same way, the same influence will attend the preaching, and the same effects will be produced under it. For, as there is no other Saviour but Jesus, so Jesus Christ saves men by delivering them from their sins, and subjecting them to himself. As Jesus He saves; as Christ, He anoints . . . as King He reigns in and over His people, subjecting everything to the mild sway of the sceptre of His righteousness.

It is in reference to this holiness and the heaven for which it prepares the soul, that the apostle adds, we preach, "Christ in you the hope of glory." For, as it was the design of the gospel to put men in possession of the Spirit and power of Christ; to make them partakers of the divine nature and thus prepare them for an eternal union with himself; so he preached this present indwelling Christ as the hope of glory; for no man can rationally hope for glory, who has not the pardon of his sins, and whose nature is not sanctified. And none can have pardon, but through the blood of His Cross; and none can have glorification but through the indwelling sanctifying Spirit of Christ. . . .

God made man in that degree of perfection which was pleasing to His own infinite wisdom and goodness. Sin defaced this divine image; Jesus Christ came to restore it. Sin must have no triumph, and the Redeemer of mankind must have His glory. But if man be not perfectly saved from all sin, sin does triumph, and Satan exult, because they have done a mischief that Christ neither can or will not remove.

To say He cannot would be a shocking blasphemy against the infinite power and dignity of the great Creator: to say He will not would be equally such against the infinite benevolence and holiness of His nature. All sin, whether in power, guilt, or defilement, is the work of the devil; and as "all unrighteousness is sin," so "His blood cleanseth from all sin," because it "cleanseth from all unrighteousness."

Perfection

Many stagger at the term *perfection* in Christianity because they think that what is implied in it is inconsistent with the state of probation; and savours of pride and presumption; but we must take good heed how we stagger at any word of God, and how . . . we deny or fritter away the meaning of any of His sayings, lest He reprove us and we be found liars before Him. But it may be that the term is rejected because it is not understood. Let us examine its import.

PERFECT LOVE

The word *perfection,* in reference to any person or thing, signifies that such person or thing is complete or finished, that it has nothing redundant, and is in nothing defective.

We count those things perfect which want nothing requisite for the end whereunto they were instituted. And to be perfect often signifies to be blameless, clear, irreproachable, and according to the above definition, a man may be said to be perfect who answers every man to his neighbour as himself, then he is a perfect man that does so; he answers the end for which God made him; and this is more evident from the nature of that love which fills his heart; for as love is the principle of obedience so he that loves his God with all his powers, will obey Him with all his powers, and he who loves his neighbour as himself, will not only do no injury to him, but on the contrary, labour to promote his best interests.

Why the doctrine which enjoins such a state of perfection as this should be dreaded, ridiculed, or despised, as a most strange thing and the opposition to it can only be from that carnal mind which is enmity to God, and had I no other proof that man is wholly fallen from God, his opposition to Christian holiness would be to me sufficient.

What Perfection Is

1. *Heart Purity.* In Matt. iv. 48, our Lord says, "Ye shall be perfect, as your Father who is in heaven is perfect." Here the word has the very same meaning as the English term; that which is complete—is in no case defective, is none redundant—and if we speak it of a Christian, he is one that is finished and completed; God has completed or finished, or made an end of His work in him—broke all the power of sin—and purified his soul from all the defilement of sin; so that he is pure and holy, and loving and beneficent in his sphere, circumstances, and nature, as God is in His. He is like his God, because he is now holy; created anew in Christ Jesus; through the power of divine grace, he has regained the image of God which he had lost.

2. *Full Obedience.* In Heb. xiii. 21, the word is used to signify the sum of obedience to the will of God, springing from the work of God in the soul.

3. *Full Health.* And in 1 Pet. v. 10, it is used to express a complete preparation for the kingdom of God. "But the God of all grace, **WHOLENESS** who hath called us unto his eternal glory by Christ Jesus, after that ye have suffered awhile, make you perfect [restore your whole disordered spirits to perfect soundness], stablish, strengthen, settle you."

And to bring a man to this state of perfect restoration to the image of God, and to fit and adapt him thoroughly to know, do, and suffer God's will, the Holy Scriptures have been given by divine inspiration, that by them, through "doctrine, reproof, correction, and instruction in righteousness, the man of God may be perfect, throughly furnished (complete in all parts) unto all good works" (2 Tim. iii. 16-17).

4. *Spiritual Maturity.* In Heb. vi. 1, the apostle exhorts the people to "go on unto perfection." They were not to rest in what might be called initiatory instructions, or the first principles of the doctrine of Christ, but to proceed to get a full, experimental and practical knowledge of all its excellence.

5. *The Whole Gospel.* Once more, the whole gospel, its blessings, and its privileges, in contradistinction from the whole Mosaic dispensation, is termed by the apostle perfection, because it brings perfect instruction in the whole will of God, perfects all revelations and dispensations that had gone before; exhibits a perfect sacrifice for all the sins of all mankind, and the complete destruction of the carnal mind, and restoration of the fallen spirit of man to the image of God, or righteousness and true holiness.

We see, therefore, that the whole design of God was to restore man to His image, and raise him from the ruins of his fall; in a word, to make him perfect; to blot out all his sins, purify his soul and fill him with holiness; so that no unholy temper, evil desire, or impure affection or passion, should either lodge or have any being within him; this and this only is true religion, or Christian perfection; and a less salvation than this would be dishonourable to the sacrifice of Christ, and the operation of the Holy Ghost, and would be as unworthy of the appellation of Christianity as it would be of that holiness of perfection. They who ridicule this are scoffers at the word of God; many of them totally irreligious men, sitting in the seat of the scornful. They who deny it, deny the whole scope and design of divine revelation and mission of Jesus Christ.

GOD'S HOLINESS

The truth is, no doctrine of God stands upon the knowledge, experience, faithfulness, or unfaithfulness of man: it stands on the veracity of God who gave it. If there were not a man to be found who was justified freely through the redemption that is by Jesus; yet the doctrine of justification by faith is true, for it is a doctrine that stands on the truth of God.

And suppose that not one could be found in all the churches of Christ whose heart was purified from all unrighteousness, and loved God and man with all his regenerated powers, yet the doctrine of Christian perfection would still be true, for Christ was manifested that He might destroy the work of the devil, and His blood cleanseth from all unrighteousness, and suppose every man be a liar, God is true.

It is not the profession of a doctrine that established its truth, it is the truth of God, from which it has proceeded. Man's experience may illustrate it, but it is God's truth that confirms it.

Conclusion

PREACHING I conclude from the whole, and trust I have satisfactorily proved it, that as Christ among and in the people, the hope of glory, was the sum and substance of the apostle's preaching, so, their redemption from *all* sin, its power, guilt, and contamination, even in this life, was the grand, the only end at which He aimed in all His ministry; and that to labour to present every man perfect in Christ Jesus, is at once, the duty and glory of every Christian preacher.

The Double Benefit of the Gospel[16]

For God so loved the world, that he gave his only begotten Son, that whosoever believeth in him should not perish, but have everlasting life (John 3:16).

This brings me to the last thing proposed, viz. That they who thus believe receive a double benefit: (1) They are exempted from eternal perdition: That they should not perish. (2) They are brought to eternal glory: That they should have everlasting life.

I have stated that this double benefit proves: (1) That man is guilty; and therefore, exposed to punishment and perdition. (2) That he is unholy; and, therefore, unfit for glory.

1. *That they should not perish.* Though we generally connect the idea of eternal destruction with the word perish, and use it to signify to run into decay, or ruin; to be cut off, to be killed, to die, and to be annihilated; yet, the literal meaning of the word is very simple; it is compounded of *per,* by or through; and *eo,* I go; and signifies no more than passing out of sight. So, in Isa. 1vii. 1, "The righteous perisheth." . . . Thus it signifies to be removed by death; to pass out of sight into the invisible world, or paradise of God.

The original word is compounded of an intensive added to the

---

16. This section forms the conclusion to Clarke's discourse on John 3:16. Abbreviated and outlined by the author.

verbs to destroy, to kill, to lose; hence, the word signifies to be utterly lost; not implying any extinction of being, but the rendering [it] useless; totally defecting the end and purpose of life.

As God created man for himself, and to be finally happy with himself; and he cannot be united to Him unless he be holy; he that sins and neglects the means of his recovery, loses the end of his living; he also passes by from the sight of men: he goes into the invisible world; but it is the blackness of darkness forever. He is annihilated: even his body rises in the great day; but his resurrection is to shame and everlasting contempt. He goes to hell, the place of the perdition of ungodly men: and there, his worm dieth not, and the fire is not quenched.

This is what the Scripture means by perdition or perishing; this is the portion of the sinner who dies unsaved; and it was to prevent this that Jesus Christ shed His sacrificial blood. As man is a sinner, he is in danger of this perdition; for this is the punishment which the divine justice has awarded to transgression: and from this punishment he who with a penitent heart believes ... on the Son of God, is saved, being truly justified from all things; and shall not thus perish. This is the first part of the benefit.

2. *But, secondly, he is to have eternal life.* His being will not only be continued, but his *well-being* shall be secured: he shall be fitted for and received into glory. This is called everlasting life, the life that always lives, it is always in being. In a word, it is eternal; for, as the design of God was to unite men eternally to himself, and He is the Author and Source of life; consequently, he who is made holy, and is thus united to God, ever lives in and by this eternal life. This is a life that cannot perish; a life that can never know decay.

Thus we see (1) That as man is guilty, he needs that pardon which preserves from the punishment of perdition. (2) As he is impure and unholy in his nature, he needs to be washed, to be cleansed from all unrighteousness, and made a partaker of the divine nature; have the very thoughts of his heart cleansed by the inspiration of the Holy Spirit, that he may be fit to dwell with God forever and ever. His being sanctified throughout body, soul, and spirit, prepares him for this state; and this is the second part of the double benefit which he receives by believing on Christ Jesus.

CLEANSING

Two Grand Doctrines of Salvation

This double benefit comprises the two grand doctrines relative to salvation, which enter into almost every Christian's creed:

1. *Justification, or the pardon of sin;* through which we are no longer subject to punishment, and are, therefore, saved from perdition.

2. *Sanctification, or the purification of the soul from all unrighteousness,* by which it is prepared for eternal glory. Without justification, or pardon, it must perish: without sanctification, or holiness, it cannot see God.

The first of these great works is usually attributed to the shedding of Christ's blood (Acts xx. 28. Rom. v. 9. See also Eph. i. 7; Col. i. 14; Heb. ix. 12); the second to the infusion of His Spirit (2 Thess. ii. 13; 1 Pet. i. 2; Rom. xv. 16). But this very Spirit comes through Christ; and is, therefore, called the Spirit of Christ, and the gift of Christ (John xv. 26; xvi. 7) and comes from the Father in the name of Christ (John xiv. 16, 26). And His gifts and graces were to be communicated in consequence of Christ's final triumph (John vii. 39; Acts ii. 33; Eph. iv. 8).

... Justification, or pardon of sin, implies no more, in itself, than the removal of that guilt and condemnation which exposed the sinner to eternal perdition. This, in itself, gives no right to eternal glory.

Sanctification, or complete holiness, is a meetness for glory; but neither does it give any right to heaven. Pardon of sin, as an act of God's mercy, does not imply the purification of the soul: the first removes the guilt, the second takes away the disposition that led to those acts of transgression by which this guilt was contracted.

SECOND BLESSING

Who supposes that the king, when, through his royal prerogative and clemency, he pardons a man who has been capitally convicted of forgery, takes as fully away the covetous principle which led him to commit the act, as by his pardon he takes away his liability to the punishment of the gallows? I produce this instance merely to show, that pardon and holiness are not so necessarily connected, as that one must imply the other. Yet there is every reason to believe, and genuine experience in divine things confirms it, that in the act of justification, when the Spirit of God, the Spirit of holiness, is given to bear witness with our spirits that we are the children of God, all the outlines of the divine image are drawn upon the soul: and it is the work of the Holy Spirit, in our sanctification, to touch off, and fill up, all those outlines, till every feature of the divine likeness is filled up and perfected.

Therefore, no believer should ever rest till he find the whole body of sin and death destroyed; and till

FOR ALL CHRISTIANS

the law of the Spirit of life in Christ Jesus have made him free from the law of sin and death.

I have said that neither justification, nor sanctification, gives a right to glory. Mere innocence is not entitled to reward; and mere meetness for a thing or place, is no proof of right to possession. The fact is, that the right to that glory comes merely by Jesus Christ, and is the effect of His infinite merit; and here the excellence and perfection of that merit appear. The merit must be infinite that can rescue the soul from deserved endless punishment; the merit must be infinite that can give a man a title to eternal glory.

Now the text states, that an exemption from endless torments, and a title to, and meetness for, eternal glory, come by Christ, as the gifts of God's love. And, as to be saved from eternal perdition is of infinite value to an immortal soul, and as the enjoyment of God in his own heavens throughout eternity is of infinite worth, and both these are attributed to Christ's giving himself for us; therefore, Christ's merit must be infinite; and it could not be so, were He not properly and essentially God.

ATONEMENT

Thus we are led back to the point from which we set out; and the postulates on the premises amount to demonstration in the conclusion. We were obliged to commence with the deity of Christ; as most obviously nothing less could have been adequate to the work which was given Him to do: and the work which He has done, and the blessings which He has acquired, demonstrate His infinite merit, and thus prove the point of His essential divinity.

I have only one word to add to what has already been said; and that shall refer to the incomprehensibility of that love which induced God to give His Son for the redemption of the world. God so loved the world, says the text, no description of this love is here attempted; its length, breadth, depth, and height, are like the nature of that God in whom it resides; all indescribable, because all incomprehensible.

To the same subject the apostle recurs (1 John iii. 1), "Behold *what manner* of love, the Father hath *bestowed* upon us!" In the *so* of the gospel, and the *what manner,* of the epistle, God has put an eternity of meaning; and has left a subject for everlasting contemplation, wonder, and praise, to angels and men: for, though not directly interested in the subject, yet these things the angels desire to look into. And to see them in all their relations, connections, and endlessly continued results, would be sufficient to constitute a heaven of heavens to all beatified spirits. . . .

Basic Principles

I shall now conclude with the principles with which I commenced: From the text and the reasonings on it, it appears evident:

1. That the world, the whole human race, was in a ruinous, condemned state, in danger of perishing everlastingly: and without power to rescue itself from the impending destruction.

2. That God, through the impulse of His own infinite love and innate goodness, provided for its rescue and salvation by giving His only begotten Son to die for it.

3. That the sacrificial death of Jesus was the only means by which the redemption of the world could have been effected: and such is the nature of this Sacrifice, that it is absolutely sufficient to accomplish this gracious design; nothing greater could be given, and nothing less could have been availing.

4. That sin is an inconceivable evil and possesses an indescribable malignity when it required no less a sacrifice to make atonement for it than that offered by God manifested in the flesh.

5. That no man is saved through this Sacrifice, but he who believes; i.e., who credits what God has spoken concerning this Christ; His sacrifice; the end for which it was offered; and the way in which it is to be applied in order to its becoming effectual.

6. That they who believe secure a double benefit: (1) They are exempted from eternal perdition—that they should not perish. (2) They are brought to eternal glory—that they should have everlasting life; this double benefit proving, (1) That man is guilty, is exposed to punishment, and needs pardon. (2) That man is impure and unholy; and, therefore, unfit for the glory of God. (3) That the merit must be infinite which procured for a fallen world such ineffable privileges, and, (4) That man owes to God His Creator, to God His Redeemer, and to God His Sanctifier; the utmost gratitude, the most affectionate obedience, and unbounded praises, throughout eternity.

Therefore, "to him who hath loved us, and washed us from our sins in his own blood, and hath made us kings and priests unto God and his Father, to him be glory and dominion, forever and ever. Amen!"

* * *

Richard Watson
(1781-1833)

Richard Watson, a Yorkshire man, was born at Barton-on-Humber, February 22, 1781. He died January 8, 1833, a true son of John Wesley.

Watson lives on in the literary gifts he left to posterity, chiefly his *Life of John Wesley,* his *Theological Institutes,* a theological dictionary, his critique of Sauthey's *Life of Wesley,* and a sizable body of sermons, essays, book reviews, and addresses. Watson also began a commentary on the New Testament with a special desire to expound Romans and Hebrews, but serious sickness and failing strength prevented the completion of this work. With Matthew through Luke completed, he passed straight to Romans but got only as far as chapter 3, verse 25: "But now a righteousness from God, apart from law, has been made known, to which the Law and the Prophets testify. This righteousness from God comes through faith in Jesus Christ to all who believe. There is no difference, for all have sinned and fall short of the glory of God, and are justified freely by his grace through the redemption that came by Christ Jesus. God presented him as a sacrifice of atonement, through faith in his blood" (Rom. 3:21-25, NIV).

Here illness compelled Watson to lay aside his versatile pen.

It was fitting that these verses should be so much on his mind, for in the glorious truth of the Atonement he had first cast the anchor of his faith. After a rather rebellious and irresponsible life as a young teenager, which gave deep grief to his Methodist father, Richard was converted largely through the influence of a sermon preached by the Rev. William Dodwell.

> The secrets of his heart were laid open; and the evils of his nature were presented to his view in a new and fearful light. . . . he could only pray "God be merciful to me a sinner." The doctrine of atonement for sin came home to his heart with a freshness and power which he had not previously experienced. . . . He put his trust in Christ for pardon, for a title to eternal life, and for that "holiness without which no man shall see the Lord." It was done unto him according to his faith. Guilty fear in his breast gave place to filial love: the Holy Ghost bore a distinct and indubitable witness with his spirit that he was a child of God; he was "filled with

Richard Watson

all joy and peace in believing"; he loved God under a deep and impressive assurance of God's love to him; and he loved all mankind for the Lord's sake.[17]

A few days later he became "a willing and happy member of the Methodist society; and meekly submitted to all the contumely and insult with which they were then treated in the city."[18] He was but 15 years of age, but began to preach almost immediately and before long was confronting both uncouth and refined opposition. Despite the plea of a Methodist minister to the London Conference, Richard was regarded as too young and inexperienced to be appointed as an itinerant. However, in 1797 he was appointed to a circuit, under the supervision of George Sargent whose ministry had played a large part in Richard's conversion.

Thus was launched the ministry of one who became an eloquent spokesman for, and systematiser of Wesleyan theology. Like Wesley he was eaten up by missionary zeal and became, with Jabaz Bunting his friend and colleague, a powerful advocate and architect of Methodist missions. He was a living example of entire sanctification. Struggling with sickness almost all of his ministerial life he was "a remarkable instance of sanctified affliction."[19]

A fitting word from his biographer sums up the central themes of Richard Watson.[20]

Theologian and Apologist

"Watson dealt with vital truths, and to him the truth of truths was the Atonement of Redeeming Love. This ran through every pamphlet, sermon, and exposition like the motif of a fugue—the soul and meaning of them all. His aim was simple—to open out the Holy Scriptures, explain and enforce them. Further than this he never went. He accepted them as a divinely inspired revelation without a shadow of reserve. 'I believe my Bible,' he would say on the platform when condemning wrong or predicting the victory of truth. 'Go, then,' says he to the youth of the *Catechism on the Evidences,* 'read, mark, learn, and inwardly digest these sacred writings. Let no sophistry of wicked

---

17. *RWW,* 1:18.
18. Ibid., 1:19.
19. Ibid., 1:475.
20. Edward J. Brailsford, *Richard Watson, Theologian and Missionary Advocate* (London: Charles H. Kelly, n. d.).

men lead you from the truth and rob you of your birthright to salvation and immortality. The Bible will be your guide through life, your comfort in affliction, and your hope in death, if you embrace the doctrines it teaches, and believe on the Saviour it sets before you.'"

Pulpit and Platform

"Watson dealt with first principles, cardinal virtues, vital truths. He hewed out colossal pillars, but could not 'carve cherry-stones.' His thoughts were massive in simple strength, and wore then the freshness of originality. But the elevated rocks of one generation make the paving-stones of the next. One thing, however, is strikingly evident: the aims of the preacher are practical. He is intensely and affectionately anxious to 'save them that hear him.' Addressing the ministers for ordination in the Manchester Conference of 1827, he says: 'Your ministrations must be pregnant with vital qualities: they are to be "clouds of blessing." Genius may mould them into various forms, and taste may illuminate and vary them with "colours dipped in heaven"; but whatever ray you cast upon the fringes of the cloud, let the body and substance of it be charged with the concentration vapours of the springs, tremulous to the impulse of every breeze, and impatient to pour the vital shower upon the thirsting earth.

"It was thus he endeavoured to preach himself, and we are more definitely reminded of his aims in the circular letter he sends to the missionaries abroad. He reminds them of Him who sent us not only to preach to men, but to persuade them; not to boast of the brightness of the weapons of our warfare and our own supposed dexterity in using them, but to subdue a rebel world to the obedience of faith and love. He preaches best, says an old divine, who saves the most souls."

A great lover of the hymns of Charles Wesley, Watson spent his final days and hours listening to those hymns being read to him by his daughter. In those hours, too, he thrilled again to the reading of John Wesley's sermon on *The Way to the Kingdom*. He died in the faith, saying:

> I shall behold His face
> I shall His power adore;
> And sing the wonders of His grace forevermore!

Following are three of his best-known sermons: (1) "The Pure in Heart"; (2) "Power from on High"; and (3) "The Right State of the Heart."

The Pure in Heart[21]

Blessed are the pure in heart—Matt. v. 8.

Here again our Lord, according to the spirit and intent of his whole discourse, turns the attention of his hearers from those outward purifications which the more superstitious Jews, and especially the Pharisees, so carefully preached, and the importance of which they so greatly exaggerated, to the purification of the *heart.* In that lies the true fountain of evil; and there the sanctification of man must begin and be completed.

This purity of heart respects the intention, in opposition to religious hypocrisy; and so consists in the simple, unmixed desire to please God in all things: it implies, also, the extirpation of all unholy desires, imaginations, tendencies, and affections. But this cannot be a negative state only; the absence of all evil is necessarily the presence of all good. Hence, in this condition of mind, truth becomes the clear light of the judgment, and the exact rule of conscience; the will is rendered cheerfully submissive to divine authority; God is loved "with all the heart, and mind, and soul, and strength, and our neighbour as ourselves"; and "whatsoever things are" externally, and in their outward, practical manifestation, "true, whatsoever things are honest, whatsoever things are just, whatsoever things are pure, whatsoever things are lovely, if there be any virtue, if there be any praise," the root of all, if they are real and not simulated virtues, is a pure heart; a nature, to use St. Paul's words, "sanctified wholly"; to effect which entire sanctification of man is the peculiar and glorious work of the Holy Ghost, through the gospel.

"For they shall see God."—This is not merely to enjoy His favour and special protection here and hereafter, as the phrase is taken by some to import. It has a larger meaning; and must be interpreted by other scriptures. Moses "endured, as seeing him who is invisible"; that is, he has respect to the power and faithfulness of a present God, and was thus preserved from fearing the wrath of Pharaoh. David had respect to God, setting him always "at his right hand," and thus, through his trust in Him, was not "moved," not agitated or oppressed, by his troubles.

---

21. *RWW,* 13:

We have also the phrases of "walking in the light of God's countenance," and of "his face being turned towards the objects of his favour"; both of which imply intimate and gracious intercourse between God and His people. An habitual regard to the invisible Creator and Preserver in His visible works, and the recognition of His agency, and a right understanding of His purposes, both in judgments and in mercies, are also acts by which we are said to see God; and rightly to understand the gospel of Christ, and so to love the truth which it reveals, and habitually and affectionately to meditate upon it, is called "beholding with unveiled face the glory of the Lord." In all these respects the pure in heart see God on earth; and the more fully and habitually so, as their purity becomes more perfect.

The promise, however, chiefly respects a future life. To see God as He manifests himself to the glorified spirits of the redeemed in heaven, has from the beginning been the crowning hope of good men, and formed their noblest conception of future felicity and glory. Thus Job, "In my flesh shall I see God"; and of the man that "walketh righteously and speaketh uprightly," Isaiah says, "Thine eyes shall *see the king* in his beauty."

Concurring with these views, and with special reference to these very words of our Saviour, St. John has the following glowing passage: "Beloved, now are we the sons of God, and it doth not yet appear what we shall be: but we know, that when he shall appear, we shall be like him; for we shall *see him as he is*. And every man that hath this hope in him purifieth himself, even as he is pure."

Those who would confine the purity of heart spoken of in this verse to purity of intention, would not greatly err, if they extended the notion as far as Bernard, who defines purity of intention to consist "in directing all our actions to the honour of God, the good of our neighbour, and the preservation of a good conscience." But how vast, how complete a change in man's moral nature does all this necessarily suppose! a change only to be accomplished by the great power of God, "working in us that which is well-pleasing in his sight, that we may be perfect in every good work to do his will."

Power from on High[22]

Watson's sermon on Pentecost is helpful to an understanding of the Wesleyan outlook on the gifts and operations of the Holy Spirit as understood by early scholars of second generation Methodism, and contributes to current studies on the Baptism with the Holy Spirit.

> *But tarry ye in the city of Jerusalem, until ye be endued with power from on high* (Luke xxxiv. 49).

These words were addressed by our Lord to the eleven Apostles, and those that were with them, when He was about to leave them; but as He had always promised the Spirit, that is, in a richer effusion than had marked any former dispensation, so now He renews the promise, and bids them wait in Jerusalem "for the promise of the Father"; a phrase which explains the text, "power from on high."

They did wait, as all must wait, for this heavenly gift; they "continued in prayer"; they were in the temple "praising and blessing God"; and "when the day of Pentecost was fully come," the gift, the great and illustrious gift, was bestowed. As then, at this season, between the resurrection and ascension, the disciples were revolving this promise in their minds, and waiting for its accomplishment, we may profitably direct our attention to its import; that, entering into its nature, we may be influenced to seek the same gift which, in His ordinary operations, is promised to us. To the expressive language of the text, I then call your attention. The Holy Spirit is the "power from on high," bestowed by God on man.

I propose to illustrate this description of the blessed Spirit,

I. By the extraordinary effects produced on the Apostles.

II. By the ordinary influence exerted on them, and on all true Christians.

I. I call your attention to the extraordinary operations of the Spirit . . . because of their use in exhibiting the evidence on which Christianity rests. Also I think it very probable that the work of the Spirit was made so strikingly visible that we might be more impressed with a

---

22. *RWW*, 3:379-84.

sense of His mighty efficacy upon the heart in His more secret workings. We should thus expect the more in our ordinary experience from His gracious influence.

Consider, then, in these extraordinary gifts which were only intended for the time, how mightily God wrought in man.

1. *Take the gift of tongues.*

He who knows the difficulty of acquiring a foreign language will perceive how unequivocal a miracle was an infusion of words into the memory, with their meanings and relations, and with that facility of applying them, which instant and rapid speech required. This gift the Spirit imparted to the Apostles.

2. *Mark the illumination of the mind with the full truth.*

The Apostles had heard Christ. They had reasoned among themselves. The sun had flamed upon the mists of their prejudices; there had sometimes been a flash of light; and then obscurity had followed. Now all was explained. The harmony of the law and the gospel, the mystery of faith, were opened to themselves, and to all by them. Here was another miracle.

3. *Mark the power with which they spake.*

All was light, all feeling. Yes, there was a rush of accompanying energy, the "demonstration of the Spirit," such as accompanied not even the words of Christ. As to those who were not obstinately blind, "they were pricked in their heart." As to others, they could not resist; but when Stephen spoke, the very gnashing of their teeth showed that the unwelcome light had penetrated their dark spirits, and that they hated the light, and hated the man. But they would have hated neither, had they not felt that the light was light from heaven, and the man a man of God.

4. *Mark their miracles of healing.*

"All the works of Christ" they did, "and greater," that is, more in number; for greater in kind they could not be. "Because," said he, "I go unto my Father," and send the Spirit. They were men, inferior to Christ, who was God-man; yet they performed the very works of divinity, because they were "endued with power from on high." The sick were healed. Virtue issued from Peter, as from His Master's garments. The dead were raised. Demons were ejected.

5. *Note their discernment of spirits, as in the cases of Ananias and Simon Magus.*

The hearts of men were opened to their eyes, not always perhaps, but on fit occasions; and man, by the "power from on high," was endued with an attribute of God, to search the heart.

6. *Finally, take their courage.*

There was courage in all; some of whom were naturally timid; the courage, not of excitement merely, but of a calm, deliberate surrender of themselves to shame, suffering, death. Not under the eye of an applauding nation, but often alone, unbefriended. "At my first answer," says St. Paul, "no man stood with me, but all men forsook me." Theirs was a courage which shrunk not in the hour of trial. There was not one apostate among them after the "power from on high" descended.

Whilst we see in all these circumstances a demonstration of the truth of the Apostles' mission, we see also what God can make man, when He vouchsafes to Him the gift of His Spirit. But we are to illustrate the phrase in the text.

II. By the ordinary influences exerted on the Apostles, and on all true Christians.

The gift of the Spirit is still "power from on high." True it is that the gifts just mentioned were extraordinary. They answered their end; they made the glory of God visible to all. When they had done this, when attention was roused, and Christianity could appeal to these demonstrations as matters of historical fact, the work was left to be carried on by more secret and invisible influences. So when the cloud of glory descended on the temple, "the Priests could not stand to minister, because of the cloud." Yet God was no less the mighty God of Israel, when invisible. The Spirit is now in the church, working all in all.

We have, indeed, been told that, the extraordinary gifts being no longer dispensed, the direct influence of the Holy Spirit was not continued. Let me refute this. It confounds two things, extraordinary and ordinary gifts. One did not necessarily imply the other. All who received the Holy Ghost, as a Teacher and Comforter, did not work miracles; and some who had gifts, had not renewing grace.

Again: If the Apostles needed the direct influence of the Holy Spirit to make them Christians, so do we. We are called to imitate them; but how can we do it, if we have not the same help? Again: We are called to be all that the gospel requires. Now, either we can attain this without the Spirit, or we cannot. If we can, man can be saved without God: If we cannot, the gospel is no longer "the power of God unto salvation"; "the glory is departed."

But all this objection is dispersed by the words of Christ: "I will pray the Father, and he shall give you another Comforter, that he may abide with you for ever." "And, lo, I am with you alway, even unto the end of the world." Thank God, if we wait, we too shall be "endued with power from on high." Let us, then, consider how this power manifests itself. And here, too, we shall see a mighty working of God in man, not inferior in real glory, and superior grace, to those extraordinary works of the Spirit.

1. *This is displayed, in the awakening of the soul of man from its deep and deadly sleep of sin.*

Who knows not that there are two states of mind, with reference to eternal things? The one is marked by unconcern and neglect. The sinner has no sense of danger, though on its very brink; no abhorrence of sin, though leprous with it; no sense of slavery, though actually bound; no shame and humiliation before God, though an ungrateful forgetfulness and rebellion shape his life.

What, then, if this sleep is broken? if the ear listens at last to the reproving, alarming voice? if the danger becomes visible? if fears are fully roused? if the heart breaks under a sense of its ingratitude? if a deep and habitual regard to the soul's interest, and to eternal things, takes full possession of the feelings? What change at the Pentecost was greater than this? What is its source?

Does man awaken himself? Does he pierce his own conscience? Does he render himself miserable and wretched? The thing is impossible and contradictory. It is the "power from on high that produces this." And, O! if by this I can obtain a soft and tender heart; if I can be kept in humiliation before God, always awake to spiritual dangers, that I may be impelled to the refuge of the atonement, always living for eternity; then let me bless God, who gives this power to man; and let me wait, in all the earnestness of prayer, until I am endued with it.

2. *Our subject is illustrated by the office of the Spirit as the Comforter.*

Here, also, are two states of mind; one of fear and alarm; the other of faith, and a joyful sense of reconciliation with God. Here is a change as marked, as miraculous, as the other. Here, too, is the "power from on high." And if this be the result; if for these doubts, I may receive assurance; if for this dread of God, I may receive the Spirit of adoption; then let me wait till I am endowed with this heavenly gift, the Spirit who cries in every believing heart, "Abba, Father."

3. *We have another instance in the office of the Spirit as the Holy Ghost the Sanctifier.*

There is not a sin from which we may not cease. But this power is not of man; it is the "power from on high," destroying the love of sin, breaking its power, and so filling the soul with the fear and love of God, that the dart of temptation falls blunted and broken, and the ennobled and freed spirit cries, "Thanks be to God, which giveth us the victory through our Lord Jesus Christ."

4. *Take a final instance from the fruits of the Spirit.*

Mark the enumeration of them: "Love, joy, peace, long-suffering, gentleness, goodness, faith, meekness, temperance." Now, when these are called the fruits of the Spirit, the expression intimates that they are not of man. Of these fruits the human heart is naturally as barren as the waste is of "corn, and wine, and oil." Even what approaches nearest to them is utterly different. Natural good temper is not "love" to God; cheerfulness of spirit is not "joy" in the Lord; tranquility is not "the peace of God, which passeth all understanding." But let the contrast be as complete as possible: Let the heart be hating and malignant; here "love" shall grow: Let it be gloomy and dark; here "joy" shall spring up: Let it be turbulent and restless; here "peace" shall establish her dominion. All this is miracle, too: It is "power from on high."

Closing Observations

I apply this subject to your edification, by observing,

1. That there is a power promised to you more glorious than all the endowments of apostolic gifts. "Though I speak with the tongues of men and of angels, and have not charity, I am become as sounding brass, or a tinkling cymbal. And though I have the gift of prophecy, and understand all mysteries, and all knowledge; and though I have all faith, so that I could remove mountains, and have not charity, I am nothing."

2. Fix the greatness of the blessing before you. The baptism of secret fire is invisible to the eye; but it works powerfully and constantly, softening the heart, kindling joy, diffusing purity, giving energy in duty, carrying you up in devout thoughts to heaven. If you seek it, all this is yours.

3. Do you ask how you are to attain it? See your example in the Apostles. Believe your Lord: "I send the promise of my Father upon

you." Wait for this, not idly, but in prayer, in the public means; for they "were continually in the temple, praising and blessing God."

4. Know, that "if any man have not the Spirit of Christ, he is none of his." Aspire, then, to this.

5. Ask the effusion of the Spirit upon your friends the whole church, the world. Even that shall come.

The Right State of the Heart[23]

> *And when he was departed thence, he lighted on Jehonadab the son of Rechab coming to meet him: And he saluted him, and said unto him, Is thine heart right?* (2 Kings x. 15).

If your hearts be right, we shall thus have the satisfaction of ascertaining it; and if they be not right, there is yet a remedy, for the gate of mercy is not closed, and the means of salvation are yet in our power. Let us seek to know our own selves, resolving to rest in nothing which comes short of a heart right with God.

For the sake of order, I bring the subject before you under four general heads of discourse. If our hearts be right, they will be right,

    I. With God.
   II. With Christ.
  III. With His church.
  IV. With themselves.

I. *If the state of our hearts be right, then will they be right with God.*

The greatest idea that can be presented to our mind is that of God. He is not a distant being, unconnected with us, unrelated to us. He it is "with whom we have to do." Such is the impressive language of Scripture. And then, the state of our hearts towards Him must always be either right or wrong. Every sentiment we cherish contains in it, as to Him, some positive good or evil.

A heart truly right with God implies,

1. *That we venerate Him.*

How little of this is expressed, or even felt, on earth! Yet in heaven, where all hearts are right, the seraphim veil their faces, and all

---

23. *RWW*, 3:148-55.

living beings fall prostrate before His throne. When, therefore, we are conscious of His presence, when we walk as under His inspection, fear His displeasure more than the frowns of the world, and, bowing before His Majesty with lowliness of mind, give unto Him the honour due unto His name, then only are our hearts right with Him.

2. *That we entirely submit ourselves to Him.*

The very word *God* is a name of dominion; and never be it forgotten that He to whom it belongs has a supreme will concerning us. There cannot be a sadder spectacle than a heart wrestling with its Maker's will. "Let the potsherds strive with the potsherds of the earth. Shall the clay say to him that fashioneth, What makest thou?" But when we recognize His will as our only rule; when we keep this before us as our supreme law, regarding it as the light and guide of our conduct; when we acknowledge His sovereignty in Providence, take our place in society as He appoints, submit to His dispensations, and in the greatest afflictions, even when nature agonizes, meekly bow like Him in the garden, and say, "Not my will, but thine be done," then is our heart right with God.

3. *That by the cultivation of a devotional spirit, we maintain a sacred intercourse with Him.*

Prayer and praise are the great instruments of the fellowship of our spirits with God; His responses of light, and love, and moral power, are the returns which the condescension of God makes to them. Ever since created intelligences existed, to desire good from God, to receive supplies of it from himself, to be devoutly grateful, and to express their love, so far as it can be expressed in praises, has been the heaven of happy spirits. It is the heaven even of earth; the only one to be enjoyed, and which all may enjoy.

How dead the heart which has no intercourse with heaven! True joy is a stranger there, and all is darkness and sin. Barren and unwatered, it bears no fruit of either righteousness or peace.

So truly is this intercourse with God the state of a heart which is right with Him, that no sooner do right principles begin their influence on it, than it moves toward Him. "I will arise, and go to my Father," is its language. Then come confessions of sin, and approaches to God through a Mediator, and unutterable longings for the dawning light of His manifested favour. Then, "as the hart pants after the waterbrooks, so pants the soul after God. The soul thirsts for God, even for the living God." And thus the true rest of the spirit is found in that state only in which we can say, "Whom have I in heaven but thee" and "there is none upon earth that I desire besides thee."

We ask, then, Is thine heart right with God? Does it venerate Him? submit to Him? aspire after Him? You know the state of your own heart: Answer these inquiries as before God.

II. *If our hearts be right, they are right with Christ.*
Till this be the case, the heart cannot even be right with God. Some have attempted, indeed, to produce a state of mind, reverential, submissive, and devotional, without respect to Christ; but the attempt has been vain. Something sentimental has been produced, perhaps, but nothing gracious. "No man cometh to the Father but by me." "No man knoweth the Father but the Son, and he to whom the Son will reveal him." That our heart be right with Christ is, therefore, the foundation of all religion. It is so,

1. *When it accepts His sacrifice as the only ground on which to claim the remission of sins.*

How many hearts are there that are not, in this respect, right with Christ! One depends on his own virtues; another on his benevolence and charities; and more still (for the heart will rest its hope somewhere), upon some undefined, unscriptural view of God's mercy. Others, more enlightened, it is true, but still egregiously wrong, repose a sort of general trust in the merits of Christ; forgetting that this trust is the personal, specific act of a broken and contrite heart, which not only flees to that all-atoning sacrifice, but, despairing of all other help, eagerly embraces this.

Brethren, a heart right with Christ in this respect has gone through the process of awakening, of arousing fears, of conviction of utter helplessness; and then surrenders its whole case to Christ, trusting solely in the merit of his death, and the power of his intercession; looking through them alone, and looking now, for the mercy of God unto eternal life.

2. *The heart is not right with Christ unless it loves Him.*

Considered abstractedly, all would pronounce it a thing monstrous, and almost a diabolical act, not to love the Saviour; and yet, sad as is this state of the heart, what can be more common? He stands before us arrayed in the perfection of virtue and holiness; and yet no form or comeliness that men should desire Him as their example. He exhibits the tenderest benevolence; but what heart is moved by it, or shows forth its praise? Men are under an infinite obligation to Him, for He died to save them; but this excites no gratitude. He holds out to them the blessings purchased by his blood, and they spurn them for every trifle. What a state of the heart is this! You see that it is wrong, awfully wrong. Yes, and it never can be right till it loves Christ supremely.

But let me caution you here. This love is not mere sentiment. It is not the mere effect which the contemplation of character, heroism, injury, suffering, may produce. It is the result of a personal experience of His benefits. He is loved as a Saviour. And it is a practical principle. It does not evaporate in feeling. He is loved above the world; that is renounced for His sake. He is loved above sin; that is mortified. He is loved above self; we are willing to labour, to suffer, and, if called, even to die for Him.

3. *When the heart is right with Christ, there is an habitual confidence in His intercession.*

This is what is called the life of faith, or, living by faith; and it is by this that the real is distinguished from the nominal believer. Faith is not one single act, but a constant reliance on the Saviour's mediation, as that which alone stands between the extreme of justice and ourselves, and by which we are looking for all good, for the supply of every want. Thus, when the heart is right with Him, it rests not in acknowledging His merit, but draws its virtue from heaven. It is not satisfied with acknowledging a fulness of spiritual blessings to be in Him, but derives them from Him through its specific and habitual exercises. In this state, we surrender every care into His hands, and are kept in peace. We leave life and death at His disposal, satisfied with this, that whether in life or death we are the Lord's.

Is thine heart thus right with Christ? Dost thou thus believe in Him? thus love Him? thus habitually confide in Him?

III. *If our hearts be right, they are right with the church of Christ.*

I mean, by this expression, the whole company of his militant and professing people here on earth; the spiritual Israel of God. Now, when the heart is in a right state,

1. *The church is avowed.*

There is the church and the world; the one is renounced, the other embraced. Baptism is not of itself a sufficient avowal. We shall unite ourselves to some portion of the visible church, and so place ourselves under its discipline. So of the Lord's supper, which will be our public declaration of communion with Christ and His church.

Where this is not the case, the heart is not right. That which keeps us in the world is some bad principle which we will not renounce; some guilty shame which we will not cast off; some sinful association which we will not break; some evil practice which we will not amend.

2. *Its members are loved.*

A new sentiment is now awakened and cherished in obedience to the commandment of Scripture: "Love one another." And this is holy charity. There would be some peculiarities in the opinions and practices of Jonadab; yet Jehu says to him, "Is thine heart right, as my heart is with thy heart? If it be, give me thine hand." Let me impress this on you, as well as a tender regard for those with whom we are more immediately connected. Remember, that the body is but one, and that it is "compacted by that which every joint supplieth."

3. *When our heart is right with the church, we feel that we are identified with it.*

We grieve at its failures: In its successes we rejoice. We say, with the Psalmist, "If I forget thee, O Jerusalem, may my right hand forget its cunning." We pray for its prosperity, and say, "Peace be within thy walls." We are willing to labour in any part which the providence of God may assign to us, if we may but promote its interests.

Here, too, let me ask, "Is thine heart right?" Dost thou avow thyself a member of Christ's church? love its members? identify thyself with its interests? and labour to promote them?

IV. *If the heart be right, it will be right with itself.*

There are strange oppositions and divisions in the heart; and this cannot be a right state of it. There is opposition between conviction and choice. Many know the good, who choose it not, who make no effort for its attainment. There is opposition between will and power. To will is indeed present with them, but how to perform they find not. There is the struggle between the flesh and the spirit; the counteraction of graces by opposite evils. There is the stunted growth. The seed is at least so far choked, that there is no fruit unto perfection. When it is thus with us, the heart is manifestly wrong. When it is right, it exerts an enlightened sway over the whole man: All its powers are in obedient order, all its graces fruitful and abundant. We therefore again ask, Is thine heart right with itself? Is it divided, and therefore faulty? or has God united it, that it may fear His name?

1. *Perhaps our heart is wrong.*

Let us be thankful that we perceive this. But be patient and persevering. Go to the very depth of its error and wrong. Heal not the wound slightly. The case may be hard; but it is not a hopeless one.

2. *Perhaps it is in part right.*

For this be thankful; but rest not here. Many evils have already given way. I see you laden with the spoils of some conquered enemies; more are nearly overthrown. O pursue the fugitives; seek them in their caves, and dens, and hiding-places. Be determined on their final, their utter extirpation.

3. *Know and use the means by which this may be accomplished.*

Exercise faith in the Saviour, live in habitual watchfulness and self-denial, "keeping the heart with all diligence, for that out of it are the issues of life."

O lovely sight, not only to men and angels, but to God also, even a heart renewed, stamped with the divine image, warmed with the divine life, and sanctified by the Holy Spirit! It is the temple of God, the glorious workmanship of Christ; and He shall exhibit it at the last day as the fruit of His passion, and the monument of His all-subduing, all-restoring grace.

6

JOHN FLETCHER
1729-85

Fletcher's Thought
The Perfection of Christ's Dispensation
Distinguishing the Three Degrees of Saving Faith
An Appeal to Matters of Fact and Common Sense
Criticism of the Doctrine of Imperfection
The Operations of the Holy Spirit

The Heart of Fletcher's Teaching
To Earnest Seekers After Entire Sanctification

John Fletcher

6 John Fletcher (1729-85)

John Fletcher, vicar of Madeley, "more apostolic than those claiming apostolic succession," was one man who seemed too good to be true. He was one man so heavenly-minded that he was of inestimable earthly worth.

If Fletcher's admirers had all been Methodists, or Anglicans, or even people religiously inclined, perhaps we would have been seriously inclined to modify their opinions. But they were not. Southey, the poet, was certainly not partial to the Methodists, but of John Fletcher he wrote:

> No age or country has ever produced a man of more fervent piety or more perfect charity; no church ever possessed a more apostolic minister. He was a man of whom Methodism may well be proud, as the most able of its defenders; and whom the Church of England may hold in remembrance, as one of the most pious and excellent of her sons.[1]

Even Voltaire thought so. The French agnostic's unfaith was threatened at least once. When asked by a friend whether he had ever met anyone like Jesus Christ he reverently answered, "I once met Fletcher of Madeley."[2]

Wesley's *Short Account of the Life and Death of the Reverend John Fletcher* was written soon after Fletcher's death in 1785. The concluding paragraph stands as the highest possible commendation of the holy character and zeal of John Fletcher.

> I was intimately acquainted with him for thirty years. I conversed with him morning, noon, and night, without the least reserve, during a journey of many hundred miles; and in all that time I never heard him speak an improper word, or saw him do an improper action. To conclude: Within fourscore years, I have known many excellent men, holy in heart and life: But one equal to him, I have not known; one so uniformly and deeply devoted to God. So unblamable a man, in every respect, I have not found either in Europe or America. Nor do I expect to find another such on this side eternity.
>
> Yet it is possible we may be such as he was. Let us, then endeavour to follow him as he followed Christ.[3]

---

1. Robert Southey, *The Life of John Wesley* (London: Hodder and Stoughton, 1882), Preface, v.
2. Quoted by W. E. Sangster, *The Pure in Heart* (London: Epworth Press, 1954).
3. *WW*, 11:364-65.

John de la Flechiere was born on September 21 in Noyon in the Swiss canton of Berne. His people were aristocrats and desired that he should become a Swiss Reformed pastor. To this end John studied at Geneva University, becoming articulate in French, Latin, German, and Greek; with a working knowledge of Hebrew also.

But John had a hankering after the military, so at 20 years of age he enlisted in the Portuguese army with the rank of captain. The war between Portugal and Brazil was on at the time and John was assigned to lead a small company. Only a series of remarkable providences kept Fletcher from traveling to Brazil. The boat on which he ought to have sailed disappeared at sea in mysterious circumstances. This, coupled with earlier deliverances from drowning impressed Fletcher that he was "a prisoner of providence."

He emigrated to England, and about 1754 became tutor to the children of Rowland Hill. In 1757 he was ordained into the ministry of the Church of England although even by then he was known to be of "Methodistical" connection.

Offered the choice of two parishes, Fletcher chose the poorer one with the smaller salary. His decision was memorable: of the richer parish he said, "Alas! Dunham will not suit me: There is too much money and too little labor!"

So Fletcher went to Madeley in Shropshire, where for 25 years, in a place no one else wanted, he served with love and patience that must impress the hardest heart.

With breathtaking diligence he cared for his populous parish; with Christlike compassion he traveled the smoky hillsides as though they were Galilee's slopes. He fed the hungry, clothed the ragged, rebuked the godless, all the while holding forth the Word of Life with a wooing and persuasive spirit. Visiting the homes of the people; preaching to help those who were present in church—and not against those who were absent; administering the sacraments; teaching the youth and consoling the dying with the solace of the gospel; dipping his pen in the ink of love and logic to write letters and books whose power still lives. What a pastor he was!

At 51 years of age, Fletcher married a longtime friend, Miss Mary Bosenquet, a godly and well-suited companion. She was saintly in attitude and disposition, utterly committed to the Lord first and thereafter to her husband. The Fletchers' married life lasted only four years, but no pastoral pair were ever more devoted to each other and to the work of God.

Fletcher, whose native tongue was French, mastered the English language so completely that his preaching was and is regarded as eloquent and powerful. His published works declare a man of philosophical ability and clarity: he wrote with devastating logic mingled with winsome serenity. Fletcher's *Works,* published in nine volumes by Joseph Benson in 1777, especially his *Checks to Antinomianism,* have stood the test of time. His exposition of *Perfect Love* stands side by side with John Wesley's *A Plain Account of Christian Perfection* as a pilot text for the understanding of Christian holiness.

Fletcher died at 55 years of age, worn out by his glorious labor but in unbelievable rapture and triumph, at 10:30 on Sunday evening, August 14, 1785. Among his final words was the hymn he loved:

> *I nothing have, I nothing am;*
> *My treasure is the bleeding Lamb,*
> *Both now and evermore!*

Is it any wonder that John Wesley's funeral sermon for Fletcher should be on Ps. 37:37: "Mark the perfect man and behold the upright: For the end of that man is peace."

Fletcher's Thought

John Fletcher became the leading frontline apologist of evangelical Arminianism and the Wesleyan message of Christian perfection. He was John Wesley's "Designated Successor," but died before his leader. His closest friend among the Methodists was, however, Charles Wesley, and the many letters that passed between them are both frank and beautiful.

Of all of John Wesley's Anglican friends and helpers no one was as useful and supportive as Fletcher of Madeley. His character adorned the doctrine of Christ, providing pragmatic proof of the actual possibilities of the grace of God in this life. His writings were splendid pieces of lucid thinking and clear expression, providing a dogmatic and apologetic of Christian perfection without peer in the defense of the Arminian-Wesleyan tradition.

Fletcher used the formularies of the Anglican Church to support his theology of entire sanctification, and to answer his chief critics who were also generally Church of England men. These Anglican formularies, however, Fletcher kept entirely subordinate to Scripture and a skillful use of church history. He was just and fair with those Calvinists who opposed the message of entire sanctification, saying that many of them were godly and pious men who were much better in character than theology.

Fletcher's great concern was that God's people should experience that Pentecostal baptism of the Holy Spirit which marks arrival in "the land of Perfection." He held that by precept and by promise the Scriptures teach freedom from all sin and complete sanctification in this life to all who diligently seek it by faith.

Wesley and Fletcher were bent and intent on declaring the great possibility of God's grace in the entire sanctification of the believing heart in this life, and that thus would the soul be entirely ready for eternity.

Wesley regarded Fletcher's *Checks to Antinomianism* as a faithful presentation and stout defense of his position both on the place of works in God's scheme of salvation, and his teaching on sanctification and perfection into which the discussion inevitably moved.

Into the *Equal Check* and the *Last Check*, Fletcher poured the riches of his thought on entire sanctification and Christian perfection. From these chiefly come our selections.

Fletcher's place in the history of the development of perfectionist theology is being more and more acknowledged and appreciated. Frank Baker draws attention to the sentiments of Asbury and Coke in this respect.[4] Outler describes Fletcher as being "the only nearly comparable theological talent" Wesley ever had.[5] Increasingly Fletcher's nomenclature of Pentecost in relation to entire sanctification receives closer attention.[6] This Fletcher nomenclature makes him extremely important with reference to the current (1980) debate on Early Methodism and the relation of Pentecostal terminology in the teaching of entire sanctification.

Timothy Smith writes:

> Fletcher developed a synthesis of the doctrine of Christian Perfection with Covenant Theology that (surprisingly to me) clearly anticipated even in the details of exposition what Charles

---

4. Frank Baker, *From Wesley to Asbury: Studies in Early American Methodism* (Durham, N.C.: Duke University Press, 1976), 166.

5. Albert C. Outler, *John Wesley* (New York: Oxford University Press, 1964), 425.

6. Cf. *Journal of the Wesleyan Theological Society*, Vol. 8, Spring 1973; Vol. 11, Spring 1976; Vol. 13, Spring 1978; Vol. 15 (1), Spring 1980.

G. Finney did, but more awkwardly because of his different view of fallen nature, and he drew the very terminology of "pentecostal" experience from Charles Wesley's early hymns and, possibly, from John Wesley's frequent use of it in reference to the general doctrine of sanctification.[7]

The Perfection of Christ's Dispensation[8]

Fletcher illustrated and supported the doctrine of Christian perfection by relating it to the three dispensations of God's revelation of himself to man, widely recognized in Christian theology. (1) Elementary revelation through nature may lead to the knowledge of God the Creator. (2) A higher revelation is given in the dispensation of Jesus Christ, the Redeemer. (3) Since Jesus' ascension, we live in the dispensation of the Holy Spirit.

Fletcher sees these three dispensations reflected in three degrees of faith in individuals today.
1. Faith in God the Father—Creator
2. Faith in God the Son—Redeemer
3. Faith in God the Holy Ghost—Sanctifier

In the following excerpts Fletcher supports his view, first from Rev. Green, a Calvinist and former assistant to George Whitefield, second from John Wesley, an Arminian.

The first quotation is selected from Rev. Green's book *Grace and Truth Vindicated:*

It appears to me, from Scripture as well as experience, that there are divers dispensations, but the same Spirit: the kingdom of heaven consists of various degrees, and different mansions. This is true, whether by the kingdom of heaven we understand the outward professors of religion and the privileges, the inward kingdom of grace, or the kingdom of glory. . . . As face answers to face in a glass, so do these respectively answer each other. Thus the outward privileges of religion from Adam to Moses were least; from Moses to Christ greater; and from Christ to the restitution of all things greatest.

Again: (1) to be a spiritual or enlightened heathen, as Socrates,

---
7. Timothy Smith, machine copy of research notes, in letter to TCM, February 8, 1979.

8. *FW*, 4:113-23.

Plato, or Cornelius before he heard Peter, is one degree or dispensation of grace. (2) To be a spiritual or enlightened Jew, and with Peter and the other disciples before the day of Pentecost to believe and acknowledge that Jesus is the Messiah, though not spiritually come, is a greater. (3) But to be a spiritual Christian, to have Christ, the exalted God-man, revealed in us from heaven, and to be sealed with the Holy Spirit of promise unto the day of the redemption of this vile body, is the last and the most perfect dispensation of grace....

It may be observed that every dispensation admits of a growth therein; and moreover, that each of them is in some sort and degree experienced by a spiritual Christian.

The second quotation is from Wesley's sermon *Salvation by Faith*[9]

My second witness is the Rev. Mr. J. Wesley, who, even in his first sermon on *Salvation by Faith,* preached near 40 years ago, clearly distinguishes Christian faith, properly so-called, or faith in Christ glorified, not only from the faith of a heathen, but also from the faith of initial Christianity, that is, "the faith which the apostles had while our Lord was upon earth."

"And first, says he, "it (the faith that saves us into the great salvation described in the second part of the sermon) is not barely the faith of a heathen. Now God requires of a heathen to believe 'that God is, that he is a rewarder of them that diligently seek him, by glorifying him as God,' and by a careful practice of moral virtue. A Greek or Roman, therefore, yea a Scythian or Indian, was without excuse if he did not believe thus much: the being and attributes of God, a future state of reward and punishment. For this is barely the faith of a heathen."

Soon after he adds: "And herein does it (this faith in Christ glorified) differ from that faith which the apostles themselves had while our Lord was upon earth, that it acknowledges the necessity and merit of his death, and the power of his resurrection."

Fletcher then continues:

The doctrine of Christian perfection is entirely founded on the privileges of the Christian dispensation in its fullness: privileges which far exceed those of the Jewish economy and the baptism of John.

---

9. *SS,* 1:37-41.

Accordingly Mr. Wesley in his sermons on Christian perfection makes the following just and scriptural distinction between those dispensations: "It may be granted, (1) That David, in the general course of his life, was one of the holiest men among the Jews. And (2) that the holiest men among the Jews did sometimes commit sin. But if you would hence infer that all Christians do, and must commit sin as long as they live; this consequence we utterly deny. It will never follow from those premises."

Those who argue thus seem never to have considered that declaration of our Lord, Matt. xi. 11, "Verily I say unto you, among them that are born of women, there hath not arisen a greater than John the Baptist. Notwithstanding, he that is least in the kingdom of heaven is greater than he." I fear indeed there are some who have imagined the kingdom of heaven here to mean the kingdom of glory: as if the Son of God had just discovered to us that the least glorified saint in heaven is greater than any man upon earth. To mention this is sufficient to refute it.

There can, therefore, no doubt be made, but the kingdom of heaven here . . . is that kingdom of God on earth, whereunto all true believers in Christ, all real Christians, belong. In these words, then, our Lord declares two things: (1) That before His coming in the flesh, among all the children of men, there had not been one greater than John the Baptist: whence it evidently follows that neither Abraham, David, nor any Jew, was greater than John. (2) That he who is least in the kingdom of God (in that kingdom which he came to set up on earth) . . . is greater than he. Not a greater prophet (as some have interpreted the word) for this is palpably false in fact: but greater in the grace of God, and the knowledge of our Lord Jesus Christ. Therefore we cannot measure the privileges of real Christians by those formerly given to the Jews. "Their ministration," or dispensation, we allow "was glorious"; but ours "exceeds in glory." So that whosoever would bring down the Christian dispensation to the Jewish standard, doth "greatly err, neither knowing the Scriptures, nor the power of God."

From these excellent quotations, therefore, it appears that you do me an honour altogether undeserved, if you suppose that I first set forth the doctrine of the dispensations. . . .

Even the apostles' creed is above the capacity of plain Christians; for that creed, the simplest of all those which the primitive Church has handed down to us, evidently distinguishes three degrees of faith: (1) Faith "in God the Father Almighty, who made heaven and earth," which is the faith of the heathens. (2) Faith in the Messiah, or "in Jesus Christ, his only begotten Son, our Lord," which is the faith of the pious Jews, of John's disciples, and of imperfect Christians, who, like the apostles before the day of Pentecost, are yet strangers to the great outpouring of the Spirit. And (3) Faith "in the Holy Ghost"; faith of the operation of God, by which Christians complete in Christ believe "according to the working of God's almighty power," and are "filled with righteousness, peace, and joy in [thus] believing."

Fletcher then turns to his treatment of degrees of faith,
1. Faith in God the Father—Creator
2. Faith in God the Son—Redeemer
3. Faith in God the Holy Ghost—Sanctifier

He closes with a comment on the ritual of confirmation in the Church of England, arguing for the need of the church for apostolic pastors full of the Spirit and power, able to lead God's people into that same fullness of the Holy Ghost.

Our church *Catechism* brings to my remembrance the ritual of confirmation. It was, it seems, originally intended to lead young believers to the fullness of the Christian dispensation, agreeably to what we read, Acts viii. 12. Peter and John went from Jerusalem to Samaria to lay their hands on the believers who had not yet been baptized with the Holy Ghost, and to "pray that they might receive him: for as yet he was fallen upon none of them, only they were baptized by Phillip in the name of the Lord Jesus."

"When the Son of man cometh, shall he find faith upon the earth?" I fear but little of the faith peculiar to his full dispensation. Most professors seem satisfied with John's baptism or Philip's baptism. The Lord raise us apostolic pastors to pray in the demonstration of the Spirit and of power. "Strengthen thy servants, O Lord, with the Holy Ghost, the Comforter; and daily increase in them thy manifold gifts of grace; the spirit of wisdom and understanding; the spirit of counsel and ghostly strength; the spirit of knowledge and true godliness; and fill them with the spirit of thy holy fear now and for ever." (Order of confirmation)

Can it be said that those in whom that prayer is not now answered live under the dispensation of Christianity perfected? Are they either established Christians or spiritual churchmen? How long shall the mystery of iniquity prevail? How long shall a pharisaic, deistical world destroy the faith of the Son, under colour of contending for faith in the Father? And how long shall a world of ... professors destroy faith in the Holy Ghost, under pretence of recommending faith in the Son? O Lord, exert Thy power. "Pour out thy Spirit upon all flesh," and give wisdom to all Thy ministers to divide the word of truth aright, and to feed Thy people according to their states and Thy dispensations.

Distinguishing the Three Degrees of Saving Faith

This remarkable essay is the conclusion to Part I of his *Equal Check*. In it Fletcher discusses the three degrees of faith in relation to the gift of the Holy Ghost. He argues from (1) New Testament teaching, (2) New Testament experience, and (3) the teachings of the catechism.

1. *New Testament Teaching*

The doctrine is expressly laid down in the New Testament. To what I have said on this head, I add here what Christ said to His disciples, "Ye believe in God, believe also in me." Here the most prejudiced may see that faith in the Father is clearly contradistinguished from faith in the Son. As for faith in the Holy Ghost, see in what manner our blessed Lord sowed the seed of it in the hearts of His disciples. "When the Comforter is come, whom I will send unto you from the Father, even the Spirit of truth, he shall testify of me. It is expedient for you that I go away: for if I go not away, the Comforter will not come unto you; but if I depart, I will send him unto you. Behold I send the promise of my Father unto you: but tarry ye in the city of Jerusalem, until ye be endued with power from on high."

HOLY SPIRIT

Nor was this great promise made to the apostles alone; for "in the last day, that great day of the feast, Jesus stood and cried, saying, If any man (not if an apostle) thirst, let him come to me and drink. He that believeth on me, as the Scripture hath said, out of his belly shall flow rivers of living water. But this he spake of the Spirit, which they that believed on Him should receive: for the Holy Ghost was not yet given (His dispensation, which is the highest of all, was not yet opened); because that Jesus was not yet glorified." And the opening of this dispensation in our hearts requires, on our part, not only faith in

Christ, but a peculiar faith in the promise of the Father; a promise . . . which has the Holy Ghost for its great object.

2. *New Testament Experience*

My second argument is taken from the experiences of those who, by the Holy Ghost, were made partakers of Christ glorified, either on the day of Pentecost, or after; and could feelingly confess Christ dying for us, and Christ living "in us, the hope of glory." In Acts ii. 5, we read of "devout men out of every nation under heaven," who were come to worship at Jerusalem. But how could they have been devout men if they had not believed in God? What could have brought them from the ends of the earth to keep a feast to the Lord, if they had been mere atheists?

And yet it is evident that through prejudice many of them rejected our Lord; putting Him to open shame and a bloody death. But when Peter preached Christ on the day of Pentecost, they at first believed on Him with a true, though not with a luminous faith. This appears from the anguish which they felt upon being charged with having "slain the Prince of life." No man in his senses can be "pricked to the heart" merely for having had a hand in the just punishment of an impostor and a blasphemer, who "makes himself equal with God." If therefore keen remorse pierced the hearts of those penitent Jews, it is evident that they looked no more upon Christ as an impostor, but already believed in Him as the true Messiah.

No sooner had they thus passed from faith in the Father to an explicit faith in the Son, but they cried out, "What shall we do?" And Peter directed them to make, by baptism, an open, solemn profession of their faith in Christ, and to believe the great promise concerning the Holy Ghost. "The promise is unto you," said he. "Be baptized every one of you, in the name of Jesus Christ, for the remission of sins; and ye (every one of you) shall receive the gift of the Holy Ghost." And upon their "gladly receiving the word," that is, upon their heartily believing the gladdening promise relating to pardon and to the Comforter; and no doubt upon their fervently praying that it might be fulfilled in them "they were all filled with the Spirit," all their hearts, overflowed with "righteousness, peace, and joy in the Holy Ghost."

St. Peter, speaking in Acts xi of a similar outpouring of the Spirit, says: "The Holy Ghost fell on them (Gentiles) as on us (Jews) at the beginning. Then remembered I the word of the Lord, how that he said, John indeed baptized with water (them that entered his dispensation), but ye shall be baptized with the Holy Ghost," when you shall enter the full dispensation of my Spirit: "God," adds Peter, "gave them the like gift as he did unto us, who believed on the Lord Jesus Christ." And when "the apostles heard these things, they glorified God" . . . by saying, "Then hath God also to the Gentiles granted repentance unto life," according to the fullness of the Christian dispensation.

That this dispensation of the Holy Ghost, this coming of Christ's spiritual kingdom with power, is attended with an uncommon degree of sanctifying grace, is acknowledged by all. The gift of tongues, which at first, on some occasions and in some persons, accompanied the baptism of the Spirit . . . was a temporary appendage, and by no means an essential part of Christ's spiritual baptism. This is evident from the merely spiritual effect which the receiving of the Holy Ghost had upon the penitent Jews, who, being "born of water and the Spirit," pressed after the apostles into the kingdom on the day of Pentecost.

"Even in the infancy of the Church," says an eminent divine, "God divided those (miraculous) gifts with a sparing hand. 'Were all (even then) prophets? Were all workers of miracles? Had all the gifts of healing? Did all speak with tongues?' No, in no wise. Perhaps not one in a thousand. Probably none but the teachers of the Church, and only some of them. It was therefore for a more excellent purpose than this that they, the brethren and apostles, 'were all filled with the Holy Ghost.' It was to give them (what none can deny to be essential to all Christians in all ages) 'the mind which was in Christ,' those holy 'fruits of the Spirit,' which whosoever hath not, is none of His; to fill them with 'love, joy, peace, long suffering, gentleness, goodness.'"

It is very remarkable, that although three thousand converts "received the gift of the Holy Ghost" on the memorable day in which Christ opened the dispensation of His Spirit, no mention is made of so much as one of them working a single miracle, or speaking with one new tongue. But the greatest and most beneficial of miracles was wrought upon them all: for "all that believed," says St. Luke, "were together; continuing daily with one accord in the temple, breaking bread from house to house, eating their meat with gladness and singleness of heart, praising God and having favour with all the people. . . . The multitude of them that believed . . . were of one heart and of one soul; neither said any of them that aught of the things which he possessed was his own; but they had all things common"; having been made perfect in one, agreeably to our Lord's deep prayer, recorded by

St. John: "neither pray I for these (my disciples) alone, but for them also who shall believe on me through their word, that they may be one; I in them (by my Spirit), and thou in me, that they may be made perfect in one."

3. *Teachings of the Catechism*

To this argument, taken from the experiences of the primitive Christians, I may add, that the doctrine of the dispensations is indirectly taught by our church even to children, in her *Catechism*, where she instructs them to say, "By the articles of my belief I learn, first, to believe in God the Father, who made me. Secondly, in God the Son, who redeemed me, and, thirdly, in God the Holy Ghost, who sanctifieth me."

These three distinctions are expressive of the three grand degrees of the faith, "whereby we inherit all the promises of God," and "are made partakers of the divine nature." They are not descriptive of faith in three gods, but of the capital manifestations of the triune God, in whose name we are baptized; and of the three great dispensations of the everlasting gospel, namely, that of the heathens, that of the Jews, and that of Spiritual Christians; the dispensation of Abraham being only a link between heathenism and Judaism; and the dispensation of John the Baptist or of Christianity begun, being only a transition between Judaism and Christianity perfected.

An Appeal to Matters of Fact and Common Sense

In 1772 Fletcher wrote:

To the principal inhabitants of the Parish of Madeley, in the County of Salop . . .

I take the liberty to present you with some of my morning meditations. May these well-meant endeavours of my pen be more acceptable to you than those of my tongue! And may you carefully read in your closets what you have inattentively heard in the church!

I appeal to the Searcher of the hearts that I had rather impart truth than receive tithes. You kindly bestow the latter upon me;

grant me, I pray, the satisfaction of seeing you favourably receive the former from.

Gentlemen,
Your affectionate minister
and obedient Servant
J. Fletcher

This is his dedication to the first edition of *An Appeal to Matters of Fact and Common Sense,* or *A Rational Demonstration of Man's Corrupt and Lost Estate.*[10] It is Fletcher's exposé of the corruption of the heart of man, the hearts of all men, and the heart of every man in the whole world through all ages from the Fall of Adam. That corruption was in Madeley in 1772—even the hearts of "the principal inhabitants"—who did not choose to attend Sunday evening service. The *Appeal* is important for an understanding of Fletcher's doctrine of sin and thus for an understanding of his teaching on full salvation.

As with Wesley we will not understand Fletcher's concept of full salvation from sin and restoration to the likeness of God unless we grasp his concept of sin and of precisely what man lost. A true understanding of our disease will assist us in grasping a sense of the magnitude of God's cure.

Fletcher and Wesley were one on this. Understand the disease if you would appreciate the cure; nevertheless to each of them the total adequacy of that cure was more important than an understanding of the genesis of the germ. But the terrible nature of the disease from which we are to be delivered assists us to more worthily appreciate and exalt the Deliverer and the means of deliverance.

John Fletcher opens his essay by claiming that the doctrine of our corruption and lost estate is "the leading principle of Christianity."

Our Lost Estate

"In every religion there is a principal truth or error, which, like the first link of a chain, necessarily draws after it all the parts with which it is essentially connected. This leading principle in Christianity, distinguished from Deism, is the doctrine of our corrupt and lost estate; for if man is not at variance with his Creator, what need of a Mediator between God and him? If he is not a depraved, undone creature, what necessity of so wonderful a Restorer and Savior as the Son of God? If he is not enslaved to sin, why is he redeemed by Jesus

---

10. *FW,* 2:5-149.

Christ? If he is not polluted, why must he be washed in the blood of that immaculate Lamb? If his soul is not disordered, what occasion is there for such a divine Physician? If he is not helpless and miserable, why is he perpetually invited to secure the assistance and consolations of the Holy Spirit? And, in a word, if he is not born in sin, why is a new birth so absolutely necessary that Christ declares, with the most solemn asseverations, without it no man can see the kingdom of God?

"This doctrine then being of such importance that genuine Christianity stands or falls with it, it may be proper to state it at large; and as this cannot be done in stronger and plainer words than those of the sacred writers, I beg leave to collect them and present the reader with a picture of our natural estate, drawn at full length by those ancient and masterly hands" (p. 9).

Fletcher, then, like his Lord, "begins with Moses and all the prophets and shews in all the Scripture" the biblical teaching on original sin. It is a rapid-fire attack and presentation. Moses, David, Ezekiel are all drawn upon, with case studies and references to Noah, Job, and others. Paul's teaching in Romans provides the cement or argument, and the words of the Lord are the peak of proof. And what is the conclusion of this biblical evidence?

"The Scriptures conclude all under sin; that there is no difference, for all have sinned and come short of the glory of God; and that the moral law denounces a general curse against its violators, that every mouth may be stopped, and all the world may become guilty before God (Rom. iii. 9-23; vi. 19; Eph. ii. 2).

"If man is thus corrupt and guilty, he must be liable to appropriate punishment. Therefore, as the prophets and apostles agree with our Lord in their dismal descriptions of his depravity, so they harmonize with him in their alarming accounts of his danger. Till he flies to the Redeemer as a condemned malefactor and secures an interest in the salvation provided for the lost, they represent him as on the brink of ruin.

"They inform us that the wrath of God is revealed from heaven, not only against some atrocious crimes, but against all unrighteousness of men (Rom. i. 18). That every transgression and disobedience shall receive a just recompense of reward (Heb. ii. 2). That the soul that sinneth shall die, because the wages of sin is death (Ezek. xviii. 4; Rom. vi. 23). They declare that they are cursed, who do err from

God's commandments; that cursed is the man whose heart departeth from the Lord; that cursed is everyone who continues not in all things which are written in the book of the law to do them; that whosoever shall keep the whole law, and yet offend in one point, is guilty of all; and that, as many as have sinned without law, shall also perish without law (Ps. cxix. 21; Jer. xvii. 5; Gal. iii. 10; James ii. 10; Rom. ii. 12).

"They entreat us to turn lest we should be found with the many in the broad way to destruction (Ezek. xviii. 23; Matt. vii. 13). They affectionately [movingly] inform us that it is a fearful thing to fall into the hands of the living God; that our God is a consuming fire to the unregenerate; that indignation and wrath, tribulation and anguish hang over every soul of man who doeth evil; that the Lord shall be revealed from heaven in flaming fire, to take vengeance on them who know Him not, and obey not the gospel; that the wicked shall be turned into hell, and all the people that forget God; that they shall be punished with eternal destruction, from the presence of the Lord, and from the glory of His power; and that they all shall be damned who believe not the truth, but have pleasure in unrighteousness (Heb. x. 31; xii. 29; Rom. ii. 9; 2 Thess. i. 8; ii. 12; Ps. ix. 17)" (p. 16).

And now through arguments universal, physical, elemental, moral, and spiritual Fletcher proceeds to shew the evidences of original sin, claiming that he is demonstrating to all persons of reason and common sense that all that the Scriptures assert about the corruption of the human heart is plainly true. Even human goodness is called to the witness stand:

"When the whole head is sick, is not the whole heart faint? Can our will, conscience, and affections run parallel to the line of duty when our understanding, imagination, memory and reason, are so much warped from original rectitude? Impossible!

"Experience, best of judges, I appeal to you. Erect your tribunal in the reader's heart and bear honest testimony of the truth of the following assertions.

"Our will, in general, is full of obstinacy; we must have our own way, right or wrong. It is inconstant, we love a thing passionately one day and tire of it the next; we form good resolutions in the morning and break them before night. It is important: when we see what is right, instead of doing it with all our might we remain as inactive as if we were bound by invisible chains. . . . We are prone to do contrary to our design those things which breed remorse and wound conscience, and we all may say,

> I do not understand my own actions. For I do not
> do what I want, but I do the very thing I hate
> *(Rom. 7:15, RSV).*

"Nor is conscience itself untainted. Alas! how slow is it to reprove in some cases: in others how apt not to do it at all. Today you may compare it to a dumb dog that does not bark at a thief: tomorrow to a snarling cur that flies alike at friend, foe, or shadow, and then madly turns upon himself and tears his own flesh.

"If conscience, the best power of the unconverted man, is so corrupt, good God! What are his affections? Almost perpetually deficient in some and excessive in others: when do they stop at the line of moderation? There is no health in us" (p. 129).

Through thirty-six arguments Fletcher presses his point until, at the conclusion of part IV he confesses that this doctrine is shocking and should drive people to self-despair:

"Yes, to a despair of being saved by their own merits and righteousness; and this is as reasonable in a sinner who comes to the Saviour as despairing to swim across is rational in a passenger that takes a ship.

"A just despair of ourselves is widely different from a despair of God's mercy and Christ's willingness to save the chief of sinners who flies to Him for mercy" (p. 129).

And now Fletcher moves to his conclusion the unspeakable advantages of acknowledging our fallen and lost estate. (Remainder directly quoted.)

No sooner is the disease rightly known, than the neglected Jesus, who is both our gracious Physician and powerful remedy, is properly valued, and ardently sought. All that thus seek, find: and all that find him, find saving health, eternal life, and heaven.

Bear your testimony with me, ye children of Abraham and of God, who see the brightness of a gospel day, and rejoice. Say, what made you first wishfully look to the hills, whence your salvation is come, and fervently desire to behold the sin-dispelling beams of the

Sun of righteousness? Was it not the deep, dismal night of our fallen nature, which you happily discovered when, awakening from the sleep of sin, you first saw the delusive dreams of life, as they appear to the dying? What was the Desire of nations to you till you felt yourselves lost sinners?

But when the storm that shook Mount Sinai overtook your careless souls, and ye saw yourselves sinking into an abyss of misery, did ye not cry out and say as the alarmed disciples, with an unknown energy of desire, Save, Lord, or we perish? And when conscious of your lost estate ye began to believe that he came to seek and to save that which was lost, how dear, how precious was he to you in all his offices. How glad were you to take guilty, weeping, Magdalene's place, and wait for a pardon at your High Priest's feet! How importunate in saying to your King, as the hapless widow, "Lord, avenge me of mine adversary," my evil heart of unbelief! How earnest, how unwearied in your applications to your Prophet for heavenly light and wisdom! The incessant prayer of blind Bartimeus was then yours, and so was the gracious answer which the Lord returned to him; you received your spiritual sight. And O! what saw you then? The sacred book unsealed! Your sins blotted out as a cloud! The glory of God shining in the face of Jesus Christ; and the kingdom of heaven open to all believers!

Then, and not till then, you could say from the heart, "This is a faithful saying, and worthy of all acceptation, that Jesus Christ came into the world to save sinners, of whom I am the chief" (1 Tim. i. 15). Then you could cry out with his first disciples, "Behold what manner of love the Father hath bestowed upon us, that we should be called the sons of God!" (1 John iii. 1). We are all the children of God by faith in Christ Jesus, "whom, having not seen, we love; in whom, though now we see him not, yet believing, we rejoice with joy unspeakable and full of glory, receiving the end of our faith, the salvation of our souls" (Gal. iii. 26; 1 Pet. i. 8). We trusted in Him, and are helped; therefore our heart danced for joy, and in our song will we praise Him (Ps. xxviii. 8). "To him that hath loved us, and washed us from our sins in his own blood, and hath made us kings and priests unto God and his Father; to him be glory and dominion for ever and ever" (Rev. i. 5).

And this will also be your triumphant song, attentive reader, if, deeply conscious of your lost estate, you spread your guilt and misery before Him who came to bind up the broken-hearted, to proclaim liberty to the captives, and the opening of the prison to them that are bound; and to comfort all that mourn, by giving them beauty for ashes, the oil of joy for mourning, and the garment of praise for the spirit of heaviness.

Nor will the blossoms of heavenly peace and joy only diffuse their divine fragrancy in your soul; all the fruits of holiness will grow together with them, to the glory of God, and the profit of mankind. We cannot be vain or despisers of others, when we see that we are all corrupted, dying shoots, of the same corrupted, dead stalk; we cannot be self-righteous when we are persuaded that the best fruit which we can naturally produce is only splendid sin, or vice, colored over with the specious appearance of virtue: we must lie prostrate in the dust when we consider the ignominious cross where our divine Surety hung, bled, and died, to ransom our guilty souls.

Once more: as soon as we can discover our spiritual blindness, we mistrust our own judgment, feel the need of instruction, modestly repair to the experienced for advice, carefully search the Scriptures, readily follow their blessed directions, and fervently pray that no false light may mislead us out of the way of salvation.

To conclude: a right knowledge that the crown is fallen from our head will make us abominate sin, the cause of our ruin, and raise in us a noble ambition of regaining our original state of blissful and glorious righteousness. It will set us upon an earnest inquiry into, and a proper use of all the means conducive to our recovery. Even the sense of our guilt will prove useful, by helping to break our obdurate hearts, by imbittering the baits of worldly vanities, and filling our souls with penitential sorrow. Before honor is humility. This happy humiliation makes way for the greatest exaltation; for thus saith the high and lofty One, that inhabiteth eternity: "I dwell in the high and holy place, with him also that is of a contrite and humble spirit, to revive the spirit of the humble, and the heart of the contrite, to fill the hungry with good things, and beautify the meek with salvation" (Isa. lvii. 15).

May the merciful and holy God, whose laws thou dost daily violate, whose word thou hourly opposest or forgettest, whose salvation thou dost every moment neglect, whose vengeance thou continually provokest, and whose cause I have attempted to plead, bear with thee and thy insults a little longer! May His infinite patience yet afford thee some means of conviction more effectual than that which is at present in thy hands! Or, shouldst thou look into this labour of love once more, may it then answer a better purpose than to aggravate thy guilt, and enhance thy condemnation, by rendering the folly of thy unbelief more glaring, and, consequently, more inexcusable! (pp. 145 ff.).

Criticism of the Doctrine of Imperfection

(From Section XIII, *The Last Check to Antinomianism*)

Like Wesley, John Fletcher faced active opposition to his teaching of Christian perfection. In this section Fletcher examines the doctrine from the standpoints of Scripture and reason. If any Christian teacher is to honestly defend a doctrine of imperfection, he must weigh carefully the force of these 14 arguments.

With passionate regard for the glory of the Lord Jesus Christ, Fletcher skillfully puts critics of perfection on the defensive.

1. *Any teaching of imperfection strikes at the doctrine of salvation by faith.*

"By grace are ye saved through faith," not only from the guilt and outward acts of sin, but also from its root and secret buds. "Not of works," says the apostle, "lest any man should (pharisaically) boast"; and may we not add, Not of *death,* lest he that had the power of death, that is, the devil, should (absurdly) boast? Does not what strikes at the doctrine of faith, and abridges the salvation which we obtain by it, equally strike at Christ's power and glory? Is it not the business of faith to receive Christ's saving word, to apprehend the power of His sanctifying Spirit, and to inherit all the great promises by which He saves His penitent, believing people from their sins?

Is it not evident that if no believers can be saved from indwelling sin through faith, we must correct the apostle's doctrine, and say, "By grace are ye saved from the remains of sin, through death"? And can unprejudiced Protestants admit so Christ-debasing, death-exalting a tenet, without giving a dangerous blow to the genuine doctrines of the reformation?

2. *The doctrine of imperfection dishonours Christ as a prophet.*

As a prophet He came to teach us to be now "meek and lowly in heart:" but the imperfect gospel of the day teaches that we must necessarily continue passionate and proud in heart till death; for pride and immoderate anger are . . . two main branches of indwelling sin. Again: my motto [text] demonstrates that He publicly taught the multitudes the doctrine of perfection. . . .

3. *Imperfection disgraces Christ as the Captain of our salvation.*

St. Paul says that our Captain furnishes us with "weapons mighty through God to the pulling down of Satan's strong holds, and to the bringing of every thought into captivity to the obedience of Christ." But our opponents represent the devil's strong hold as absolutely impregnable. No weapons of our warfare can pull down Apollyon's throne. Inbred sin shall maintain its place in man's heart, and in man's heart strike the victorious blow. . . .

4. *Imperfection pours contempt upon Him as the surety of the New Covenant.*

In this covenant God has engaged himself to deliver obedient believers "from their enemies, that they may serve him without (tormenting) fear, all the days of their lives." For how does He execute His office in this most oppressive and inveterate enemy, indwelling sin? Or if that deliverance take place only at death, how can they, in consequence of their death-freedom, "serve God without fear all the days of their lives"?

5. *Imperfection affronts Christ as a King.*

It represents the believer's heart, which is Christ's spiritual throne, as being necessarily full of indwelling sin, a spiritual rebel, who, notwithstanding the joint efforts of Christ and the believer, maintains his power against them both during the term of life . . . Does not a good king deliver his loyal subjects from oppression, and avenge them of a tyrannical adversary, when they cry to him in their distress? But does our Lord show himself such a king, if he never avenge them, nor turn the usurper, the murderer, sin, out of their breasts? . . .

6. *The teaching injures Christ as a restorer of pure, spiritual worship.*

It indirectly represents him as a pharisaic Saviour who made much ado about driving . . . harmless sheep and oxen out of His Father's material temple; but who gives full leave to Satan . . . to harbour and breed there during the term of life, the swelling toad, pride; and the hissing viper, envy; to say nothing of the greedy dog, avarice, and the filthy swine, impurity. . . .

7. *Imperfection insults Christ as a Priest.*

Our Melchisedec shed His all-cleansing blood upon the cross, and now pours His all-availing prayer before the throne; asking, that . . . we may now be "cleansed from all unrighteousness, and perfected in one." But if we assert that believers, let them be ever so faithful, can never be thus cleansed and perfected . . . till death comes to the Saviour's assistance, do we not place our Lord's cleansing blood, and powerful intercession, and of consequence His priesthood, in an unscriptural and contemptible light?

Four Comments on Paragraph 7.

(a) Perfect Christians need as much the virtue of Christ's blood, to prevent the guilt and pollution of sin from returning, as imperfect Christians want (need) it to drive that guilt and pollution away. It is not enough that the blood of the true paschal Lamb has been sprinkled upon our souls to keep off the destroyer; it must still remain there to hinder his coming back "with seven other spirits more wicked than himself." . . .

ATONEMENT

(b) The hearts of perfect Christians are cleansed and kept clean by faith; and Christian perfection means the perfection of Christian faith, whose property it is to endear Christ and His blood more and more; nothing then can be less reasonable than to say that, upon our principles, perfect believers have done with the atoning blood.

FAITH

(c) Such believers continually "overcome the accuser of the brethren through the blood of the Lamb; there is no moment, therefore, in which they can spare it: they are feeble believers who can yet dispense with its constant application; and hence it is that they continue feeble. None make so much use of Christ's blood as perfect Christians. Once it was only their medicine, which they took now and then, when a fit of fear, or a pang of guilt obliged them to it; but now it is the divine preservative which keeps off the infection of sin. Now it is the reviving cordial, which they take to prevent their "growing weary, or faint in their minds." Now it is their daily drink; now it is what they sprinkle their every thought, word, and work with. . . .

(d) Lastly: are not the saints before the throne perfectly sinless? And who are more ready than they to extol the blood and sing the song of the Lamb: "To him that loved us, and washed us from our sins in his blood, be glory"? If an angel preached to them the modern gospel, and desired them to plead for the remains of sin, lest they should lose their peculiar value for the atoning blood; would not they all suspect him to be an angel of darkness, transforming himself into an angel of light? And shall we be the dupes of the tempter, who deceives good men, that they may deceive us by a similar argument?

8. *Imperfection discredits Christ as the fulfiller of the Father's promise.*

Christ sends the indwelling, abiding Comforter in order that our joy may be full. For the Spirit never takes His constant abode as a Comforter in a heart full of indwelling sin. If He visit such a heart with His consolations, it is only "as a guest that tarrieth but a day. When he enters a soul fraught with inbred corruption, he rather acts as a reprover than as a Comforter; throwing down the tables of the spiritual money changers ... and expelling, according to the degree of our faith, whatsoever would make God's house "a den of thieves."

But instead of this, Mr. Hill's doctrine considers the heart of a believer as a "den of lions"; and represents Christ's Spirit, not as the destroyer, but as the keeper of the wild beasts, and evil tempers which dwell therein.... O, ye preachers of finished salvation, we leave it to your candour to decide which of these doctrines brings most glory to the saving name of Jesus.

9. *The doctrine of our necessary continuance in indwelling sin makes us despise God's perfect holiness.*

It naturally defeats the full effect of evangelical truths and ministerial labours; an effect which is thus described by St. Paul; "teaching every man in all wisdom, that we may present every man perfect in Christ Jesus." ... Again: "The Scripture is profitable for instruction in righteousness, that the man of God may be perfect, throughly furnished to all good works" (2 Tim. iii. 16). Now we apprehend that the perfection which thoroughly furnishes believers unto all good works, is a perfection productive of all the "good works" evangelically as well as providentially "prepared that we should walk in them" before death: because ... the Scriptures say, "Whatsoever thy hand findeth to do, do it with thy might; for there is no work nor device" in death, that is, "in the grave whither thou goest." For as the tree falls, so it lies: if it falls full of rottenness with a brood of vipers, and a neverdying worm in its hollow centre, it will continue in that very condition; and woe to the man who trusts that the pangs of death will kill the worm, or that a purgative fire will spare the rotten wood and consume the vipers!

10. *Imperfection defeats in part the end of the gospel.*

"All the law, the prophets," and the apostolic writings, "hang on these two commandments: Thou shall love the Lord thy God with all thy heart, and thy neighbour as thyself," through penitential faith in the light of thy dispensation; that is, in two words, thou shalt be evangelically perfect. Now, if we believe that it is absolutely impossible to be thus perfect by keeping these two blessed commandments in faith, we cannot but believe also that God, who requires us to keep them is defective in wisdom, equity, and goodness, by requiring us to do what is absolutely impossible....

11. *The teaching of imperfection has a necessary tendency to unnerve our deepest prayers.*

How can we pray in faith that God would help us to "do his will on earth as it is done in heaven," or that He would "cleanse the thoughts of our hearts, that we may perfectly love him and worthily magnify his holy name"; how can we, I say, ask this in faith, if we disbelieve the very possibility of having these petitions answered? And what poor encouragement has Epaphras ... "always to labour fervently for the Colossians in prayer, that they might stand perfect and complete in the will of God"; or St. Paul to wish that "the very God of peace would sanctify the Thessalonians wholly, and that their whole spirit, and soul, and body, might be preserved blameless," if these requests could not be granted before death?

12. *This false teaching soothes lukewarm, unholy professors.*

It encourages them to sit quietly ... under the baneful influence of their unbelief and indwelling sin; nothing being more pleasing to the carnal mind than this siren song: "It is absolutely impossible that the thoughts of your hearts should be cleansed in this life. God himself does not expect that you should be purified from all iniquity on this side the grave. It is proper that sin should dwell in your hearts by unbelief, to endear Christ to you, and so to work together for your good."

The preachers of Christian imperfection tell their hearers that nobody can be cleansed from heart sin before death. This new doctrine makes them secretly trust in a death purgatory, and hinders them from pleading in faith the promises of full sanctification before death stares them in the face....

13. *Preachers of Christian imperfection discourage willing seekers.*

... Nothing is more proper to damp their ardour than such a speech as this: "You may strive against your corruptions and evil tempers as long as you please: but you shall never get rid of them; the Jericho within is impregnable: it is fenced up to heaven, and garrisoned by the tall, invincible, immortal sons of Anak: so strong are these adversaries, that the twelve apostles, with the help of Christ and the Holy Ghost, could never turn one of them out of his post....

14. *To conclude*

The modish doctrine of Christian imperfection and death purgatory is so contrived that carnal men will always prefer the purgatory of the Calvinists to that of the Papists. For the Papists prescribe I know not how many cups of divine wrath and dire vengeance, which are to be drunk by the souls of the believers who die half purged....

But our opponents have found out a way to deliver half-hearted believers out of all fear in this respect. Such believers need not "utterly abolish the body of sin" in this world. The inbred man of sin not only may, but he shall live as long as we do. You will possibly ask, "What is to become of this sinful guest? Shall he take us to hell, or shall we take him to heaven? If he cannot die in this world, will Christ destroy him in the next?" No; here Christ is almost left out of the question.... Our indwelling adversary is not destroyed by the brightness of the Redeemer's spiritual appearing, but by the gloom of the appearance of death. Thus they have found another Jesus: another Saviour from sin. The king of terrors comes to the assistance of Jesus' sanctifying grace, and instantaneously delivers the carnal believer from indwelling pride, unbelief, covetousness, peevishness, uncharitableness, love of the world and inordinate affection.

Fletcher brings this section of his *Last Check* to a conclusion by offering a number of arguments against the necessity of continuance in sin and sin's necessary continuance in regenerate persons. We select three remarks on what he describes as the absurdity of such a proposition.

1. Mark the inconsistency of our opponents.... They blame us for making use of Christ's law, to spur believers: and yet they ... do not blush to preach openly the law of sin to believers; insisting that its working in their members is necessary to "make them long for the land of promise, as for the land of rest, and for the speedy possession of that great good which God has laid up for them." We are heretics for preaching the law of Christ, the law of liberty; they who preach the law of sin, the law of bondage, are orthodox, and engross to themselves the glorious title of gospel ministers!

2. *How absurd is it to prop up the throne of indwelling sin* in the hearts of believers, that its tyrannical law may make them long for

heaven! Did not Christ long for heaven without indwelling sin? Do not the holiest believers, who are most free from indwelling sin, long most for the beatific vision? And do we not see that fallen believers, who are most filled with indwelling sin, are most apt to be lovers of sin and the world "more than lovers of God" and heaven? . . .

3. *Is not indwelling sin a clog,* rather than a spur, to the heavenly racers? If sin be of such service to us, to make us run the career of holy longing after heavenly rest, why does the apostle exhort us to "set aside every weight and the sin which does so easily beset us"? If we want a spur to make us mend our pace, need we keep the spur of indwelling sin? Is it not more likely to spur us to hell than to heaven? . . .

If you ask, What are the sinless spurs of believers? We reply, all the toils, infirmities, and pains of our weary, decaying, mortal bodies: all the troubles, disappointments, and sorrows, which arise as naturally out of our present circumstances as sparks do out of fire: a share of the dreadful temptations which harassed Christ in the wilderness: and frequent tastes of the bitter cup which made him sweat blood in the garden, and cry out on Calvary. . . . Surely indwelling sin was never one of Christ's afflictions. . . .

I grant that all true believers have not these thorns in the flesh, and feel not the spurs . . . but, at the best of times, they have, or should have David's affliction, "My eyes run down with water because men keep not thy law"; they have, or should have Jeremiah's grief, "O that my head were waters, and mine eyes a fountain of tears, that I might weep, day and night, for the desolation of Jerusalem, or for the slain of the daughter of God's people!" . . .

To suppose, I say, that we must keep the sting of indwelling sin on these accounts is absurd.

The Operations of the Holy Spirit

(From *The Portrait of Paul*)[11]

It was John Fletcher's intention that his work on Paul should be published in his native country, hence it was written in French and brought close to completion during his search for health in Mayon

---

11. *FW,* 5:420-23.

1779-80. He returned to Madeley still a very sick man, and the manuscript was laid to one side. It was found bit by bit by Mrs. Fletcher after John's death. Only the industrious skill of the translator let it loose into the English-speaking world in a style and manner of which its author would have approved.

The translator, Mr. Gilpin, wrote in his introduction: "It contains Mr. Fletcher's last and best thoughts upon some of the most important subjects that can occupy the human mind."

The specimens here given present Fletcher's teaching on entire sanctification and Christian perfection. He is counseling us on understanding and recognizing the gifts of the Spirit, while emphasizing the inward operation of that Spirit. Fletcher's note is strongly ethical: inward and outward holiness is his message—holiness of heart, mind, and life. Only that which produces and promotes a holy walk with God will Fletcher regard as the operation of the indwelling Spirit. To him the pouring out of the Pentecostal Spirit was "in order to sanctification," it was "to shed the love of God abroad" in human hearts, to make intercession for believers who "know not how to pray" as they ought, and to give full and perfect assurance that nothing and no one can separate us from the love of Christ! Fletcher writes:

> To reject the Son of God manifested in the Spirit, as worldly Christians are universally observed to do, is a crime of equal magnitude with that of the Jews, who rejected Christ manifested in the flesh. Nevertheless, in vain has the Apostle Paul informed us, that "Jesus Christ is a priest forever, after the order of Melchisedic" (Heb. vii. 17); "The same yesterday, today, and forever" (Heb. xiii. 8). In vain has John the Baptist declared that "he shall baptize us with the Holy Ghost and with fire" (Matt. iii. 11). In vain has Christ himself made a gracious offer of this baptism to all nations (Matt. xxviii. 19). In spite of all these declarations, our incredulity still seeks out some plausible reason for rejecting the dispensation of the Spirit....

The Gift of the Holy Spirit[12]

That the extraordinary gifts of the Holy Spirit were peculiarly necessary to the apostles, and that they were actually put in possession of such gifts, we readily allow. But, at the same time, we consider those gifts as entirely distinct from the Spirit itself. When the Spirit of grace

---

12. Headings provided by the editor.

takes the full possession of a particular person, he may, if the edification of the Church requires it, bestow upon that person an extraordinary gift in an instantaneous manner: as the prince, who honours any subject with an important commission, invests him with sufficient power for the execution of such commission.

But the presents of a prince do not always demonstrate his actual presence; since it is very possible for a prince to lodge with one of his subjects, upon whom he has conferred no inestimable favour; while he makes a magnificent present to another, whom he has never condescended to visit in person. Thus the Holy Spirit descended upon Mary the mother of Jesus, together with several other holy women, as well as upon the apostles, with whom they continued in earnest supplication and prayer: nevertheless, it does not appear that any one of them received even the gift of tongues.

On the other hand, we are well assured that many persons who never received the Spirit of holiness, were yet outwardly distinguished by several extraordinary gifts of the Holy Ghost. The first king of Israel gave rise to that memorable proverb, "Is Saul also among the prophets?" (1 Sam. x. 12). Jonah, though he possessed neither the faith nor the charity which are common to many Christians of this age, was yet commissioned to visit Nineveh with an extraordinary message from heaven. And we are informed that Judas was endued with the power of performing miracles, as Balaam had before been honoured with the gift of prophecy. But, notwithstanding these external appearances, we may rest assured that neither Saul, nor Balaam, nor Judas had fully experienced that happy estate which the meanest among the primitive Christians were permitted to enjoy.

When, therefore, we assert that every sincere believer becomes a "temple of the Holy Ghost" (1 Cor. vi. 19); it is not to be understood by such expression that they have received the power of working miracles: since in this sense St. Paul himself was not always replenished with the Spirit. But it should rather be understood, that the same Spirit of humility, of zeal, of faith, and of charity, which so eminently dwelt in Christ, continually flows from Him to the meanest of His spiritual members, as the sap is known to pass from the trunk of a vine into the least of its branches (John xv. 5).

The Old and New Testament sufficiently prove that the special influences of the Spirit are to be universally experienced by the faithful in every age. Isaiah promises this invaluable blessing to those who are athirst for God (Isa. xliv. 3). Ezekiel announces the same blessing in a variety of passages to all those who enjoy the privileges of the new covenant. The Prophet Joel more directly promises the extraordinary effusion of the Holy Spirit to "the young and the old (among the people of God); to their sons and their daughters, their servants and their handmaids" (Joel ii. 28-29).

John the Baptist expressly repeats the same promise to all those who partake of his inferior baptism (Luke iii. 16). Our Lord invites every believer freely to come and receive the long-expected blessing (John vii. 37, 39). St. Peter unreservedly offers it to the truly penitent (Acts ii. 38); and St. Paul everywhere declares that it is the common privilege of Christians to "be filled with the Spirit" (Eph. v. 18; 1 Cor. vi. 19). Nay, he even intimates that the name of Christian should be refused to those who have not received the promise of the Father (Rom. viii. 9). These few passages abundantly testify, how strangely those professors deceive themselves, who confidently affirm that the Holy Spirit was promised to the apostles alone.

Why the Holy Spirit Was Given at Pentecost

Revelation is no sooner admitted, but reason itself confirms the very truth for which we contend. Why was the Holy Spirit to be poured out in its full measure upon the first followers of Christ? If in order to their sanctification, have we less need of holiness than the apostles had? If it was to shed abroad in their hearts the love of God, is that love less necessary for us than for them? If to make intercession for them with groanings which cannot be uttered, were the apostles supposed to stand in greater need of such intercession than all other men?

Lastly, if the Holy Ghost was given that believers might be enabled to cry, "Who shall separate us from the love of Christ? Shall tribulation, persecution, or death? O death, where is thy sting? O grave, where is thy victory? Thanks be to God, who giveth us the victory through our Lord Jesus Christ"—if so, then it should seem that the apostles alone were called to suffer and die in a manner so perfectly worthy of Christians.

The Gift Is for Every Christian

The more we meditate upon the Scriptures of truth, the more we shall be convinced that the experience of real Christians, and the reason of natural men coincide with that sacred volume in demonstrating that the grand promise of a Comforter must respect every sincere believer, as well as the first disciples of Jesus. To reject, then, this precious gift, is to trample under foot the pearl of great price, and to despise the Redeemer himself in that spiritual appearance which is of far greater importance to us than His outward manifestation in Judea. Farther: to insinuate among Christians that the promise of Christ's spiritual coming is no longer in force, is to enervate the glorious gospel of God, and to maintain in His Church that detestable lukewarmness which will ultimately prove the ground of its condemnation. It is to surpass the Jews in their obstinate rejection of our only Lord and Saviour.

There was no need, says the incredulous Jew, that the Messiah should suffer and die for our sins: nor is there any need, says the carnal Christian, that the Saviour should come in a spiritual manner to reign in my heart. The one destroys the body, the other the soul of Christianity; and both are equally strangers to the renovating power of the gospel.

Let Everything Be Done Decently and in Order

In every Christian country there are not wanting such as have rendered the dispensation of that Spirit contemptible by their ridiculous and impious pretensions. . . . The enthusiast extinguishes the torch of reason that he may have opportunity to display in its room the vain flashes of his own pretended inspirations. The "enlightened Christian" entertains a just respect for reason following it as the surest guide, so far as it is able to direct him in the search of truth; and whenever he implores a superior light, it is merely to supply the defects of reason.

The one destroys the clear sense of Scripture language, that a way may be made for his own particular manifestations: the other refers every thing "to the law, and to the testimony," fully satisfied, that if high pretenders . . . "speak not according to this word, it is because there is no light in them" (Isa. viii. 20). The former flatters himself, that while the means are neglected, the end may be obtained, presuming that God will illuminate him in a miraculous manner without the help of prayer, study, meditations, sermons, or sacraments. The latter unpresumingly expects the succours of grace in a constant use of the appointed means; and, conscious that "the Holy Scriptures are able to make him wise unto salvation" (2 Tim. iii. 15), he takes them for the subject of his frequent meditation, the ground of his prayers, and the grand rule of his conduct.

The fanatic imagines himself independent of superior powers both in Church and state. The real Christian, a constant friend to truth and order, looking upon himself as the servant of all, not only acknowledges the respect due to his superiors, but is ready to give them an account either of his faith or his conduct, with meekness and submission; he is anxious to have his principles supported by appeals to the reason and conscience of his adversaries, as well as by the testimony of revelation.

The fanatic pays but little regard to the inestimable grace of charity. Like Simon, the sorcerer, he aspires after the extraordinary gifts of the Spirit, and seduced by a vain imagination, forsakes the substance that he may pursue the shadow. The true Christian, without despising the most inconsiderable spiritual gifts, implores only those which may assist him in the discharge of his several duties, and peculiarly that of charity, which is to be ranked as high above the performance of miracles, as miracles are to be esteemed above the tricks of jugglers.

The fanatic conceives himself to be animated by the Spirit of God, when his body is agitated by a rapid motion of the animal spirits, excited by the sallies of an overheated imagination.... The judicious Christian detests this enthusiasm, which, covering religion with a veil of delusion and frenzy, renders it contemptible in the eyes of those who are ever ready to treat devotion as fanaticism.

It appears, from the writings of St. Paul, that enthusiasm had once risen to so great a height in the Corinthian church that the communion was polluted by the members of that church, and its public services thrown into the utmost disorder. Now, if the apostle had himself been an enthusiast, he would have seen these disorders without regret; or had he been like the ministers of the present day, he would have rejoiced at the pretext afforded him by the fanatical Corinthians, for turning into ridicule devotion and zeal, the power of prayer, and the gift of exhortation.

But, equally attached both to order and zeal, he wrote to them in the following terms: "I would that ye all spake with tongues, but rather that ye prophesied: for he that prophesieth edifieth the church. Forasmuch, then, as ye are zealous of spiritual gifts, seek that ye may excel to the edifying of the Church. Brethren, be not children in understanding, but men. Ye may all prophesy, that all may learn, and all may be comforted." And observe this, that "the spirits of the prophets are subject to the prophets: for God is not the author of confusion, but of peace, as in all churches of the saints. If any man think himself to be a prophet, or spiritual, let him acknowledge that the things I write unto you are the commandments of the Lord. Let all things be done decently, and in order" (1 Cor. xiv).

It is by adopting the admirable method of this apostle, that the good pastor endeavours to root up the tares of enthusiasm, without injuring the invaluable grain of devotion.

Here it may, perhaps, be inquired, "If particular manifestations of the Spirit are admitted, how is it possible to shut the door against dangerous illusions? Would it be wiser entirely to reject the dispensation of the Spirit, while it is attended with so many difficulties? And would it not make for the happiness of the church were every member of it to rest contented with having all the Holy Scriptures explained according to the best rules of reason and criticism?"

We answer, By no means. Bad money, indeed, is frequently put into our hands; but is it necessary on this account to obstruct the free course of that which is intrinsically good? And would it be reasonable to refuse a sovereign prince the right of coining for the state lest that coin should be counterfeited or defaced? As in society, after warning the public of their danger, we content ourselves with apprehending the man who attempts to impose upon us in this way; so we may rest fully satisfied with adopting the same mode of conduct in regard to the Church of God.

The More Excellent Way

Let it be here observed, that the operations of the Holy Spirit upon the hearts of believers are to be distinguished from the effects of enthusiasm in the imagination of visionaries, just as readily as we distinguish health from sickness, wisdom from folly, and truth from falsehood. The believers of Rome could say, "The Spirit itself beareth witness with our spirit, that we are the children of God" (Rom. viii. 16). "By one Spirit are we baptized," say the Corinthians, "and have been all made to drink into one Spirit" (1 Cor. xii. 13). And St. Paul could testify, that many of the Ephesians were "sealed by the Holy Spirit of God, unto the day of redemption" (Eph. iv. 30).

"These were all enthusiasts," says a modern doctor, "unless they could restore sight to the blind, raise the dead from their grave, and fluently converse in a variety of languages which they had never taken the trouble to study."

No, insinuates the apostle, you forget the essential for the accessory, and found your system upon false suppositions. "Are all workers of miracles? Have all the gifts of healing? Do all speak with tongues?" There must, then, be some more indubitable method of distinguishing those whose bodies are become temples of the Holy Ghost; and "I show unto you this more excellent way" (1 Cor. xii. 29-31).

What was meant by this excellent way may be satisfactorily discovered by an attentive perusal of the following chapter (1 Cor. 13). Here the apostle would have the examination to turn, not upon the gift of prophecy, and much less that of languages, but essentially upon all the characters of charity.

* * *

The Heart of Fletcher's Teaching

Volume six of the *Works of John Fletcher* is the most important of all his writings on Christian perfection, or entire sanctification. In the lengthy earlier sections, Fletcher argues eloquently that the best way of opposing the opposers of Christian perfection as being attainable in this life is to set the teaching in a proper light. With much Scripture and vigorous reasoning he covers ground-arguments often employed by Wesley, and quotes Wesley frequently. He also uses some Anglican writers to support his views. These men he describes as good Calvinists such as Bishop Hopkins and Archbishop Leighton whom Fletcher maintains "plead for the same perfection we maintain."[13]

He then endeavors to remove four objections to his concept of sin and Christian maturity (Pars. 1-4), and 10 more in the succeeding chapters with 11 probing questions put to the critics. Sections IV through X bring the apostles Paul and John as witnesses to and preachers of entire sanctification. Section XI shows how much of the opposition to perfection is due to a misunderstanding of the Old

---
13. See opening paragraphs of sec. II.

Testament. In section XIII, he dwells on the absurdity of supposing that death or a fictitious purgatory will be effective in cleansing the soul from all sin.

In two sections, XIX and XX, quoted below, we find Fletcher's positive instructions under the appealing title, "To Earnest Seekers After Entire Sanctification." These sections from *The Last Check to Antinomianism* are in Fletcher's own words, howbeit paragraphed and abbreviated for plainer reading.

To Earnest Seekers After Entire Sanctification

Faith's Foundation in Scripture

Your regard for Scripture and reason, and your desire to answer the end of God's predestination by "being conformed to the image of his Son," have happily kept or reclaimed you from antinomianism.

You see the absolute necessity of personally "fulfilling the law of Christ"; your bosom glows with desire to "perfect holiness in the fear of God"; and, far from blushing to be called "perfectionists," ye openly assert that a perfect faith, productive of perfect love of God and man is the pearl of great price for which you are determined to sell all; and which, next to Christ, you will seek early and late as the one thing needful for your spiritual and eternal welfare. Some directions, therefore, about the manner of seeking this pearl cannot but be acceptable to you if they are scriptural and rational; and such, I humbly trust, are those which follow:

First, if ye would attain an evangelically sinless perfection, let your full assent to the truth of that deep doctrine firmly stand upon the evangelical foundation of a precept and a promise. A precept without a promise would not sufficiently animate you; nor would a promise without a precept properly bind you; but a divine precept and a divine promise form an unshaken foundation. Let, then, your faith deliberately rest her right foot upon these precepts:

"Hear, O Israel: Thou shalt love the Lord thy God with all thine heart, and with all thy soul, and with all thy might" (Deut. vi. 4-5).

"Thou shalt not hate thy neighbour in thy heart: thou shalt in any wise rebuke thy neighbour, and not suffer sin upon him. Thou shalt not avenge, nor bear any grudge against the children of thy people; but thou shalt love thy neighbour as thyself: I am the Lord. Ye shall keep My statutes" (Lev. xix. 17-19).

"And now, Israel, what doth the Lord thy God require of thee, but to fear the Lord thy God, to walk in His ways, and to love Him, and to serve the Lord thy God with all thy heart and with all thy soul, to keep the commandments of the Lord thy God, and His statutes, which I command thee this day for thy good." "Circumcise therefore the foreskin of your heart, and be no more stiff-necked" (Deut. x. 12, 16).

"Serve God with a perfect heart and a willing mind; for the Lord searcheth all hearts, and understandeth the imaginations of the thoughts" (1 Chron. xxviii. 9).

Should unbelief suggest that these are only Old Testament injunctions, trample upon the false suggestion, and rest the same foot of your faith upon the following New Testament precepts:

"Think not that I am come to destroy the law, or the prophets." I say unto you, "Love your enemies, bless them that curse you, do good to them that hate you, that ye may be the children of your Father who is in heaven." "For if ye love them which love you, what reward have ye? Do not even the publicans the same?" "Be ye therefore perfect, even as your Father which is in heaven is perfect" (Matt. v. 17, 44).

"If thou wilt enter into life, keep the commandments" (Matt. xix. 17).

"Bear ye one another's burdens, and so fulfill the law of Christ" (Gal. vi. 2).

"This is my commandment, that ye love one another, as I have loved you" (John xv. 12).

"He that loveth another hath fulfilled the law. For this, Thou shalt not commit adultery," "Thou shalt not covet; and if there be any other commandment, it is briefly comprehended in this saying, Thou shalt love thy neighbour as thyself." "Love worketh no ill to his neighbour: therefore love is the fulfilling of the law" (Rom. xiii. 8-10).

"This commandment we have from him, that he who loves God, love his brother also" (1 John iv. 21).

"If ye fulfill the royal law, Thou shalt love thy neighbour as thyself, ye do well. But if ye have respect to persons ye commit sin, and are convinced of the law as transgressors" (James ii. 8-9).

"Circumcision is nothing, uncircumcision is nothing," comparatively speaking; but, under Christ, "the keeping of the commandments of God" is the one thing needful (1 Cor. vii. 19).

"For the end of the commandment is charity out of a pure heart, and of a good conscience, and of faith unfeigned" (1 Tim. i. 5).

"Though I have all faith . . . and have not charity, I am nothing" (1 Cor. xiii. 2).

"Whosoever shall keep the whole law" of liberty, "and yet offend in one point" (in uncharitable respect of persons), "he is guilty of all." "So speak ye, and so do, as they that shall be judged by the law of liberty," which requires perfect love, and therefore makes no allowance for the least degree of uncharitableness (James ii. 10, 12).

When the right foot of your faith stands on these evangelical precepts and proclamations, lest she should stagger for want of a promise every way adequate to such weighty commandments, let her place her left foot upon the following promises, which are extracted from the Old Testament:

"The Lord thy God will circumcise thine heart, and the heart of thy seed, to love the Lord thy God with all thine heart, and with all thy soul, that thou mayest live" (Deut. xxx. 6).

"Come now, and let us reason together, says the Lord: though your sins be as scarlet, they shall be as white as snow; though they be red like crimson, they shall be as wool" (Isa. 1. 18). That this promise chiefly refers to sanctification is evident (1) From the verses which immediately precede it: "Make you clean," etc. "Cease to do evil, learn to do well," etc. And (2) From the verses which immediately follow it: "If ye be willing and obedient, ye shall eat the good of the land; but if ye refuse and rebel," or disobey, "ye shall be devoured with the sword."

Again: "I will give them an heart to know me, that I am the Lord: and they shall be my people, and I will be their God," in a new and peculiar manner: "for they shall return unto me with their whole heart." "This shall be the covenant that I will make with the house of Israel: After those days, says the Lord, I will put my law in their inward parts, and write it in their hearts; and will be their God, and they shall be my people" (Jer. xxiv. 7; xxxi. 33).

"Then will I sprinkle clean water upon you, and ye shall be clean: from all your filthiness, and from all your idols, will I cleanse you. A new heart also will I give you, and a new spirit will I put within you: and I will put away the heart of stone out of your flesh, and I will give you an heart of flesh. And I will put my Spirit within you, and cause you to walk in my statutes, and ye shall keep my judgments, and do them" (Ezek. xxxii. 25-27).

And let nobody suppose that the promises of the "circumcision," the "cleansing," the "clean water," and the "Spirit" which are mentioned in these scriptures, suppose that these glorious promises belong only to the Jews; for their full accomplishment peculiarly refers to the Christian dispensation. Besides, if sprinkling of the Spirit were sufficient under the Jewish dispensation to raise the plant of Jewish perfection in Jewish believers, how much more will the revelation of "the horn of our salvation," and the outpourings of the Spirit, raise the plant of Christian perfection in faithful Christian believers!

That this revelation of Christ in the Spirit, as well as in the flesh, these effusions of the water of life, these baptisms of fire which burn up the chaff of sin, throughly purge God's spiritual floor, save us from all our uncleannesses, and deliver us from all our enemies; that these blessing, I say, are peculiarly promised to Christians, is demonstratable by the following cloud of New Testament declarations and promises:

SCRIPTURAL

"Blessed be the Lord God of Israel; for he hath raised up an horn of salvation for us, as he spake by the mouth of his holy prophets, that we, being delivered out of the hands of our enemies, might serve him without" unbelieving "fear," that is, with perfect love, "in holiness and righteousness before him, all the days of our life" (Luke i. 68-75).

"Blessed are the poor in Spirit," who "thirst after righteousness: for they shall be filled" (Matt. v. 3, 6).

"If thou knowest the gift of God," etc., "thou wouldest have asked of him, and he would have given thee living water." "And the water that I shall give him, shall be in him a well of water springing up to everlasting life" (John iv. 10, 14).

"Jesus stood and cried, saying, If any man thirst, let him come to me and drink. He that believeth on me," when I shall have ascended up on high, to receive gifts for men, "out of his belly shall flow rivers of living water," to cleanse his soul, and to keep it clean. "But this he spake of the Spirit, which they that believe on him shall receive; for the Holy Ghost was not yet given" in such a manner as to raise the plant of Christian perfection, "because Jesus was not yet glorified," and his spiritual dispensation was not yet fully opened (John vii. 37).

Always rest the doctrine of Christian perfection on the scriptural foundation, and it will stand as firm as revelation itself.

The Promise of the Father

It is allowed on all sides, that the dispensation of John the Baptist exceeded that of the other prophets, because it immediately introduced the gospel of Christ, and because John was not only appointed to "preach the baptism of repentance," but also clearly to point out the very person of Christ, and to "give knowledge of salvation to God's people by the remission of sins" (Luke i. 77). And, nevertheless, John only promised the blessing of the Spirit, which Christ bestowed when He had received gifts for men. "I indeed," said John, "baptize you with water unto repentance: but he that cometh after me is mightier than I; he shall baptize you with the Holy Ghost, and with fire" (Matt. iii. 11). Such is the importance of this promise, that it is particularly recorded not only by the three other evangelists (see Mark i. 8, Luke iii. 16, and John i. 26), but also by our Lord himself, who said, just before His ascension, "John truly baptized with water; but ye shall be baptized with the Holy Ghost not many days hence" (Acts i. 5).

So capital is this promise of the Spirit's stronger influences to raise the rare plant of Christian perfection, that when our Lord speaks of this promise he emphatically calls it "the promise of the Father"; because it shines among the other promises of the gospel of Christ as the moon does among the stars. Thus, Acts i. 4: "Wait," says He, "for the promise of the Father, which ye have heard of me." And again, Luke xxiv. 49: "Behold, I send the promise of my Father upon you."

Agreeably to this, St. Peter says, "Jesus being by the right hand of God exalted, and having received of the Father the promise of the Holy Ghost, he has shed forth this." He has begun abundantly to fulfill "that which was spoken by the prophet Joel." "And it shall come to pass in the last days, saith God, that I will pour out" (bestow a more abundant measure) "of my Spirit upon all flesh." "Therefore repent and be baptized," that is, make an open profession of your faith, "in the name of the Lord Jesus for the remission of sins; and ye shall receive the gift of the Holy Ghost. For the promise is unto you, and to your children, and to as many as the Lord our God shall call" to enjoy the full blessings of the Christian dispensation (Acts ii. 16-17, 33-39).

This promise, when it is received in its fullness, is undoubtedly the greatest of all the "exceedingly great and precious promises" which "are given to us, that by them you might be partakers of the divine nature," that is, of pure love and unmixed holiness (2 Pet. i. 4). Have, therefore, a peculiar eye to it, and to these deep words of our Lord: "I will ask the Father, and he shall give you another Comforter, that he may abide with you forever; even the Spirit of truth" and power, "whom the world knows not," etc.: "but ye know him; for he remaineth with you, and shall be in you." "At that

HOLY SPIRIT

day ye shall know that I am in my Father, and you in me, and I in you." For "if any man," that is, any believer, "love me, he will keep my words: and my Father will love him, and we will come to him, and make our abode with him" (John xiv. 16-23). "Which," says Mr. Wesley, in his note on the place, "implies such a large manifestation of the divine presence and love, that the former, in justification, is as nothing in comparison of it."

Agreeable to this, Wesley expresses himself thus in another of his publications: "These virtues"—meekness, humility, and true resignation to God—"are the only wedding garment; they are the lamps and vessels well furnished with oil. There is nothing that will do instead of them; they must have their full and perfect work in you, or the soul can never be delivered from its fallen, wrathful state. There is no possibility of salvation but in this. And when the Lamb of God has brought forth His own meekness in our souls, then are our lamps trimmed, and our virgin hearts made ready for the marriage-feast. This marriage-feast signifies the entrance into the highest state of union that can be between God and the soul in this life. This birthday of the Spirit of love in our souls, whenever we attain, will feast our souls with such peace and joy in God as will blot out the remembrance of everything that we called peace or joy before."

And now a fuller answer is given to His deep request. Take it in the words of the inspired historian: "And when they had prayed, the place was shaken where they were assembled together; and they were" once more "filled with the Holy Ghost, and they spake the word with" still greater "boldness. And the multitude of them that believed were of one heart, and of one soul: neither said any of them, that ought of the things which he possessed was his own; but they had all things common," etc. "And great grace was upon them all" (Acts iv. 31-33). Who does not see in this account a specimen of that grace which our Lord had asked for believers, when He had prayed that His disciples, and those who would believe on Him through their word, might be "perfected in one"!

The Cleansing Baptism

Upon the whole, it is, I think, undeniable, from the four first chapters of the Acts, that a peculiar power of the Spirit is bestowed upon believers, under the gospel of Christ; that this power, through faith on our part, can operate the most sudden and surprising change in our souls; and that, when our faith shall fully embrace the promise of full sanctification, or of a complete circumcision of the heart in the Spirit, the Holy Ghost, who kindled so much love on the day of Pentecost, that all the primitive believers loved, or seemed to love, each other perfectly, will not fail to help us to "love one another" without sinful self-seeking; and as soon as we do so "God dwelleth in us, and His love is perfected in us" (1 John iv. 12; John xiv. 23).

Should you ask, "How many baptisms, or effusions of the sanctifying Spirit, are necessary to cleanse a believer from all sin, and to kindle his soul into perfect love?" I reply, that the effect of a sanctifying truth depending upon the ardour of the faith with which that truth is embraced, and upon the power of the Spirit with which it is applied, I should betray a want of modesty if I brought the operations of the Holy Ghost, and the energy of faith, under a rule which is not expressly laid down in Scripture. If you asked your physician how many doses of physic you must take before all the crudities of your stomach can be carried off, and your appetite perfectly restored, he would probably answer you, that this depends upon the nature of those crudities, the strength of the medicine, and the manner in which your constitution will allow it to operate; and that, in general, you must repeat the dose, as you can bear, till the remedy has fully answered the desired end.

I return a similar answer: If one powerful baptism of the Spirit "seals you unto the day of redemption," and "cleanses you from all" moral "filthiness," so much the better. If two or more are necessary, the Lord can repeat them; "His arm is not shortened that it cannot save," nor is His promise of the Spirit stinted: He says, in general, "Whosoever will, let him come and take of the water of life freely." "If you, being evil know how to give good gifts to your children, how much more will your heavenly Father," who is goodness itself, "give his Holy" sanctifying "Spirit to them that ask him"?

I may, however, venture to say, in general, that, before we can rank among perfect Christians, we must receive so much of the truth and Spirit of Christ by faith, as to have the pure love of God and man shed abroad in our hearts by the Holy Ghost given unto us, and to be filled with the meek and lowly mind which was in Christ. And if one outpouring of the Spirit, one bright manifestation of the sanctifying truth, so empties us of self as to fill us with the mind of Christ, and with pure love, we are undoubtedly Christians, in the full sense of the word.

Understand the Promise

When you firmly assent to the truth of the precepts and promises on which the doctrine of Christian perfection is founded, when you understand the meaning of these scriptures—"Sanctify them through thy truth: thy word is truth"; "I will send the Comforter" (the Spirit of truth and holiness) "unto you"; "God has chosen you to" eternal "salvation, through sanctification of the Spirit, and belief of the truth"—when you see that the way to Christian perfection is by the word of the gospel of Christ, by faith, and by the Spirit of God; in the next place, get tolerably clear ideas of this perfection.

This is absolutely necessary. If you will hit a mark, you must know where it is. Some people aim at Christian perfection, but, mistaking it for angelical perfection, they shoot above the mark, miss it and then peevishly give up their hopes. Others place the mark as much too low: hence it is that you hear them profess to have attained Christian perfection, when they have not so much as attained the mental serenity of a philosopher, or the candour of a good-natured, conscientious heathen. In the preceding pages, if I am not mistaken, the mark is fixed according to the rules of scriptural moderation: it is not placed so high as to make you despair of hitting it, if you do your best in an evangelical manner; nor yet so low as to allow you to presume that you can reach it without exerting all your abilities to the uttermost, in due subordination to the efficacy of Jesus' blood, and the Spirit's sanctifying influences.

Grace, Freewill, and Faith

Should we ask, "Which is the way to Christian perfection? Shall we go to it by internal stillness or shall we press after it by an internal wrestling, according to these commands of Christ?—'Strive to enter in at the strait gate.' 'The kingdom of heaven suffereth violence, and the violence taketh it by force,'" etc.

According to the evangelical balance of the doctrine of free grace and free will, I answer, that the way to perfection is by the due combination of prevenient, assisting free grace, and of submissive, assisting free will. Antinomian stillness, therefore, which says that free grace must do all, is not the way; pharisaic activity, which will do most, if not all, is not the way. Join these two partial systems, allowing free grace the lead and high pre-eminence which it so justly claims, and you have the balance of the two gospel axioms; you do justice to the doctrines of mercy and justice, of free grace and free will, of divine faithfulness, in keeping the covenant of grace, and of human faithfulness in laying hold on that covenant and keeping within its bounds: in short, you have the scripture method of waiting upon God, which Mr. Wesley describes thus—

> *Restless, resign'd, for God I wait;*
> *For God my vehement soul stand still.*

Would you then wait aright for Christian perfection? Impartially admit the two gospel axioms and faithfully reduce them to practice. In order to do this let them meet in your hearts as the two legs of a pair of compasses meet in the rivet which makes them one compound instrument. Let your faith in the doctrine of free grace, and Christ's righteousness, fix your mind upon God as you fix one of the legs of your compass immovably in the centre of the circle which you are about to draw; so shall you stand still according to the first texts produced in the question. And then, let your faith in the doctrine of free will and evangelical obedience make you steadily run the circle of duty around that firm centre; so shall you imitate the other leg of the compass, which evenly moves around the centre, and traces the circumference of a perfect circle. By this activity subordinate to grace, you will "take the kingdom of heaven by force."

When your heart quietly rests in God by faith, as it steadily acts the part of a passive receiver, it resembles the leg of the compass which rests in the centre of the circle; and then the poet's expressions, "restless, resigned," describe its fixedness in God. But when your heart swiftly moves towards God by faith, as it acts the part of a diligent worker; when your ardent soul follows after God as a thirsty deer does after the water-brooks, it may be compared to the leg of the compass which traces the circumference of the circle: and then these words of the poet, "restless" and "vehement," properly belong to it.

To go on steadily to perfection, you must therefore endeavour steadily to believe, according to the doctrine of the first gospel axiom; and, as there is opportunity, diligently to work, according to the doctrine of the second. And the moment your faith is steadily fixed in God as in your centre, and your obedience swiftly moves in the circle of duty from the rest and power which you find in that centre you have attained, you are made perfect in the faith which works by love. Your humble faith saves you from pharisaism, your obedient love from antinomianism; and both (quiet trust and earnest seeking), in due subordination to Christ, constitute you a just man made perfect according to dispensation.

Instantaneous and Gradual

Another question has also puzzled many sincere perfectionists; and the solution of it may remove a considerable hindrance out of your way. "Is Christian perfection," say they, "to be instantaneously brought down to us? or are we gradually to grow up to it? Shall we be made perfect in love by a habit of holiness suddenly infused into us, or by acts of feeble faith and feeble love so frequently repeated as to become strong, habitual, and evangelically natural to us, according to the well-known maxim, 'A strong habit is a second nature'?"

IN A MOMENT

Both ways are good; and instances of some believers gradually perfected, and of others, comparatively speaking, instantaneously fixed in perfect love, might probably be produced, if we were acquainted with the experiences of all those who have died in a state of evangelical perfection. It may be with the root of sin as it is with its fruit: some souls parley many years before they can be persuaded to give up all their outward sins; and others part with them as it were instantaneously. You may compare the former to those besieged towns which make a long resistance, or to those mothers who go through a tedious and lingering labour; and the latter resemble those fortresses which are surprised and carried by storm, or those women who are delivered almost as soon as labour comes upon them.

Travellers inform us that vegetation is so quick and powerful in some warm climates, that the seeds of some vegetables yield a salad in less than twenty-four hours. Should a northern philosopher say "Impossible!" and should an English gardener exclaim against such mushroom salad, they would only expose their prejudices, as do those who decry instantaneous justification, or mock at the possibility of the instantaneous destruction of indwelling sin.

For where is the absurdity of this doctrine? If the light of a candle brought into a dark room can instantly expel the darkness; and if, upon opening your shutters at noon, your gloomy apartment can instantaneously be filled with meridian light, why might not the instantaneous rending of the veil of unbelief, or the sudden and full opening of the eye of your faith instantly fill your soul with the light of truth and the fire of love; supposing the Sun of Righteousness arise upon you with powerful healing in His wings? May not the Sanctifier descend upon your waiting soul as quickly as the Spirit descended upon our Lord at His baptism? Did it not descend as a dove, that is, with the soft motion of a dove, which swiftly shoots down, and instantly lights?

A good man said once, with truth, "A mote is little when it is compared to the sun; but I am far less before God." Alluding to this comparison, I ask, If the sun could instantly kindle a mote; nay, if a burning glass can in a moment calcine a bone and turn a stone to lime; and if the dim flame of a candle can in the twinkling of an eye destroy the flying insect which comes within its sphere, how unscriptural and irrational is it to suppose that when God fully baptizes a soul with His sanctifying Spirit with the celestial fire of His love, He cannot in an instant destroy the man of sin, burn up the chaff of corruption, melt the heart of stone into a heart of flesh, and kindle the believing soul into pure seraphic love!

An Illustration

An appeal to parallel cases may throw some light upon the question which I answer. If you were sick, and asked of God the perfect recovery of your health, how would you look for it? Would you expect to have your strength restored you at once, without any external means, as the lepers who were instantly cleansed; and as the paralytic, who, at our Lord's word, took up the bed on which he lay, and carried it away upon his shoulders; or, by using some external means of a slower operation, as the ten lepers did, who were more gradually cleansed "as they went to show themselves to the priests"? or, as King Hezekiah, whose gradual but equally sure recovery was owing to God's blessing upon the poultice of figs prescribed by Isaiah? Again: if you were blind, and besought the Lord to give you perfect human sight, how should you wait for it? as Bartimeus, whose eyes were opened in an instant? or, as the man who received his sight by degrees? At first he saw nothing; by and by he confusedly discovered the objects before him; but at last he "saw all things clearly"! Would ye not earnestly wait for an answer to your prayers now; leaving to divine wisdom the particular manner of your recovery? And why should ye not go and do likewise, with respect to the dreadful disorder which we call indwelling sin?

Now Is the Time

If your hearts are "purified by faith," as the Scripture expressly testifies; if the faith which peculiarly purifies the heart of Christians is a faith in "the promise of the Father," which promise was made by the Son, and directly points at a peculiar effusion of the Holy Ghost, the purifier of spirits; if we may believe in a moment; and if God may, in

IN A MOMENT a moment, seal our sanctifying faith by sending us a fullness of His sanctifying Spirit; if this, I say, is the case, does it not follow that to deny the possibility of the instantaneous destruction of sin is to deny, contrary to Scripture and matter of fact, that we can make an instantaneous act of faith in the sanctifying promise of the Father, and in the all-cleansing blood of the Son, and that God can seal that act by the instantaneous operation of His Spirit? which St. Paul calls "the circumcision of the heart in" or by "the Spirit," according to the Lord's ancient promise: "I will circumcise thy heart, to love the Lord thy God with all thy heart." Where is the absurdity of believing that the God of all grace can now give an answer to the poet's rational and evangelical request?

> *Open my faith's interior eye;*
> *Display Thy glory from above,*
> *And sinful self shall sink and die,*
> *Lost in astonishment and love.*

If a momentary display of Christ's bodily glory could in an instant turn Saul, the blaspheming, bloody persecutor, into Paul, the praying, gentle apostle; if a sudden sight of Christ's hands could, in a moment, root up from Thomas's heart that detestable resolution, "I will not believe," and produce that deep confession of faith, "My Lord and my God!" what cannot the display of Christ's spiritual glory operate in a believing soul, to which He manifests himself, "according to that power whereby he is able to subdue all things to himself"? Again: if Christ's body could, in an instant, become so glorious on the mount, that His very garments partook of the sudden irradiation, became not only free from every spot, but also "white as the light," "shining exceeding white as snow, so as no fuller on earth can white them"; and if our bodies "shall be changed," if "this corruptible shall put on incorruption, and this mortal shall put on immortality, in a moment, in the twinkling of an eye, at the last trump," why may not our believing souls, when they fully submit to God's terms, be fully changed, fully "turned from the power" of Satan unto God?

When the Holy Ghost says, "Now is the day of salvation," does He exclude salvation from heart iniquity? If Christ now deserves fully the name of Jesus, because He fully "saves His" believing "people from their sins"; and if now the gospel trumpet sounds and sinners arise from the dead, why should we not, upon the performance of the conditions, be changed in a moment from indwelling sin to indwelling holiness? Why should we not pass in the twinkling of an eye, or in a short time, from indwelling death to indwelling life?

This is not all: if you deny the possibility of a quick destruction of indwelling sin, you send to hell, or to some unscriptural purgatory, not only the dying thief but also all those martyrs who suddenly embraced the Christian faith and were instantly put to death by bloody persecutors for confessing the faith which they had just embraced. And if you allow that God may "cut His work short in righteousness" in such a case, why not in other cases? why not especially, when a believer confesses his indwelling sin, ardently prays that Christ would, and sincerely believes that Christ can now "cleanse from all unrighteousness"?

The Work of Faith

On the other hand, to deny that imperfect believers may and do gradually grow in grace, and, of course, that the remains of their sins may and do gradually decay, is as absurd as to deny that God waters the earth by daily dews, as well as by thunder showers: it is as ridiculous as to assert that nobody is carried off by lingering disorders, but that all men die suddenly, or a few hours after they are taken ill.

I use these comparisons about death to throw some light upon the question which I solve, and not to insinuate that the decay and destruction of sin run parallel to the decay and dissolution of the body, and that, of course, sin must end with our bodily life. . . .

From the preceding observations it appears that believers generally go to Christian perfection, as the disciples went to the other side of the Sea of Galilee. They toiled some time very hard, and with little success; but, after they had "rowed about twenty-five or thirty furlongs, they saw Jesus walking on the sea. He said to them, It is I; be not afraid. Then they willingly received him into the ship; and immediately the ship was at the land whither they went." Just so we toil till our faith discovers Christ in the promise, and welcomes Him into our hearts; and such is the effect of His presence, that immediately we arrive at the land of perfection. Or, to use another illustration, God says to believers, "Go to the Canaan of perfect love. Arise; why do ye tarry? Wash away the remains of sin . . . believing, "on the name of the Lord." And if they submit to the obedience of faith, He deals with them as He did with the evangelist Philip, to whom He had said, "Arise, and go towards the south"; for, when they arise and run, as Philip did, the Spirit of the Lord takes them, as He did the evangelist, and they are found in the New Jerusalem, as "Philip was found at Azotus." They dwell in God, or in perfect love; and God, or perfect love, dwells in them.

Hence it follows, that the most evangelical method of following after the perfection to which we are immediately called is that of seeking it now, by endeavouring fully to lay hold on the promise of that perfection, through faith, just as if our repeated acts of obedience could never help us forward. But, in the meantime, we should do the work of faith, and repeat our internal and external acts of obedience with as much earnestness and faithfulness, according to our present power, as if we were sure to enter into rest merely by a diligent use of our talents and the faithful exertion of the powers which divine grace has bestowed upon us. If we do not attend to the first of these directions, we shall seek to be sanctified by works, like the Pharisees; and if we disregard the second, we shall slide into solifidian sloth with the antinomians (i.e., faith without effort).

AVAILABLE NOW

Balance Free Grace and Free Will

"Much diligence," says á Kempis, "is necessary to him that will profit much. If he who firmly purposeth often faileth, what shall he do who seldom or feebly purposeth anything?" But, I say it again and again, do not lean upon your free will and good purposes, so as to encroach upon the glorious pre-eminence of free grace. Let the first gospel axiom stand invariably in its honourable place. Lay your principal stress upon divine mercy; and say, with the good man whom I have just quoted, "Help me, O Lord God, in Thy holy service, and grant that I may now this day begin perfectly."

GRACE

In following this method, ye will do the two gospel axioms justice: ye will so depend upon God's free grace, as not to fall into pharisaic running; and ye will so exert your own free will, as not to slide into antinomian sloth. Your course lies exactly between these rocks. To pass these perilous straits, your resolving heart must acquire a heavenly polarity. Through the spiritually magnetic touch of Christ, "the corner-stone," your soul must learn to point towards faith and works, or, if you please, towards a due submission to free grace, and a due exertion of free will, as the opposite ends of the needle of a compass point towards the north and the south.

In—But Not of Yourselves

From this direction flows the following advice: Resolve to be perfect in yourselves, but not of yourselves. The antinomians boast that they are perfect only in their heavenly Representative. Christ was filled with perfect humility and love; they are perfect in His person; they need not a perfection of humble love in themselves. To avoid their error, be perfect in yourselves, and not in another; let your perfection of humility and love be inherent; let it dwell in you. Let it fill your own heart, and influence your own life; so shall you avoid the delusion of the virgins, who give you to understand that the oil of their perfection is all contained in that sacred vessel which formerly hung on the cross, and therefore their salvation is finished; they have oil enough in that rich vessel.

They say Christ's heart was perfect; and theirs may safely remain imperfect, yea, full of indwelling sin, till death, the messenger of the Bridegroom, come to cleanse them, and fill them with perfect love at the midnight cry. Delusive hope! Can anything be more absurd than for a sapless, dry branch to fancy that it has sap and moisture enough in the vine which it cumbers? or for an impenitent adulterer to boast that "in the Lord he has" chastity and "righteousness"? Where did Christ ever say, "Have salt in another"? Does He not say, "Take heed that ye be not deceived"? "Have salt in yourselves"? (Mark ix. 50). Does He not impute the destruction of stony ground hearers to their "not having root in themselves"? (Matt. xiii. 21) . . .

But is it enough to have the root in ourselves? Must we not also have "the fruit"; yea, "be filled with the fruits of righteousness"? (Phil. i.11). Is it not St. Peter's doctrine, where he says "If these things be in you, and abound, ye shall neither be barren, nor unfruitful in the knowledge of Christ"? (2 Peter i. 8). And is it not that of David where he prays, "Create in me a clean heart"? Away, then, with all antinomian refinements; and if, with St. Paul, you will have salvation and rejoicing in yourselves, and not in another, make sure of holiness and perfection in yourselves, and not in another.

But while you endeavour to avoid the snare of the antinomians, do not run into that of the Pharisees, who will have their perfection of themselves, and therefore, by their own unevangelical efforts, self-concerted willings, and self-prescribed runnings, endeavour to "raise sparks of their own kindling," and to "warm themselves by" their own painted fires, and fruitless agitations. Feel your impotence. Own that "no man hath quickened" and perfected "his own soul." Be contented to invite, receive, and welcome the light of life; but never attempt to reform or to engross it.

It is your duty to wait for the morning light, and to rejoice when it visits you: but if you grow so self-conceited as to say, "I will create a sun: let there be light"; or if, when the light visits your eyes, you say, "I will bear a stock of light; I will so fill my eyes with light today, that tomorrow I shall almost be able to do my work without the sun, or at least without a constant dependence upon its beams," would ye not betray a species of self-deifying idolatry and satanical pride?

If our Lord himself, as "Son of Man," would not have one grain of human goodness of himself; if He said, "Why callest thou me good? there is none good," self-good, or good of himself, "but God," who can wonder enough at those proud Christians, who claim some self-originated goodness, boasting of what they have received, as if they had not received it; or using what they have received, without a humble sense of their constant dependence upon their heavenly Benefactor.

To avoid this horrible delusion of the Pharisees, learn to see, to feel, and to acknowledge that of the Father, through the Son, and by the Holy Ghost, are all your . . . "lights" and "perfections." And while the Lord says, "From me is thy fruit found" (Hosea xiv. 8), bow at His footstool, and gratefully reply, "Of thy fulness have all we received, and grace for grace" (John i. 16). For Thou art "the Father of lights, from whom cometh every good and perfect gift" (James i. 17). "Of Thee, and through Thee, and to Thee, are all things. To Thee," therefore, "be the glory for ever. Amen" (Rom. xi. 36).

Repentance in Believing

You will have this humble and thankful disposition if you let your repentance cast deeper roots. For if Christian perfection implies a forsaking all inward as well as outward sin; and if true repentance is a grace "whereby we forsake," it follows, that to attain Christian perfection we must so follow our Lord's evangelical precept, "Repent, for the kingdom of heaven is at hand," as to leave no sin, no bosom sin, no heart sin, no indwelling sin, unrepented of, and, of consequence, unforsaken. He whose heart is still full of indwelling sin has no more truly repented of indwelling sin, than the man whose mouth is still defiled with filthy talking and jesting has truly repented of his ribaldry. The deeper our sorrow for and destestation of indwelling sin, the more penitently do we confess "the plague of our heart"; and when we properly confess it, we inherit the blessing promised in these words: "If we confess our sins, he is faithful and just to forgive us our sins, and to cleanse us from all unrighteousness."

To promote this deep repentance, consider how many spiritual evils still haunt your breast. Look into the inward chamber of imagery, where assuming self-love, surrounded by a multitude of vain thoughts, foolish desires, and wild imaginations keep her court. Grieve that your heart which should be all flesh is yet partly stone; that your soul which should be only a temple for the Holy Ghost is yet so frequently turned into a den of thieves . . . for the remains of envy, jealousy, fretfulness, anger, pride, impatience, peevishness, formality, sloth, prejudice, bigotry, carnal confidence, evil shame, self-righteousness, tormenting fears, uncharitable suspicions, idolatrous love, and I know not how many of the evils which form the retinue of hypocrisy and unbelief.

CARNALITY

Through grace, detect these evils by a close attention to what passes in your own heart at all times, but especially in an hour of temptation. By frequent and deep confession, drag out all these abominations; these sins, which would not have Christ to reign alone over you, bring before Him, place them in the light of His countenance; if you do it in faith, that light and the warmth of His love will kill them, as the light and heat of the sun kill the worms which a plough turns up to the open air in a dry summer's day.

Nor plead that you can do nothing; for by the help of Christ who is always ready to assist the helpless, ye can solemnly say upon your knees what ye have probably said in an airy manner to your professing friends. If ye ever acknowledge to them that your heart is deceitful, prone to leave undone what ye ought to do and ready to do what ye ought to leave undone, ye can undoubtedly make the same confession to God. Complain to Him who can help you, as ye have done to those who cannot; lament as you are able, the darkness of your mind, the stiffness of your will, the dullness or exorbitancy of your affections; and importunately entreat the God of all grace to renew a right spirit within you. If ye "sorrow after this godly sort, what carefulness" will be "wrought in you, what indignation, what fear, what vehement desire, what zeal, yea, what revenge"! Ye will then sing in faith what the imperfectionists sing in unbelief:

> O how I hate those lusts of mine
> That crucified my God;

> *Those sins that pierced and nail'd His flesh*
> *Fast to the fatal wood!*
>
> *Yes, my Redeemer, they shall die,*
> *My heart hath so decreed;*
> *Nor will I spare those guilty things*
> *That made my Savior bleed.*
>
> *Whilst with a melting, broken heart,*
> *My murder'd Lord I view,*
> *I'll raise revenge against my sins,*
> *And slay the murderers too.*

Self-denial

Closely connected with this deep repentance is the practice of a judicious, universal [complete] self-denial. "If thou wilt be perfect," says our Lord, "deny thyself, take up thy cross daily and follow me." "He that loveth father or mother"—much more, he that loveth praise, pleasure, or money "more than me, is not worthy of me." Nay, "whosoever will save his life, shall lose it; and whosoever will lose it for my sake, shall find it." Many desire to live and reign with Christ, but few choose to suffer and die with Him. However, as the way of the cross leads to heaven, it undoubtedly leads to Christian perfection.

To avoid the cross, therefore, or to decline drinking the cup of vinegar and gall which God permits your friends or foes to mix for you . . . it is to refuse a medicine which is kindly prepared to restore your health and appetite; in a word, it is to renounce the Physician who heals all our infirmities, when we take His bitter draughts, submit to have our abscesses opened by His sharp lancet, and yield to have our proud flesh wasted away by His painful caustics. Our Lord "was made" a "perfect" Saviour "through sufferings"; and we may be made perfect Christians in the same manner; we may be called to suffer, till all that which we have brought out of spiritual Egypt is consumed . . . on a shameful Calvary.

Should this lot be reserved for us, let us not imitate our Lord's imperfect disciples, who "forsook Him, and fled"; but let us stand the fiery trial till all our fetters are melted, and all our dross is purged away. Fire is of a purgative nature; it separates the dross from the gold; and the fiercer it is, the more quick and powerful is its operation. "He that is left in Zion, and he that remaineth in Jerusalem, shall be called holy," etc., "when the Lord shall have washed away the filth of the daughters of Zion, and shall have purged the blood of Jerusalem, by the spirit of judgment and by the spirit of burning" (Isa. iv. 3-4). "I will bring the third part through the fire," saith the Lord, "and will refine them as silver is refined, and will try them as gold is tried: they shall call on my name, and I will hear them; I will say, It is my people; and they shall say, The Lord is my God" (Zech. xiii. 9).

Therefore, if the Lord should suffer the best men in His camp, or the strongest men in Satan's army, to cast you into a furnace of fiery temptations, come not out of it till you are called; "let patience have its perfect work"; meekly keep your trying station till your heart is disengaged from all that is earthly, and till the sense of God's preserving power kindles in you such a faith in His omnipotent love as few experimentally know but they . . . who can say with St. Paul, "We are killed all the day long; and, behold, we live!"

"Temptations," says á Kempis, "are often very profitable to men, though they be troublesome and grievous: for in them a man is humbled, purified, and instructed. All the saints have passed through, and profited by many tribulations; and they that could not bear temptations became reprobates and fell away." "My son," adds the author of Ecclesiasticus (ii. 1-5), "if thou come to serve the Lord," in temptation, "set thy heart aright; constantly endure; and make not haste in the time of trouble. Whatever is brought upon thee take cheerfully, and be patient when thou art changed to a low estate. For gold is tried and purified "in the fire, and acceptable men in the furnace of adversity." And therefore, says St. James, "Blessed is the man that endureth temptation; for, when he is tried," if he stands the fiery trial, "he shall receive the crown of life, which the Lord has promised to them that love him" with the love which "endureth" temptation and "all things," that is, with perfect love (James i. 12). Patiently endure, then, when God "for a season, if need be," will suffer you to "be in heaviness, through manifold temptation." By this means, "the trial of your faith, being much more precious than that of gold which perisheth, though it be tried in the fire, will be found unto praise, and honour, and glory, at the appearing of Jesus Christ" (1 Pet. i. 7).

Faith and Cleansing

Deep repentance is good, gospel self-denial is excellent, and the degree of patient resignation in trials is of unspeakable use to attain the perfection of love; but as "faith" immediately "works by love," it is of far more immediate use to purify the soul. Hence it is that Christ, the prophets, and the apostles so strongly insist upon faith; assuring us, that "if we will not believe, we shall not be established"; that "if we will believe, we shall see the glory of God," "we shall be saved," and the "rivers of living water shall flow from our inmost souls"; that "our hearts are purified by faith"; and that "we are saved by grace through faith." They tell us that "Christ gave himself for the Church, that He might sanctify and cleanse it by the Word, that He might present it to himself a glorious Church, not having spot, or wrinkle or any such thing," but that it should be "holy and without blemish."

Now, if believers are to be cleansed and made without blemish by the Word, which testifies of the all-atoning blood, and the love of the Spirit, it is evident that they are to be sanctified by faith; for faith, or believing, has as necessary a reference to the Word as eating has to food. For the same reason the apostle observes, that "they who believe enter into rest"; that, "a promise being given us to enter in," we should "take care not to fall short of it through unbelief"; that we ought to take warning by the Israelites, who "could not enter" into the land of promise "through unbelief"; that we are "filled with all joy and peace in believing"; and that "Christ is able to save to the uttermost them who come unto God through him."

Now, "coming," in the scripture language, is another expression for believing: "He that cometh to God," says the apostle, "must believe." Hence it appears that faith is peculiarly necessary to those who will be "saved to the uttermost," especially a firm faith in the capital promise of the gospel of Christ, the promise of "the Spirit of holiness," from the Father, through the Son. For "how shall they call on him in whom they have not believed?" Or how can they earnestly plead the truth, and steadily wait for the performance, of a promise in which they have no faith? This doctrine of faith is supported by Peter's words: "God, who knoweth the hearts" of penitent believers, "bare them witness, giving them the Holy Ghost, and purifying their hearts by faith" (Acts xv. 8-9). For the same Spirit of faith which initially purifies our hearts when we cordially believe the pardoning love of God, completely cleanses them, when we fully believe His sanctifying love.

Twofold Operation of the Spirit

The doctrine of this address exactly coincides with Mr. Wesley's, with this verbal difference only, that what he calls "faith implying a twofold operation of the Spirit, productive of spiritual light and supernatural sight," I have called "faith apprehending a sanctifying baptism, or outpouring, of the Spirit."

HOLY SPIRIT

I have already pointed out the close connection there is between an act of faith which fully apprehends the sanctifying promise of the Father, and power of the Spirit of Christ which makes an end of moral corruption by forcing the lingering man of sin instantaneously to breathe out his last.

The Promise and Prayer

Social prayer is closely connected with faith in the capital promise of the sanctifying Spirit; and therefore I earnestly recommend that means of grace (group prayer) where it can be had, as being eminently conducive to the attaining of Christian perfection. When many believing hearts are lifted up, and wrestle with God in prayer together, you may compare them to many diligent hands which work a large machine. At such times, particularly, the fountains of the great deep are broken up, the windows of heaven are opened, and "rivers of living water flow" from the heart of obedient believers.

SEEKING AND FINDING

> *In Christ when brethren join,*
>   *And follow after peace,*
> *The fellowship divine*
>   *He promises to bless,*
> *His chiefest graces to bestow*
> *Where two or three are met below.*
>
> *Where unity takes place,*
>   *The joys of heaven we prove;*
> *This is the gospel grace,*
>   *The unction from above,*
> *The Spirit on all believers shed,*
> *Descending swift from Christ their Head.*

Accordingly we read that, when God powerfully opened the kingdom of the Holy Ghost on the day of Pentecost, the disciples "were all with one accord in one place." And when He confirmed that kingdom, they were lifting up "their voice to God with one accord" (Acts ii. 1 and iv. 24). Thus also the believers at Samaria were filled with the Holy Ghost, the Sanctifier, while Peter and John prayed with them, and laid hands upon them.

Faith Expectant

Up, then, thou sincere expectant of God's kingdom; let thy humble, ardent, free will meet prevenient, sanctifying, free grace . . . as the Father of the faithful met the Lord, when He "appeared to him in the plain of Mamre." "Abraham lifted up his eyes, and looked; and, lo, three men stood by him"; so does free grace, if I may venture upon the allusion, invite itself to thy tent; nay, it is now with thee in its creating, redeeming, and sanctifying influences. "And when he saw them, he ran to meet them from the tent door, and bowed himself towards the ground": "Go, and do likewise"; if thou seest any beauty in the humbling "grace of our Lord Jesus Christ," in the sanctifying "love of God," and in the comfortable "fellowship of the Holy Ghost," let thy free will "run to meet them, and bow itself toward the ground." Oh for a speedy going out of thy tent, thy sinful self! Oh for a race of desire in the way of faith! Oh for incessant prostrations! Oh for a meek and deep bowing of thyself before thy divine Deliverer!

And Abraham said, "My Lord, if now I have found favour in thy sight, pass not away, I pray thee, from thy servant." Oh for the humble pressing of a loving faith! Oh for the faith which stopped the sun when God avenged His people in the days of Joshua! Oh for the important faith of the two disciples who detained Christ when "He made as though he would have gone farther! They constrained him, saying, Abide with us; for it is towards evening, and the day is far spent. And he went in to tarry with them." He soon, indeed, "vanished out of their" bodily "sight," because they were not called always to enjoy His bodily presence.

Far from promising them that blessing, He had said, "It is expedient for you that I go away: for if I go not away, the Comforter will not come unto you, but if I depart, I will send Him unto you, that He may abide with you forever. He dwelleth with you, and shall be in you." This promise is still "yea and amen in Christ": only plead it according to the preceding directions; and as sure as our Lord is "the true and faithful Witness," so sure will "the God of hope" and love soon "fill you with all joy and peace, that ye may abound in" pure love, as well as in confirmed "hope, through the power of the Holy Ghost." Then shall you have an indisputable right to join the believers who sing . . .

> *Many are we now, and one,*
> *We who Jesus have put on:*
> *There is neither bond nor free,*
> *Male nor female, Lord, in Thee*

> *Love, like death, hath all destroy'd,*
> *Render'd all distinctions void;*
> *Names and sects, and parties fall;*
> *Thou, O Christ, art All in all.*

In the meantime you may sing:

> *O for a heart to praise my God,*
>   *A heart from sin set free,*
> *A heart that's sprinkled with the blood*
>   *So freely spilt for me;*
>
> *A heart resign'd, submissive, meek,*
>   *My dear Redeemer's throne,*
> *Where only Christ is heard to speak,*
>   *Where Jesus reigns alone;*
>
> *An humble, lowly, contrite heart,*
>   *Believing, true, and clean,*
> *Which neither life nor death can part*
>   *From Him that dwells within;*
>
> *A heart in every thought renew'd,*
>   *And fill'd with love divine,*
> *Perfect, and right, and pure, and good,*
>   *A copy, Lord, of Thine!*
>
> *My heart, Thou knowest, can never rest*
>   *Till Thou create my peace;*
> *Till, of mine Eden repossess'd,*
>   *From self and sin I cease.*
>
> *Thy nature, gracious Lord, impart;*
>   *Come quickly from above;*
> *Write Thy new name upon my heart,*
>   *Thy new, best name of love.*

Here is undoubtedly an evangelical prayer for the love which restores the soul to a state of sinless rest and evangelical perfection. . . . Nor can ye wait for an answer to the prayer contained in the preceding hymn in a more scriptural manner, than by pleading the "promise of the Father" in such words as these

Love divine, all loves excelling,
   Joy of heaven, to earth come down;
Fix in us Thine humble dwelling,
   All Thy faithful mercies crown:
Jesus, Thou art all compassion,
   Pure, unbounded love Thou art!
Visit us with Thy salvation,
   Enter every trembling heart.

Breathe, O breathe Thy loving Spirit
   Into every troubled breast!
Let us all in Thee inherit,
   Let us find Thy promised rest:[14]
Take away the power of sinning,[15]
   Alpha and Omega be,
End of faith as its beginning,
   Set our hearts at liberty.

Come, Almighty, to deliver,
   Let us all Thy life receive;
Suddenly return, and never,
   Never more Thy temples leave:
Thee we would be always blessing,
   Serve Thee as Thine hosts above;
Pray, and praise Thee without ceasing,
   Glory in Thy precious love.

Finish then Thy new creation,
   Pure, unspotted, may we be;
Let us see Thy great salvation,
   Perfectly restored by Thee:
Changed from glory into glory,
   Till in heaven we take our place;
Till we cast our crowns before Thee,
   Lost in wonder, love, and praise.

---

14. Fletcher comments here: "Mr. Wesley says 'second rest,' because an imperfect believer enjoys a first, inferior rest; if he did not, he would be no believer."

15. "Is not this expression too strong?" asks Fletcher. "Would it not be better to soften it as Mr. Hill has done, by saying 'Take away the love of (or the bent to) sinning'? Can God take away from us our 'power of sinning,' without taking away our power for free obedience?"

Faith Fortified

Hear this encouraging gospel: "Ask, and you shall have; seek, and you shall find; knock, and it shall be opened unto you. For every one that asketh, receiveth; and he that seeketh, findeth; and to him that knocketh, it shall be opened." "If any of you" believers "lack wisdom" (indwelling wisdom; "Christ, the wisdom and the power of God, dwelling in his heart by faith"), "let him ask of God who giveth to all men, and upbraideth not; and it shall be given him. But let him ask" as a believer, "in faith, nothing wavering; for he that wavereth is like a wave of the sea, driven with the wind and tossed; for let not that man think that he shall receive the thing which he" thus "asketh." But "whatsoever things ye desire when ye pray, believe that ye receive them, and ye shall have them." For "all things" commanded and promised "are possible to him that believeth."

He who has commanded us to be "perfect" in love "as our heavenly Father is perfect," and He who has promised "speedily to avenge his elect, who cry to him night and day," He will speedily avenge you of your grand adversary, indwelling sin. He will say to you, "According **CLEANSING** to thy faith be it done unto thee; for he is able to do far exceeding abundantly above all that we can ask or think"; and "of his fulness" we may "all receive grace for grace"; we may all witness the gracious fulfillment of all the promises which He has graciously made, "that by them we might be partakers of the divine nature," so far as it can be communicated to mortals in this world.

You see that, with men what you look for is impossible: but show yourselves believers; take God into the account and you will soon experience that "with God all things are possible." Nor forget the omnipotent Advocate whom you have with Him. Behold, He lifts His once pierced hands, and says, "Father, sanctify them through thy" loving "truth, that they may be perfected in one"; and, showing to you the fountain of atoning blood, and purifying water, whence flow the streams which cleanse and gladden the heart of believers, He says, "Hitherto ye have asked nothing in my name; whatsoever ye shall ask the Father in my name, he will give it to you." "Ask," then, "that your joy may be full."

I Believe!

In the meantime, be not afraid to "give glory to God" by believing in hope against hope. Stagger not at the "promise" of the Father and the Son, "through unbelief"; but trust the power and faithfulness of your Creator and Redeemer, till your Sanctifier has fixed His abode in your heart. Wait at mercy's door, as the lame beggar did at the "beautiful gate of the temple. Peter, fastening his eyes upon him, with John, said, Look on us: and he gave heed to them, expecting to receive something of them." Do so too; give heed to the Father in the Son, who says, "look unto me, and be ye saved." Expect to receive the "one thing" now "needful" for you—a fullness of the sanctifying Spirit; and though your patience may be tried, it shall not be disappointed. The faith and power which, at Peter's word, gave the poor cripple a perfect soundness in the presence of all the wondering Jews, will give you at Christ's word a perfect soundness of heart, in the presence of all your adversaries.

FINDING

> *Faith, mighty faith the promise sees,*
> *And looks to that alone,*
> *Laughs at impossibilities*
> *And cries, It shall be done.*
>
> *Faith asks impossibilities;*
> *Impossibilities are given:*
> *And I, even I, from sin shall cease,*
> *Shall live on earth the life of heaven.*

The Victory Is the Lord's

Ye have not sung the preceding hymns in vain, O ye men of God, who have mixed faith with your evangelical requests. The God who says, "Open thy mouth wide and I will fill it"; the gracious God who declares, "Blessed are they that hunger after righteousness, for they shall be filled"—and that faithful, covenant-keeping God has now "filled you with all righteousness, peace, and joy in believing." The brightness of Christ's appearing has destroyed the indwelling man of sin. He who had slain the lion and the bear, He who had already done so great things for you, has now crowned all His blessings by slaying the Goliath within. Aspiring, unbelieving self is fallen before the victorious Son of David. The "quick and powerful word of God," which is "sharper than any two-edged sword," has "pierced even to the dividing asunder of soul and spirit."

ASSURANCE

The carnal mind is cut off; "the circumcision of the heart, through the Spirit," has fully taken place in your breast; and now "that mind is in you which was also in Christ Jesus"; ye are spiritually minded; loving God with all your heart, and your neighbour as yourselves, ye are full of goodness, ye keep the commandments, ye observe "the law of liberty," ye "fulfill the law of Christ." Of Him ye have "learned to be meek and lowly in heart." Ye have gladly "taken his yoke upon you"; in so doing, ye have "found" a sweet abiding "rest unto your souls"; and from blessed experience ye can say, "Christ's yoke is easy, and His burden is light"; His "ways are ways of pleasantness, and his paths are peace"; "all the paths of the Lord are mercy and truth, unto such as keep his covenant and his testimonies."

The beatitudes are sensibly yours; and the charity described by St. Paul has the same place in your breast which the tables of the law had in the ark of the covenant. Ye are the living temple of the Trinity; the Father is your life, the Son your light, the Spirit your love; ye are truly baptized into the mystery of God, ye continue to "drink into one Spirit," and thus ye enjoy the grace of both sacraments.

There is an end of your "lo here!" and "lo there!" "The Kingdom of God is" now established "within you." Christ's "righteousness, peace, and joy" are rooted in your breast "by the Holy Ghost given unto you" as an abiding guide and indwelling Comforter. Your introverted eye of faith looks at God, who gently "guides you with His eye into all the truth" necessary to make you "do justice, love mercy, and walk humbly with your God." Simplicity of intention keeps darkness out of your mind, and purity of affection keeps wrong fires out of your breast. By the former ye are without guile; by the latter ye are without envy.

Your passive will instantly melts into the will of God; and on all occasions you meekly say, "Not my will, O Father, but thine be done": thus are ye always ready to suffer what you are called to suffer. Your active will evermore says, "Speak, Lord, thy servant heareth: what wouldest thou have me to do? It is my meat and drink to do the will of my heavenly Father"; thus are ye always ready to do whatsoever ye are convinced that God calls you to do; and "whatsoever ye do, whether ye eat, or drink, or do anything else, ye do all to the glory of God, and in the name of our Lord Jesus Christ; rejoicing evermore; praying without ceasing; in everything giving thanks; solemnly "looking for, and hasting unto," the hour of your dissolution, and "the day of God, wherein the heavens being on fire shall be dissolved," and your soul, being clothed with a celestial body, shall be able to do celestial services to the God of your life.

Think on These Things

Adam, ye know, lost his human perfection in paradise: Satan lost his angelic perfection in heaven; the devil thrust sore at Christ in the wilderness, to throw Him down from His mediatorial perfection; and St. Paul, in the same epistles where he professes not only Christian but apostolic perfection also (Phil. iii. 15; 1 Cor. i. 6; 2 Cor. xii. 11), informs us that he continued to "run for the crown of heavenly" perfection like a man who might not only lose his crown of Christian perfection, but become a reprobate, and be cast away (1 Cor. ix. 25-27). And therefore so run ye also, "that no man take your crown" of Christian perfection in this world, and "that ye may obtain" your crown of angelic perfection in the world to come. Still keep your body under. Still guard your senses. Still watch your own heart; and "steadfast in the faith," still "resist the devil," that he may "flee from you"; remembering, that if Christ himself, as Son of Man, had "conferred with flesh and blood," refused to deny himself, and avoided taking up His cross, He had lost His perfection, and sealed up our original apostasy.

GROWTH

"We do not find," says Mr. Wesley, in his *Plain Account of Christian Perfection*, "any general state described in Scripture from which a man cannot draw back to sin. If there were any state wherein this was impossible, it would be that of those who are sanctified, who are fathers in Christ, who 'rejoice evermore, pray without ceasing, and in everything give thanks.' But it is not impossible for these to draw back. They who are sanctified may yet fall and perish (Heb. x. 29). Even fathers in Christ need that warning, 'Love not the world' (1 John ii. 15). They who 'rejoice, pray, and give thanks, without ceasing,' may, nevertheless, 'quench the Spirit' (1 Thess. v. 16, etc.). Nay, even they who are 'sealed unto the day of redemption' may yet 'grieve the Holy Spirit of God' (Eph. iv. 30)."

The doctrine of the absolute perseverance of the saints is the first card which the devil played against man: "'Ye shall not surely die,' if ye break the law of your perfection." This fatal card won the game. Mankind and paradise were lost. The artful serpent had too well succeeded at his first game to forget that lucky card at his second. See him "transforming himself into an angel of light" on the pinnacle of the temple. There he plays over again his old game against the Son of God. Out of the Bible he pulls the very card which won our first parents, and swept the stake . . . "Cast thyself down," says he; "for it is written," that all things shall work together for Thy good, Thy very falls not excepted: "He shall give his angels charge concerning thee, and in their hands they shall bear thee up, lest at any time thou dash thy foot against a stone." The tempter, thanks be to Christ, lost the game at that time; but he did not lose his card; and it is probable that he will play that round against you all, only with some variation.

Let me mention one among a thousand. He promised our Lord that God's angels should bear Him up in their hands, if He threw himself down; and it is not unlikely that he will promise you greater things still. Nor should I wonder if he was bold enough to hint that when you cast yourselves down, God himself shall bear you up in His hands, yea in His arms of everlasting love. Oh, ye men of God, **DANGERS** learn wisdom by the fall of Adam. Oh, ye anointed sons of the Most High, learn watchfulness by the conduct of Christ. If He was afraid to "tempt the Lord His God," will ye dare to do it? If He rejected as poison the hook of the absolute perseverance of the saints, though it was baited with scripture, will ye swallow it?

No: "through faith in Christ the Scriptures have made you wise unto salvation"; you will not only fly with all speed from evil, but from the very appearance of evil. And when you stand on the brink of a temptation, far from entering into it, under any pretence whatever, ye will leap back into the bosom of Him who says, "Watch and pray, lest ye enter into temptation"; "for" though "the spirit is willing, the flesh is weak."

I grant that, evangelically speaking, the weakness of the flesh is not sin; but yet the "deceitfulness of sin" creeps in at this door; and by this means not a few of God's children, "after they had escaped the pollutions of the world, through the" sanctifying "knowledge of Christ," under plausible pretences, "have been again entangled therein and overcome." Let their falls make you cautious. Ye have put on the whole armour of God: Oh, keep it on, and use it "with all prayer" that ye may, to the last, "stand complete in Christ" and be "more than conquerors" through Him that has loved you.

Remember that "every one who is perfect shall be as his Master." Now, if your Master was tempted and assaulted to the last; if to the last He watched and prayed, using all the means of **CHRISTLIKENESS** grace himself, and enforcing the use of them upon others; if to the last He fought against the world, the flesh, and the devil, and did not "put off the harness" till He had put off the body, think not yourselves above Him, but "go and do likewise." If He did not regain paradise, without going through the most complete renunciation of all the good things of this world, and without meekly submitting to the severe stroke of His last enemy, death, be content to be "perfect as He was"; nor fancy that your flesh and blood can inherit the celestial kingdom of God, when the flesh and blood which Emmanuel himself assumed from a pure virgin could not inherit it without passing under the cherub's flaming sword; I mean, without going through the gates of death.

Ye are not complete in wisdom. Perfect love does not imply perfect knowledge; but perfect humility, and perfect readiness to receive instruction. Remember, therefore, that if ever ye show that ye are above being instructed, even by a fisherman who teaches according to the divine anointing, ye will show that ye are fallen from a perfection of humility into a perfection of pride.

Never Farther than the Cross

Do not confound angelical with Christian perfection. Uninterrupted transports of praise and ceaseless raptures of joy do not belong to Christians but to angelical perfection. Our feeble frame can bear but a few drops of that glorious cup. In general, that "new wine" is too strong for our "old bottles"; that power is too excellent for our earthen cracked vessels; but weak as they are, they can bear a fullness of meekness, of resignation, of humility, and of that love which is willing to obey unto death. If God indulges you with ecstasies and extra ordinary revelations, be thankful for them, but be "not exalted above measure by them"; take care lest enthusiastic delusions mix themselves with them; and remember that your Christian perfection does not so much consist in "building a tabernacle" upon Mount Tabor, to rest and enjoy rare sights there, as in resolutely taking up the judgment-hall of an unjust Pilate, and [climbing] to the top of an ignominious Calvary.

HUMANITY

Ye never read in your Bibles, "Let that glory be upon you, which was also upon St. Stephen, when 'he looked up steadfastly into heaven, and said, Behold, I see the heavens opened, and the Son of Man standing on the right hand of God.'" But ye have frequently read there, "Let this mind be in you, which was also in Christ Jesus, who made himself of no reputation, took upon him the form of a servant, and, being found in fashion as a man, humbled himself, and became obedient unto death, even the death of the cross."

CHRISTLIKENESS

See Him on that ignominious cross: He hangs, abandoned by His friends, surrounded by His foes, condemned by the rich, insulted by the poor. He hangs, a worm, and no man! a very scorn of men, and the outcast of the people! "All they that see Him laugh Him to scorn. They shoot out their lips and shake their heads saying, He trusted in God that He would deliver Him; let Him deliver Him, if He will have Him." "There is none to help Him." One of His apostles denies, another sells Him, and the rest run away.

He is poured out like water; His heart in the midst of His body is like melting wax; His strength is dried up like a potsherd; His tongue cleaveth to His gums; He is going into the dust of death. His hands and feet are pierced. You may tell all His bones. They stand staring and looking upon Him. They part His garments among them, and cast lots for the only remainder of His property, His plain, seamless vesture. Both suns, the visible and the invisible, seem eclipsed. No cheering beam of created light gilds His gloomy prospect. No smile of His heavenly Father supports His agonizing soul. No cordial unless it be vinegar and gall, revives His sinking spirits. He has nothing left, except His God. But His God is enough for Him.

In His God He has all things. And though His soul is "seized with sorrow, even unto death," yet it hangs more firmly upon His God by a naked faith, than His lacerated body does on the cross by the clinched nails. The perfection of His love shines in all its Christian glory. He not only forgives His insulting foes and bloody persecutors, but in the highest point of His passion He forgets His own wants, and thirsts after their eternal happiness. Together with His blood, He pours out His soul for them; and, excusing them all, He says, "Father, forgive them, for they know not what they do." Oh, ye adult sons of God, in this glass "behold all with open face the glory" of your Redeemer's forgiving, praying love; and, as ye behold it, "be changed into the same image from glory to glory, by the loving Spirit of the Lord."

The Fellowship of His Sufferings

This lesson is deep; but He may teach you one deeper still: by a strong sympathy with Him in all His sufferings He may call you to know Him every way crucified. Stern justice thunders from heaven, "Awake, O sword, against the man who is my fellow!" The sword awakes, the sword goes through His soul, the flaming sword is quenched in His blood. But is one sinew of His perfect faith cut, one fibre of His perfect resignation injured, by the astonishing blow? No; His God slays Him, and yet He trusts in His God. By the noblest of all ventures, in the most dreadful of all storms, He meekly bows His head, and shelters His departing soul in the bosom of His God: "My God! my God!" says He, "though all thy comforts have forsaken me, and all thy storms and waves go over me, yet into thy hands I commend my spirit." "For thou wilt not leave my soul in hell, neither wilt thou suffer thine Holy One to see corruption. Thou wilt show me the path of life: in thy presence is fulness of joy, and at thy right hand," where I shall soon sit, "there are pleasures for evermore."

What a pattern of perfect confidence! Oh, ye perfect Christians, be ambitious to ascend to those amazing heights of Christ's perfection; "for even hereunto were ye called, because Christ also suffered for us, leaving us an example, that ye should follow his steps; who knew no sin; who, when he was reviled, reviled not again; when he suffered, he threatened not, but committed himself to him that judgeth righteously." If this is your high calling on earth, rest not, oh ye fathers in Christ, till your patient hope and perfect confidence in God have got their last victory over your last enemy—the king of terrors.

Divine Love

"The ground of a thousand mistakes," says Mr. Wesley, "is, the not considering deeply that love is the highest gift of God, humble, gentle, patient love; that all visions, revelations, manifestations whatever, are little things compared to love. It were well you should be thoroughly sensible of this: the heaven of heavens is love. There is nothing higher in religion; there is, in effect, nothing else. If you look for anything but more love, you are looking wide of the mark, you are getting out of the royal way. And when you are asking others, 'Have you received this or that blessing?' if you mean anything but more love, you mean wrong; you are leading them out of the way, and putting them upon a false scent. Settle it, then, in your heart, that, from the moment God has saved you from all sin, you are to aim at nothing but more of that love described in 1 Cor. xiii. You can go no higher than this, till you are carried into Abraham's bosom."

PERFECT LOVE

Love is humble: "Be therefore clothed with humility," says Mr. Wesley; "let it not only fill but cover you all over. Let modesty and self-diffidence appear in all your words and actions. Let all you speak and do show that you are little, and base, and mean, and vile in your

ATTITUDES own eyes. As one instance of this, be always ready to own any fault you have been in: if you have at any time thought, spoken, or acted wrong, be not backward to acknowledge it; never dream that this will hurt the cause of God: no; it will further it. Be therefore open and frank when you are taxed with anything: let it appear just as it is; and you will thereby not hinder, but adorn, the gospel."

Why should ye be more backward in acknowledging your failings, than in confessing that ye do not pretend to infallibility? St. Paul was perfect in the love which casts out fear, and therefore he boldly reproved the high priest. But when he had reproved him more sharply than the fifth commandment allows, he directly confessed his mistake, and set his seal to the importance of the duty in which he had been inadvertently wanting: "Then Paul said, I knew not, brethren, that he was the high priest: for it is written, Thou shalt not speak evil of the ruler of thy people."

St. John was perfect in the courteous, humble love which brings us down at the feet of all. His courtesy, his humility, and the dazzling glory which beamed forth from a divine messenger, whom he apprehended to be more than a creature, betrayed him into a fault contrary to that of St. Paul; but, far from concealing it, he openly confessed it, and published his confession for the edification of all the churches. "When I had heard and seen," says he, "I fell down to worship before the feet of the angel who showed me these things. Then saith he unto me, See thou do it not; for I am thy fellow servant." Christian perfection shines as much in the childlike simplicity with which the perfect readily acknowledge their faults, as it does in the manly steadiness with which they "resist unto blood, striving against sin."

If humble love makes us frankly confess our faults, much more does it incline us to own ourselves sinners, miserable sinners, before that God whom we have so frequently offended. I need not remind you that your "bodies are dead because of sin"; you see, you feel it: and therefore, so long as you dwell in prison of flesh and blood, which death the revenger of sin is to pull down; so long as your final justification, as pardoned and sanctified sinners, has not taken place; yea, so long as you break the law of paradisic perfection, under which you were originally placed, it is meet, right, and your bounden duty to consider yourselves as sinners, who, as transgressors of the law of innocence and the law of liberty, are guilty of death, of eternal death.

St. Paul did so, after he was "come to Mount Sion and to the spirits of just men made perfect": he still looked upon himself as the "chief of sinners," because he had been a daring blasphemer of Christ, and a fierce persecutor of his people: "Christ," says he, "came to save sinners, of whom I am chief." The reason is plain. . . . According to the doctrines of grace and justice and before the throne of God's mercy and holiness, a sinner pardoned and sanctified must, in the very nature of things, be considered as a sinner; for if you consider him as a saint, absolutely abstracted from the character of a sinner, how can he be a pardoned and sanctified sinner?

To all eternity, therefore, but much more while "death, the wages of sin," is at your heels, and while ye are going to "appear before the judgment seat of Christ," to receive your final sentence of absolution or condemnation, it will become you to say with St. Paul, "We have all sinned, and come short of the glory of God; being justified freely," as sinners, by his grace, through the redemption that is in Jesus Christ"; although we are justified judicially; as believers, through faith; as obedient believers, through the obedience of faith; and as perfect Christians, through Christian perfection.

Humble love "becomes all things to all men," although it delights most in those who are most holy. Ye may, and ought to, set your love of peculiar complacence upon God's dearest children, upon those who, like yourselves, excel in virtue; because they more strongly reflect the image of the God of love, the Holy One of Israel. But if ye despise the weak, and are above lending them a helping hand, ye are fallen from Christian perfection, which teaches us to "bear one another's burdens," especially the burdens of the weak. Imitate, then, the tenderness and wisdom of the Good Shepherd who "carries the lambs in His bosom, gently leads the sheep which are big with young," feeds with milk those who cannot bear strong meat, and says to His imperfect disciples, "I have many things to say to you, but ye cannot bear them now."

Catholic Love

"Where the loving Spirit of the Lord is, there is liberty"; keep therefore at the utmost distance from the shackles of a narrow, prejudiced, bigoted spirit. The moment ye confine your love to the people who think just as you do, and your regard to the preachers who exactly suit your taste, you fall from perfection and turn bigots. "I entreat you," says Mr. Wesley, in his *Plain Account,* "beware of bigotry. Let not your love or beneficence be confined to Methodists (so called) only; much less to that very small part of them who seem to be renewed in love, or to those who believe yours and their report. Oh, make not this your 'shibboleth.'" On the contrary, as ye have time and ability, "do good to all men." Let your benevolence shine upon all; let your charity send its cherishing beams towards all, in proper degrees; so shall ye be "perfect as your heavenly Father," who "makes his sun to shine upon all," although He sends the brightest and warmest beams of His favour upon the household of faith, and reserves His richest bounties for those who lay out their five talents to the best advantage.

Love, pure love, is satisfied with the supreme Good, with God. "Beware, then, of desiring anything but Him. Now you desire nothing else: every other desire is driven out; see that none enter in again. Keep thyself pure: let 'your eye remain single, and your whole body shall be full of light.' Admit no desire of pleasing food, or any other pleasure of sense; no desire of pleasing the eye, or the imagination; no desire of money, of praise, or esteem; of happiness in any creature. You may bring these desires back, but you need not: you may feel them no more. Oh, 'stand fast in the liberty wherewith Christ hath made me free.' Be patterns to all of denying yourselves, and taking up your cross daily. Let them see that you make no account of any pleasure which does not bring you nearer to God, nor regard any pain which does; that you simply aim at pleasing Him, whether by doing or suffering; that the constant language of your heart, with regard to pleasure or pain, honour or dishonour, riches or poverty, is

> *All's alike to me, so I*
> *In my Lord may live and die.*

The best soldiers are sent upon the most difficult and dangerous expeditions; and as you are the best soldiers of Jesus Christ, ye will probably be called to drink deepest of His cup, and to carry the heaviest burdens. "Expect contradiction and opposition," says Wesley, "together with crosses of various kinds. Consider the words of St. Paul: 'To you it is given in the behalf of Christ,' for His sake, as a fruit of His death and intercession for you, 'not only to believe, but also to suffer for his sake' (Phil. i. 29). 'It is given'—God gives you this opposition or reproach; it is a fresh token of His love. And will you disown the giver? or spurn His gift, and count it a misfortune? Will you not rather say, 'Father the hour is come, that thou shouldest be glorified. Now thou givest thy child to suffer something for thee. Do with me according to thy will.' Know that these things, far from being hindrances to the work of God, or to your soul, unless by your own fault, are not only unavoidable in the course of providence, but profitable, yea necessary, for you; therefore, receive them from God, not from chance, with willingness, with thankfulness; receive them from men with humility, meekness, yieldingness, gentleness, sweetness."

Love can never do nor suffer too much for its divine Object. Be then ambitious, like St. Paul, to be made perfect in sufferings. I have already observed that the apostle, not satisfied to be a perfect Christian, would also be a perfect martyr, earnestly desiring to "know the fellowship of Christ's" utmost "sufferings." Follow him, as he followed his suffering, crucified Lord. "Your feet are shod with the preparation of the gospel of peace": run after them both in the race of obedience, for the crown of martyrdom, if that crown is reserved for you. And if ye miss the crown of those who are martyrs indeed, ye shall, however, receive the reward of those who are martyrs in intention—the crown of righteousness and angelical perfection.

But do not so desire to follow Christ to the garden of Gethsemane, as to refuse following Him now to the carpenter's shop, if Providence now calls you to do it. Do not lose the present day by idly looking back at yesterday, or foolishly antedating the cares of tomorrow; but wisely use every hour, spending them as one who stands on the verge of time, on the border of eternity, and who has his work cut out by a wise Providence from moment to moment. Never, therefore, neglect using the two talents you have now, and doing the duty which is now incumbent upon you. Should ye be tempted to it under the plausible pretence of waiting for a greater number of talents, remember that God doubles our talents in the way of duty. . . .

Says Mr. Wesley, "grace flies a vacuum, as well as nature; the devil fills whatever God does not fill." "As 'by works faith is made perfect,' so the completing or destroying the work of faith, and enjoying the favour or suffering the displeasure of God, greatly depends on every single act of obedience." If you forget this, you will hardly do now whatsoever your hand findeth to do. Much less will you do it with all your might for God, for eternity.

Let Your Light Shine

WITNESSING

Love is modest; it rather inclines to bashfulness and silence than to talkative forwardness. "In a multitude of words there wanteth not sin": be, therefore, "slow to speak," "nor cast your pearls before" those who cannot distinguish them from pebbles.

Nevertheless, when you are solemnly called upon to bear testimony to the truth, and to say what great things God has done for you, it would be cowardice, or false prudence, not to do it with humility. Be, then, "always ready to give an answer to every man who" properly "asketh you a reason of the hope that is in you, with meekness" without fluttering anxiety, "and with fear," with a reverential awe of God upon your minds (1 Pet. iii. 15).

The perfect are "burning and shining lights"; and our Lord intimates that, as "a candle is not lighted to be put under a bushel, but upon a candlestick, that it may give light to all the house," so God does not light the candle of perfect love to hide it in a corner, but to give light to all those who are within the reach of its brightness. If diamonds glitter, if stars shine, if flowers display their colours, and perfumes diffuse their fragrance, to the honour of the Father of lights, and Author of every good gift, if, without self-seeking, they disclose His glory to the utmost of their power, why should ye not "go and do likewise"?

Gold answers its most valuable end, when it is brought to light and made to circulate for charitable and pious uses; and not when it lies concealed in a miser's strong box or in the dark bosom of a mine. . . .

Love, or "charity, rejoiceth in the" display of an edifying "truth." Fact is fact all the world over. If you can say to the glory of God, that you are alive, and feel very well when you do so, why could you not also testify to His honour that you live not, but that Christ liveth in you, if you really find that this is your experience? Did not St. John say, "Our love is made perfect, because, as he is, so are we in this world"? Did not St. Paul write, "The righteousness of the law is fulfilled in us, who walk after the Spirit"? Did he not with the same simplicity aver that, although he "had nothing," and was "sorrowful," yet he "possessed all things," and was "always rejoicing"?

Hence it appears that, with respect to the declaring or concealing what God has done for your soul, the line of your duty runs exactly between the proud forwardness of some stiff Pharisees and the voluntary humility of some stiff mystics. The former vainly boast of more than they experience; and by that means they set up the cursed idol, self: the latter ungratefully hide the wonderful works of God, which the primitive Christians spoke of publicly in a variety of languages; and by this means they refuse to exalt their gracious benefactor, Christ.

The first error is undoubtedly more odious than the second; but what need is there of leaning to either? Would you void them both? Let your tempers and lives always declare that perfect love is attainable in this life; and when you have a proper call to declare it with your lips and pens, do it without forwardness, to the glory of God; do it with simplicity, for the edification of your neighbour; do it with godly jealousy. . . . How properly does St. Peter charge believers to give with fear an account of the grace which is in them! and how careful should ye be to observe this important charge!

[marginal note: WRITING]

Grace and Gratitude

Follow an excellent direction of Mr. Wesley. When you have done anything for God, or "received any favour from Him, retire, if not into your closet, into your heart, and say, 'I come, Lord, to restore to Thee what Thou hast given, and I freely relinquish it, to enter again into my own nothingness. For what is the most perfect creature in heaven or earth in Thy presence but a void, capable of being filled with Thee and by Thee, as the air which is void and dark is capable of being filled with the light of the sun? Grant therefore, O Lord, that I may never appropriate Thy grace to myself, any more than the air appropriates to itself the light of the sun, who withdraws it every day to restore it the next; there being nothing in the air that either appropriates His light or resists it.

"'Oh, give me the same facility of receiving and restoring Thy grace and good works! I say, Thine; for I acknowledge that the root from which they spring is in Thee, and not in me.' The true means to be filled anew with the riches of grace is thus to strip ourselves of it: without this it is extremely difficult not to faint in the practice of good works." "And therefore, that your good works may receive their last perfection, let them lose themselves in God. This is a kind of death to them, resembling that of our bodies which will not attain their highest life, their immortality, till they lose themselves in the glory of our souls, or rather of God, wherewith they shall be filled. And it is only what they had of earthly and mortal which good works lose by this spiritual death."

Paul's Pursuit of a Higher Perfection

Would ye see this deep precept put in practice? Consider St. Paul. Already possessed of Christian perfection, he does good works from morning till night. He "warns every one night and day with tears." He carries the gospel from east to west. Wherever he stops, he plants a church at the hazard of his life. But instead of resting in his present perfection and in the good works which spring from it, "he grows in grace and in the knowledge of our Lord Jesus Christ"; unweariedly "following after, if that he may apprehend that" perfection "for which also he is apprehended of Christ Jesus," that celestial perfection of which he got lively ideas when he was "caught up to the third heaven, and heard unspeakable words, which is not lawful for a man to utter."

GROWTH

With what amazing ardour does he run his race of Christian perfection for the prize of that higher perfection! How does he forget the works of yesterday, when he lays himself out for God today! "Though dead, he yet speaketh"; nor can an address to perfect Christians be closed by a more proper speech than his. "Brethren," says he, "be followers of me." "I count not myself to have apprehended" my angelical perfection; "but this one thing I do, forgetting those things which are behind," settling down in none of my former experiences, resting in none of my good works, "and, reaching forth unto those things which are before, I press towards the mark, for the" celestial "prize of the high calling of God in Christ Jesus. Let us therefore, as many as are perfect, be thus minded; and if in anything ye be otherwise minded, God shall reveal even this unto you."

In the meantime you may sing the following hymn of the Rev. Mr. Charles Wesley, which is descriptive of the destruction of corrupt self-will, and expressive of the absolute resignation which characterizes a perfect believer:

> *To do or not to do; to have*
> *Or not to have, I leave to Thee;*
> *To be or not to be, I leave;*
> *Thy only will be done in me.*
> *All my requests are lost in one;*
> *Father, Thy only will be done.*
>
> *Suffice that, for the season past,*
> *Myself in things divine I sought,*
> *For comforts cried with eager haste,*
> *And murmur'd that I found them not.*
> *I leave it now to Thee alone:*
> *Father, Thy only will be done.*

> Thy gifts I clamour for no more,
>   Or selfishly Thy grace require,
> An evil heart to vanquish o'er;
>   Jesus, the Giver, I desire;
> After the flesh no longer known:
> Father, Thy only will be done.
>
> Welcome alike the crown or cross;
>   Trouble I cannot ask, nor peace,
> Nor toil, nor rest, nor gain, nor less,
>   Nor joy, nor grief, nor pain, nor ease,
> Nor life, nor death; but ever groan,
> "Father, Thy only will be done."

This hymn suits all the believers who are at the bottom of Mount Sion, and begin to join the spirits of just men made perfect. But when the triumphal chariot of perfect love gloriously carries you to the top of perfection's hill; when you are raised far above the common heights of the perfect; when you are almost translated into glory like Elijah, then you may sing another hymn of the same Christian poet:

> Who in Jesus confide,
> They are bold to outride
> The storms of affliction beneath;
>   With the prophet they soar
>   To that heavenly shore,
> And outfly all the arrows of death.
>
> By faith we are come
> To our permanent home;
> By hope we the rapture improve;
>   By love we still rise,
>   And look down on the skies;
> For the heaven of heavens is love!
>
> Who on earth can conceive
> How happy we live
> In the city of God the great King;
>   What a concert of praise,
>   When our Jesus's grace
> The whole heavenly company sing!

What a rapturous song,
When the glorified throng
In the spirit of harmony join!
Join all the glad choirs,
Hearts, voices and lyres,
And the burden is "Mercy divine"!

That your earthen vessels may be filled with this love till they break, and you enjoy the divine Object of your faith without an interposing vest of gross flesh and blood, is the wish of one who sincerely praises God on your account, and ardently prays—

Make up Thy jewels, Lord, and show
The glorious, spotless Church below;
The fellowship of saints make known;
And, O my God, might I be one!

O might my lot be cast with these,
The least of Jesu's witnesses!
O that my Lord would count me meet
To wash His dear disciples' feet!

To wait upon His saints below,
On gospel errands for them go;
Enjoy the grace to angels given,
And serve the royal heirs of heaven.

7

FRANCIS ASBURY AND HIS ASSOCIATES IN AMERICA

Francis Asbury (1745-1816)
Asbury's Experience and Holiness Preaching

Asbury's Associates:
- Phillip Gatch
- William Watters
- William Thatcher
- Freeborn Garrettson
- Ezekiel Cooper
- Daniel Hitt
- William McKendree

Francis Asbury, Prophet of the Long Road

7 Francis Asbury and His Associates in America

Francis Asbury
(1745-1816)

What Wesley was to England, Asbury was to America—but much more so.

An Englishman by birth; an American by calling and choice; an apostle by election and passion, Asbury was the architect of the Methodist Episcopal Church, which became the womb of a score or more modern evangelical holiness churches and denominations. Francis Asbury was Methodism incarnate let loose on the American continent.

Asbury was born in the midlands in a humble home on the outskirts of Birmingham, even then a spreading smoky symbol of industrial England.

Born in a year of political revolution and the infamous '45 Rebellion, he spent his youthful years in the midst of an industrial revolution. He then held on with his witnessing way during the major political revolution of modern Western history; he was a lonely, threatened, and harassed Englishman who symbolized the tyranny of George III to colonists eager to sever every possible link with England.

In the long run, Asbury became the general-in-chief of a religious revolution that first loosened the hand of Wesley on colonial Methodism, and then shook it off completely so far as any constitutional links were concerned. He was a religious combination of Paul Revere, George Washington, and Thomas Jefferson. Asbury's is the profile on the coin of Methodist independence.

And yet Francis Asbury had no such ideas in mind when he rose at Wesley's bidding, and came to the American colonies in 1771. Rather, the burning urge and convictions that made him a Methodist preacher in England in his youth were what brought him to America as a young man.

In England, at 23 years of age he had written to his parents:
Let others condemn me as being without natural affection, as

being stubborn, disobedient to parents, or say what they please. It does not alter the case, for it is a small matter with me to be judged of man. I love my parents and friends, but I love my God better and his service, because it is perfect freedom, and he does not send me away at my own cost, for he gives me to prove, as my day is, my strength is, and it is my meat and drink to do his will. And tho I have given up all I do not repent, for I have found it all.[1]

That was in October 1768. In September 1771, just four days after sailing out of "a port near Bristol," he confided to his newly started *Journal:*

I will set down a few things that lie on my mind. Whither am I going? To the New World. What to do? To gain honour? No, if I know my own heart. To get money? No: I am going to live to God, and to bring others to do so.[2]

The keyword here is "others," a truly Wesleyan word.

Asbury landed at Philadelphia in October 1771, and here he remained until his death on March 21, 1816. He never lost the fiery zeal that had gripped him when first he heard the Methodist, Alexander Mather preach:

Mr. Mather (one of Wesley's itinerants), came into those parts when I was about fifteen; and young as I was, the word of God soon made deep impressions on my heart, which brought me to Jesus Christ, who graciously justified my guilty soul through faith in his precious blood, and soon showed me the excellency and necessity of holiness.[3]

For 45 years he rode up, down, and across the colonies preaching the gospel of full salvation from all sin for all men. He counseled hundreds of converts, organized and supervised scores of Societies. In travel, he outdid even Wesley, riding almost 280,000 miles on horseback. That averages about 6,000 miles a year; the equivalent of a round trip across the United States every year for 45 years. He sat in at least 224 Annual Conferences, and ordained 4,000 ministers.

Asbury was ordained bishop when he was 39 years of age; at that time the Methodists of America numbered about 14,000 members and 80 preachers. He laid his armor down at 71 when the church had almost 212,000 members and more than 700 itinerant preachers. He did for America what Wesley could never have done with the ideas and procedures that worked so well in England. It took a man whose heart

---

1. Francis Asbury, ed. by Elmer T. Clark, *Journal and Letters of Francis Asbury* (Nashville: Abingdon Press, 1958), 3:4. Hereafter referred to as JFA.
2. Ibid., 1:4.
3. Ibid.

was fused to America and to the cause of Christ here. He saw very clearly that the Methodists must be adaptable to the everchanging and spreading of the political and social frontiers.

Even in his ordination as bishop he had insight to break with Wesley's procedure. He refused to accept the position of superintendent unless he should be elected to it by his brethren. This decision was probably the taproot of the General Conference of the Methodist Church.

Asbury held a high view of the episcopacy, and indeed of the Christian ministry. When speaking of the passion that propelled him ceaselessly for a lifetime, he wrote: "I have done it for souls; had I done it for silver, there is not enough in New York to pay me."

The bishop was a man without house or home because his home was wherever he could do the most good. He was a warmly welcomed visitor in the frontier log cabins and in the mansions of the planters. Though not a father, he had a remarkable love for little children, and they for him: he took time to read to them when he could, and instructed them in the way of the Lord.

He did his work on a salary of $64.00 a year, and yet there are numerous instances of his generosity to others, especially his preachers.

In 1800 a friend asked him for a loan, or gift, of 50 pounds:
> He might as well have asked me for Peru. I showed him all the money I had in the world, about 12 dollars, and gave him 5.
> At the session of the Western Conference in 1806, some of the preachers were in want and could not purchase decent clothes. So I parted with my watch, my coat, and my shirt.[4]

The self-sacrifice, the sagacity, the courage, the endurance and suffering—but above all the sanctity and spirituality of Asbury—justifies the claim made in all humility and for the glory of God: "the marks of an apostle have been seen in me."

He finished his earthly course in Spottsylvania on March 31, 1816. If John Wesley's horse went to heaven, Asbury's did also! The Bishop was "on the road" when his Master called "Come up higher!" Are there roads in glory? If so, you will know where to find Francis Asbury, "The prophet of the long road."

---

4. Ibid., 2:517.

Asbury's Experience and Holiness Preaching

The early Methodist preachers in America were not merely speculative and systematic in their theology of heart holiness. They were dynamic. Their chief concern was the message of salvation from sin to godliness; and their gospel although deeply personal was powerful in social effect.

The appeal was primarily to Scripture and experience, but Asbury, Coke, Wright, McKendree, and Garrettson were eminently reasonable men. They had the special help of what so many reasonable men lack—"The wisdom of the Holy Spirit," the "wisdom that is from above."

Asbury's experiential appeal and evangelical pragmatism were exactly suited to the conditions and culture in which he served up and down the frontier and on the seaboard. His so-called exaggeration of the subjective experience of grace and his "tendency to accentuate its emotional requirements"[5] might with equal strength be levelled at the apostle Paul. Probably the criticism would please Asbury. It was certainly an advantage to early Methodism in America that her early preachers and architects gave loyal adherence to Wesley's criteria, "Scripture, Reason, and Experience." It was this that enabled them to dig deep and to lay firm foundations sunk in divine grace and reliance on the operation and guidance of the Holy Spirit.

Asbury's personal experience and testimony, or lack of it, to Christian perfection has had much criticism and analysis. Like Wesley he left no precisely worded confession: he left only strong hints, clues, and indications. We might wish that both had had foresight enough to have left what possibly might have satisfied the wise critics blessed with hindsight. We must however be satisfied with what we have.

And what do we have? We have literally scores of sermon outlines on sanctification and Christian perfection; we have urgent appeals to the Methodist preachers never to cease preaching perfect love; we have reports of scores of believers being entirely sanctified; we have recorded regrets of what transpires when the call to Christian per-

---

5. R. E. Chiles, *Theological Transition in American Methodism, 1790-1855* (New York: Abingdon Press, 1965), 42 ff.

fection is either stifled or neglected; we have rejoicings of how the work of God prospers where the message is preached and received; we have it written into the *Form of Discipline,* that great fertilizer at the roots of 19th-century Methodism.

And we have Asbury's yearnings, prayers, and affirmations. He believed himself to have been made perfect in love, and his selfless life of incredible devotion and sacrifice leave us no room for doubt, and little for criticism. His, however, was a living and growing experience. Like Charles Wesley he was never satisfied with the experience of the present moment: whatever he had grasped, he was still reaching. He obeyed Paul "Let us therefore, as many as be perfect, be thus minded" (Phil. 3:10-16). "One day's profession, therefore, became the next day's petition. It was not vacillation but aspiration."[6] All along his path it was, "O give me Jesus. Give me more!"

Asbury was first and foremost a herald and prophet. With a glorious monotony the words "I preached" open chapter after chapter and paragraph after paragraph in his *Journal.* He believed that he had power and authority from God to preach and had been divinely ordained and commissioned to preach, so that was what he did. He was born to preach, lived to preach, and died preaching.

For upwards of half a century he preached, wore his body out, getting where people needed to hear his message. He preached almost 17,000 sermons; some two hours in length but most of them much shorter. He preached from his Bible only—"a man of one book" as closely as Wesley. He did not need a meeting house nor a pulpit, although grateful when those were available: a barn, an arbor, a kitchen, a tree stump; he used them all.

And what did he preach? He preached the gospel of holiness! The following extracts are but crumbs from the constant supply of the bread of life that Asbury held forth to those who hungered and thirsted after righteousness.

Ezekiel Cooper said of him in his funeral discourse:

> He was careful to regulate all his religious tenets and doctrines by the Book of God, and to discard everything that was incompatible with the divine law and testimony. Mr. Wesley's *Sermons,* and *Notes on the Scriptures,* and Fletcher's *Checks,* exemplify his leading doctrines. The articles of religion, in the *Form of Discipline,* and what is commonly called, the *Apostles' Creed,*

---

6. John L. Peters, *Christian Perfection and American Methodism* (New York: Abingdon Press, 1956), p. 218.

contain a brief summary of his faith and doctrines. In his public ministry, in his conference communications, and examinations of candidates for the ministry; in his addresses to the societies, and his private and social interviews, and in his sentimental conversations, we have often heard him, instructively and entertainingly, profess, declare, and enforce his opinions and doctrines. We have fully known them.[7]

I have gathered some of the abundant material contained in this holy man's *Journal* and *Letters,* and allowed him to speak for himself. I have tried to let the emphasis fall on the mature Asbury while not neglecting the young preacher who came to America with Wesley's blessing; and stayed when his preacher friends went home.

Sept. 4, 1771: ON THE WAY TO AMERICA

On Wednesday, September 4, we set sail from a port near Bristol and having a good wind, soon passed the channel. For three days I was very ill with the seasickness; and no sickness I ever knew is equal to it. The captain behaved well to us. On the Lord's day, September 8, brother Wright preached a sermon on deck, and all the crew gave attention.

Thursday, 12. In America there has been a work of God: some moving first amongst the Friends, but in time it declined; likewise by the Presbyterians, but amongst them also it declined. The people God owns in England, are the Methodists. The doctrines they preach, and the discipline they enforce, are, I believe, the purest of any people now in the world. The Lord has greatly blessed these doctrines and this discipline in the three kingdoms: they must therefore be pleasing to Him. If God does not acknowledge me in America, I will soon return to England. I know my views are upright now; may they never be otherwise.

On the Lord's day, September 15, I preached on Acts xvii. 30: "*But God now commandeth all men everywhere to repent.*" The sailors behaved with decency. My heart's desire and prayer for them was, and is, that they may be saved: but O! the deep ignorance and insensibility of the human heart!

March, 1775: IN MARYLAND

Friday, 17. The glory of God and the salvation of men were my

---

7. Ezra S. Tipple, *Francis Asbury: The Prophet of the Long Road* (New York and Cincinnati: Methodist Book Concern, 1916), 227.

principal objects. I went to preach at the Point, but they were training the militia, so that the town seemed all in confusion.

Saturday, 18. Peace and pure desires filled my soul; and Christ was the object of my love. Glory be to Thee, O Lord! The next day the Spirit of the Lord God was with me in preaching at the Point; and with great pathos I was enabled to deliver the truth at night in town. Many of the audience felt the weight of God's word. May they yield to the sacred touch, and be saved! On Monday and Tuesday, I made a small excursion into the country, and laboured to bring souls to Christ at Mr. Rodger's and Mr. Taylor's. It seems Caleb Dorsey has not lost all the concern he felt some time ago. I afterward returned safe to town in the evening; and spent a part of the next day in reading Taylor's *Treatise on Holy Living*. This book was made a blessing to me above seven years. I preached in the evening from 1 Samuel x. 6: "The Spirit of the Lord will come upon thee, and thou shalt prophesy with them, and shalt be turned into another man." Here I took occasion to show,

I. The operations of the Spirit on the heart of man—to convince, convict, and convert, and sanctify.

II. The effects of these operations.

1. A strong inclination to speak for God. This is the duty of every Christian.

2. A great change—in judgment, desire, spirit, temper, and practice.

I found myself much indisposed when I returned to my lodgings, and the disorder of my body depressed my spirits.

Friday, 24. I ventured to Patapsco Neck, and had a full house at Captain Ridgley's, whose wife is brought by grace to the knowledge of God in Christ Jesus.

Lord's day, 26. My heart was delightfully taken up with God. In the time of preaching at the Point this morning, my spirit was tender, and many of the audience were much melted. I also found myself greatly drawn out in preaching at night in town.

Extract from the
Preface to the Sixth Edition of the DISCIPLINE, *1790.*

And we humbly believe that God's design in raising up the preachers called Methodists in America, was to reform the continent, and spread scriptural holiness over these lands. As a proof hereof, we have seen in course of 22 years, a great and glorious work of God, from New York through the Jersies, Pennsylvania, Maryland, Virginia, North and South Carolina, and Georgia; as also the extremities of the Western Settlements.

We also esteem it our duty and privilege most earnestly to recommend to you as members of our church, our *Form of Discipline,* which has been founded on the experience of 50 years in Europe, and of 20 years in America; as also on the observations and remarks we have made on ancient and modern churches. We have made some little alterations in the present edition, yet such as effect not in any degree the essentials of our doctrines and discipline. We think ourselves obliged to view and review annually the whole order of our church, always aiming at perfection, standing on the shoulders of those who have lived before us, and taking the advantage of our former selves.

We wish to see this little publication in the house of every Methodist, and the more so as it contains our plan of Collegiate and Christian education, and the articles of religion maintained more or less, in part or in the whole, by every reformed church in the world. We would likewise declare our real sentiments concerning the scripture doctrine of election and reprobation; as also on the infallible unconditional perseverance of all that ever have believed, or ever shall; and lastly, on the doctrine of Christian perfection.

THOMAS COKE
FRANCIS ASBURY[8]

February, 1797: IN SOUTH CAROLINA

Sunday, 12. I attended my station, and stood upon my watchtower. My subject was Eccles. v. 1: *"Keep thy foot when thou goest into the house of God."*

I. The house of God—the temples, the first and second, and the synagogues, were called houses of God. A place built for the worship and service of the Lord; the congregation and church.

II. The exercises and ordinances of the house of God: reading and preaching the word of God; prayer and praises; baptism and the Lord's supper. In his temple every one shall speak of his glory.

III. The manifestations that God is pleased to make of himself in his own house to the souls of his people.

IV. How people should prepare for, and behave in, the house of

---

8. *JFA,* 3:84.

God. To keep their eyes and ears—fix their attention on the Lord and Master of the house.

V. The wicked called fools, and the sacrifice they make. Ignorant of themselves, of God, of Christ, and true religion, and the worship of the Lord, and do not consider it is God, Christ, and sacred things they make light of.

We were full, and I put my strength to the test. In the afternoon, from Ezek. xxxvi. 25-27. I showed the evils God threatened, and prophesied the removal of, by His servant to His nominal professed people, Israel.

I. Their stony heart—their idols and filthiness.

II. The blessings promised and prophesied—a new heart, a new spirit, the indwelling and sanctifying influence of the Spirit.

III. The blessed consequential effects—*"I will cause you to walk in my statutes, and ye shall keep my judgments to do them."* The law, the judgments of God, because of the penalty annexed—thus saith the Lord to the renewed soul, "Thou shalt have none other gods but me." "Lord," saith the Christian, "I want none other but thee." Saith Jehovah, "Thou shalt not make to thyself any graven image." The pious soul saith, "I will not; the work of my hands cannot save my soul: I will not take thy name in vain. I love thy day—thy love hath written thy law upon my heart, and love to my neighbour engages me to fulfill my duty to him also." "The meek shall inherit the earth," as a sacred chapter from the Lord—this is their claim, security, and defence.

I was wearied with the duties of the day, and had only retired to rest when the alarm of fire was called—it proved only to be a kitchen and by the activity of the people it was soon extinguished.

December, 1797: IN VIRGINIA

Friday, 15. Was my well day; I took some of the powders, had good nursing, and got rest. I only read the Bible and the *Form of Discipline.* I write, ride, and talk a little with the women, children, and Africans. My thoughts were led to meditate upon 1 Tim. iv. 16: *"Take heed unto thyself and unto the doctrine; continue in them; for in doing this thou shalt both save thyself and them that hear thee."*

I. "Take heed to thyself"—in religion, as in nature, self-preservation is one of the first laws. Take heed that thy experience in religion and doctrine be sound; that thou hast a good heart, and a good head, and a good life, and a good conversation, ministerial diligence and fidelity in every part of Christian and pastoral duty. Saved already by grace, thou shalt be preserved from all the snares set for thy feet, and not backslide as a Christian minister, but feel persevering, sanctifying, glorifying, and crowning grace.

II. Thou shalt "save them that hear thee" from lukewarmness and backsliding; legality on the one hand, and making void the law through faith on the other; that they profess and possess, live and walk as it becometh the gospel of Christ.

III. "Continue in them"—in all the doctrines, ordinances, and duties of the gospel: the same gospel, the same ordinances, the same duties which are designed to complete the work in the souls of ministers as Christians, are as needful to continue the work of grace as to begin it; and not only continue, but to finish and bring on the headstone with shouting.

A Dumb Day!

Saturday, 16. I employed myself as much as my health would admit, in reading the Bible and writing such observations thereon as were suggested to my mind.

Sunday, 17. I had to keep in the house; O dumb day! I am better, yet it is not safe for me to go out in such very cold weather. I read the word of God and preached.

January, 1799: In South Carolina

Sabbath day, 6. Very cold, sleet in the streets, and dangerous walking. We had a solemn sacramental season; and a goodly number of "Ethiopians stretched out their hands to the Lord."

Saturday, 12. My time has been chiefly taken up in composing and selecting from Cave's *Lives of the Fathers,* showing the primitive episcopacy. We are laid up for winter, when it is like summer. I hope to labour upon the Lord's day in the churches, so called.

Sabbath day, 20. I preached at Bethel: my subject was Mark xi. 17: "*And he taught, saying unto them, Is it not written, My house shall be called of all nations the house of prayer? but ye have made it a den of thieves.*" At the old church my subject was 2 Pet. i. 16. A group of sinners gathered around the door, and when I took the pulpit they went off with a shout: I felt what was coming. In the evening there was a proper uproar, like old times. I employed the last week of reading, writing, visiting, and attending feasts of charity; one with the white society and the other with the Africans.

Sabbath day, 27. I preached in the morning at Bethel, from Heb. xiii. 20-21.

I. It was a prayer: as he, Paul, had asked their prayers, he gave them his.

II. "The God of peace": the gracious relation of the Hebrews as reconciled to God.

III. "Brought again from the dead"; when it might be thought, all was lost when Jesus was dead; again He had brought the Hebrews from a state of death in trespasses and sins.

IV. This was more than bringing the apostle to them, although he might be given to them of God according to their prayers.

V. "Great Shepherd of the sheep"—all the sheep, Jews, and Gentiles. The Shepherd of the shepherds; doing really, what they, under-shepherds, do instrumentally: he seeketh, keepeth, feedeth, and watcheth his ordained flock against those who would steal or kill them, and alienate them from Jesus, or the true fold and faithful pastors.

VI. "Through the blood of the everlasting covenant," see Exod. xxiv. 3; Moses said, *Behold the blood of the covenant, when he sprinkled the people; it is this that meriteth, sealeth, and sanctifieth.*

VII. "Make you perfect in every good work" as to the quantity and quality of good works: and,

Lastly, "pleasing to God" in gracious affections, purity of intention, and uniformity of conduct; and all by the merit and intercession of Jesus Christ. In the afternoon I preached in Cumberland street meeting house on Deut. iv. 9.

February, 1799: IN SOUTH CAROLINA

Sunday, February 3. By riding until ten o'clock in the night, we came, fifty miles, to Mr. Boon's. On Saturday I rode alone to Georgetown: we have made it nearly eighty miles from Charleston to this place. I preached on Gal. v. 24-26: First, They that are Christ's in a special spiritual sense: His sheep, redeemed, sought, and saved; His children, bearing his image. Secondly, How they are to be distinguished: they crucify the flesh with the passions and desires thereof; the sinful love of the world, with the sinful fear and joy also. Thirdly, Let us walk in the Spirit, as an evidence that we live in the Spirit.

Fourthly, Let us not be "desirous of vain glory"; in forms, ordinances, or any outward appearances of men and things. Fifthly, let us not by such mean measures "provoke one another," or envy one another. In the afternoon I preached on Isa. lxvi. 5.

August, 1801: IN MARYLAND

I continued at Perry Hall, from August 3d to Saturday the 15th. An intermittent fever came upon me every morning, and indisposed my stomach: it was with difficulty I could attend to the performance of family and closet duties being much unfitted for reading or writing. I got through a part of Doddridge's *Rise and Progress,* and some of *Young's Night Thoughts.* The great engagedness of the African part of the family was delightfully pleasing. Gough Holliday professed to find the Lord, and one or two more of the family appear to be earnestly seeking Him. I preached, read, prayed, exhorted, and conversed; but it was not much I could do. Our family, when in the chapel, makes a respectable congregation.

Sunday, 16. I spent this day in Baltimore. My indisposition of body was amply compensated by the consolation I felt whilst holding forth upon Matt. v. 8: "Blessed are the pure in heart, for they shall see God."

I. The character of those who by justification are, in a special manner, called to be pure in heart; called by promise, by privilege, by duty.

II. The purity of the gospel in authority, in example, precept, and spirit; in its operative influence on the understanding, conscience, intentions, will, hopes, fears, joys, sorrows, and affections, producing the sanctification of the soul in a deliverance from all sin.

III. The visions: in what manner the pure in heart should see God; they shall see Him in His perfections, in His providence, in His works of nature, and the operations of His grace, and they shall see Him in His glory!

I had a desire to preach in the market house upon Howard's Hill. I spoke to hundreds, perhaps thousands, upon Luke xiv. 21: *"Go out quickly into the streets and lanes of the city, and bring in hither the poor, and the maimed, and the halt, and the blind."* I thought it my duty, and I felt it a delight to sanction what the preachers do in preaching abroad: I wish to do it in Philadelphia, and had appointed it, but some of my brethren made strong objections, and it was abandoned. We have peace, health, and union in Baltimore.

May, 1803: IN NEW YORK

Sunday, 22. I preached at the old church, John Street, from James iii. 17.

I. "The wisdom that cometh from above" is revealed and inspired; it is "pure"—negatively: it is not mixed by its divine Author with that wisdom which is "earthly, sensual, and devilish"; it is not mixed with the policy, or pleasures, or prophets of this world; or of sin, which is of hell. The apostle hath written "pure religion," and this it cannot be when mingled with such qualities, all of which spring from men or devils.

II. "The wisdom that cometh from above is pure"—positively; it is pure in conviction, repentance, faith, regeneration, and sanctification: it is the operative principle of grace in the soul, as internally, and externally manifested. It is "peaceable" in relation to God, and all mankind, to the church, and the world, and the tranquil state of the soul. It is "gentle," soft, amiable in all its administrations, never stormy, or sour, or haughty, or over bearing.

"Easy to be entreated," to do and suffer anything that is right and reasonable, for the glory of God, and for the good of our own, and the souls of others.

"Impartiality," this is the Christian dress: not bound and pinched by countries, names, forms, and opinions; neither does it envy the rich on account of their riches, nor neglect the poor on account of their poverty.

"Without hypocrisy," sincerity is the incontestable evidence of God and man of our possession of the heavenly treasure of "that wisdom that cometh from above"; and people may go upon fancies, and be ready to die with raptures but if they are turbulent, ungovernable, self-willed, and false towards their fellow men, or towards their God, their religion is vain; whatever it may once have been, it is not the gold of the sanctuary now, but a counterfeit, alloyed by a mixture of the wisdom of this world.

ATTITUDES

After Brother Whatcoat had preached in the afternoon, I gave them an exhortation.

I. The excellencies of this salvation: it is a common salvation, a great salvation, the salvation of God.

II. The nature of this salvation: in its degrees of justification, sanctification, and glorification.

III. The present subjects of salvation—infants and believers. The ample means furnished to all, that they may see this salvation—faithful ministers, faithful, consistent, praying professors, and all the holy ordinances of the Church. I was greatly assisted in speaking. I warmly exhorted our friends in Norfolk to build a tabernacle in some part of the town.

Monday, 11. At Joliff's chapel I spoke on an appropriate text, from Isa. xlix. 20; the house is not half large enough. We dined at brother Denbigh's, and came on to the widow Reddick's: she and her sister are both professors.

Tuesday, 12. At Suffolk, brother Whatcoat preached a very appropriate sermon. At Murphy's, work revives; a new house is in preparation: the place is too strait: we must make room for them to dwell. My subject here was 1 Tim. ii. 3-4.

We have made one hundred miles of these roads in three days: poor men! poor horses! We are housed with Elias Clark, Esq., near Chester Gap.

Sabbath, 24. Having taken cold in my head, I was very unwell; I [forced myself] to preach at Pennell's. On Monday we crossed the ridge at Chester Gap, passing the head spring of the north branch of the Rappahannock River. We stopped at Front Royal or Lucetown; I preached at three o'clock; and brother Whatcoat at night.

My subject was Rom. xii. 1-2: *"I beseech you, therefore, brethren, by the mercies of God, that ye present your bodies a living sacrifice, holy, acceptable to God, which is your reasonable service. And be not conformed to this world, but be ye transformed by the renewing of your mind, that ye may prove what is that good, and acceptable, and perfect will of God."*

It was observed, that the apostle's form of address was excellent, and particularly directed to the Christian believers—the subjects of grace. That the people of the "world" who lived in conformity to its manners and maxims, lived in their proper element—"but ye (said our Lord in addressing believers) are not of the world, as I am not of the world, because I have called you out of the world."

The apostle had in view one thing, in two parts, namely: the devotion of the whole man, body and soul, to God; without which the man cannot be a Christian, perfect and entire. "Present your bodies a living sacrifice"—this can only be done by abstaining from all things sinful in practice. We must not only not live in the use of unlawful things, but we must not indulge in the unlawful use of lawful things: it is lawful to eat, but not to gluttony; it

CONSECRATION

is lawful to drink, but not to drunkenness; it is lawful to be married, but it is unlawful for either husband or wife to idolize the other.

We ought to make the faculties of our bodies subservient to the worship and service of God—our eyes to see for God; our ears to hear; our hands to be liberal; our feet to move for God, so as to do or suffer—this is "reasonable service"; and thus occupied, the "mercies of God" excite us properly, and we are "not conformed to this world."

That we be "renewed in our minds"—that all the powers of the soul be given in love and service to the Lord; in conviction for indwelling sin, the repentance of believers; in sanctification; persevering grace; perfect love; and the fruition—perfect and eternal glory; we "prove the will of God" by this—to be good, to be "acceptable" to our own souls; and to be "perfect" in our Christian perfection, holiness, and holiness eternal.

December, 1804: IN SOUTH CAROLINA

Wednesday, 19. I preached at Rembert's chapel: we had a cold rain—it chills the people; they cannot hear to profit: my subject was 1 Thess. v. 24: *"Faithful is he that calleth you, who also will do it": that is, give you entire sanctification, and persevering grace to the end.*

Thursday, 20. We had snow four inches deep: I felt thankful that I had a house, and all things necessary to temporal enjoyment and comfort. Next day it cleared away; my soul is happy in God—purity of heart is my joy, and prayer my delight. I feel as if God would sanctify all the conferences in the South: O may it, in answer to my unceasing prayers, be a great time with the Lord's prophets. It is nine hundred miles from Wheeling on the Ohio, to Charleston, South Carolina: from Baltimore thither, by this route, about 1,200 miles.

On Thursday, Saturday, and Sabbath day, I rested: Jonathan Jackson preached at Rembert's chapel on Monday, and on Tuesday, Christmas day, I gave them a sermon upon Isa. ix. 6: *"For unto us a child is born, unto us a son is given; and the government shall be upon his shoulders; and his name shall be called Wonderful, Counsellor, the Mighty God, the Everlasting Father, the Prince of Peace."*

A "child," after his human nature; a "son" of God. "The government shall be upon his shoulders"—upon the shoulder it was that ancient temporal governors carried their badge of office. His "shoulders" shall be strong enough for the thousands of His faithful ministers, and the millions of His faithful people in His Church militant, who shall confide in His strength.

"His name shall be called"—that is, He shall in reality be what He is called. "Wonderful"—that is, a mysterious and miraculous person in His manifestations—in His birth, spiritual and holy; and in His miracles, notable, perfect, and undeniable.

"Counsellor"—this may refer to His ministry—His prophetic, priestly, and kingly offices. "Mighty God"—mighty in the power of His grace. "The Everlasting Father"—as such, giving life, and life eternal. "Prince of Peace"—and preserving peace in His kingdom; and thus contradistinguished from temporal princes, who are so generally promoters of war.

Wednesday, 26. We set out for Charleston; the rain overtook us, and we passed Sumter court house dripping. We dined with Mr. Bradford, and pursued our journey, wet as it was: stopping at a house where we might have remained for the night, we were driven off by a drunken madman who went on like a fiend: it was dark, and we had rain above, and mud and water below; the elements appeared to be at war with us: at length Mr. Boyd saw us in our deep distress, and led us to his house, and treated us very kindly. I was wet; I was blistered; I was skinned.

February, 1805: IN VIRGINIA

Sunday, 10. I preached at Norfolk, upon Rom. xiii. 11-14: "That knowing the time," etc. Slumbering, sleeping professors are called, by the signs of the time, to "awake—to cast off the works of darkness," as they would clothes which no longer suited their characters, garments no longer appropriate to their profession, and "to put on the armour of light—the whole armour of God"; to "walk honestly," that is, decently as it becometh the true, consistent, dignified, Christian character, to avoid the sensualities of the world, and the sins and indulgences of the flesh and spirit; to "put on the Lord Jesus Christ," to be dressed, decked, adorned with Jesus Christ, and filled with His Spirit; "to make no provision for the flesh," with the intent of fulfilling its lusts.

At Portsmouth I preached upon Luke iii. 6: *"All flesh shall see the salvation of God."*

October, 1814: IN TENNESSEE

Here he preached on John viii. 31-32: *"Ye shall know the truth, and the truth shall make you free."* How to know the truth? By continuing under gospel ministry, and using gospel means. Ye shall know the truth—of the gospel; feelingly, experimentally, practically. "Make you free"—What the freedom wrought consists in. It is an entire deliverance from sin—from its guilt, power, and inbeing. A freedom embracing the privileges of pardon, peace, patience, meekness, perfect love, joy on earth, and everlasting glory in heaven.

We hasted away, after meeting, to William Cunningham's.

October, 1814: IN NORTH CAROLINA

(Here is one of the many grateful tributes paid by Asbury to his traveling companions who cared for him during his incredible journeys under hardship and much sickness.—Editor)

Tuesday, 18. Our ride brought us to Jarratt's, on Pigeon River. O my excellent son, John Bond! A tree had fallen across our way—what was to be done? Brother Bond sprung to the axe fastened under our carriage. Mounted upon the large limbs, hewing and hacking, stroke after stroke, without intermission, until he had cut away five of them, hauling them on one side as he severed them, so that we passed without difficulty.

Is there his equal to be found in the United States? He drives me along with the utmost care and tenderness, he fills my appointments by preaching for me when I am disabled, he watches over me at night after the fatigue of driving all day, and if, when he is in bed, and asleep, I call, he is awake and up in the instant to give me medicine, or to perform any other services his sick father may require of him; and this is done so readily, and with so much patience, when my constant infirmities and ill health require so many and oft-repeated attentions.

We have had a great drought; I think I never saw the rivers so low. The asthma presses sorely upon my panting breast: Lord, sanctify all my afflictions!

Letter to Rev. Henry Smith, Baltimore
My very dear Smith:

May great grace attend you. I consent to what you say, in general. O, purity! O, Christian perfection! O, Sanctification! It is heaven below to feel all sin removed. Preach it, whether they will bear or forbear. Preach it. You have never experienced the realities of heaven or hell, but preach them. Some have professed it (perfect love), but have fallen from it; others profess, but do not possess it. They trifle away life. They seldom use the gift God hath given them. I think we ought modestly to tell what we feel in the fullest. For two years past, amidst incredible toils, I have enjoyed almost inexpressible sensations. Our Pentecost is come, in some places, for sanctification.

I have good reason to believe that upon the Eastern Shore 4,000 have been converted since the first of May last, and 1,000 sanctified, besides souls convicted, and quickened, and restored: Oh glory, it will come across the Bay. I have reason to believe that at the Philadelphia Conference many of the preachers were powerfully blest in their own souls and convenanted to use ordinary and extra-ordinary means. Brother Chandler has been 40 nights and days in the woods at camp and quarterly meeting, and possibly will be 110 more before November. Ten campmeetings are planned north of New York in about 2 months and more laid out now.

I think we congregate 2 millions in a year; and I hope for 100,000 souls convicted, converted, restored, or sanctified. The whole continent is awake. I am on a route of 3,000 miles from and to Baltimore. Such a work of God, I believe, was never known for the number of people. The preachers will die in harvest field, as it lasts all the year. I believe Brother Whatcoat died a martyr for the work. Farewell in Jesus. I am still thine.

F. Asbury

P.S. I had to speak two hours today on the drought and was so worn out I had to write to forget myself.

December 30, 1802
In general I am persuaded we have not preached sufficiently on baptism and Christian perfection.

F. A.

November, 1815: In North Carolina
(The final outline in Asbury's *Journal* is of the sermon he preached on Sunday, November 19, 1815, in North Carolina.— Editor)

Sabbath, 19. I preached upon Acts xxvi. 17-18. Many were the instances of deliverance; they bound Him and scourged Him, yet had the Jews no power over His life, which they so often sought. And the Gentiles, to whom He was especially sent by the Son of God, what a description is given of their deplorable state! what blindness of mind, ignorance, idolatry, superstition, complicated and unaccountable wickedness! "The power of Satan"—completely in his possession, body, soul, and spirit, in all their powers and passions—in infidelity and impenitence, and under the guilt of actual transgression.

Thus gospel truth and gospel ministers find sinners; and they must be preached to with energy. And these ministers must be sent; and to be qualified for this mission, they must, like Paul, be convinced, convicted, and converted, and sanctified. Like him they must be preserved from the violence of the people; but especially from their indulgences and flatteries. "Turning them from darkness to light, and from the power of Satan unto God." A faithful minister will have these signs to follow him.

I die daily—am made perfect by labour and suffering, and fill up still what is behind. There is no time or opportunity to take medicine in daytime, I must do it at night. I am wasting away with a constant dysentery and cough.[9]

The sick and homeless prophet was still tenacious of his holiness message, passionate in his delivery of it, and jealous for its continued proclamation by his beloved Methodist preachers. The preachers were left in no doubt but that the ultimate authentication of a Spirit-filled ministry is in lives convicted of sin, converted to God, and sanctified wholly under that ministry.

Asbury's Last Days

The final entry in Asbury's *Journal* comes almost as suddenly as the passing of Moses. It is dated December 7, 1815. Asbury had still four months to live and serve, and he was determined that his usefulness to God and his life would end together. Comforted and strengthened by his Methodist family, he maintained his zeal to the very end.

Asbury preached his last sermon on March 24, 1816, in Richmond, Va. The indomitable Methodist apostle was carried to the pulpit, where, seated at a table for support, he preached from Rom. 9:28: *"For he will finish the work and cut it short in righteousness: because a short work will the Lord make upon the earth."*

Having preached for an hour he was carried from the pulpit to a carriage and taken to his lodging. He made the effort to get on to Fredericksburg, but it was too much. Asbury turned in to his last staging post in George Arnold's home surrounded by his fighting com-

---

9. *JFA*, 2:796.

panions of the Holy War. He passed peacefully away with hands raised to heaven.

Charles Wesley's triumphant hymn would surely have been most appropriate:

> *Rejoice for a brother deceased!*
> *Our loss is his infinite gain!*

But upon whom did the mantle of the prophet fall?

* * *

Asbury's Associates

In *The History of American Methodism* there is a brief but beautiful section titled "The Deeper Work of Grace." Enshrined within it are some striking testimonies from Asbury's men regarding their personal experience of the second definite work of God's grace. The author, Leland Scott, was at the time of publication director of the Wesley Foundation of the University of Arizona. He writes:

> For the early American Methodists, Wesley's emphasis on the gracious possibility of full salvation was nothing less than divinely inspired. Who could limit the extent to which the love of God could captivate—and thus cleanse and release—one's inner life! Indeed, Wesley insisted the power and assurance of divine love could enter the believer's heart at any moment in such fullness that the responsive love to God and man simply replaced all sinful actions, thought, and tempers. "I think I shall never be satisfied," exclaimed Freeborn Garrettson, "until I have a deeper work of grace in my soul."
>
> As with the blessing of forgiveness, so it was with the blessing of sanctification: ask, in the miserable awareness of one's desperate need, and the gift could be expected. Once having entered into the life of faith, through conviction and conversion, believers were to be encouraged to consider the yet more glorious privileges offered to them in the gospel.
>
> The Methodist preacher, in his work with believers, "must not spare the remaining man of sin; he must anatomize the human

heart, and follow self-will and self-love through all their windings
... with great tenderness. ... He must hold forth Christ as an
all-sufficient Saviour. ... He must describe to them, in all its
richest views, the blessing of perfect love." Indeed, he must declare
how the Savior "is this moment able and willing to reduce the
mountain into a plain."

Coke has a moving reminder of the promise of sanctification
in "The Substance of a Sermon on the Godhead of Christ,"
preached at Baltimore ... on the 26th day of December, 1784,
before the General Conference of the Methodist Episcopal
Church: "Yea, thou shalt sweetly and experimentally know of
thine own self, that the blood of Jesus Christ cleanseth from all sin.
Thou shalt be one with him, and he will be one with thee; thine
heart shall be his constant home."

Preceded by a depressing realization of the weight of sin still
clinging to one, such an experience of the whole of grace was the
occasion for grand rejoicing no less than experiences of initial
assurance.[10]

Scott proceeds by condensing the testimonies of Phillip Gatch,
William Watters, William Thatcher, and Freeborn Garrettson. He
concludes an impressive section with quotations from two letters, one
from Ezekiel Cooper, Asbury's friend, and the other from Daniel
Hitt's letter to Asbury.

The witness of these four saintly circuit preachers of holiness is
sufficient to demonstrate and illustrate Asbury's assertion: "It is true,
real religion cannot exist without peace, and love, and joy. But then,
REAL religion is REAL HOLINESS. And all sensations without a strong
disposition for holiness are but delusive."[11]

Phillip Gatch

Phillip Gatch was commissioned to preach by Thomas Rankin,
Wesley's emissary. He writes of the hunger of his heart in the pursuit
of holiness after his liberation by grace:

> I labored under a sense of want, but not of guilt. I needed
> strength of soul ... The struggle was severe but short. I spent the
> most of my time in prayer, but sometimes only with groans that I
> could not utter. I had neither read nor heard much on the subject,
> till in the midst of my distress a person put into my hand Mr.
> Wesley's sermon on "Salvation by Faith." I thought, if salvation was

---

10. *History of American Methodism* (New York and Nashville: Abingdon Press, 1964), 1:301 ff. Hereafter referred to as HAM.

11. *JFA*, 1:127.

to be obtained by faith, why not now? I prayed, but the Comforter tarried....

God had his way in the work; my faith was strengthened and my hope revived.

Thus it was that one evening Phillip was overcome under the sense of his need, and although it was the time of family worship, he prayed desperately for himself; and as he did so:

the Spirit of the Lord came down upon me, and the opening heavens shone around me. By faith I saw Jesus at the right hand of the Father. I felt such a weight of glory that I fell with my face to the floor, and the Lord said by his Spirit, "You are now sanctified, seek to grow in the fruit of the Spirit." ... This work and the instruction of divine truth were sealed on my soul by the Holy Ghost. My joy was full. I related to others what God had done for me. This was in July, a little more than two months after I had received the Spirit of justification.

William Watters

It is written of William Watters, "His piety was of a choice and unquestionable type. To prayer and thanksgiving of a sanctified heart he added that other grace of spiritual energy which delights itself in doing good. Christ the Savior engaged in doing good was his ideal. With the Holy Ghost love in his heart, he strove to be like him in works of mercy and help to our suffering humanity.[12]

In 1807 Watters wrote to Phillip Gatch:

Your remarks on the necessity and the effects of preaching and pressing on believers a present and full salvation from sin, I think are perfectly correct. I have generally, for many years, found that in proportion to my own enjoyment of the mind which was in the blessed Jesus, I have held forth the great and precious promises of the gospel to my brethren.[13]

William Thatcher

Thatcher was converted in 1790, entirely sanctified in 1793, and became a local preacher in 1795. He died in 1856. Asbury lodged in his home upon occasion and wrote to him as presiding elder on the New York district. Asbury wrote of that district in 1806:

We had great order and great power from beginning to end (of the Camp Meeting): I judge two hundred souls were made the

---

12. D. A. Watters, *The First American Itinerant of Methodism: William Watters* (Cincinnati: Printed for the author by Curts and Jennings, 1898).

13. *HAM*, 1:303.

subjects of grace in its various operations of conviction, conversion, sanctification, and reclamation. Glory! Glory![14]

Thatcher himself wrote:

> Having the charge of a store (Petersburg, Virginia), and being the only religious person in the family, on closing the store at dusk, my custom was, to lock myself in and pray privately. At one of these seasons of retirement, as soon as the door was fastened, suddenly such a sense of inward corruption took possession of my heart, as brought me to the floor on my face, merely from self-abhorrence. No consciousness of guilt, or doubt of my state of justification was the cause of my mental anguish; but such a view of the evils of my heart, as was never before shown me.
>
> I rose from my prostration to my knees and began to pray, and this text was applied—"If the prophet had bid thee do some great thing, wouldst thou not have done it? How much rather when he saith to thee, Wash and be clean?" My next thought was, "If washing in Jordan, at the command of the prophet would cleanse Naaman how much more shall the blood of Christ, who through the Eternal Spirit offered himself without spot to God, purge my conscience from dead works to serve the living God!"
>
> O what a view of the fullness of Christ I then had! The all-sufficiency of the infinite merits of our Saviour was then spread before me; my soul was all imprisoned by his life; my unbelief gave way; faith grasped the prize! The witness of full sanctification was given, O astonishing love divine! Redeeming love! Glory be to God, I now know that the blood of Jesus Christ cleanseth from all sin. . . . Humbled in the dust, my heart could say, "To me, who am less than the least of all saints is this grace given."[15]

Freeborn Garrettson

Garrettson (1752-1827) was the son of a prosperous Maryland family. He was converted in 1775 and immediately united with the Methodist Conference. Ordained by Thomas Coke during the famous Christmas Conference in 1784, he became the Methodist apostle of the northeast traveling as far as Lake Champlain, and working extensively in Eastern New York, Connecticut, and Vermont. His three-year mission in Nova Scotia meant an increase of 600 new members for the Societies. He stood tall among Asbury's American-born preachers, and was a competent leader under the pressures of the Revolutionary War.

Garrettson was firm in his conviction and experience of Christian

---

14. *JFA*, 2:505 ff.
15. *HAM*, 1:303.

perfection. Being fully persuaded that the promise of God is full deliverance from all sin Garrettson defended the Wesleyan message with vigor. When confronted with the idea that perfection is unattainable before death he replied:

> Our Lord "came to destroy the works of the devil"; and do you suppose he will call death to his assistance? Death in Scripture is called the last enemy, and we learn, that as death leaves us, judgment will find us; and that there is no knowledge or work in the grave. And if we die in our sins, where the Lord is we cannot come: I want to know how death is to bring this about. Why, at the article of death, sin is done away, and not till then?
>
> The Papists say we must be refined by the fire of purgatory: the Universalists, that the last farthing will be paid in hell; and you say, Nay, death will do it; but we profess to hold with the Holy Scriptures, which say, that "his name shall be called Jesus, for he shall save the people from their sins." Do you not, said I, believe that the Lord is able to wash and cleanse the soul from all sin one minute before death? To this he agreed. And if a minute, why not a day, a month, yea, why not seven years? The apostle saith "Behold now is the accepted time! Behold now is the day of salvation!" How dare any man limit the Holy One of Israel!

Years later, reflecting upon this experience, he wrote:

> We were both beginners in the great work of the ministry, and probably a few years' longer experience, and we should have been capable of handling the controversy more profitably. God alone is absolutely perfect. Among finite intelligences perfection can only be in degrees. . . . Christians may be perfect in their measure, and what we call Christian perfection is a high degree of piety—to love God with every power of the soul, and to be saved from all sin, properly so called.[16]

Ezekiel Cooper

One man who was profoundly moved by the powerful preaching of Garrettson was Ezekiel Cooper, who entered the Methodist ministry in 1785. Known among his fellow preachers as "a living encyclopedia," he became American Methodism's first native-born book agent, an office he filled most efficiently from 1799-1808.

In a letter (1786) to a member of the New Jersey Assembly, Ezekiel Cooper speaks to the assertion that no one could live without sin:

> Dear Sir: I am sorry to find one who professes to be a child of God, yet espouses the infidel's cause, and openly proves an advocate for sin, even while the word of God loudly demonstrates

---

16. Ibid., 1:232, 323.

that "He that committeth sin is of the devil," 1 John iii. 8; and, verse 9, "Whosoever is born of God doth not commit sin."

Cooper points to the distinction between sin and temptation. "The devil presents something of the world or flesh to the mind. Here temptation begins, but while the mind opposes the evil we do not sin." With "Christ helping him," man is enabled to "overcome sin and the false spirit."

> Take heed that you do not lay a stumblingblock in your neighbor's way, or be instrumental, through your friendship to sin, in stopping any in the pursuit of holiness, by getting that dangerous notion in their heads "that there is no living without sin," and so they may say, "I'll not strive after that which is not attainable," and give way to sin, as (the more is the pity) too many do.
>
> I beg that you will serve God and prepare to meet him for "without holiness no man shall see the Lord."[17]

Daniel Hitt

Hitt became associate editor and book steward with John Wilson upon the resignation of Ezekiel Cooper in 1808. He was a man of whom Asbury had high opinion. Hitt's name appears frequently in the *Journal* and *Letters*. He was often Asbury's traveling companion and was at one time appointed by the Conference to accompany Asbury. He had a sincere concern for Church Order,[18] and also for the preaching of heart holiness as is shown in the following extract from a letter to Asbury, March 15, 1803:

> Since my last to you, we have had glorious times in truth.... The other day, I was [in] Alexandria, and ... Brother Rowen told me ... they had taken upwards of three hundred, far the greater part of whom profess to be converted ... the others appear to be thoroughly convinced of their lost and undone situation by sin, and earnestly engaged for redemption in the blood of the Lamb.
>
> On the fifth of February the quarterly meeting for Rockingham circuit began.... It was impossible correctly to ascertain the number converted, but I think there must have been thirty or upwards, with a number of sanctifications. I was very much pleased to find in the friends, such a hungering and thirsting for the mind which was in Christ Jesus. I think there are no surer marks of a genuine work, than to see them eager to be made perfect in love.[19]

---

17. *JFA*, 1:346-47.
18. *JFA*, 1:378 ff.
19. *HAM*, 1:307.

William McKendree

McKendree was the first American-born bishop of the Methodist Episcopal Church. He was, next to Asbury, the architect of the Methodist Church in America, and "may be justly awarded the distinction of carrying forward the work and securing its permanency and success by his remarkable legislative and administrative abilities."[20]

It is certain that Methodism has had no more devoted and zealous servant than this vigorous Virginian. He gave himself to the extension and consolidation of the work of evangelism with a loyalty to the church, her Lord, and her leader Asbury with a passion and industry not surpassed by any of his contemporaries. Born in Richmond, Va., in 1757, the son of a planter, he died in 1835 in the full assurance of faith, repeating Charles Wesley's words:

> *Not a cloud can arise to darken my skies,*
> *Or hide for a moment my Lord from my eyes!*

He is variously described as "a son to Asbury," "the major general" of the great Western advance; "His intellect was bright and his thoughts diamond-pointed."[21] We call this outstanding preacher as a witness to two clear works of grace in his heart and as a consistent preacher of holiness:

> I resolved to seek religion, and began in good earnest, to pray for it that evening.
>
> Tuesday I went to church, fasting and praying. Mr. Easter preached from John iii. 19-22, "And this is the condemnation, that light has come into the world," etc. The word reached my heart. From this time I had no peace of mind; I was completely miserable. My heart was broken up, and I saw that it was evil above all things, and "desperately wicked." A view of God's forbearance, and of the debasing sin of ingratitude, of which I had been guilty in grieving the Spirit of God, overwhelmed me with confusion.
>
> Now my conscience roared like a lion. "The pains of hell got hold of me." I concluded that I had committed the "unpardonable sin," and had thoughts of giving up all for lost. For three days I might have said, "My bed shall comfort me, then thou scarest me with

---

20. Robert Paine, *The Life and Times of William McKendree* (Nashville: Publishing House of the Methodist Episcopal South, 1880), 7.
21. See *HAM*, 1:100 ff.

dreams, and terrifiest me through visions, so that my soul chooseth strangling and death rather than life." Job. vii. 7-15.

But in the evening of the third day deliverance came. While Mr. Easter was preaching, I was praying as well as I could, for I was almost ready to despair of mercy. Suddenly doubts and fears fled, hope sprung up in my soul, and the burden was removed. I knew that God was love—that there was mercy even for me, and I rejoiced in silence.

[A few days of uncertainty followed, however, before he received the witness of the Holy Spirit:]

But deliverance was at hand. Mr. Easter came round, and his Master came with him, and in the time of meeting the Lord, who is merciful and kind, blessed me with the witness of the Spirit; and then, sir, I could rejoice indeed—yes, with joy unspeakable and full of glory!

Within twenty-four hours after this I was twice tempted to think my conversion was delusive, and not genuine, because I did not receive the witness of the Spirit at the same time.

But I instantly applied to the throne of grace, and, in the duty of prayer, the Lord delivered me from the enemy, and from that day to this I have never doubted my conversion. I have pitied, and do still pity, those who, under the influence of certain doctrines, are led to give the preference to a doubting experience, and therefore can only say, "If I ever was converted," "I hope I am converted," "I fear I never was converted," etc., but can never say, "We know that we have passed from death unto life." In this respect, "darkness, in part, has happened to Zion," but I hope the time is not far distant when truth and religion shall triumph over error and form.

Not long after I had confidence in my acceptance with God, Mr. Gibson preached us a sermon on sanctification, and I felt its weight. When Mr. Easter came, he enforced the same doctrines. This led me more minutely to examine the emotions of my heart.

SECOND BLESSING I found remaining corruption—embraced the doctrine of sanctification, and diligently sought the blessing it holds forth. The more I sought the blessing of sanctification, the more I felt the need of it—and the more important did that blessing appear. In its pursuit, my soul grew in grace and in the faith that overcomes the world. But there was an aching void which made me cry.

> 'Tis worse than death my God to love,
> And not my God alone.

FINDING One morning I walked into the field, and while I was musing, such an overwhelming power of the divine Being overshadowed me, as I had never experienced before. Unable to stand, I sunk to the ground, more than filled with transport. My cup ran over, and I shouted aloud.

Had it not been for a new set of painful exercises which now came upon me, I might have rejoiced "evermore;" but my heart was enlarged, and I saw more clearly than ever before the danger of an unconverted state. For such persons I prayed with anxious care. At times, when called upon to pray in public, my soul would get into an agony, and the Lord would, in great compassion, pour out his Spirit; souls were convicted and converted, and Zion rejoiced abundantly in those days.

WITNESSING Without a thought of preaching, I began to tell my acquaintances what the Lord had done for me, and could do for them. It had its effect, and lasting impressions were made. Thus I was imperceptibly led on until the preachers and people began to urge me to speak more publicly.

[McKendree's biographer writes of his preaching ministry:][22]

PREACHING Daily self-denial, frequent, fervent, and protracted prayer, "in fastings often," "preaching the word in season and out of season," reproving, rebuking, exhorting, as "need required and occasion was given," combined with a constant study of the Bible and devout meditation, were the means by which our fathers in the ministry "wrought wonders." Their preaching was plain and in faith: they felt the force of the momentous truths which they uttered.

They realized the presence of God, and expected the aid of the Holy Spirit to attend the divinely-appointed means. They looked for present effects, and they were not disappointed. Sinners were convicted and converted under the word, and the lukewarm and self-satisfied were stimulated to seek for holiness. God honored the men, by giving them the signs and seal of his favor, who honored him by their confidence in his truth and power. So it has ever been, and so it will be to the end of time.

---

22. Paine, *Life and Times of William McKendree*, 83 ff.

With the profiles, confessions, testimonies, and records of such men before him can any reasonable person come to any conclusion other than that Wesley's American sons and their "people called Methodist" heartily believed, experienced, and propagated the gospel of entire sanctification, perfect love, Christian perfection—"the second blessing properly so-called"?

Bibliography

BOOKS

Abbey and Overton. *The English Church in the Eighteenth Century.* London: Longmans, 1902.

Allen, Brigadier Margaret. *Fletcher of Madeley.* London: Salvation Army 1905. (reprinted by Alleghany Wesleyan Methodist Connexion, 1974).

Armstrong, Anthony. *The Church of England, the Methodist and Society.* London: University Press, 1973.

Asbury, Francis. *Journal and Letters of Francis Asbury.* 3 vols. Edited by Elmer T. Clark. Nashville: Abingdon Press, 1958.

Baker, Frank. *The Methodist Pilgrim in England.* London: Epworth Press, 1951.

———. *A Charge to Keep.* London: Epworth Press, 1947.

———. *Representative Verse of Charles Wesley.* London: Epworth Press, 1962.

———. *Charles Wesley's Verse.* London: Epworth Press, 1964.

———. *Charles Wesley's Theology as Revealed by His Letters.* London: Epworth Press, 1948.

———. *From Wesley to Asbury: Studies in Early American Methodism.* Durham, N.C.: Duke University Press, 1976.

———. *William Grimshaw, 1708-63.* London: Epworth Press, 1963.

Baker, Eric S. *A Herald of the Evangelical Revival.* London: Epworth Press, 1963.

———. *The Faith of a Methodist.* London: Epworth Press, 1958.

Belden, Albert D. *George Whitefield the Awakener.* London: Rockcliffe, 1953.

Bennett, R. *The Early Life of Howell Harris.* London: Banner of Truth Trust, 1962.

Benson, Joseph. *Life of Fletcher.* vol. 1 of *Fletcher's Works.* London: Hodder and Stoughton, 1832.

Beynon, T. *Howell Harris in London.* Aberystwyth (Wales): Camprian News Press, 1960.

Bett, Henry. *The Spirit of Methodism.* London: Epworth Press, 1937.

Body, A. *John Wesley and Education.* London: Epworth Press, 1936.

Brailsford, Edward J. *Richard Watson, Theologian and Missionary Advocate.* London: Charles Kelly, n.d.

Brailsford, Mabel R. *A Tale of Two Brothers.* London: Rupert Hart-Davis, 1954.

12Bready, J. Wesley. *England Before and After Wesley.* London: Hodder and Stoughton, 1938.

Burtner, R. W. and Chiles, R.E., eds. *A Compend of Wesley's Theology.* Nashville: Abingdon Press, 1954.

Butler, Rev. D. *Thomas á Kempis: A Religious Study.* Edinburgh and London: Oliphant, Anderson, and Ferrier, 1908.

Cameron, Richard M. *The Rise of Methodism.* New York: Philosophical Library, 1954.

Cannon, William Ragsdale. *The Theology of John Wesley.* Nashville: Abingdon Press, 1946.

Carroll, H. K. *Francis Asbury in the Making of American Methodism.* New York: Methodist Book Concern, 1923.

Carter, Charles W. *The Person and Ministry of the Holy Spirit.* Grand Rapids: Baker Book House, 1974.

Carter, Henry. *The Methodist Heritage.* London: Epworth Press, 1951.

———. *The Methodist.* London: Epworth Press, 1914.

Cell, Croft. *The Rediscovery of John Wesley.* New York: Henry Holt and Co., 1935.

Chiles, R. E. *Theological Transition in American Methodism.* New York: Abingdon Press, 1965.

Clarke, Adam. *Memoirs of the Wesley Family.* London and New York: Lane and Scott, 1851.

———. *Christian Theology.* London: Wesleyan Office, 1835.

Clarke, J. B. B. (ed.) *An Account of the Infancy, Religious, and Literary Life of Adam Clarke, LL.D., F.A.S.* New York: D. Appleton and Co., 1833.

———. (ed.) *An Account of the Religious and Literary Life of Adam Clarke, LL.D., F.A.S.* New York: Carlton and Phillips, 1854.

Coke, T. and Moore, H. *The Life of Rev. John Wesley, A. M.* London: Robins and Co., 1823.

Cox, Leo George. *John Wesley's Concept of Perfection.* Kansas City: Beacon Hill Press, 1964.

Cragg, George G. *Grimshaw of Haworth.* London: Canterbury Press, 1947.

Crook, W. *The Ancestry of the Wesleys.* London: Epworth Press, 1938.

Curtis. L. P. *Anglican Moods of the Eighteenth Century.* New Haven, Conn.: Archon Books, 1966.

Cumming, J. Elder. *Holy Men of God.* London: Hodder and Stoughton, 1893.

Davies, Rupert E. *Methodism.* London: Epworth Press, 1963.

Davies, Rupp, ed., *History of the Methodist Church in Britain,* vol. 1. London: Epworth Press, 1965.

Deschner, John. *Wesley's Christology.* Dallas: Southern Methodist University Press, 1960.

Dimond, S. G. *The Psychology of the Methodist Revival.* London: Oxford University Press, 1926.
——. *Psychology of Methodism.* London: Epworth Press, 1932.
Doughty, W. L. *John Wesley, Preacher.* London: Epworth Press, 1955.
Drakeford, John W. *Take Her, Mr. Wesley.* Waco, Tex.: Word Books, 1973.
DuBose. *Francis Asbury: A Biographical Study.* Nashville: Methodist Episcopal Publishing House, 1916.
Dunn, S. *Christian Theology by Adam Clarke, LL.D., F.A.S.* London: Tegg and Son, 1835. (Reprinted by Schmul, Salem, Ohio, 1967.)
Edwards, Maldwyn. *John Wesley and the Eighteenth Century.* London: Epworth Press, 1955.
——. *John Wesley, the Astonishing Youth.* London: Epworth Press, 1959.
——. *Family Circle.* London: Epworth Press, 1949.
——. *Sons to Samuel.* London: Epworth Press, 1961.
——. *This Methodism.* London: Epworth Press, 1939.
——. *Francis Asbury.* Manchester, England: Penwork, 1972.
Evans, Eifion. *Howell Harris Evangelist.* Cardiff, Wales: University of Wales Press, 1974.
Fitchett, W. H. *Wesley and His Century.* London: Smith Elder and Co., 1906.
Fletcher, John. *The Works of John Fletcher,* 9 vols. London: Wesleyan Conference Office, 1877.
——. *An Appeal to Matters of Fact and Common Sense.* Titusville, Pa. Allegheny Wesleyan Methodist Connection, 1973.
——. *The Portrait of St. Paul,* or the true model for Christians and pastors, translated from a French manuscript of the late Rev. John William De La Flechere, vicar of Madeley, by the Rev. John Gilpin. Salem, Ohio: Convention Bookstore, n.d.
Flew, R. Newton. *The Idea of Perfection in Christian Theology.* London: Oxford University Press, 1934.
Gee, H. L. *Easter at Epworth.* London: Epworth Press, 1944.
Gill, Frederick C. *In the Steps of John Wesley.* London: Lutterworth Press, 1962.
——. *Charles Wesley, The First Methodist.* London: Epworth Press, 1964.
——. *The Prayers of John Wesley.* London: Epworth Press, 1951.
Gould, J. Glenn. *Healing the Hurt of Man.* Kansas City: Beacon Hill Press of Kansas City, 1971.
Greathouse, William M. *From the Apostles to Wesley.* Kansas City: Beacon Hill Press of Kansas City, 1979.
Green, J. Brazier. *John Wesley and William Law.* London: Epworth Press, 1945.
Green, John Richard. *A Short History of the English People.* London and New York: Harper and Brothers, 1898.
Green, Richard. *Oxford Studies.* London: Macmillan, Vol. 3, 1901.

———. *John Wesley Evangelist*. London: Religious Tract Society, 1905.

Green, V. H. H. *The Young Mr. Wesley*. London: Edwin Arnold, 1961.

———. *A History of Oxford University*. London: Batsford, 1974.

———. *Religion at Oxford and Cambridge*. London: S. C. M. Press, Ltd., 1964.

Hamilton, J. T. and K. G. *History of the Moravian Church*. Winston-Salem, N.C.: Moravian Church in America, 1967.

Harmon, Rebecca. *Susanna, Mother of the Wesleys*. Nashville: Abingdon Press, 1968.

Harrison, G. Elsie. *Son to Susanna*. London: Nicholson and Watson, 1937.

———. *Methodist Good Companion*. London: Epworth Press, 1955.

Hildebrandt, Franz. *I Offered Christ*. London: Epworth Press, 1967.

———. *From Luther to Wesley*. London: Lutterworth Press, 1951.

———. *Christianity According to the Wesleys*. London: Epworth Press, 1956.

House of Shirley. *Life and Times of the Countess of Huntingdon*. 2 vols. London: W. E. Painter, 1840.

Hutton, J. E. *A History of the Moravian Church*. London: Moravian Publication Office, 1909.

Jackson, Thomas. *Life of Charles Wesley*. 2 vols. London: John Mason, 1841.

———, ed. *Memoirs of Rev. Charles Wesley, M.A.* London: John Mason, 1848.

———, ed. *Journal of Rev. Charles Wesley, M.A.*, 2 Vols. London: John Mason, 1849.

———, ed. *The Lives of Early Methodist Preachers*. 6 vols. London: Wesleyan Conference Office, 4th edition 1871-72.

Jones, D. M. *Charles Wesley*. London: Sharp., n.d.

Jones, M. H. *The Trevecca Letters*. Bangor and Caernarvon: Welsh Calvinistic Methodist Bookroom, 1932 and 1962.

Kent, John. *The Age of Disunity*. London: Epworth Press, 1966.

Kirby, G. W. *The Elect Lady*. Croydon, England: Trustees of Countess of Huntingdon Connexion, 1972.

Kirk, Rev. John. *Charles Wesley the Poet of Methodism*. London: Hamilton Adams, 1860.

———. *The Mother of the Wesleys*. London: Charles Kelly, 1864.

Knight, Helen C. *Lady Huntingdon and Her Friends*. New York: American Tract Society 1853.

Knox, Ronald. *Enthusiasm*. London: Oxford University Press, 1950.

Koerber, Carolo. *The Theology of Conversion According to John Wesley*. New York: Neo-Eboraci, 1967.

Langton, Edward. *History of the Moravian Church*. London: Allen and Unwin, 1956.

Law, William. *A Serious Call to a Devout and Holy Life.* Everymans edition. London: Dent and Co., 1906.

Lawson, A. B. *John Wesley and the Christian Ministry.* London: SPCK, 1963.

Lawton, George. *Shropshire Saint.* London: Epworth Press, 1960.

Lee, Umphrey. *The Lord's Horseman.* New York: Abingdon Press, 1954.

———. *John Wesley and Modern Religion.* Nashville: Abingdon-Cokesbury Press, 1936.

———. *The Historical Background of Methodist Enthusiasm.* New York: A. M. S. Press, 1967.

Lewis, A. J. *Zinzendorf, the Ecumenical Pioneer.* London: S.C.M. Press, 1962.

Lindstrom, Harald. *Wesley and Sanctification.* Stockholm, Sweden: Nya Bokforlags Aktiebolaget, 1946.

Mains, George D. *Francis Asbury.* London: Robert Culley, 1909.

McDonald, H. D. *Theories of Revelation.* Grand Rapids: Baker Book House, 1979.

McDonald, W. *John Wesley.* New York: Methodist Book Concern, 1899.

McDowel, W. F. *Creative Men.* New York: Abingdon Press, 1934.

Meredith, William H. *Jesse Lee, Apostle of Methodism.* New York: Eaton and Mains, 1909.

Mitchell, T. Crichton. *Mr. Wesley.* Kansas City: Beacon Hill Press, 1957.

———. *Meet Mr. Wesley.* Kansas City: Beacon Hill Press of Kansas City, 1982.

Monk, Robert C. *John Wesley, His Puritan Heritage.* London: Epworth Press, 1966.

Moore, Henry. *Life of Mrs. Fletcher.* London: Wesleyan Methodist, 1817.

Morgan, Irwony. *'Twixt the Mount and Multitude.* London: Epworth Press, 1957.

Newton, John. *Susanna Wesley, Puritan Maid.* London: Epworth Press, 1968.

Nuttall, G. F. *Howell Harris, 1714-1773.* Cardiff, Wales: University of Wales Press, 1965.

Outler, Albert C. *John Wesley.* New York: Oxford University Press, 1964.

———. *Theology in the Wesleyan Spirit.* Nashville: Tidings, 1975.

———. *Evangelism in the Wesleyan Spirit.* Nashville: Tidings, 1971.

Overton, John Henry. *The Evangelical Revival in the Eighteenth Century.* New York: Randolph and Company, 1886.

———. *The English Church in the Eighteenth Century.* London: Longmans and Green, 1902.

Paine, Robert. *The Life and Times of William McKendree.* Nashville: Publishing House of the Methodist Episcopal Church South, 1880.

Parris, John R. *John Wesley's Doctrine of the Sacraments.* London: Epworth Press, 1963.

Paul, Robert J. *The Atonement and the Sacraments.* London: Hodder and Stoughton, 1961.

Perkins, Harold W. *The Doctrine of Christian Perfection.* London: Epworth Press, 1927.

Peters, John L. *Christian Perfection and American Methodism.* Nashville: Abingdon, 1956.

Piette, Maximin. *John Wesley in the Evolution of Protestantism.* London: Sheed and Ward, 1938.

Purkiser, W. T.; Taylor, R. S.; Taylor, W. H. *God, Man, and Salvation, A Biblical Theology.* Kansas City: Beacon Hill Press of Kansas City, 1977.

Rattenbury, J. Ernest. *The Conversion of the Wesleys.* London: Epworth Press, 1958.

———. *Wesley's Legacy to the World.* London: Epworth Press, 1928.

———. *The Evangelical Doctrines of Charles Wesley's Hymns.* London: Epworth Press, 1941.

Roberts, Gomer Morgan, trans. and annot. *Selected Trevecka Letters (1747-1794).* Caernarvon Wales: Calvinistic Methodist Bookroom, 1962.

Sangster, W. Eawin. *The Path to Perfection.* London: Hodder and Stoughton, 1943.

———. *The Pure in Heart.* London: Epworth Press, 1955.

———. *Methodisn Can Be Born Again.* London: Epworth Press, 1938.

Schmidt, Martin. *John Wesley, A Theological Biography.* 3 Vols. London: Epworth Press, 1962, 1971, 1973.

Seed, T. Alexander. *John and Mary Fletcher.* London: C. H. Kelly, n.d.

Semmel, Bernard. *The Methodist Revoltuion.* London: Heinemann, 1974.

Simon, John S. *John Wesley.* 5 vols. London: Epworth Press, 1921-34

———. *The Revival of Religion in the Eighteenth Century.* London: Robert Culley, n.d.

Slatte, H. A. *The Arminian Arm of Theology.* Washington: University of America, 1977.

———. *Fire in the Brand.* New York: Exposition Library, 1963.

Starkey, Lycurgus M. *The Holy Spirit at Work in the Church.* New York: Abingdon Press, 1965.

———. *The Work of the Holy Spirit, A Study in Wesleyan Theology.* New York: Abingdon Press, 1962.

Stevens, Abel. *History of Methodism to Death of Wesley.* London: William Tegg, 1864.

Stevenson. *Memorials of the Wesley Family.* London: S. W. Partridge and Co., 1876.

Telford, J. *The Life of John Wesley.* New York: Eaton and Mains, n.d.

Tipple, Ezra S. *Freeborn Garrettson.* New York: Eaton and Mains, 1910.

———, ed. *The Heart of Asbury's Journal*. New York: Eaton and Mains, 1904.

———. *Francis Asbury: The Prophet of the Long Road*. New York and Cincinnati: Methodist Book Concern, 1916.

Todd, John M. *John Wesley and the Catholic Church*. London: Hodder and Stoughton, 1958.

Towlson, C. W. *Moravian and Methodist*. London: Epworth Press, 1957.

Townsend, W. J.; Workman, H. B.; Eayrs, G., eds. *New History of Methodism*. London: Hodder and Stoughton, 1909.

Tracy, Wesley. *When Adam Clarke Preached, People Listened*. Kansas City: Beacon Hill Press of Kansas City, 1981.

Turner, George Allan. *The Vision Which Transforms*. Kansas City: Beacon Hill Press of Kansas City, 1970.

———. *Christian Holiness in Scripture, in History, and in Life*. Kansas City: Beacon Hill Press of Kansas City, 1977.

Tuttle, Robert G. *John Wesley: His Life and Theology*. Grand Rapids: Zondervan, 1978.

Tyerman, Luke. *The Oxford Methodists*. London: Hodder and Stoughton, 1973.

———. *The Life and Times of the Rev. John Wesley, M.A.* 3 vols. New York: Harper and Bros., 1872.

———. *The Life and Times of George Whitefield*. 2 vols. London: Hodder and Stoughton, 1876.

———. *Wesley's Designated Successor*. London: Hodder and Stoughton, 1882.

Upham, Francis B., *Thomas Coke*. London: Robert Culley, 1910.

Venn, Rev. Henry. *The Life and a Selection from the Letters of the Late Rev. Henry Venn, M.A.* London: John Hatchard and Son, 1835.

Vickers, John. *Thomas Coke, Apostle of Methodism*. Nashville: Abingdon Press, 1969.

Wakefield, G. *Methodist Devotion*. London: Epworth Press, 1966.

Walker, A. K. *William Law, His Life and Work*. London: SPCK, 1973.

Watters, D. A. *The First American Itinerant of Methodism: William Watters*. Cincinnati: 1898.

Watson, Philip. *The Message of the Wesleys*. New York: The Macmillan Co., 1964.

Watson, Richard. *Richard Watson's Works*. 13 vols. London: John Mason, 1858.

Weakley, Clare, ed. *The Holy Spirit and Power*. Plainfield, N.J.: Logos International, 1977.

Wearmouth, Robert F. *Methodism and the Common People of the Eighteenth Century*. London: Epworth Press, 1945.

Wesley, John. *Wesley His Own Biographer*. London: C. H. Kelly, 1891.

―――. *Standard Sermons of John Wesley.* 2 vols. Edited by Edward H. Sugden, M.A., B.Sc., Litt. D. London: Epworth Press, 1921. (First annotated edition.)

―――. *Journal of John Wesley,* Standard Edition. Edited by Nehemiah Curnock. 8 vols. London: Epworth Press, 1938.

―――. *Letters of John Wesley,* Standard Edition. Edited by John Telford. London: Epworth Press, 1931.

―――. *Works of John Wesley,* Oxford Edition.
Vol. 11. *The Appeals to Men of Reason and Religion.* Edited by Gerald R. Cragg. Oxford: University Press, 1975.
Vol. 25. *Letters I, 1721-1739.* Edited by Frank Baker. Oxford: University Press, 1980.
Vol. 26. *Letters II, 1740-1755.* Edited by Frank Baker. Oxford: University Press, 1982.

―――. *Wesley's Works.* 3rd edition. 14 vols. London: John Mason, 1829.

―――. *Sermons on Several Occasions by the Rev. John Wesley, M.A.* 3 vols. with a life of the author, by the Rev. John Beecham, D.D. London: Wesleyan Office, 1866.

―――. *The Epistles of the Apostolical Fathers.* St. Clement, St. Ignatius, St. Polycarp, and the martyrdom of St. Ignatius and St. Polycarp: partly translated and partly abridged. Also *The Homilies of Macarius* and *John Arndt's True Christianity.* Compiled and arranged by the Rev. John Wesley, M.A. London: Houlston and Stoneman, 1845.

―――. *Explanatory Notes upon the New Testament.* 1st ed. London: William Bower, 1755.

―――. *Explanatory Notes upon the Old Testament.* 1st ed. Bristol: William Pine, 1765.

―――. *Hymns for the Use of the People Called Methodists.* London: 1780 (and various editions).

―――. *The Doctrine of Original Sin, According to Scripture, Reason, and Experience.* 1st ed. Bristol: E. Farley, 1757.

―――. *Letter to a Roman Catholic.* Edited by Michael Hurley, S.J., London: Geoffrey Chapman, 1968.

Wesley, John and Charles. *The Poetical Works.* 13 vols. Collected and arranged by G. Osborn, D.D. London: Wesleyan-Methodist Conference Office, 1868-72.

―――. *Hymns on the Lord's Supper.* London: G. Paramore, 1794.

Whaling, Frank, ed. *John and Charles Wesley.* New York: Paulist Press, 1981.

Wiley, H. Orton. *Christian Theology.* 3 vols. Kansas City: Nazarene Publishing House, 1940-45.

Williams, Colin W. *John Wesley's Theology Today.* London: Epworth Press, 1960.

Wilson, D. Dunn. *Many Waters Cannot Quench.* London: Epworth Press, 1969.

Winchester, C. T. *The Life of John Wesley.* London: Macmillan and Co., 1915.
Wiseman, Luke. *Charles Wesley.* London: Epworth Press, 1932.
———. *Charles Wesley and His Hymns.* London: Epworth Press, 1938.
Wood, A. Skevington. *The Inextinguishable Blaze.* London: Paternoster Press, 1960.
———. *The Burning Heart.* London: Paternoster Press, 1967.
Wynkoop, Mildred Bangs. *A Theology of Love.* Kansas City: Beacon Hill Press of Kansas City, 1972.
———. *John Wesley: Christian Revolutionary.* Kansas City: Beacon Hill Press of Kansas City, 1970.
Yates, Arthur S. *The Doctrine of Assurance.* London: Epworth Press, 1952.
Zinzendorf, Count Nikolaus Ludwig von. *Nine Public Lectures.* Translated and edited by George W. Forell. Iowa City, Ia.: University of Iowa Press, 1973.

ARTICLES

Wesleyan Theological Journal: Bulletin of the Wesleyan Theological Society.
    Vol. 3, No. 1, Spring 1968. William M. Arnett, Ph.D. "John Wesley and the Bible." Robert A. Mattke, "John Fletcher's Methodology in the Antinomian Controversy of 1770-76."
    Vol. 14, No. 2. Laurence W. Wood, "Exegetical-Theological Reflections on the Baptism with the Holy Spirit."
    Vol. 15, No. 1. John A. Knight, "The Supreme Pursuit."
    Vol. 16, No. 1. Timothy L. Smith, "Notes on the Exegesis of John Wesley's *Explanatory Notes upon the New Testament.*"
    Vol. 13, Spring 1978. Allan Coppedge, "Entire Sanctification in Early American Methodism."
    Vol. 10, Spring, 1975. Mildred Bangs Wynkoop, "John Wesley—Mentor or Guru?"
    Vol. 8, Spring 1973. William M. Arnett, "A Study in John Wesley's *Explanatory Notes upon the Old Testament.*"
Proceedings of the Wesley Historical Society
    Vol. XXX, Part 4, December 1955. Irene Longstaff, "The Archives of the Methodist Missionary Society."
    Vol. XXXII, Part 5, March 1960. B. C. Drury, "John Wesley, Hymnologist (I)."
    Vol. XXXII, Part 6, June 1960. B. C. Drury, "John Wesley, Hymnologist (II)."
    Vol. XXXIII, Part 2, June 1961. Frank Baker, "The Early Experience of Fletcher of Madeley."
    Vol. XXXIV, Part 2, June 1963. George Lawton, "A Wesley Autograph on Sinless Perfection."
    Vol. XXXV, Part 7, September 1966. Peter W. Grant, "The Wesleys' Conversion Hymn."

The Evangelical Quarterly (ed. F. F. Bruce)
  Vol. XLVI, No. 4. Mark A. Noll, "Romanticism and the Hymns of Charles Wesley."
  Vol. XLVII, No. 1. Irwin W. Reist, "John Wesley and George Whitefield: A Study in the Integrity of Two Theologies of Grace."

The London Quarterly and Holborn Review
  April 1934. W. F. Lofthouse, "Wesley's Doctrine of Christian Perfection."
  October 1940. Oliver A. Beckerlegge, "John Wesley and the German Hymns."
  July 1940. Henry Bett, "John Wesley's Translation of German Hymns."
  October 1957. Issue commemorating Charles Wesley.
    Leslie G. Church, "Charles Wesley—the Man."
    T. S. Gregory, "Charles Wesley's Hymns and Poems."
    Frank Baker, "The Prose Writings of Charles Wesley."
    Wesley F. Swift, "Brothers Charles and John."
    Oliver A. Beckerlegge, "Charles Wesley's Politics."

Methodist Recorder
  December 12, 1907. Florence Bone, "The Charm of Charles Wesley."
  "When was Charles Wesley born? A chat with John J. Telford."
  October 7, 1937. J. Ernest Rattenbury, "A word for Brother Charles."
  October 22, 1936. F. L. Wiseman, "All Saints Day: Suitable Hymns."
  March 31, 1933. F. L. Wiseman, "Charles Wesley's Hymns on Last Things."
  Centenary Issue: "The Homes, Habits, and Friends of John Wesley."

Author Index

à Kempis, Thomas 23
Asbury, Francis 459
Baker, Frank 386
Barber, Thomas 333
Bardsley, Samuel............... 264
Bastable, Cornelius 264
Bell, George 102, 260
Bengelius..................... 231
Bennis, Mrs................... 266
Benson, Joseph............ 270, 385
Bohler, Peter.................. 306
Bosenquet, Mary 384
Brettel, John 333
Briggs, Betsy 272
Briggs, Philothea 268
Bunting, Jabaz 365
Bunyan, John 141
Clarke, Adam 332
Coke, Thomas 466, 481
Cooke, Mary 334
Cooper, Ezekiel 463, 482, 483
Dodwell, William............... 363
Downes, John................. 264
Fletcher, John............. 158, 383
Fletcher, Mary 260
Flew, R. Newton 159, 308
Furley, Dorothy 263
Garrettson, Freeborn........... 481
Gatch, Phillip 479
Gradin, Arvid 157, 162
Gwynne, Sally 307
Hitt, Daniel 483
Law, William................ 28, 281
Macarius..................... 108
Mather, Alexander............. 460
Maxfield, Thomas 102, 260
McKendree, William 484
Middleton, Dr. Conyers 273
Newton, John............. 157, 265
Rankin, Thomas................ 479
Sargent, George 365
Smith, Henry 475
Smith, Timothy 386
Thatcher, William 480
Tyerman, Luke 158
Walpole, Horace 259
Walsh, Thomas................ 146
Watson, Richard............... 363
Watters, William 480
Wesley, Charles.. 158, 180, 260, 305, 385, 453, 463
Wesley, John .... 36 ff.
Wesley, Susanna 305
Whitefield, George 387
Wiseman, Luke 305

Subject Index

A Serious Call......... 30, 160, 265
Advice for the Entirely Sanctified . 204
Appeals to Men of Reason
  and Religion 281
Assurance 55, 59, 68, 115, 187, 194, 200, 267, 287, 440
Atonement 113, 183, 197, 270, 361, 403
Attitudes... 119, 196, 276, 447, 471

Bengel's Gnomon 231
Books, how to read 24
Cameo of a True Christian 273
Carnality 88, 93, 108, 119, 404, 406, 431
Catholic Spirit 73, 448
Character of a Methodist, The ... 163
Checks to Antinomianism .. 385, 386, 401
Christian Perfection, Thoughts On 182
Christian perfection 159, 284, 352, 401
Christian Perfection, Sermon On . 166
Christians Pattern 160

Children, The 297
Christlikeness 58, 131, 139, 145,
    153, 168, 341, 376, 443, 444
Christ's dispensation (Fletcher)... 387
Cleansed in this life 168, 344
Cleansing ..61, 88, 91, 97, 124, 140,
    270, 271, 283, 286, 345,
    359, 420, 433, 439
Circumcision of the Heart, The ...50, 161
Consecration 140, 375, 432, 472

Dangers...................... 443
Division...................... 209
Discipline, The Form of.....463, 465

*Earnest Appeal to the
    Children of God, An* 220
Eleven Propositions on Perfection. 217
Ethics 408
Evil speaking................. 120
Experiencing holiness 280

Faith 54, 109, 111, 116, 125,
    147, 261, 279, 284, 321,
    322, 403, 422, 427, 434
Fanaticism.......190, 205, 281, 412
*Farther Thoughts on
    Christian Perfection* 194
Farther Appeal, A............... 285
Finding 435, 440, 486
For all Christians . 59, 134, 150, 154,
    286, 360, 410
Freewill 422, 428

God's holiness 335, 357
Grace...... 122, 127, 422, 428, 452
Growth . 55, 109, 145, 214, 442, 453

Helping seekers 189
Holiness in the hymns......169, 240
Holiness is reasonable 138, 220
Holy Living and Dying 160
Holy Club, The 306
Holy Spirit .336, 346, 349, 355, 369,
    391, 408, 410, 419, 435
Homo unius libri 46, 463
Humanity 172, 183, 197, 198,
    261, 263, 433, 444
Hunger 126, 139, 193, 277, 283
Hymns for ... Methodists 255

Imitation of Christ.............. 24
In a moment.... 115, 147, 218, 262,
    346, 424, 426
"Is thine heart right?" 75

Jane Cooper's testimony 193
Justification 107

Letters of John Wesley 259
Life that pleases God............ 33
Lordship 60
Love 207, 342

Man's lost estate 395
Marks of the New Birth, The 64
Methodist Conferences......... 175

More Excellent Way, The........ 148
Notes on the New Testament 230
Notes on the Old Testament 229
Now is the time 115, 260, 352,
    425, 428

*Office of the Holy Spirit,
    The Grand* 335
On Patience 142
On Perfection 127
On the Wedding Garment 151
Original sin 80, 91

Patience...................... 213
Pentecost 327, 369
Pentecostal baptism............ 386
Perfect love... 56, 60, 109, 131, 198,
    261, 269, 270, 275,
    323, 338, 355, 446
Perfection described 129, 166
Perfection, objections 133
*Plain Account of
    Christian Perfection*.......... 155
Plain Questions of a Plain Man .. 191
Poor, The 295, 299
Prayer 213
Preaching, Wesley's 45
Preaching 177, 219, 264, 272,
    358, 462, 475, 486
*Preface to Volume 2, Hymns
    for Methodists* 250
Pride 204
Pure in Heart, The..........61, 367

Recommended Reflections 211
Remains of sin 91
Repentance of Believers, The 116
Right intention 33
Rules for singing 258

"Scripture, Reason, and
   Experience" 462
Scripture Way of Salvation, The .. 101
Scripture, how to read 228
Scripture, authority of 225
Scriptural 114, 178, 219,
                 278, 347, 418
Second blessing . 122, 147, 188, 254,
              262, 272, 360, 485
Seeking 188, 272, 310, 329, 348,
          351, 352, 415, 435, 436
Self-will 85, 118
Self-denial 432
Sick, The 294
Simplicity of intention ... 25, 30, 160

Sin in Believers 90, 91
Sin, a voluntary transgression 135,
                140, 184, 268
Social implications of
   entire sanctification 290
Suffering 212, 445, 450

Temptation 26, 199, 215, 273
Tolerance 47, 74
Translated hymns .... 242 ff.

Use of money 33, 298, 299, 301

Wholeness 146, 343, 356
Widows, The 296
Witnessing 138, 185, 210, 267,
         273, 293, 315, 450, 486
Works of John Fletcher 414
Writing 452

Zeal for God 341

Index of Scripture References

Genesis
1:27   132
6:5   81

Exodus
24:3   469

Leviticus
6:13   318
19:17-19   415

Deuteronomy
4:9   469
6:4   415
6:5   175, 415
10:12, 16   416
30:6   123, 133, 178, 417

1 Samuel
10:6   465
10:12   409

1 Kings
18:38-39   318

2 Kings
10:15   74, 374
10:29   76

Job
7:7-15   485

Psalms
9:17   397
28:8   399
37:37   385
51:5   229
51:6-17   230
63:5   70
119:21   397
130:8   134, 178

Ecclesiastes
2:1-5   433
5:1   466

The Song of Solomon
1:7   325

Isaiah
1:18   417
4:3-4   433
8:20   411
9:6   473
44:3   409
49:20   472

57:15   400
66:5   470

Jeremiah
17:5   397
24:7   417
31:31   192
31:33   417
35:6-8   75

Ezekiel
18:4   396
32:25-27   417
36:23   311
36:25   123, 134, 178, 203, 229
36:25-27   134, 467
36:26   203, 229
36:27-28   229
36:29   176, 229

Hosea
14:8   430

Joel
2:28-29   347, 410
2:30   347
2:32   347

Zechariah
12:8 167
12:10 287
13:9 433

Matthew
3:11 319, 408, 419
4:48 356
5:3 418
5:6 418
5:8 61, 231, 367, 470
5:13-16 291
5:17 416
5:28 72
5:44 416
5:48 179, 231
6:1, 10 232
7:13 397
11:11 389
13:21 429
19:17 416
22:12 151
22:37 133, 179
28:19 408

Mark
1:8 419
1:15 117
9:50 429
11:17 468
11:24 321

Luke
1:68 124, 418
1:69 179, 418
1:73-75 134, 418
1:77 419
3:6 474
3:16 410, 419
14:21 470
24:49 369, 419

John
1:12-13 65
1:26 419
3:8 64
3:16 358
3:19-22 484
4:10, 14 418
7:37 410, 418
7:39 191, 360, 410
8:31-32 474
14:12 186
14:16 287, 288, 289, 360, 420
14:23 421
14:26 287, 360
14:27 67
15:5 409
15:12 416
15:26 360
16:7 360
16:13 288
16:22 69
16:33 67
17:17 320
17:20-23 179

Acts
1:4-5 419
2:1 435
2:5 392
2:16-17 419
2:33 360, 419
2:38 410, 419
4:24 435
4:31-33 420
8:12 390
11:16-17 392
17:30 464
20:28 360
26:17-18 476
26:18 353

Romans
1;18 396
2:9 397
2:12 397
2:29 51
3:9-23 396
3:21-25 363
5:1 67
5:2, 5 69
5:9 360
6:6 232
6:19, 23 396
7:4 192
7:15 398
8:1 97
8:3-4 178, 232
8:9 410
8:14-16 68, 287
8:16-17 68, 200, 413
8:27 287
8:29-30 233
8:34 287
9:5 353
9:28 477
10:4 194
12:1-2 472
13:8 416
13:9 196, 416
13:11-14 474
13:10 184, 196, 416
15:16 360

1 Corinthians
1:2 93
1:6 442
2:12 200
3:1-3 93
6:9-11 96
6:19 96, 409, 410
7:19 416
9:21 195
9:25-27 442
12:13 413
12:25 205
12:31 149, 414
13:1-3 148, 417

2 Corinthians
1:22 202
5:17 91, 96
7:1 94, 178
12:11 442

Galatians
3:10 397
3:26 65, 399
4:6 69
5:5 193
5:17 93
5:24 98, 469
6:2 416

Ephesians
1:7 360
1:13 202
2:2 396
2:8 106
2:22 347
3:8 353
3:14 179
4:8 360
4:21-24 133
4:30 201, 413, 442
5:18 410
5:25, 27 98, 178

Philippians
1:11 429
1:29 210, 449
3:10-16 463
3:12 128
3:15 217, 442

Colossians
1:14 360
1:16-17 353
1:24 97
1:27-28 352
2:9 353
3:9 98

1 Thessalonians
5:16   201, 218, 442
5:23   132, 179, 233
5:24   234, 473

2 Thessalonians
1:8   397
2:12   397
2:13   360

1 Timothy
1:5   196, 417
1:15   399
2:3-4   472
4:16   467
6:15   353

2 Timothy
3:15   411
3:16   404

Titus
2:11-14   179, 347

Hebrews
6:1   128, 129, 217
6:11   68
7:17   408
8:10   192
9:12   360
10:14   198
10:22   68
10:29   201, 442
10:31   397
12:14   234
12:22   97
12:24   234
12:29   397
13:8   408
13:20-25   234, 356, 469

James
1:4   142
1:12   433
2:8-9   416
2:10   397, 417
2:12   417
4:4   72

1 Peter
1:2   360
1:3   68
1:7   433
1:8   399
1:11   192
1:15   132
2:5   132
3:15   431
5:10   356

2 Peter
1:3-4   348, 419
1:8   429
1:16   468

1 John
1:1-9   234, 322
2:1-11   235
2:15   201, 442
2:27   288
3:1-2   66, 361, 399
3:4-5   236
3:6-7   67, 236
3:8   178, 237
3:9   66, 237
3:11   74
3:14   70
3:15   72
3:16   70, 74
3:21, 24   237
4:7   70, 74, 237
4:8   237
4:12   237, 421
4:13   70
4:14   237
4:16   237
4:17   179, 238
4:18   218, 238
4:21   416
4:19   238
5:1   65, 70
5:5-7   238
5:15   69, 239
5:17   239
5:18   67, 239
5:19   200, 239, 333
5:20-21   239

Revelation
1:5   399
2:2-4   93
2:13   94
2:16   94
3:2-3   94